Caribbean Jewish Crossings

New World Studies

J. Michael Dash, Editor

Frank Moya Pons and
Sandra Pouchet Paquet,
Associate Editors

Caribbean Jewish Crossings

LITERARY HISTORY AND
CREATIVE PRACTICE

Edited by Sarah Phillips Casteel
and Heidi Kaufman

University of Virginia Press
Charlottesville and London

University of Virginia Press
© 2019 by the Rector and Visitors of the University of Virginia
All rights reserved
Printed in the United States of America on acid-free paper

First published 2019

ISBN 978-0-8139-4328-2 (cloth)
ISBN 978-0-8139-4329-9 (paperback)
ISBN 978-0-8139-4330-5 (e-book)

9 8 7 6 5 4 3 2 1

Library of Congress Cataloging-in-Publication Data
is available for this title.

Cover art: "Telescope," Anna Ruth Henriques, from *Exodus II*, 2000. (Courtesy of the artist)

*In memory of J. Michael Dash—
generous mentor and field-shaping scholar*

Contents

Foreword   xi
Natalie Zemon Davis

Acknowledgments   xv

Introduction: Crossing Disciplines, Cultures, Geographies   1

Part I.   **The Emergence of Caribbean Jewish Literary Culture**

The Portuguese Jewish Nation: An Enlightenment Essay on the Colony of Suriname   29
Ineke Phaf-Rheinberger

Henrik Hertz and Racial Imagination in the Nineteenth-Century Danish Caribbean   46
David Gantt Gurley

Jamaican Jewish Tricksters: Philip Cohen Labatt's Literary Crossings   66
Heidi Kaufman

Translating Cuba: Language, Race, and Homeland in Cuban-Yiddish Poetry of the 1930s   89
Rachel Rubinstein

Part II.	Revisiting the Inquisition and the Sephardic Caribbean	
	David Dabydeen's Hogarth: Blacks, Jews, and Postcolonial Ekphrasis *Sarah Phillips Casteel*	113
	Jubanidad and the Literary Transmission of Cuban Crypto-Judaism *Leonard Stein*	135
	Diaspora and Hybridity: Jewish American Women Write the Caribbean *Linda Weinhouse and Efraim Sicher*	154
Part III.	Colonialism and Caribbean Holocaust Memory	
	Splattering the Object: Césaire, Nazi Racism, and the Colonial *Ben Ratskoff*	177
	From Shtetl to Settler Colony and Back: André Schwarz-Bart's *The Morning Star* *Kathleen Gyssels*	198
	Raphaël Confiant and Jewishness: The Fraught Landscapes of French, Martinican, and Franco-Martinican Intellectualisms *Alessandra Benedicty-Kokken*	220
	Caryl Phillips's Post-Holocaust/Decolonized Interstices and the Levinasian Subjective in *Higher Ground* and *The Nature of Blood* *Neil R. Davison*	248
Part IV.	Contemporary Voices: Narrative and Poetry	
	Ema *Anna Ruth Henriques*	273
	Meeting with Judith *Cynthia McLeod*	285

Jewish-Cuban Poems: "Dream of Sefarad," "The Last
Perera," "A Father's Tattoo," "Saying Goodbye to La
Habana in May"   289
Ruth Behar

On *The Nature of Blood* and the Ghost of Anne Frank   295
Caryl Phillips

Afterword   301
Bryan Cheyette

Notes on Contributors   311

Index   319

Foreword

Natalie Zemon Davis

IN 1837–38, THE Jewish artist Isaac Mendes Belisario published his *Sketches of Character in Illustration of the Habits, Occupation and Costume of the Negro Population in the Island of Jamaica*. There he offered (with commentary sometimes supercilious and sometimes appreciative) striking images of the festive and urban work life of the recently emancipated Blacks of his native Jamaica. In 1820, the baptized artist Gerrit Schouten, great-grandson of an emancipated slave, Isaac, and cousin of free Jews of color, gave expression to the Jewish presence in Suriname in his diorama of the waterfront of Paramaribo. There he included the textile shop of the Ashkenazi Abraham Hartog de Vries, with three Caribs standing in its doorway. Some thirty years earlier Schouten's uncle Philip Hansen—the first Surinamese of color to get a law degree from the University of Leiden—and the Jewish physician David de Isaac Cohen Nassy had been members of the Suriname Friends of Letters. At one of the society's meetings, Hansen heard Nassy discuss uses of the word "romance" from the troubadours through Pierre de Marivaux's *Marianne*.[1]

Thus, the literary "crossings" to which Sarah Phillips Casteel and Heidi Kaufman so compellingly summon us have an early expression in Caribbean life, marked by stark racist asymmetries and anti-Semitism though it was. I discovered these figures late in my own quest as a historian. As Casteel and Kaufman say, the Caribbean was long absent from courses in Jewish studies in North America. When Mark Cohen, Theodore Rabb, and I teamed up in 1979 to teach a Princeton University course on the Jews in early modern Europe, we were innovative in bringing sources on women and gender, patterns of literacy, and other social history themes to our undergraduates, but we did nothing on colonial matters. It was gender that first led me there in 1989. Hoping to learn more of the life of the seventeenth-century entomologist-artist Maria Sibylla Merian, I followed her to Suriname and discovered the ancestors of David de Isaac Cohen Nassy, early settlers in that Dutch colony and major plantation owners, along with other families at Jews' Savannah.[2]

Jewish slave owners in the Caribbean of early modern times! I had not dreamed that they existed. By 1989, there was in fact considerable publication on Jews in the Caribbean, much of it local. It would increase in the next years, especially in the wake of the 1997 conference at the John Carter Brown Library on "The Jews and the Expansion of Europe to the West," which was published as book a few years later.[3] This literature deepened our knowledge of the place of European Jews in establishing colonies, of the structure of Jewish communities and their privileges or rights within colonies, and of Jewish entrepreneurship. But authors often trod carefully around the subject of Jewish-Black relations in the Caribbean, especially in regard to the sensitive subject of slavery and its aftermath. Seymour Drescher and Eli Faber were among those who cleared the way here, with their studies on the role of Jews in the cross-Atlantic and cross-Caribbean purchase and sale of slaves (their statistics showed the Jewish role was on the whole "modest"). Jonathan Schorsch then centered on Jewish relations with enslaved persons, including religious relations, in his searching *Jews and Blacks in the Early Modern World* (2004). Now scholars such as Aviva Ben-Ur and others are giving us a wider picture, frank and nuanced, of the history of Jewish-Black relations in the Caribbean, on the plantations, in the synagogues, and on the city streets.[4]

As for the publication from Black scholars in the Caribbean itself, the great figures such as Anton de Kom in his *Wij Slaven van Suriname* (We slaves of Suriname, 1934) and Eric Williams in his *History of the People of Trinidad and Tobago* (1962) did not single out Jews from other settlers in their consideration of white/black relations. A pioneer here was R. A. J. van Lier, himself born in Paramaribo of both Black and Jewish ancestry. In his *Frontier Society: A Social Analysis of the History of Surinam* (1949), van Lier compared Jews and Blacks in Suriname, using quotations from the *Essai historique* of David de Isaac Cohen Nassy himself. He also drew a portrait of a group that illustrates well the Black/Jewish crossing: "the free mulattoes," a number of whom were Jewish.[5]

Especially interesting are the varied comments about Jews made by Blacks from earlier times. On the one hand, there were the Suriname slaves who got revenge against the racist sentiments of owners by using language offensive to Jews, the one group of whites they could most easily insult. "Smous" was an anti-Semitic word introduced from seventeenth-century Europe: in 1782, slaves from a Christian plantation accosted slaves owned by Jews, who were thus "Smouse Neegers." The former knocked off the hats of the latter and shouted "Smous, Smous." On the other hand, in 1793, the Jews of color, many of them recently emancipated, demanded of the rectors of the Jewish nation (including Nassy himself) that they be granted equal treatment in the congregation, and quoted Scripture: "One law and one manner shall be for you, and the stranger that sojourneth with you."[6]

Finally, there are similarities between Blacks and Jews suggested by Blacks themselves. In his *Interesting Narrative* of 1789, Olaudah Equiano, having noted parallels in the customs of Jews and Blacks, remarked that "the strong analogy which . . . appears to prevail in the manners and customs of my countrymen and those of the Jews . . . would induce me to think that the one people had sprung from the other." In the next century in the south of the United States, the biblical Exodus became the model inspiring runaway slaves and their prayers. Closer to our own time, the Holocaust has offered an event through which Black writers could characterize the trauma of the Middle Passage. Toni Morrison dedicated her novel *Beloved* to "Sixty Million and more."[7] Through this collection of essays, Sarah Phillips Casteel and Heidi Kaufman lead us on another kind of voyage.

Notes

1. Tim Barringer, Gillian Forrester, and Barbara Martinez Ruiz, eds., *Art and Emancipation in Jamaica: Isaac Mendes Belisario and His Worlds* (New Haven, CT: Yale University Press, 2007); Clazien Medendorp, *Kijkkasten uit Suriname: De Diorama's van Gerrit Schouten* (Amsterdam: KIT, 2008), 9–15, 27; Cynthia McLeod, *Elisabeth Samson: Een vrije, zwarte Vrouw in het 18e-eeuwse Suriname* (Schoorl: Conserve, 1996), 35, 40–41, 44–47; *Letterkundige uitspanningen van het Genootschap de Surinaamsche Lettervrienden* 4 (1787), "Naamlyst der Leden"; David de Isaac Cohen Nassy, "Onderzoek over de Woorden Roman en Romance," *Letterkundige uitspanningen* (1787): 49–63.

2. Natalie Zemon Davis, *Women on the Margins: Three Seventeenth-Century Lives* (Cambridge, MA: Harvard University Press, 1995), 173, 176. For detail on the Nassy family in the early decades of European settlement in Suriname, see Natalie Zemon Davis, "Regaining Jerusalem: Eschatology and Slavery

in Jewish Colonization in Seventeenth-Century Suriname," *Cambridge Journal of Postcolonial Literary Inquiry* 3 (2016): 11–38.

3. Mordechai Arbell, *Spanish and Portuguese Jews in the Caribbean and the Guianas: A Bibliography* (New York: Interamericas, 1999); Paolo Bernardini and Norman Fiering, eds., *The Jews and the Expansion of Europe to the West* (Oxford: Berghahn, 2001).

4. Seymour Drescher, "Jews and New Christians in the Atlantic Slave Trade," in Bernardini and Fiering, *Jews,* 439–70; Eli Faber, *Jews, Slaves, and the Slave Trade* (New York: New York University Press, 2000); Jonathan Schorsch, *Jews and Blacks in the Early Modern World* (Cambridge: Cambridge University Press, 2004); Aviva Ben-Ur, "A Matriarchal Matter: Slavery, Conversion, and Upward Mobility in Colonial Suriname," in Richard Kagan and Philip Morgan, eds., *Atlantic Diasporas: Jews, Conversos, and Crypto-Jews in the Age of Mercantilism, 1500–1800* (Baltimore: Johns Hopkins University Press, 2000), 152–69. I have given some further bibliography in Davis, "Regaining Jerusalem," 12n5.

5. Anton de Kom, *Wij Slaven van Suriname* (Houten: Het Wereldvenster, [1934] 1988); Eric Williams, *History of the People of Trinidad and Tobago* (New York: Frederick Praeger, 1962); R. A. J. van Lier, *Frontier Society: A Social Analysis of the History of Suriname*, trans. M. J. L. van Yperen (The Hague: Martinus Nijhoff, 1971), 91–95, 108–13; first Dutch edition: *Samenleving in een Grensgebied* (The Hague: Martinus Nijhoff, 1949).

6. Natalie Zemon Davis, "Creole Languages and their uses: the example of colonial Suriname," *Historical Research* 82 (2009): 278; Robert Cohen, *Jews in Another Environment: Surinam in the Second Half of the Eighteenth Century* (New York: E. J. Brill, 1991), 167–68.

7. Olaudah Equiano, *The Interesting Narrative and Other Writings*, ed. Vincent Carretta (New York: Penguin, 2003), 43–44; Kenneth Chelst, *Exodus and Emancipation: Biblical and African-American Slavery* (Jerusalem: Urim, 2014), 123; Maria Diedrich, Henry Louis Gates Jr. and Carl Pedersen, eds., *Black Imagination and the Middle Passage* (Oxford: Oxford University Press, 1999), 58–61; Toni Morrison, *Beloved* (New York: Alfred A. Knopf, 1987), dedication.

Acknowledgments

THROUGHOUT THE PROCESS of editing this book, we have been grateful for the encouraging and enthusiastic responses we have received to our efforts to bring attention to a topic that hitherto remained largely unrecognized: the literary representation of Caribbean Jewish connections. Our warm thanks to the late J. Michael Dash, and to Eric Brandt, Morgan Myers, and Helen Chandler at the University of Virginia Press, for their support for this project and for shepherding it so expertly through the various stages of the process. We are also deeply indebted to the press's two anonymous readers, whose insightful and constructive feedback helped us to negotiate the difficult challenge of creating a scholarly conversation across fields that have rarely talked to one another. Above all, we want to thank the contributors to this volume who were part of the original ACLA seminar that we organized at Harvard University in 2016 on "Caribbean/Jewish Intersections in (Post)Colonial Literary and Print Cultures," as well as those contributors who came on board later.

We are particularly honored to be able to include in this volume the work of several Caribbean and Caribbean diaspora creative writers and artists from whose work our own scholarship has drawn much inspiration. We wish to thank Cynthia McLeod for generously translating her short story into English for this volume, to Ruth Behar for sharing her wonderful poetry, and to Anna Ruth Henriques for contributing not only her writing but also her beautiful artwork. Caryl Phillips, whose fiction has done more than any other work to singlehandedly open up scholarly discussion of Caribbean Jewish intersections, very kindly allowed us to reprint his essay, which originally appeared as "On 'The Nature of Blood,'" *CommonQuest* 3, no. 2 (1998): 4–7.

We thank John Benjamins Publishing Company for permitting us to reprint Ineke Phaf-Rheinberger's essay, which originally appeared as

"Essay on the Colony of Suriname," *A History of Literature in the Caribbean,* vol. 2, ed. A. James Arnold (Amsterdam: John Benjamins, 2001), 491–503. Sarah Phillips Casteel's essay originally appeared as "David Dabydeen's Hogarth: Blacks, Jews, and Postcolonial Ekphrasis," *Cambridge Journal of Postcolonial Literary Inquiry* 3, no. 1 (January 2016): 117–33. Sarah thanks Ato Quayson and Willi Goetschel for commissioning this article for a special issue on "Jewish Studies and Postcolonialism." We are also very grateful to Kate Huber for her expert translation and editing assistance in the preparation of the manuscript. We wish to thank the Oregon Humanities Center and the College of Arts and Sciences at the University of Oregon, as well as the Office of the Dean, Faculty of Arts and Social Sciences at Carleton University, for their generous subvention support.

We would like to acknowledge the warm welcome we have received over the past decade from Jewish communities in the Caribbean, in particular in Jamaica, Curaçao, and Suriname. In Jamaica, Ainsley Henriques has been a tireless supporter of academic research in the rich history of the Jewish Caribbean; indeed, it was the 2010 conference on "The Jewish Diaspora of the Caribbean" that Ainsley co-organized in Kingston with historians Jane Gerber and Stan Mirvis that first brought the two of us together. We also want to express our gratitude to Rachel Frankel and CVE (Caribbean Volunteers Expeditions) for including us in their important, multiyear project documenting Jewish cemeteries in Jamaica.

Finally, as always, our deepest thanks go to our families for their unflagging patience, understanding, and support.

Caribbean Jewish Crossings

Introduction

Crossing Disciplines, Cultures, Geographies

IN A RECENT blog post, Jamaican author Marlon James writes about the challenge of confronting racism in the work of canonical authors. Adopting an analogy to draw out the point, he explains, "My being expected to tolerate or even like Flannery O'Connor, or any other racist on the grounds of aesthetic excellence may be admirable in theory but it's as ludicrous in practice as a Jewish person writing about the structural brilliance of Albert Speer."[1] The focus on anti-Semitism in James's post may seem curious, considering the range of racist histories he might otherwise have recalled. Why the Holocaust? And what do we make of a Jamaican writer's choice to use the Holocaust to explain the challenge of reading racist texts? In another recent example of cross-cultural referencing, Haitian writer Louis-Philippe Dalembert's novel *Avant que les ombres s'effacent* (Before the shadows fade, 2017) centers on a Polish Jewish refugee who, fleeing the Nazis, makes his way to Port-au-Prince in 1939. Again, this may seem a rather unexpected choice on the part of a writer who comes from a region whose history was shaped primarily by the violent upheavals of the transatlantic slave trade rather than the Holocaust. Do these texts simply reflect the problematic status in contemporary culture of the Holocaust as a litmus test for other historical traumas? Or do they signal a more specific set of connections between Caribbean literary culture and Jewish historical experiences?

James and Dalembert, in fact, connect two histories that have long been entangled both within Caribbean culture and in representations of that culture. William Makepeace Thackeray's *Vanity Fair* (1847–48) offers a well-known example of how Jewishness and the Caribbean become associated with one another in colonial-era literature. Thackeray describes his character Miss Rhoda Swartz as "the rich woolly-haired mulatto from St. Kitt's." The narrator adds, "Her father was a German Jew—a slave-owner they say—connected with the Cannibal Islands in some way or other."[2] Thackeray's account of Swartz's provenance reflects the historical presence (albeit in relatively small numbers) of Jewish slaveholders throughout the Caribbean colonial world.[3] Indeed, Sephardim (Iberian Jews) and, later, Ashkenazim (Eastern European Jews) have been a continuous presence in the Caribbean since the seventeenth century. Their connections to the region are registered not only by European authors such as Thackeray, but also by colonial and postcolonial Caribbean authors.

In his classic essay "The Muse of History" (1974), Derek Walcott describes African slaves as feeling an "identification with Hebraic suffering, the migration, the hope of deliverance from bondage." He writes that "the passage over our Red Sea was not from bondage to freedom but its opposite, so that the tribes arrived at that New Canaan chained."[4] Concretizing this analogy, Walcott's early play *Drums and Colours* (1958) features a Sephardic Jewish protagonist who, escaping the Inquisition, boards a Spanish slave ship in 1510 bound for the Caribbean. *Caribbean Jewish Crossings* takes up these and other points of intersection between African and Jewish diasporic experiences, both historical and symbolic. One of this volume's central goals is to understand how Caribbean writers such as James, Dalembert, and Walcott articulate these diasporic cultures' divergences, similarities, and mutually constituted representations. We consider how the incorporation of such cross-cultural references supports the development of a Caribbean poetics from the era of European Atlantic slavery until the present. As the essays in this collection illustrate, not only Jewish-descended but also non-Jewish Caribbean authors have a long tradition of weaving together African and Jewish diasporic narratives and, in the process, have identified or forged cultural and historical connections between them. Moreover, within a creolized context characterized by the cultural mixing of Indigenous, African, Asian, European, and other populations, sharp distinctions between Jewish and non-Jewish Caribbean authorship can be difficult to draw and can obscure points of mutual engagement. Our volume acknowledges these historical and discursive Caribbean Jewish intersections—or crossings—as marking a significant and understudied dimension of both Caribbean and Jewish literary history and culture.[5] The essays and creative writing collected in this volume point to a range of ways in which literary culture both registers and is energized by such crossings.

Critical Ambivalences

The extensive scholarship on Black-Jewish literary relations has traditionally focused on the United States. By contrast, this volume of essays identifies the Caribbean as an important alternative site in which to anchor and reframe discussions of Black-Jewish literary relations as well as comparative postcolonial Jewish scholarship. *Caribbean Jewish Crossings* highlights both the historical convergence of African, Jewish, and other diasporic and Indigenous populations in the Caribbean region since the seventeenth century, and the symbolic resonances among Black and Jewish cultural narratives of oppression, migration, and survival. In recent years, historians of the Jewish Atlantic have successfully worked toward the recovery of Jewish experience in the early modern Caribbean.[6] Yet the relationship of Jewishness to colonial and postcolonial Caribbean literary and print cultures has not received anywhere near the same degree of attention. The critical silence from scholars of both Caribbean and Jewish literature on the place of Jewishness in Caribbean literary history—or the place of the Caribbean in Jewish literary history—contrasts sharply with contemporary Caribbean creative writers' frequent invocations of Jewishness. It is this gap between scholarship and creative practice that our collection seeks to address, with the hope that future scholarship will advance the concerns raised in this volume.

One of the few critics to identify the significance of Jewishness in African diaspora intellectual history beyond a US national framework is Paul Gilroy. In his frequently cited concluding chapter to *The Black Atlantic,* Gilroy observes, "It is often forgotten that the term 'diaspora' comes into the vocabulary of black studies and the practice of pan-Africanist politics from Jewish thought."[7] He adds, "The concept of diaspora can itself provide an underutilised device with which to explore the fragmentary relationship between blacks and Jews and the difficult political questions to which it plays host."[8] Taking up Gilroy's call to more fully acknowledge African diaspora engagements with Jewishness and Jewish thought, this volume investigates the diaspora concept and other points of intersection in order to bring to light how Jewishness is invoked by writers from multiple Caribbean language and literary traditions. The work of well-known contemporary Caribbean writers such as Caryl Phillips, David Dabydeen, Cynthia McLeod, Achy Obejas, Raphaël Confiant, and Maryse Condé, as well as less discussed earlier Caribbean literary figures such as the Trinidadian novelist and historian E. L. Joseph (1792–1838) and Jamaican writers and editors Philip Cohen Labatt (1823–1854) and

H. G. de Lisser (1878–1944), encourages us to read across disciplinary boundaries and traditional literary categories, and to place in dialogue Atlantic, Caribbean, Latin American, Jewish, and postcolonial studies.

As a cross-disciplinary project, our volume confronts a number of methodological challenges, including how to excavate literary histories and texts that are not readily accessible or legible, and how to bridge the respective vocabularies and investments of Caribbean and Jewish studies. Initially and importantly focused on the African heritage of Caribbean culture and its contestatory relationship with the colonial European inheritance, Caribbean literary scholarship has more recently moved to address the South Asian, Chinese, and Irish dimensions of Caribbean literary history.[9] Yet despite this productive expansion of the field, writing by European-descended Caribbean authors continues to occupy a marginal and problematic space within discussions of Caribbean literature. As Alison Donnell, Maria McGarrity, and Evelyn O'Callahan observe in their introduction to their 2015 edited collection *Caribbean Irish Connections,*

> the defining lines of racial power between white and non-white in the Caribbean have made the study of white ethnic minorities a less compelling field within the general push to decolonize historiography. Very recently, works on Jewish populations in the Caribbean and other white minorities such as the Portuguese have begun to emerge. Yet the broad divide in historiographical interest between those who were victims of colonialism in the Caribbean and those who benefited from it does not easily accommodate a study of the Irish. The particular and stubborn riddle of the Irish is that they fell on both sides of this divide, identified by an ethnic label—*Irish*—that was itself radically unstable and constantly called upon to do the work of paradox.[10]

Here, Donnell, McGarrity, and O'Callahan identify the ambiguous positioning of the Irish as somewhat unique. Yet Caribbean Jewishness, too, is characterized by significant ambiguities with respect to race and power that present similar challenges for the project of incorporating Jewish authors and themes into a literary history of the Caribbean. Like the Irish, Jews were, according to historian Jonathan Israel's eloquent phrase, "both agents and victims of empire."[11] Early modern Jews participated in the colonial project as merchants, brokers, and, more rarely, as slave traders and planters. In some cases Jews enjoyed new freedoms in the Caribbean colonies that had been unavailable to them in Europe. Most notably, the Jewish agricultural settlement of Jodensavanne (Jew's Savannah), founded in the 1680s in Suriname, was granted near-autonomy by the colonial authorities. Yet colonial Jewry also suffered from renewed or continuing forms of oppression in the Caribbean in the form of special taxes and limits on property ownership and voting rights. In the British Caribbean colony of Jamaica, as historian Jane Gerber notes, Jews acquired full civil rights only in 1831, "six months after the free blacks and three years before the general abolition of slavery."[12] Still more drastically, Jews were expelled from the French Caribbean with the *Code noir* in 1685 and were prohibited from professing their faith openly in the Spanish Caribbean by the Inquisition. In the Spanish Caribbean, the fate of Jews became complexly intertwined with those of other Others, with 1492 marking the onset of linked processes of expulsion, forced conversion, and genocide that variously affected Indigenous peoples, Africans, and Jews in the Old and New Worlds. Yet as speculation about Columbus's possibly crypto-Jewish origins suggests, the status of Jewishness with respect to these forces of colonization remains difficult to define.

Historical evidence suggests that colonial Jewry both challenged and supported the Caribbean colonial project. For example, in his biography of Toussaint Louverture, Philippe Girard recounts the story of Isaac Sasportas, a Sephardic merchant who "revered the French Revolution because it had proclaimed the civil emancipation of the Jews."[13] In 1799, Sasportas developed a plan to export the revolution to Jamaica, where he hoped to foment a slave revolt. He traveled to Jamaica for that purpose, where he was arrested, convicted of treason, and hanged after his plan was leaked by Louverture. A half-century later, Sidney Levien, a Jewish owner and editor of the Jamaican newspaper the *County Union*, was imprisoned in the months following the Morant Bay Rebellion, which began on October 11, 1865. Immediately following the rebellion, Governor Edward John Eyre used brutal force to punish those he believed to be involved. His violence led to controversy, outrage, and an official inquiry from England. According to Gad Heuman, Governor Eyre viewed Levien as a threat both because he aided political dissidents supporting the rebellion and because he used his newspaper to criticize Eyre's leadership.[14]

In other cases, however, colonial Jewry helped to quash slave and Maroon revolts, as we learn from the *Essai historique sur la colonie de Surinam* published by the Surinamese Jewish community in 1788 (discussed in the present volume by Ineke Phaf-Rheinberger). The authors of the *Essai* proudly note their military contribution to the efforts to suppress the Maroons, asserting that the Jewish colonists "equal the Christians in courage, in discipline, and in their burning zeal to serve the colony."[15] As evidence of the strength of the Sephardic community's devotion to the colony, the *Essai* includes a description of Captain David Cohen Nassy's 1743 victorious attack against the Maroons, which was carried out despite the fact that it fell on *Yom Kippur,* a Jewish holy day.[16]

Such conflicting examples leave us wondering whether figures such as Sasportas and Levien were outliers in Caribbean Jewish communities in their resistance to colonial power. Or were there other examples of Caribbean Jews who led campaigns to fight or overthrow colonial rule? And how has literary culture tended to this history? The uncertainty surrounding such questions reflects, in part, the ambiguous position that Jews occupied in colonial Caribbean hierarchies, somewhere in between the ruling white classes and the colored and slave classes. Jewish difference, with its tendency to destabilize racial and other categories of identity, might be understood as a threat to homogeneity and therefore potentially capable of undermining colonial authority. Conversely, Jewishness might be read as participating in and shoring up white power or as aspiring to do so. The essays in this collection show that despite—or perhaps because of—their fluctuating racial and political status in the early modern Atlantic world, Jews have played a significant role in colonialist expressions of power, the development of Caribbean Creole culture under those powers, and the rise of postcolonial Caribbean literary aesthetics and concerns.

Yet, at the same time, the ambiguous status of Jewishness in Caribbean society has contributed to the ambivalent critical reception of Caribbean Jewish intersections precisely because Jewish writers tend to be perceived as uniformly white or as always writing from a position of power. Combined with the more general tendency of Caribbean literary studies until recently to focus on twentieth-century and especially post–World War II writing, this critical inattention has meant that early Caribbean Jewish authors are now nearly forgotten. This pattern of omitting Jewishness as a dimension of Caribbean literary history continues in the scholarship on twentieth-century literary culture, which has at times responded ambivalently to white or mixed-race Caribbean authors who engage with Jewish themes, such as John Hearne and Michelle Cliff.[17] For example, in her prose poem "If I Could Write This in Fire, I Would Write This in Fire," Cliff associates the racially unstable identities of light-skinned middle-class Jamaican Creoles with the religious fluidity of Marranos (forcibly converted Sephardic Jews). Sarah Phillips Casteel has argued elsewhere that "it is no accident that Jewishness is a persistent trope in the work of writers such as Hearne, Walcott, and Cliff, who have on occasion been accused of inauthenticity, conservatism, and of an insufficiently Afrocentric perspective. . . . The presence of Jewish themes in these authors' writing reflects the exposure to European literary and artistic traditions that their class backgrounds and colonial educations afforded them. In such works Jewishness is an intermediary term, a channel through which to incorporate the European into the African or to consider the ambiguous status of those light-skinned Creole subjects who are both European and not, white and not white."[18]

Perhaps also contributing to this critical reluctance to address Jewish presences within Caribbean literary history are critiques of Zionism and contemporary Israeli politics that have made it difficult for postcolonial studies more broadly to address linkages with Jewish experiences of Othering and racialization. As Jonathan Boyarin, Bryan Cheyette, Michael Rothberg and others have discussed, postcolonial studies and Jewish or Holocaust studies have, until recently, had little to say to one another.[19] Holocaust studies has only recently begun to undergo what Rothberg describes as a "colonial turn."[20] For its part, despite the early postwar engagement of anticolonial theorists such as Aimé Césaire and Frantz Fanon with Jewishness and the Holocaust (discussed in this collection by Ben Ratskoff), postcolonial studies as it was institutionalized in the academy has largely neglected linkages between colonial racism and European fascism. As we indicated above, the significant historical presence of Jews in the Caribbean region notwithstanding, Caribbean literary studies has largely followed suit. This may reflect a concern with Israeli policy toward Palestine that variously figures in the work and reception of writers discussed in this volume, such as Raphaël Confiant, André Schwarz-Bart, and Caryl Phillips. It may also reflect an awareness of the presence of Jews within contemporary Caribbean national elites and of the fact that Jewish participation in structures of power in the Caribbean extends beyond the colonial period. While the reasons for this critical silence are understandable, the result has been that Jewishness has remained largely invisible in studies of nineteenth- and twentieth-century Caribbean literary history and culture.

If Caribbeanists have tended not to address Jewishness, scholars of Jewish American literature are only just beginning to understand their field in hemispheric and multilingual terms and to engage with the Caribbean. American studies' traditional insularity, exceptionalism, and monolingualism was challenged in the mid-1990s by the hemispheric turn, which embraced a transnational and comparative mode of reading of the field and interrogated the ideological underpinnings of the term "America." The rise of hemispheric American studies responded to calls such as that of Shelly Fisher Fishkin in her 2004 presidential address to the American Studies Association to consider "what . . . the field of American studies [would] look like if the *trans*national rather than the national were at its center."[21] Yet, with a few exceptions, in contrast to Jewish American historiography, Jewish American literary studies has been slow to respond to this call to internationalize the field.[22] As Dalia Kandiyoti has observed, "Jewish literature of the Americas is a body of writing connected by its histories of migration, minoritization, and creolization, but it hardly enters the horizons of 'Jewish American Studies' even though its writers hail from 'America,' whether as inhabitants of or exiles from Argentina, Mexico or Cuba."[23] This stubborn adherence to national boundaries has become all the more questionable in light of literary studies' current embrace of World Literature. Moreover, the persistence of a methodological nationalism is also paradoxical, for, as Lital Levy and Allison Schachter have argued, with their mobility and multilingualism, Jewish literatures are particularly well positioned to contribute to a critical reassessment of the World Literature paradigm.[24]

Recentering discussions of Jewish literary history on the Caribbean encourages a hemispheric reading of Jewishness that challenges the methodological nationalism that has conventionally shaped the field of Jewish American studies. Moreover, such a move not only reframes Jewish American studies in transnational terms, but also recasts the categories of Jewish identity and Jewish authorship. For if rereading Jewish American literary studies through a Caribbean lens generates an alternative understanding of *America,* it also promotes a reexamination of the field's other key term: *Jewishness.* In particular, the history of the Sephardic Caribbean as it is recovered and reimagined by contemporary Caribbean writers (such as those discussed in part 2 of this volume) reveals the significant (yet largely overlooked) role of Jews in the linguistic and cultural creolization of the colonial Caribbean that we discuss below. Relatedly, Caribbean literature highlights the presence of Jewish lineage among Caribbean populations, including in the family trees of a number of Caribbean authors, thereby drawing attention to Jews of color. Yet when the St. Kitt's-born British writer Caryl Phillips recounts the story of his belated discovery as an adult that he had a Sephardic grandfather, he introduces this anecdote not so much to establish his Jewish credentials, but rather to explain in very personal terms how he came to a fuller understanding of the phenomenon of Caribbean creolization: "I now understood that the cultural hybridity that is the quintessential Caribbean condition had certainly marked my person, and the quality of the blood that flowed through my veins was doggedly 'impure.'"[25]

The insight that Caryl Phillips gains into the profoundly creolized nature of identity—an insight that has been one of the primary contributions of Caribbean studies to cultural theory—encourages a less ethnocentric and identitarian model than the one that has traditionally defined Jewish American literary studies. Indeed, in the Caribbean context, which famously confounds notions of purity, distinctions between the categories of *Jewish* and *non-Jewish* writing are difficult to uphold. Thus, while the Black-Jewish relations discussion in the United States, for example, has tended to present "Black" and "Jew" as sharply delineated categories, Caribbean literary discourse about Jewishness calls binary constructions of this kind into question. In so doing, Caribbean literature raises questions about the definition of Jewishness that underpins the field of Jewish American literary studies—questions that Benjamin Schreier has recently urged us to consider.[26] Just as Phillips's discovery of his Jewish ancestry yields insight into what he calls the "quintessential Caribbean condition" of creolization, so making space for the Caribbean in Jewish American literary studies can help the field to denaturalize the categories of Jewish identity and Jewish authorship.

Crossings

Caribbean Jewish Crossings invokes the idea of *crossings* in multiple senses. First and foremost, our title references the historical movement of populations across geographies and oceans that brought Jews into contact with other displaced and Indigenous populations in the early modern Caribbean and that later writers would respond to in their work. Subsequent historical periods saw further waves of internal and external migration by these groups that led to new and diverse forms of cross-cultural encounter both in the Caribbean and in its diaspora. It is against a historical background patterned by intersecting and repeated migrations that the literary corpus examined in this volume was produced.

In her giclée print "Telescope" from *Exodus II*, Jamaican Jewish visual artist and writer Anna Ruth Henriques turns sideways and collages together images of European sailing vessels with a colonial map. In the upper left-hand corner of "Telescope" is a double portrait of Ferdinand and Isabella, whose images reappear upside down in the lower right-hand corner. In the center of the work is a male European figure holding a telescope—an instrument of naval navigation. This central figure, whose face has been obscured, is painted onto a gold-colored Jamaican chocolate wrapper and encircled with gold coins to suggest the spices and financial networks that fueled the Europeans' conquest of the Americas as well as Jewish resettlement in the New World. The title of Henriques's series weaves together the Biblical Exodus of the Jewish people—a story retold each year during the Jewish holiday of Passover—with the forced exodus imposed on Sephardic Jews in the late fifteenth century by the Spanish Inquisitors. The Iberian expulsion was not only tied historically to the Spanish conquest of Jamaica but also to Henriques's Jewish ancestors' flight to Jamaica on the occasion of the Inquisition's violence.[27] "Telescope" is thus doubly suggestive of the oppressive colonial regimes that landed Sephardic Jews and enslaved Africans, as well as indentured populations from Asia in subsequent years, throughout the Caribbean. The collage technique that Henriques adopts vividly registers in particular the way in which both Jewish and African diaspora peoples work through inherited memories of their forced exiles through repeated retellings of the biblical story.

Through its aesthetic of collage, the *Exodus II* series visually positions Sephardic Jews as part of the cultural matrix of the Caribbean. As Henriques remarks on her website, "These works represent a synthesis of culture—the integration of belief systems, symbolisms, and sensibilities of a multitude of peoples present in the Caribbean."[28] The Jewish communities that resulted from these transoceanic migrations became part of a vast Atlantic network of what historians refer to as "port Jews." Across this network circulated people, capital, goods, and, most significantly for our purposes, a variety of forms of Caribbean Jewish periodical culture such as Jamaica's *Daily Gleaner*, later shortened to the *Gleaner* (1834–present), and *First Fruits of the West*, the first Jewish literary journal in the Caribbean (1844). This history of Jewish print culture in the Caribbean features in Andrea Levy's historical novel *The Long Song* (2010), which is set in colonial Jamaica and centers on the relationship between the slave author July and her son Thomas Kinsman, a printer. In the novel, Thomas Kinsman's success as a printer is ensured when he finally secures his first customer, a Jew named Cecil Levy, who "required . . . a press for the first edition of a newspaper he was to publish which was to be called *The Trelawney Mercury*."[29]

Understood in the sense of physical journeys and their literary representation, *crossings* signals the idea of diaspora itself as one of the fundamental linking concepts that carries across Caribbean literary culture. As Stuart Hall remarks in his classic essay "Cultural Identity and Diaspora," the problem of how to narrativize the identity of a dispersed people and its relationship to home is one that confronts not only the Jewish diaspora but Caribbean society more broadly.[30] While Hall distances a

"Telescope," Anna Ruth Henriques, from *Exodus II*, 2000. (Courtesy of the artist)

Caribbean conception of diaspora from what he views as a more conservative Jewish conception, this common challenge becomes a potential site of cross-cultural sympathy or identification in many of the literary texts considered herein. Accordingly, diaspora and diasporism—the valorization of life in the diaspora over an emphasis on returning to an ancestral homeland—emerge as central concerns in several of this volume's essays. Notably, diaspora is not understood in our collection as a normative concept that originates in Jewish experience and subsequently is taken up, borrowed, and adapted by non-Jewish writers and thinkers. Rather than adopting a unidirectional and diachronic understanding of what Gilroy calls the "intercultural history of the diaspora concept," the literary examples examined in this collection illustrate how a Caribbean poetics of diaspora is produced reciprocally and cross-culturally.[31]

Yet while *crossings* invokes physical journeys and the dispersion of populations across space (the Exodus narrative), it also suggests the centrality of cultural transaction, translation, and exchange to the literary representation and production of the Jewish Caribbean. Accordingly, as we discuss further below, this collection draws attention to the significant, albeit neglected, relationship of Jews to Caribbean creolization, both cultural and linguistic. Moreover, the essays that follow detail various acts of cultural and linguistic translation in which diverse and entangled Caribbean experiences are read and reinterpreted through the lens of the Other. Indeed, often in the texts discussed here, these historical experiences are analogized and or made to stand in for one another.

Finally, our title is intended to evoke the myriad exchanges among disciplines, as well as between scholarly and creative practice, that the topic of our volume requires. This collection demonstrates the value of bringing the methods of literary criticism to bear on a subject—the resettlement of Jewish populations in the Caribbean—that has up until now largely been the province of historians.[32] At the same time, the essays are deeply engaged with such disciplines as art history, philosophy, history, and anthropology. Ultimately, however, they suggest that imaginative literature has a privileged role to play in a context in which historical records and ethnographic information are difficult to retrieve. Accordingly, we devote significant space in the collection to creative writing, poetry, and memoir by contemporary Caribbean and Caribbean diaspora writers. While scholars have tended to neglect the cultural formation of the Jewish Caribbean, which falls between the cracks of the disciplines of Jewish studies and Caribbean or postcolonial studies, creative writers have long been alert to its presence and history. The creative writing included in our volume not only makes visible this presence, but also does its own kind of theoretical work that complements and expands some of the ideas addressed in the scholarly essays. Moreover, the creative writers themselves cross over the boundaries of media and disciplines within their respective oeuvres (e.g., between text and visual art, or between poetry and anthropology). For the literary history of Caribbean Jewish crossings and its relationship to larger Caribbean cultural formations is too fragmentary and multilayered, our volume suggests, to be told through the resources of a single discipline, medium, or genre.

Caribbean Jewish Creolization

Caribbean Jewish Crossings begins with an acknowledgment that Jewish, African, Asian, and other cultures of the Caribbean are not mutually exclusive. Rather, these cultural fields have been deeply imbricated with one another over the last three hundred years. Evidence of this imbrication may be found in the history of the development of Creole languages among other arenas. Linda M. Rupert, for example, notes that "the earliest known document written in Papiamentu, a vibrant creole language that today is spoken by approximately 200,000 people of all ethnicities and social classes on the Dutch Caribbean islands of Curaçao, Aruba and Bonaire," is a fragment of a 1775 love letter between two Sephardic Jews who were living in Curaçao.[33] In an essay on Creole languages in colonial Suriname, historian Natalie Zemon Davis explains that in the late seventeenth century, a distinctive Creole language developed on Jewish-owned plantations that incorporated Portuguese and African lexicons as well as English words. This Creole, known as Dju-tongo (the Jewish tongue), traveled with those slaves who managed to escape the Jewish plantations.[34] The anthropologist Richard Price details in his ethnography of Maroons in Suriname how, as a result of patterns of Jewish settlement and slaveholding there, the Hebrew term *treef* (treif) entered the Creole Sranan-Tongo language and was used to refer to food taboos.[35] Other Jewish cultural practices such as cleansing after menstruation also were adopted by some Maroon groups who had been exposed to them while living on the plantations.[36] For as Davis writes, "Many Jewish practices seeped into plantation custom by the rhythm of everyday life, accompanied by directions in Dju-tongo: the keeping of Jewish holidays, Kosher food preparation at the big house, slave assistance at the Mikvah bath and the house of the dead and the like."[37]

Yet, despite such striking examples, with the possible exception of the Dutch Caribbean, Jewishness has been largely absent from discussions of Caribbean creolization. Beginning with Edward Kamau Brathwaite's seminal work *The Development of Creole Society in Jamaica, 1770–1820*, which identified a reciprocal (albeit asymmetrical) process of intercultural change and indigenization, the study of creolization has been driven by efforts to understand the genesis and vitality of Caribbean language and culture. As Alison Donnell and Sarah Lawson Welsh have argued of the Anglophone Caribbean, studies of creolization have reflected "a desire to decolonize and indigenize imaginatively and to claim a voice for history, a geography and a people which had been dominated by British Victorians—both literally and literarily."[38] Accordingly, the terms *creole* and *creolization* are traditionally defined by their ties to African slavery and the plantation. As Neil Roberts explains, "Although notions of hybridity, *mestizaje,* and douglarization have a family resemblance to creolization, creolization itself has a particular lineage grounded in the slave ship, the plantation, and post-plantation politics, out of which debates have ensued concerning its meaning and utility."[39] We don't dispute this lineage, but we want to highlight some of the ways in which slavery and postemancipation cultural and political developments remain tied, in many cases, to Jewish slaveholders or mixed-race Afro-Jewish Caribbean subjects with connections to multiple Caribbean histories.

Wieke Vink has defined "creole Jews" as a term applying to those "members of the white Jewish group, born and bred in the New World, who had the self-consciousness of a colonial elite, as well as to those Jews of mixed Afro-Jewish descent who retained an ambiguous position in the Surinamese Jewish community."[40] Vink's study of colonial-era Suriname recalls earlier meanings of the word *creole,* which referred to white-skinned Europeans born in the Caribbean "who had lived there so long that they had acquired certain characteristics viewed by their European counterparts as 'native.'"[41] Wieke adds, "The term had a negative connotation, as it implied that someone had forgotten how to be a 'proper' Frenchman or Englishman, or in the case of the Surinamese Jew, how to be a 'good Jew.'"[42] The presence of Creole Jews in the colonial Caribbean meant that Black-Jewish cross-cultural encounter was a feature of many of these societies and contributed to their development.

By way of illustration, we might recall the early pan-Africanist thinker Edward Wilmot Blyden. In *The Jewish Question* (1898), Blyden reflects on the biographical origins of his interest in Judaism and in the Zionist movement:

> I was born in the midst of Jews in the Danish island of St. Thomas, West Indies. For years, the next-door neighbors of my parents were Jews. I played with Jewish boys, and looked forward as eagerly as they did to the annual festivals and feasts of their church. I always went to the Synagogue on the solemn Day of Atonement—not inside. I took up an outside position from which I could witness the proceedings of the worshippers, hear the prayers and the reading, the singing and the sermon. The Synagogue stood on the side of a hill; and, from

a terrace immediately above it, we Christian boys who were interested could look down upon the mysterious assembly, which we did in breathless silence, with an awe and a reverence which have followed me all the days of this life.[43]

As Blyden's account testifies, disciplinary silos can prevent us from seeing how Jews, Blacks, and other diasporic peoples not only lived alongside one another in the colonial Caribbean, but participated in one another's cultural activities. In the childhood scene that Blyden recounts, he is pushed to the edges of the event not primarily because he's Black, but because he's a Christian witnessing a Jewish religious observance. Blyden's simultaneous sense of wonder and distance reminds us of the range of ways in which identity and culture were produced and expressed in the Caribbean through the performance and witnessing of spectacles such as the "mysterious assembly" of the Jewish "church" service. While Blyden emphasizes in *The Jewish Question* that "the history of the African race . . . closely resembles that of the Jews," we suggest that to recover points of intersection among diasporic populations living under colonial regimes is not necessarily to argue that they had something in common.[44] Rather, we are interested in understanding how Caribbean writers have viewed Jews as participants in the development of a shared or overlapping society—one that cannot be easily contained by the binaries of white/Black, master/slave, or Christian/Jew. Blyden's record points to some of the important ways that these categories intersected in the colonial Caribbean.

In her reading of the performance of Purim in the colonial Dutch Caribbean, historian Aviva Ben-Ur observes that "the annual celebration of the deliverance of the Jews of an ancient Persia from annihilation in the fifth or fourth century BCE, as narrated in the biblical book of Esther" was not just celebrated, but performed in Suriname and Curacao in the eighteenth and nineteenth centuries by all members of society, including Jews and Christians as well as slaves.[45] Ben-Ur explains,

> In Suriname, Purim lasted nearly a week and sometimes longer. Crowds of masked Jews, young and old, poured into the streets of Paramaribo, yelling out obscene declarations against Christianity. Surrounding them were bands of field slaves pulling wagons laden with costumed Jews and their domestic bondsmen. Sometimes these bondsmen circled the masquerading Jews, shouting and singing through the streets. Intoxicated Jewish men dressed up as armed soldiers, sailors, and even Maroons and Indians, and women donned men's clothing their female slaves following suit. Christians purchased masks

from Jewish vendors and disguised themselves, with the suspected intention of attacking their enemies incognito.⁴⁶

Purim is one of many examples, Ben-Ur argues, in which Caribbean slaves were not passively engaging with Jewish cultural expressions under the force of their masters. Instead,

> Purim is a prism through which to understand how the cultural domains of enslaved and free people in Surinamese society became imbricated. Jews extended their ethnoreligious heritage to unfree people by naming some of their slaves Prim or Harbona and by allowing their bondsmen and bondswomen not only leisure time but also participation in the holiday merrymaking. In their rebellious behavior, whether by challenging masters or mistresses on Jewish holidays, absconding into the wilderness with a meguila, or synchronizing their communal celebrations with Jewish festive days, slaves owned by Jews demonstrated an awareness and understanding of Jewish heritage. Public celebration of Purim reached a new zenith in the early 1800s and, with the participation of Christians, slaves, and domestic bondsmen, shows strong signs of having become the colony's carnival, an ecumenical festivity with pronounced Afro-Creole attributes.⁴⁷

Ben-Ur's recovery of this creolized tradition elucidates not just the expression of Jewish culture on a Jewish-owned plantation, and not just the coparticipation of enslaved peoples within asymmetrical relations of power, but also the mixing of these worlds through the performance of the Purim story. The result is a reenactment of a text, the Book of Esther, framed by cultural convergences and the *process* of intersection. Here, transmission, translation, and adaptation not only change the performance, but shape the cultures and self-perceptions of the performers. We therefore draw inspiration from postcolonial critic Gauri Viswanathan's model of cultural analysis in which "one culture is studied as at once the condition and the effect of the other."⁴⁸ At the same time, we heed Viswanathan's warning that "what might thus appear as interdependence will be more accurately understood as mutual limitation."⁴⁹ Accordingly, this collection asks: What can the intersection or collision of Jewish and other Caribbean diasporic cultures help us to understand about Caribbean literary history, the rise of Creole culture, and the role of colonialism in shaping racial knowledge and class structures to consolidate its power? Our interest in a Jewish Caribbean Creole culture highlights the forms of cultural expression and performance produced by Black, Jewish, and other crossings in the colonial Caribbean. Simultaneously, this volume addresses postcolonial writing that registers these kinds of intersections as part of a larger matrix of Caribbean creolization and as contributing to the dynamics of exchange in Caribbean literary culture.

Ben-Ur's evocation of biblical Persian Jewish experience reconstructed on a Surinamese plantation stands as a perfect emblem of the blurring of categories that this collection registers. In so doing, the collection seeks to draw attention to the presence of Creole Jews in the Caribbean as well as mixed-race Jewish populations and their contribution to the production of a Caribbean literary culture. However, we are also interested in literary texts without any Jewish characters or authorship that narrate stories through a Jewish lens; or, alternately, how the story of slavery turns to the Holocaust for the language of analogy; or how contemporary Afro- and Indo-Caribbean writers blend Jewish and Black stories in novels critical of colonialism. This study represents an attempt to chart new methodological possibilities for recovering and interpreting these rich and largely unexamined crossings in the literary culture of the Caribbean over the last three hundred years.

The Essays and Creative Writing

Caribbean Jewish Crossings takes a pan-Caribbean approach rather than focusing on a single island, linguistic region, or colonial power. Indeed, one of the advantages of tracing the literary legacy of the peripatetic Jewish presence in the Caribbean is that it reveals how this legacy—real and imagined—cuts across the imperial map of the Caribbean and its linguistic and political divisions. Therefore, while not attempting to offer a comprehensive account of Caribbean Jewish literary intersections, this collection targets significant historical moments, writers, and regions whose literary output calls out for further consideration.

The opening section of the volume recovers a series of moments in the literary histories of Suriname, St. Thomas, Jamaica, and Cuba from the late eighteenth century through the early twentieth century. This section stands in for a much longer and larger understudied preindependence literary history in which writers explored links between Jewish and Black culture in the Caribbean. Ineke Phaf-Rheinberger's "The Portuguese Jewish Nation: An Enlightenment Essay on the Colony of Suriname" focuses on the eighteenth-century Surinamese author David Nassy, who was born in 1741 and whose *Essai historique* (1788) represents what she calls the "specific standpoint of the Portuguese Jewish Nation."

Phaf-Rheinberger's essay explores the profound influence that Nassy's *Essai historique*, a seminal text for the study of New World and Jewish Caribbean literary culture, would have over the Sephardic Atlantic world. Tracing Nassy's condemnation of anti-Jewish discrimination, Phaf-Rheinberger shows that he not only "laments this lack of respect" but maintains that it "caused a permanent internal rivalry in the colony, which manifested itself acutely in periods of economic crisis." In "Henrik Hertz and Racial Imagination in the Nineteenth-Century Danish Caribbean," David Gantt Gurley reads a little-known novel, Henrik Hertz's *De Frifarvede* (The free-colored, 1836), as a political gesture. The novel is set in the Danish West Indies and explores relations between a white plantation owner's son and his biracial cousin. Gurley argues that the novel offers both a sharp critique of colonialism and a scathing commentary on the Crown's policies regarding slavery. At the same time, Gurley compellingly shows how this colonial critique is tied to Danish domestic debates about Jewish emancipation.

Heidi Kaufman's "Jamaican Tricksters: Philip Cohen Labatt's Literary Crossings" approaches Jewish and Black intersections from the perspective of a little-studied Jamaican Jewish writer. While considering Labatt's perspective as a writer who may have been biracial but was probably never enslaved, Kaufman argues that Labatt's story "Curgy's Funeral" exposes a form of literary creolization shaped by a Jewish writer's exploration of enslavement and resistance, and illustrates in particular Labatt's "use of racial stereotypes in a work that blends a number of written and oral literary cultures." Kaufman raises the question of the role of Jewishness in the formation of Caribbean creolization in Jamaica. The final essay in this section, Rachel Rubinstein's "Translating Cuba: Language, Race, and Homeland in Cuban-Yiddish Poetry of the 1930s," explores the work of Yiddish Cuban writers who found ways to authenticate their "visions of Cuban citizenship." Rubinstein's discussion focuses on the 1931 poem *Hatuey* by Oskar Pinis (also known as Ascher Penn) and the 1932 poem *Maceo* by Eliezer Aronowsky, which she describes as "epic poems with popular indigenous and Afro-Cuban revolutionary subjects." Both Yiddish writers turn to national heroes: Hatuey, the sixteenth-century Taino Indian and protorevolutionary, and Maceo, the symbol of Cuban struggles for independence. Rubinstein's sensitive reading of these texts draws productively on Ortiz's concept of transculturation to theorize the translational dimensions of Yiddish literature in 1930s Cuba.

Part 2 examines the afterlife of the Spanish Inquisition in contemporary Caribbean literature and the relationship of Sephardic Jewishness to Caribbean spaces. Sarah Phillips Casteel's "David Dabydeen's Hogarth: Blacks, Jews, and Postcolonial Ekphrasis" draws attention to Jewish and Sephardic figures in two novels by Guyanese British writer David Dabydeen, *A Harlot's Progress* and *Johnson's Dictionary*. Dabydeen's ekphrastic novels invoke the eighteenth-century satirical artist William Hogarth—in particular, plate 2 of his 1732 series *A Harlot's Progress*, which depicts the encounter of a cuckolded Jewish merchant, his mistress, and a turbaned slave boy. In her essay, Casteel argues that Dabydeen's "strategy of introducing visual intertexts into his fiction" enables a "comparative reading of the representational regimes that historically have shaped popular perceptions of Blacks and Jews." Casteel recalls the centrality of visual culture, of seeing and being seen, within the linked histories of colonialism, slavery, and crypto-Jewry. Leonard Stein's *"Jubanidad* and the Literary Transmission of Cuban Crypto-Judaism" reads crypto-Jewry from the perspective of Cuban Jewish writers Achy Obejas's semi-autobiographical *Days of Awe* and Genie Milgrom's memoir *My 15 Grandmothers*. Stein makes a persuasive case for reading Jewishness as a process of transmission, or what he calls "the conveyance of preserved information, genetic or constructed, through intimate relationships with others; the passage of history through unspoken traditions; the transference and dissemination of the hidden to the revealed." Obejas's novel also features in Linda Weinhouse and Efraim Sicher's essay, "Diaspora and Hybridity: Jewish American Women Write the Caribbean," which considers how expressions of secret Jewish observance shape depictions of diasporic culture in novels by Jewish Caribbean and Jewish American women writers. Their discussion of Achy Obejas's *Days of Awe* and Alice Hoffman's *The Marriage of Opposites* explore women characters with a *converso* or crypto-Jewish background who engage in imagined returns to lands that they have never before visited. For Weinhouse and Sicher, these returns evoke and rework Jewish memorial and diasporic narratives within Caribbean contexts.

Part 3 turns to the question of colonialism and its relationship to Holocaust memory, with a particular emphasis on theory and on the Francophone Caribbean. Ben Ratskoff's "Splattering the Object: Césaire, Nazi Racism, and the Colonial" revisits a seminal figure both in Caribbean poetics and in discussions of postcolonial-Jewish intersections: the Martinican poet and theorist Aimé Césaire. Ratskoff brings a fresh and nuanced perspective to Césaire's classic text *Discourse on Colonialism* by attending to questions of translation and Césaire's surrealist style. Ratskoff's close reading of this text traces how Césaire "deexceptionalizes the Jewish experience of Nazism as racism's urtext while suggesting the incorporation of European Jewish history into anticolonial critique." Kathleen Gyssels's "From Shtetl to Settler Colony and Back: André Schwarz-Bart's *The Morning Star*" draws attention to the French Jewish writer André Schwarz-Bart, who married and collaborated with the important Guadeloupean author Simone Schwarz-Bart. Examining André Schwarz-Bart's posthumously published and little-known works, Gyssels illustrates how he elaborated a cross-cultural vision. Gyssels shows how Schwarz-Bart turned to Guadeloupe as an alternative to both Europe and Israel while also problematizing the critical reception of his work.

Alessandra Benedicty-Kokken's "Raphaël Confiant and Jewishness: The Fraught Landscapes of French, Martinican, and Franco-Martinican Intellectualisms" highlights another key figure from the Francophone Caribbean—Raphaël Confiant. Benedicty-Kokken's thoughtful discussion of the controversy surrounding Confiant's allegedly anti-Semitic remarks traces a more ambivalent dimension of Caribbean literary discourse about Jewishness, which she situates in terms of a larger Francophone Caribbean literary tradition as well as with respect to the Créolité movement (to which Confiant has been a key contributor). Ultimately, she argues that "the scholarly treatment of the scandal surrounding his work points to an extreme paucity in our ability to deal with questions of Otherness, difference, race, and religion." Rounding out this section of the collection, Neil R. Davison addresses the writer who has inspired perhaps the most critical discussion of Jewish-postcolonial literary intersections: Caryl Phillips. Synthesizing the substantial critical reception of Phillips's novels, in "Caryl Phillips's Post-Holocaust/Decolonized Interstices and the Levinasian Subjective in *Higher Ground* and *The Nature of Blood*," Davison introduces a new and valuable dimension to the discussion by rereading Phillips through the lens of philosopher Emmanuel Levinas. In Davison's reading, Phillips's fiction provides "an entrance into a space in which an older notion of an absolute yet nontranscendent humanity is rediscovered through a disturbing yet inviolable individuality that aligns with the Levinasian concept of alterity."

Finally, in recognition of the fact that creative writers have long registered the Caribbean Jewish presences and intersections that scholars have tended to overlook, our last section features the contemporary voices of Caribbean writers who address Jewishness in their poetry and fiction. This section signals the importance of literary production as a corrective to some of the blind spots of what Bryan Cheyette calls "disciplinary thinking" as well as literary culture's value as a site for alternative forms of theoretical discourse.[50] Jamaican Jewish visual artist and writer Anna Ruth Henriques, whose beautiful artwork graces the cover of our volume, has also contributed a short biography of her Jamaican Jewish grandmother, Evelyn Matalon, who passed away in 2017. "Ema" not only presents the life of a person through the lens of her family, but reads twentieth-century Jamaican Jewish culture through the perspective of a single family history. Surinamese novelist and historian Cynthia McLeod, who traces Jewish lineage in her own family tree, recalls in her autobiographical story "Meeting with Judith" (translated here for the first time into English) the impact of her childhood friendship with a Dutch Jewish girl whose family moved to Suriname in 1938. McLeod's story movingly recounts her reunion with her childhood friend some fifty years later as well as how this friendship provided inspiration for her historical novel about Jewish plantation life, *Hoe duur was de suiker? (The Cost of Sugar,* 1987).

In her sequence of poems, the Cuban American anthropologist and writer Ruth Behar, author of *An Island Called Home: Returning to Jewish Cuba* (2007), writes about the condition of nostalgia, of a Sephardic longing for a lost home. Calling upon symbolic systems and languages—tattoos, keys, and the sea—Behar weaves together both her sense of Cuban Jewish heritage and the loss of home against and through which that heritage was born. Finally, in his essay "On *The Nature of Blood* and the Ghost of Anne Frank," originally published in 1998, Caryl Phillips reflects on his important novel *The Nature of Blood* (1997; discussed by Neil Davison in this volume). Addressing the question "Why would a writer from the Caribbean want to write about the Holocaust?" Phillips recounts how he came to identify as a child with Jewish victims of the Holocaust in a society in which "colonial history was not taught." Phillips describes his visits to the Anne Frank House in Amsterdam and his sense of indebtedness to the Jewish diarist while also commenting on the plight of Palestinians and the treatment of Black Jews in Israel.

Our hope with this collection is to open up a space of intersection and dialogue between Caribbean and Jewish studies and to lay the groundwork for future research. While there remains more material to recover and address, our collection reveals some of the significant ways in which Jewish culture took hold in the Caribbean while in turn helping to shape narratives of Caribbeanness. For example, as Rachel Rubinstein's essay in this collection illustrates, Jewish languages (Yiddish and Hebrew) were used to articulate Cuban cultural narratives while Cuban national myths were simultaneously adapted and incorporated into Yiddish literary tradition. Also noteworthy, as many of the essays in this volume suggest, are the longstanding effects of the Inquisition's creation of crypto-Jewry. Under the pressure of the Inquisition, Jews were forced to convert to Christianity to avoid torture and death. The generations that followed continued to observe Jewish rituals in private, in some cases with little knowledge of the forces that pushed their traditions into hiding. Thus, Jewish Caribbean writers such as Achy Obejas narrate the experience of Jewish hiding or of belatedly discovering their Jewish heritage and family. Hidden, submerged identities are one of the hallmarks of Jewish Caribbean intersections and overlap powerfully with African diaspora narratives of passing and cultural survival. Alongside these motifs, the biblical story of Exodus has remained a significant point of intersection for writing about slavery and emancipation. While Jewish and African diaspora experiences and histories diverge significantly from one another and from those of other outsider groups, they have in common a narrative of being at sea, exiled from home, or wandering in deserts, literal or figurative, in search of a new sense of belonging. Finally, several essays in this collection remind us how writers and theorists from the Caribbean have turned to the Sephardic expulsion and the Holocaust to bolster their critiques of European colonialism and racism. An intellectual trajectory that divides Jewish, African, Asian and other diasporic cultural expressions misses an opportunity to see how they have crossed in Caribbean literary history, or, as Aviva Ben-Ur puts it, have formed a pattern of "latticework" that opens up new ways of reading beyond "the separate spheres, ordered upon hierarchy and violence."[51]

Notes

1. Marlon James, "Bigots on My Bookshelf," *Marlon James Among Other Things,* September 19, 2017, http://marlon-james.blogspot.com.au/2009/03/bigots-on-my-bookshelf.html.

2. William Makepeace Thackeray, *Vanity Fair: A Novel Without a Hero,* 2 vols. (London: Smith Elder, 1869), vol. 1, 219.

3. Eli Faber, *Jews, Slaves, and the Slave Trade: Setting the Record Straight* (New York: New York University Press, 1998).

4. Derek Walcott, "The Muse of History," in *What the Twilight Says* (New York: Farrar, Straus & Giroux, 1998), 54–56.

5. While several important studies focus on the intersection of Jewish and Caribbean history, discussions of this intersection from a literary perspective are rare. Moreover, few such literary discussions extend beyond the analysis of a single text (such as Caryl Phillips's *The Nature of Blood*). Among the few to do so are: Celia Britton, "Exile, Incarceration and the Homeland: Jewish References in French Caribbean Novels," in *Comparing Postcolonial Diasporas*, ed. Michelle Keown, David Murphy, and James Proctor (New York: Palgrave Macmillan, 2009), 149–67; Sarah Phillips Casteel, *Calypso Jews: Jewishness in the Caribbean Literary Imagination* (New York: Columbia University Press, 2016); Sue Greene, "The Use of the Jew in West Indian Novels," *World Literature Written in English* 26, no. 1 (1986): 150–69; Kathleen Gyssels, *Marrane et marronne: La co-écriture réversible d'André et de Simone Schwarz-Bart* (Amsterdam: Rodopi, 2014); and Bénédicte Ledent, "Caribbean Writers and the Jewish Diaspora: A Shared Experience of Otherness," in *The Invention of Legacy: Essays in Memory of Hena Maes-Jelinek*, ed. Gordon Collier, Geoffrey V. Davis, Marc Delrez, and Bénédicte Ledent (Boston: Rodopi, 2015), 229–50.

6. See, for example, Jonathan Schorsch, *Jews and Blacks in the Early Modern World* (Cambridge: Cambridge University Press, 2004); *The Jews in the Caribbean*, ed. Jane S. Gerber (Oxford: Littman Library of Jewish Civilization, 2014); E. L. Joseph, *Warner Arundell: The Adventures of a Creole*, ed. Lise Winer (Kingston, JA: University of West Indies Press, 2001); and *Art and Emancipation in Jamaica: Isaac Mendes Belisario and His Worlds*, ed. Tim Barringer, Gillian Forrester, and Barbaro Martinez-Ruiz (New Haven, CT: Yale University Press, 2007).

7. Paul Gilroy, *The Black Atlantic: Modernity and Double Consciousness* (Cambridge, MA: Harvard University Press, 1993), 205.

8. Gilroy, *Black Atlantic*, 207.

9. See, for example, Brinda Mehta, *Diasporic (Dis)locations: Indo-Caribbean Women Writers Negotiate the Kala Pani* (Kingston, JA: University of West Indies Press, 2004); and Anne-Marie Lee-Loy, *Searching for Mr. Chin: Constructions of Nation and the Chinese in West Indian Literature* (Philadelphia: Temple University Press, 2010).

10. *Caribbean Irish Connections: Interdisciplinary Perspectives*, ed. Alison Donnell, Maria McGarrity, and Evelyn O'Callighan (Kingston, JA: University of the West Indies Press, 2015), 1–2.

11. Jonathan Israel, *Diasporas within a Diaspora: Jews, Crypto-Jews, and the World of Maritime Empires: 1540–1740* (Leiden: E. J. Brill, 2002), 1.

12. Jane S. Gerber, "Introduction," in *The Jews in the Caribbean*, ed. Jane S. Gerber (Oxford: Littman Library of Jewish Civilization, 2014), 11.

13. See Philippe Girard, *Toussaint Louverture: A Revolutionary Life* (New York: Basic Books, 2016), 184.

14. Gad Heuman, *"The Killing Time": The Morant Bay Rebellion in Jamaica* (Knoxville: University of Tennessee Press, 1994), 153.

24 Introduction

15. David Isaac de Cohen Nassy, *Historical Essay on the Colony of Surinam* (1788), trans. Simon Cohen (Cincinnati: American Jewish Archives, 1974), 66.

16. See Schorsch, *Jews and Blacks*, 283–84, for a discussion of this episode. See also Natalie Zemon Davis, "Regaining Jerusalem: Eschatology and Slavery in Jewish Colonization in Seventeenth-Century Suriname," *Cambridge Journal of Postcolonial Literary Inquiry* 3, no. 1(January 2016): 11–38, where she discusses what she terms the "Passover conundrum." Davis writes that "there is no sign that the Nassys and their fellow Jews saw a contradiction between their struggle for equal status as free people living 'in their own manner' and their purchase of captive Africans" (26).

17. See Hearne's novel *Land of the Living* (London: Faber & Faber, 1961) and Cliff's novels *Abeng* (New York: Plume, [1984] 1995) and *Free Enterprise* (New York: Plume, 1993) and poems "A Visit to the Secret Annex," *The Land of Look Behind* (Ithaca, NY: Firebrand, 1985), 104–7, and "If I Could Write This in Fire, I Would Write This in Fire," in *The Land of Look Behind* (Ithaca, NY: Firebrand, 1985), 57–76. See Casteel, *Calypso Jews*, chapters 2 and 7, for in-depth discussions of Jewish themes in Cliff's fiction and poetry, and chapter 5 for a discussion of Hearne's novel.

18. Casteel, *Calypso Jews*, 274.

19. See Jonathan Boyarin, "The Other Within and the Other Without," in *Storm from Paradise: The Politics of Jewish Memory* (Minneapolis: University of Minnesota Press, 1992), 77–98; Bryan Cheyette, *Diasporas of the Mind: Jewish and Postcolonial Writing and the Nightmare of History* (New Haven, CT: Yale University Press, 2013); and Michael Rothberg, *Multidirectional Memory: Remembering the Holocaust in the Age of Decolonization* (Stanford, CA: Stanford University Press, 2009).

20. Rothberg, *Multidirectional Memory*, 101.

21. Shelley Fisher Fishkin, "Crossroads of Cultures: The Transnational Turn in American Studies: Presidential Address to the American Studies Association, November 12, 2004," *American Quarterly* 57, no. 1(March 2005): 17–57, 21.

22. See Jennifer Glaser, "Invisible Hebrews: Jews in Early America," *Early American Literature* 49, no. 1 (2014): 201–11, 202–3; and Dalia Kandiyoti, "What Is the 'Jewish' in 'Jewish American Literature'?" *Studies in Jewish American Literature* 31, no. 1 (2012): 48–60, 55.

23. Kandiyoti, "What Is the 'Jewish,'" 55.

24. Lital Levy and Allison Schachter, "Jewish Literature/World Literature: Between the Local and the Transnational," *PMLA* 130, no. 1 (2015): 92–109.

25. Caryl Phillips, *A New World Order* (New York: Vintage, 2001), 130.

26. See Benjamin Schreier's *The Impossible Jew: Identity and the Reconstruction of Jewish American Literary History* (New York: New York University Press, 2015).

27. Personal correspondence with Anna Ruth Henriques, August 12, 2017.

28. See https://www.henriquesart.com/exodus-ii.

29. Andrea Levy, *The Long Song* (London: Headline Review, 2010), 302.

30. Stuart Hall, "Cultural Identity and Diaspora," *Identity: Community, Culture, Difference,* ed. Jonathan Rutherford (London: Lawrence & Wishart, 1990), 222–37.

31. Gilroy, *Black Atlantic,* 211.

32. See, for example, the work of historians Jonathan Schorsch and Aviva Ben-Ur cited in the present essay. Other studies that address the history of the Jewish Caribbean include Laura Leibman's *Messianism, Secrecy, and Mysticism: A New Interpretation of Early American Jewish Life* (London: Vallentine Mitchell, 2013), which adopts a material culture approach, and Barry Stiefel's architectural history *Jewish Sanctuary in the Atlantic World* (Columbia: University of South Carolina Press, 2014).

33. Linda M. Rupert, "Trading Globally, Speaking Locally: Curaçao's Sephardim in the Making of a Caribbean Creole," in *Jews and Port Cities, 1590–1990: Commerce, Community, and Cosmopolitanism,* ed. David Cesarini and Gemma Romain (London: Vallentine Mitchell, 2006), 109–22, 110.

34. Natalie Zemon Davis, "Creole Languages and their Uses: The Example of Colonial Suriname," *Historical Research* 82 (May 2009): 1–17, 4.

35. Richard Price, *Alabi's World* (Baltimore: Johns Hopkins University Press, 1990).

36. Schorsch, *Jews and Blacks,* 229.

37. Zemon Davis, "Creole Languages," 15.

38. Alison Donnell and Sarah Lawson Welsh, eds., *The Routledge Reader in Caribbean Literature* (New York: Routledge, 1996), 4.

39. Neil Roberts, *Freedom as Marronage* (Chicago: University of Chicago Press, 2015), 145.

40. Wieke Vink, *Creole Jews: Negotiating Community in Colonial Suriname* (Leiden: KITLV, 2010), 10.

41. Wieke, *Creole Jews,* 9.

42. Wieke, 9–10.

43. Edward Blyden, "The Jewish Question," in *Black Spokesman: Selected Writings of Edward Wilmot Blyden,* ed. Hollis R. Lynch (London: Frank Cass, 1971), 209–14.

44. Blyden, "The Jewish Question," 211.

45. Aviva Ben-Ur, "Purim in the Public Eye: Leisure, Violence, and Cultural Convergence in the Dutch Atlantic," *Jewish Social Studies* 20, no. 1 (Fall 2013): 32–76, 33.

46. Ben-Ur, "Purim in the Public," 32–33.

47. Ben-Ur, 61–62.

48. Gauri Viswanathan, *Outside the Fold: Conversion, Modernity, and Belief* (Princeton, NJ: Princeton University Press, 1998), 4.

49. Viswanathan, *Outside the Fold,* 4.

50. Cheyette, *Diasporas of the Mind,* 6.

51. Ben-Ur, "Purim in the Public," 34.

PART I

The Emergence of Caribbean Jewish Literary Culture

The Portuguese Jewish Nation
An Enlightenment Essay on the Colony of Suriname

Ineke Phaf-Rheinberger

IN THE SECOND half of the eighteenth century, the spirit of Enlightenment reached Suriname, much as it did the United Provinces and the rest of Europe. An important essay authored by David (Isaac de Cohen) Nassy in 1788 both incorporates an Enlightenment worldview and served as a major document on the colony of Suriname to that date. Jonathan Israel, in his monumental *The Dutch Republic: Its Rise, Greatness, and Fall (1477–1806)*, praises Nassy as one of "the leading figures of the Dutch colonial Enlightenment."[1] Nassy's *Essai historique sur la colonie de Surinam* (Historical essay on the colony of Surinam), written in the universal language of the Enlightenment, has also been mined as a source for recent literature and scholarship. Cynthia McLeod mentions the *Essai historique* as one of the main inspirations for her novel, *Hoe duur was de suiker? (The Cost of Sugar,* 1987).[2] The eminent cultural anthropologist Richard Price, in *First-Time* (1983), uses Nassy's essay to verify much of the information obtained from his Saramacca Maroon informants. Such an enduring interest in the *Essai historique* justifies our reserving a special place for it in the early history of literature in the region of the Caribbean colonized by the Dutch.

The *Essai historique* is written from the specific standpoint of the Portuguese Jewish Nation, the community into which David Nassy was born in 1741. The Jew's Savannah, as his birthplace was called, was a village on the Suriname River three hours by boat from Paramaribo. The Nassy family was very prominent. One of their forefathers had been an outstanding leader of the first colonists of Suriname to whom freedom of religion had been granted, first under English rule, then under the Dutch. The principal synagogue, Beracha Ve Shalom (Blessing and Peace), was inaugurated in the Jew's Savannah in October 1685, on land donated by the Nassy family, then the richest planter family in the region. David

Nassy did not belong to the wealthy branch of the family, however. His father, Isaac, became an administrative official of the Jewish Nation in Suriname in 1754 and remained in his office until his death in 1774. David began his working life as his father's clerk in 1765. In 1770 he decided to buy the coffee plantation Tulpenburg (Tulip bourg). He was not successful as a planter. Bijlsma recalls the reason why Nassy was unable to continue the exploitation of the plantation: "A terribly high death rate struck the blacks of Tulpenburg. Rumor had it that one of the blacks had poisoned his fellow slaves and the doctor who came to see Nassy found him depressed about the persistent loss of his workers."[3] Nassy was forced to sell his property at a very unfavorable price in 1773; he first moved to Paramaribo but fled back to the Jew's Savannah to avoid imprisonment for debt in early 1776. In the meantime, he worked as official translator of Spanish and Portuguese for the Council of Police and, as a result, was constantly consulted on questions involving the members of the Portuguese Jewish Nation.

When the French functionary Malouet, a royal commissioner-general and administrator (and, as such, not a promoter of the rights of the Jews in Christian countries), visited Suriname in 1777, he made acquaintance with a certain Isaac Nassy in the Jew's Savannah. Bijlsma concludes that this was none other than the author of the *Essai historique;* he reproduces a lengthy text in which Malouet describes the qualities of this "homme extraordinaire."[4] Malouet notes that Nassy aimed to elevate the general level of instruction and knowledge of the Jewish Nation and, therefore, studied in his cabinet at least eight hours a day. At the time when Nassy was able to return to Paramaribo in 1782 the city had become susceptible to such intellectual endeavors. Governor Wiebers founded a Society for Natural Sciences and supported initiatives for improvement of general education. Together with other members of the government, Wiebers had attended the celebrations for the centenary of the synagogue Beracha Ve Shalom, in October 1785, which was witnessed by more than 1,600 guests at the Jew's Savannah. Notwithstanding these high numbers in attendance, the glory days of the Portuguese Jews in Suriname were already past. Henceforth, their general board, the *mahamad,* gathered exclusively in the thriving capital of Paramaribo and had to confront totally new questions of social mobility.

There is no doubt that the Nassy family has been instrumental in the rise and fall of the Jew's Savannah. The *Essai historique,* on many of its pages, refers to their strong leadership in agricultural, financial, military, governmental, and intellectual matters successively. David Nassy's contribution was in this last domain, the one that concerns us here. He was appointed to the salaried position of secretary of the *mahamad* in 1778, and he was largely responsible for the reform of the *askamoth* between 1785 and 1788. He was cofounder of the learned society Docendo Docemur in Paramaribo, where important works were discussed by members of the government, administrators, planters, and other interested Christian and Jewish people. It was in this capacity that Nassy wrote the *Essai historique* in 1788. The book was published anonymously in Amsterdam in 1789, and on the cover of the original edition appear the names of the members of the *parnassim,* or leaders of the community: Mos. Pa. de Leon, Samuel Hco. de la Parra, Ishak de la Parra, David de Is. C. Nassy, Samual Whel. Brandon. The essay came out in a Dutch translation in 1791, apparently without Nassy's knowledge, and was well received in the Netherlands. There is slim evidence of any reaction to the book in Suriname at that time.

The organization of the *Essai historique* displays its dual aim: to instruct and enlighten. The essay is divided into two parts, which are preceded by a preface and an introduction. The copies of several original documents are added as an appendix. The frontispiece presents a veritable summary of the book's contents with respect to interpreting the early history of Suriname:

> Its foundation, its revolutions, its progress, from its origin until our days, as also the causes which since some years have stopped the course of its prosperity, with the description and the actual state of the Colony, as well as the annual revenues, the charges and taxes which have to be paid, and equally several other civil and political objectives; also a tableau des moeurs of its inhabitants in general, WITH the History of the Portuguese and German Jewish Nation and Established, their Privileges, immunities and franchises; their political and moral State, old as well as modern. The role they played in the defense and the progress of the Colony.[5]

R. A. J. van Lier, who published *Frontier Society: A Social Analysis of the History of Surinam* in 1971, quotes liberally from Nassy in order to call attention to his own disagreement with anti-Semitism in his native country.[6] He conceives the eighteenth century as a crucial moment for anti-Semitism:

> The prejudices against the Jews had gradually assumed a stereotyped form. They were held responsible for the running away of slaves, as they had sent a number of their slaves into the jungle during the French invasion in 1712 so as to

reduce their share in the levy imposed by the French admiral. After that they supposedly caused a marked increase in the number of deserters because of the cruel treatment to which they subjected their slaves, amongst whom they failed to keep discipline, moreover, as a result of the large number of Jewish feasts on which work was at a standstill. Some accused them of too great a familiarity with their slaves, others of excessive cruelty. They were said to be bad farmers who had only themselves to blame for their ruin. The authors of the *Essai Historique* have produced sufficient evidence to disprove these views. These persisted until Emancipation, however, and claimed many innocent victims among the Jews. Especially the view that Jews were exceptionally cruel masters for their slaves constantly recurs in the literature on Surinam. We find allusions to this in the writings of Hartsinck and Stedman, while even as late as the 19th century Teenstra wrote about the cruel treatment which slaves received especially at the hand of Jewish owners.[7]

Nassy, in his time, perceived those prejudices as a personal affront and attributed their existence to the severe economic crisis that lasted from 1765 to 1775; it affected all planters, but the Jews in particular. The dramatic nature of their situation is evident in these significant details related by van Lier: "In 1760 Jews still owned around 115 of the 591 estates, the majority of which were sugar estates, which [sic] by 1788 this number had dwindled to 46, including 16 sugar and coffee estates, the remainder consisting mostly of timber estates."[8] In order to frame this drama for the Portuguese Nation, Nassy recalls the expulsion of the Jews from Spain in 1492, and from Portugal in 1496–97 in the first part of the *Essai historique*. Through their contacts in the Flemish cities of Antwerp, Bruges, and Ghent the Portuguese Jews were familiar with the details of the liberation struggle in the north and, when Antwerp fell to the Spanish in 1585, they began to move to Amsterdam. Representatives of this Jewish group participated in the Dutch conquest of Brazil and, due to their insistence, the Portuguese New Christians were accorded freedom of religion from 1636 until 1654. Formerly despised by "real" Christians, they now met with "real" Jews from the Portuguese Nation in Amsterdam who helped them with the organization of their synagogue and cemetery. In exchange, the Dutch could count on their loyalty as well as their international expertise and language skills. After the reconquest of Recife by the Portuguese, in 1654, a group of these Portuguese Jews moved to Cayenne and, afterward, to Suriname, where their privileges were guaranteed, first by the English and, after 1667, by the Dutch.

Early in his essay Nassy condemns the discrimination and even hatred on the part of the Christians toward the Jewish people in Europe and toward the Jewish colonists in Suriname in particular. He laments this lack of respect in consideration of the numerous examples that demonstrated the loyalty and responsibility of the Jews for Christian government in the past. Furthermore, in Nassy's opinion, this attitude had caused a permanent internal rivalry in the colony, which manifested itself acutely in periods of economic crisis. Nassy writes that frequently the governor of the colony himself or even the Dutch government had to intervene in order to reconcile the two white groups and to assure the Jewish Nation that they would keep their privileges. In order to illustrate his arguments, Nassy counters the misunderstanding of the Suriname colony in contemporary Dutch history, citing numerous studies published in Amsterdam and other European capitals.

We know that Nassy was extremely well read. Robert Cohen has published a catalogue of 433 titles in Nassy's library, as well as a list of 90 other titles mentioned in the *Essai historique*.[9] Because of his manifest interest in contemporary philosophy and science, and in the context of his efforts to improve the condition of Jews in Suriname, Nassy enthusiastically introduced Christian Wilhelm Dohm's *Die bürgerliche Verbesserung der Juden* (The civil improvement of the Jews)—published in Berlin in 1781 to his own readers. In his analysis of the position of the Jews in European countries, Dohm had questioned their absence from public service, the military, craft trades, and farming. He concluded that the Jews had never possessed equal civil rights in Europe, notwithstanding abundant proof of their capability, loyalty, and erudition. Dohm's classical Enlightenment essay occasioned many contradictory discussions in Berlin and Vienna before it arrived in Suriname in the French translation of 1785. Early in 1786 Nassy presented Dohm's book to his fellow intellectuals in Paramaribo; its thesis was publicly discussed in the learned society "Docendo docemur." Dohm's arguments were so well received that the *parnassim* decided to write Dohm a letter on March 10, 1786, to express gratitude for his valuable observations. By way of response, Dohm on January 29, 1787, sent a letter back to Paramaribo, which arrived on June 29th of that year. In it he requested further information about the history of Jewish privileges in Suriname. This correspondence was included in the *Essai historique,* since it supported the main arguments of Nassy's book.[10]

Alongside his statement of aims in writing the essay, Nassy assured his readers that he had verified his facts through extensive consultation of the archives of the Portuguese Nation, which had seldom been consulted by Dutch historians. This last argument refers, in particular, to another typical treatise of the Dutch Enlightenment, *Beschrijving van Guiana* (Description of Guiana), which Jan Hartsinck published in Amsterdam in 1770. Nassy protests against the tendentious nature of Hartsinck's representation of the military activities of members of the Portuguese Jewish Nation. He argues to the contrary that, from the very beginnings of the colony, Christian and Jewish colonists organized the defense of the plantation areas together, initially against the Amerindians. His forefather Samuel Nassy, who spoke their language, arranged peace treaties between the Amerindians and Governor Van Sommelsdyk, who received in exchange the daughter of an Amerindian chief as his wife. Afterward, and in the eighteenth century in particular, Jews and Christians fought the Maroons, who increasingly threatened the prosperity and peace of the country. The nation participated in this defense at the cost of an extraordinarily high economic investment, which Nassy illustrates in his text.

The first part of the *Essai historique* leaves no doubt that the Portuguese Jewish Nation had the position of a minority, always subject to discrimination and loss of respect for their traditions in the Christian colony of Suriname. Nassy mentions, for instance, the constant debate over Sunday as a working day for the Jews, who often sacrificed their own Sabbath to participate in the duties they had in common with the Christians. For the Protestant planters, however, Sunday was the day dedicated to the worship of their God and, jealous of the success of the Jewish planters, they forbade work on all the plantations of the colony on their holy day.

In contrast, the tone in part 2 of the *Essai historique* is completely different. It is conceived as a hymn to the colony of Suriname. According to Nassy, one would probably not find "in any colony of the Americas other than Suriname plantations which are regulated better, or are more beautiful, and with many magnificent buildings and gardens of such a sumptuosity that they are beyond compare."[11] The structure of the work reveals Nassy's intention to counter, in the second part, the negative image of Suriname in Europe. To that end he provided detailed data concerning costs and prices of crop production as well as signs of tolerance toward different religions, which led to the Catholics establishing a church of their own in Paramaribo in 1787. He took care to supply information on political government, taxes, population, institutions, literature, and science as well.

The style in this second part of Nassy's essay is that of a proud colonist of Suriname, eager to show his superiority to the French colonists of Saint-Domingue. This recurrent reference to Saint-Domingue is noteworthy; it can be explained by the rivalry between these two Caribbean plantation societies in the eighteenth century. Amsterdam, with the income from its East and West Indian plantations, practically monopolized the European sugar markets from 1667 until approximately 1750, as Fernand Braudel demonstrated in a fascinating chapter of his *Civilisation matérielle, économie et capitalisme XVe–XVIIe siècles, tome 3: Le Temps du monde* (*Civilization and Capitalism, 15th–18th Century, vol. 3: The Perspective of the World,* 1979). By 1750 the Dutch had lost their monopoly to the French, whose colony of Saint-Domingue was emerging as the most lucrative in the world, a position it maintained until the revolution in 1791. Like Paramaribo, Cap François—the main export town in Saint-Domingue—was expanding rapidly in the second half of the eighteenth century. Its urban life (commerce, theater, churches, architecture, public life, science, and humanities) was just as carefully described by Médéric Moreau de Saint-Méry in his *Description topographique, physique, civile, politique et historique de la partie française de l'isle Saint-Domingue* (Topographical, physical, civil, political, and historical description of Saint-Domingue), the two volumes of which were published in Philadelphia in 1797–98. This author, born in Martinique, occupies a position in the historiography of eighteenth-century Saint Domingue similar to Nassy's for Suriname. McClellan even claims that Moreau de Saint-Méry dominates "the contemporary historiography, and readers should know of the extraordinary role he played in preserving Saint Domingue from historical oblivion."[12]

Moreau de Saint-Méry wrote his *Description topographique* while in exile in Philadelphia, after having fled the revolution in France. He was understandably nostalgic over the loss of the colony where he had spent many good years of his life. Nassy, in contrast, had never left his native country when he formulated his arguments in response to the prejudices against the Jews there. Suriname, like Saint-Domingue, was at war. McClellan, quoting from Moreau de Saint-Méry, depicts the organization of Saint-Domingue as that of a military camp. Nassy likewise refers frequently to military actions, their purposes and results, because the role of the Jews in the struggle against the Maroons was one of the key issues used against the Portuguese Jewish Nation. In reality, of course, colonial policies were at stake and nothing was specifically Jewish about that.

An important thematic nexus exists between this eighteenth-century historiography and twentieth-century fiction. Moreau de Saint-Méry, as is well known, describes the complex relationship among slaves, mulattos, and white Creoles. That relationship entailed numerous violent forms of resistance on the part of the slaves. Poisoning, which was a major problem for Nassy on his Tulpenburg plantation, as we have seen above, was one of the most conspicuous forms of this resistance. Alejo Carpentier, in *El reino de este mundo* (*The Kingdom of This World*, 1949), used Moreau de Saint-Méry's *Description topographique* to flesh out his fictional plot based on the revolt fomented in Saint-Domingue by the Maroon Mackandal. The historic Mackandal was famous for the poisonings that spread terror among the slaves and made them all obey him. This story line parallels a similar plot device, based in Suriname in the same historical period: the celebrated—and very widespread—stereotype of the cruel white mistress who takes revenge on the slave woman who was "courted" by her husband. Moreau de Saint-Méry adds a historical dimension to this stereotype in his chapter on Creole women, in which he emphasizes their extremely jealous character: "And nothing can equal the anger of a Creole woman who is punishing a slave whom her husband has forced to soil the marriage bed. In her jealous rage she knows only how to devise means to satiate her vengeance. These frightful scenes which were very rare are becoming more like daily occurrences."[13]

Neither Moreau de Saint-Méry nor David Nassy write from a contemporary postcolonial perspective, which condemns slavery and colonialism as a crime. In both cases, their position as white colonists represents the opposite of what C. L. R. James, in *The Black Jacobins,* or Richard Price, in *First-Time,* intend to explain by focusing on the inner dynamics of the struggle against slavery. However, James and Price also make use of the information given by our two eighteenth-century authors. Moreau and Nassy wish to place their arguments within the norms of public opinion in Europe and the United States in their day, according to which not slavery itself but the excesses of the system were considered questionable. Whereas both focus on the rivalry between the white Creoles and the free mulattos or Blacks, for Nassy these white Creoles are the Portuguese Jews and not the Christians. As a prominent member of the former group, he has perceived the deterioration of the position of the Jews at the same time that the freedmen were gaining ground in public life in Paramaribo. Nassy's point is not that he disagrees with these changes, but that they imply a negative judgment of the Jews. Therefore, he is at pains to counter Hartsinck's argument concerning the privileged position of the Jews:

> What does it mean nowadays to have the privilege of contributing to the nomination of the colony's magistrates? A Free Negro who owns a shack or a

piece of land, does he not have the same right? This type of democratic liberty conceded by the legislative power to the inhabitants of a Colony who work equally hard for their happiness as well as that of the Mother Country, is it susceptible to such childish and unjust observations? Mr. Hartsink, unwilling to acknowledge the truth of this fact, and possibly led on by his own prejudice, says that this liberty given to the Jews still wounds the heart of the other inhabitants. Why did he not add but one word of disapproval in order to show his impartiality?[14]

Passages such as this one demonstrate that Nassy was very much in touch with Enlightenment philosophy concerning political renewal; he even speaks of democratic liberty prior to the French Revolution. Robert Cohen, in *Jews in Another Environment: Surinam in the Second Half of the Eighteenth Century* (1991), makes these same urban social dynamics a crucial issue in his book. He bases his analysis on three points. In the first place, he observes that Suriname in those days represented a major emigration destination for the Jews of Amsterdam. Cohen argues that the Sephardis had to deal with a considerable economic burden because of the influx of poor Ashkenazi Jews who had fled pogroms and war in Germany and Poland. Jonathan Israel also explains that, in times of economic decay, the "Amsterdam Sephardic community in the 1740s stepped up its policy of assisting emigration of members who lacked employment opportunities in the Republic to Surinam and Curaçao."[15] These Jewish immigrants, once arrived in Suriname, generally chose to stay in Paramaribo without considering the possibility of doing business in the interior. In this sense, the economic burden moved with them from Amsterdam to Paramaribo and fell upon the Jewish organizations in that city as well.

In the second place, Cohen distinguishes his own reading of Surinamese urbanization patterns from Nassy's interpretation of the same phenomena. Nassy understood his position primarily as a part of Jewish history without questioning the colonial experience as such. Cohen claims that this attitude has lost its legitimacy. For this reason, he analyzes the drive for internal coherence on the part of the *mahamad* from a contemporary, postcolonial point of view. Cohen also takes a critical position toward the Jewish elite and their denial of the legitimate claims of mixed-race Jews. Finally, as a historian Cohen laments the fact that most of his colleagues do not address the ambiguous position of the Jews and the Jewish mulattos. This is why he carefully lays out the dynamics of their social life:

> If we compare the structure of a plantation society to a broad-based triangle intersected by two lines parallel to the base, we find a small apex, a middle sector and a large base, respectively representing the white European community, the free colored, and the slaves. Color is the dividing line between the two top sectors and legal status the lines between the bottom and middle section.... Jews, being white, undoubtedly belonged to the small apex of the societal model. They had more in common with the ruling elite than just their color. They were but a small group of the population, whose socio-economic position had little to do with their numerical strength. But in spite of their color, Jews did not enjoy full political and social acceptance in white society. As whites, they could not and did not belong to the lower strata. As Jews, they could not belong to the white apex. The Jewish mulattos found themselves in a similar societal bind. As free men or women their place was undoubtedly among the middle sectors, but through their association with the Jewish community they were placed, or put themselves, in a separate category within the small middle section.[16]

In Cohen's view, the problem of the Jewish mulattos was a major challenge for the Jewish regents. With the help of Sephardis and Ashkenazis, the Jewish mulattos had founded the association *Darhe Jesarim* (Way of the Righteous), in Paramaribo in 1759. They also had a synagogue of their own and certainly felt encouraged to claim equal rights for their congregation in view of their being—albeit a separate—part of the new urban group of free mulattos and Blacks, which had begun to play a role in public life in Paramaribo. This exceptional status of the Jewish mulattos became apparent in the sociopolitical issues raised by the claims of Elisabeth Samson, a free Black woman. She was one of the richest women in Paramaribo when she announced her intention to marry a European, first in 1764 and then in 1767, when the marriage actually took place. Cynthia McLeod, who conducted extensive archival research into Samson's family background, demonstrates that Elisabeth had important allies.[17] She lived as a child in the house of her older sister Maria, who had married a Dutch member of the Council of Police, the highest administrative body in the colony. By 1750 at the latest, Elisabeth herself had shared her household with Carl Otto Creuz, a German. Creutz came to Suriname in 1733 with a contract as a soldier from the Society of Suriname in Amsterdam. In 1749 he was charged with peace negotiations with the Maroons, which he carried out so successfully that he was appointed to the Council of Police, a position he held until his death in 1762. One of Elisabeth Samson's close family members was married to Hendrik Schouten, the Dutch poet who wrote about the ins and outs of marriage in Suriname. Schouten was cofounder in 1775 of a theater in Paramaribo from which Jews were banned. This theater is said to have been unsuccessful in comparison with the theater founded by the Jews in 1776 in response to this exclusion. At the height of these social tensions some local authorities even considered creating a special quarter for Jews in Paramaribo.

The push for the creation of a middle class of free mulattos and Blacks was nurtured by the very large number of white emigrants from Suriname during the years of financial crisis in the 1770s. Some local officials went so far as to propose that all female slaves who were made pregnant by their owners should be declared free ipso jure together with their unborn children. This proposal was never put in practice but the philosophy behind it evidences the changes which were to affect the Jewish Nation. Cohen reproduces the results of a population survey of the Jew's Savannah in 1762; it listed twenty-seven free mulattos and Blacks, one-third of them children under ten years of age.[18] Most of them moved to Paramaribo in the 1770s, where they advanced to positions of affluence. Of course, this group could not be satisfied with the lack of democracy in the Jewish congregation, where they were not admitted as full members. Discussion of this issue was intense from 1790 to 1794, when the petition to officially recognize a separate Jewish mulatto community was dismissed by decree of the governor. The internal cohesion of the colony took precedence at a time when revolution raged in the French colony of Saint-Domingue and could reasonably be expected to sweep over Suriname as well.

In his *Essai historique* Nassy merely alludes to this conflict. His point is to complain about the "mépris continuel" (continuous disdain) against the Jews in Paramaribo, where it became popular to address Jews using disparaging names. The former contacts between Christians and Jews had deteriorated to such a degree that they stopped visiting each other: "They were even treated with arrogance, and sometimes the Jews have experienced (with the exception of judicial condemnation) what Candide said when he came to Suriname."[19] The reference to Voltaire's naive hero is initially obscure to today's reader. On the one hand, Candide's first words on seeing Suriname were: "Our troubles are at an end and our period of happiness is just beginning."[20] On the other, after hearing the story of the Black slave who had been rendered disabled from the violence of his Dutch master, Candide finally admitted to his traveling companion Cacambo that optimism "is the madness that maintains that all is well when one is suffering."[21] Voltaire's *Candide* (1759) would have been a universal reference for Nassy's Enlightenment readers who could be presumed to grasp his real intention, which was to rhetorically appropriate the most advanced thinking of the day on behalf of the Portuguese Jewish Nation in Suriname. The initial obscurity of the reference to Voltaire serves as an example of literary camouflage by a group that finds itself oppressed.

Nassy, of course, does not speak here only in his individual capacity. As a member of the Jewish elite in Paramaribo, he had to deal with the directives emanating from his coreligionists in Amsterdam. Yosef Kaplan, in *Judíos nuevos en Amsterdam: Estudio sobre la historia social e intelectual del judaísmo sefardí en el siglo XVII* (New Jews in Amsterdam: A study of the social and intellectual history of Sephardic Judaism in the seventeenth century) has analyzed this question from the perspective of the Municipal Archive in Amsterdam. According to Kaplan's data obtained from the archive, among the Blacks and mulattos in Amsterdam there were Jewish converts who were not well received and suffered discrimination at the hands of the *mahamad*. Furthermore, Kaplan mentions the fact that, from April 29, 1647, a special section of the Jewish cemetery in Ouderkerk in Holland had been reserved for Blacks and mulattos.[22] The cemetery question was equally ardent in Suriname. It motivated the Jewish mulattos to express their wishes for recognition to the governor in a letter dated September 2, 1793: "They could not understand why the Jews could arrogate themselves more privileges than the Christian community, which is so far superior to them and whose members constitute the lawful authorities of this country and under whose protection the Jewish nation exercises its religion."[23]

Kaplan also mentions other interesting facts. Mulattos, born Jewish, whose parents were married according to the Jewish rituals, or mulattos who were married to whites in a Jewish ceremony, were not excluded from full membership in the nation. This implies that marriages between whites and converted Blacks or mulattos were not forbidden by religious laws, and that the converted people of color who were married to whites were significantly better off. This factor should be emphasized because it demonstrates that the Jewish variant of the "Surinamese marriage"—legal marriage or concubinage between a European man and a native woman of color—would have been possible legally, although it seems to have been little practiced by the Jews of Suriname. Cohen mentions that in the archives of the Sephardic Jews he consulted in Suriname, the first marriage of a Sephardi man with a free Jewish woman of color took place only in 1817. These were the years when religious barriers were breaking down. Another first marriage—of a Sephardi with an Ashkenazi—took place in 1811; and the first marriage of a Sephardi with a Christian woman took place in 1820. In the latter case, the woman converted to the religion of her husband.

Since the best-known model of social mobility in Suriname—the Surinamese marriage—was no alternative for the Jewish population, what then did Nassy have in mind as a creative alternative for the future? Without any doubt, he interpreted the plans for the reform of the congregation extremely seriously with respect to the plea for the improvement of education. His *Essai historique* states that this was a family tradition. A forefather had established a school in the Jew's Savannah as early as 1667, but no further details are provided. The David Nassy of the eighteenth century, however, already knew how to expand his educational efforts beyond the Portuguese Jewish Nation. In 1785 he proposed a reading list to Governor Wichers for use in a night school planned for Paramaribo. The list contains the following items in this chronological order: classical history, Jewish history, Dutch history, commerce, navigation, agriculture, philosophy, medicine, literature, and politics. Rather than a public school, Nassy suggested establishing a night school where members of the Docendo Docemur society might read important works together with the pupils of both "sexes of the age of puberty and of all religions without distinction." The lectures were to be given in French and Dutch, with the possibility of translation into Spanish and Portuguese for those who knew neither of the main languages.[24] In his answer, the governor proposed adding geography as a priority, without even mentioning the possibility of including religion in the program. Cohen comments that this educational program, with Jewish history presented prior to Dutch history, seems to point to an "Enlightenment Surinam style, where Jews formed an integral part of the select intellectual circle."[25] Nassy's second plan dates from 1797, when, following his stay in Philadelphia, he considered opening a college of humanities in the Jew's Savannah for the "children of all ranks and classes without exemption of Nation and religion."[26] His model was Harvard or Princeton, with free entrance for the poor. In 1797, he presented a rather different curriculum to the governor: Dutch, French, basic English, writing, ethics, history, arithmetic, geography, and mathematics. This time Nassy received no answer to his suggestions.

These endeavors on behalf of enlightened and modern education do not, however, suggest that the Portuguese Jewish Nation excluded knowledge originating with the Afro-Surinamese. On the contrary, the author of the *Essai historique* gives examples of the great influence of such knowledge in the Jew's Savannah where everybody lived closely together, and the typical caste divisions were less explicitly felt. This is especially important with respect to Nassy's interest in medicine. Bijlsma focuses on his pharmaceutical knowledge, gained in the 1770s in the Jew's Savannah. When Nassy decided in 1792 to leave Suriname for the first time in his life, he sailed to Philadelphia—then the capital of the United States—where he established himself as a doctor. Coming back to Suriname before the end of 1795, he kept the title Dr. Nassy. The coincidences with Saint-Domingue are, once again, surprising. McClellan, who praises the information provided by Moreau de Saint-Méry, describes the "mad-for-science-summer" of 1784 in Cap François, when the Cercle des Philadelphes was born, with close connections to scholars in the United States. Colonial problems could be overcome through science! Nassy's interest in medicinal plants and public health is evident in the *Essai historique*, where two chapters deal with medicinal plants and healing techniques. While in Philadelphia, the temple of American science, Nassy was elected a member of the American Philosophical Society (APS) and served as its first medical correspondent. He also published under the auspices of the APS a study concerning an epidemic in Philadelphia. Further research is necessary in order to assess the source of Nassy's knowledge. It is certainly no accident that Moreau de Saint-Méry also published the first edition of his landmark book on colonial Saint-Domingue in this same city.

Although it is not the foremost aspect of his *Essai historique,* Nassy provides fascinating material for a future literary history of Sephardic Jews in the seventeenth century. Kaplan has argued that there are stylistic regularities in the writing of this community that can be attributed to their efforts to negotiate their needs from a minority position. Harm den Boer, in *La literatura sefardí de Amsterdam (The Sephardic Literature of Amsterdam,* 1995), confirms this hypothesis and identifies the panegyric as the typical genre of the Amsterdam Sephardic writers. According to Den Boer, the panegyric was borrowed from Spanish literature of the Golden Age, then adapted to Jewish political practices in negotiating their position in Suriname. Kaplan and den Boer emphasize the politics of literary camouflage in terms of the special bond the Sephardim of Amsterdam retained with Iberian and Spanish reality in particular, despite the upheavals of the Inquisition that had brought about their own expulsion at the end of the fifteenth century. The poet Miguel de Barrios was the popular voice of this cultural movement. He was born in Andalusia, fought as a captain in the service of the Spanish Hapsburgs in Flanders, and subsequently moved to Amsterdam in order to be able to confess his Jewish religion openly. Nassy refers to him frequently and even quotes some of his verses at the beginning of the *Essai historique:* "With the Dutch in ardent Brazil / the Holy Nation opposes the Portuguese / and this year breaks the imperial power, / which threatens to subdue it."[27] Although den Boer does not stress the importance of extra-European events in his book, the necessity of maintaining a web of international friends in politics constantly shines through. With respect to this point, Kaplan found a very pertinent quotation in a poem by Miguel de Barrios: "One People judges you negatively / because you put yourself aside from them, / and others consider you unfaithful / because they saw you as hypocritical."[28] Barrios's use of *fingir* as feigning, in the sense of hypocrisy and simulation, is in line with the new historicism's stress on the negotiating postures of minority cultures. Sephardic literature of the seventeenth century can be seen as its early exponent; Nassy in the *Essai historique* is the heir of the colonial Enlightenment in this respect.

Notes

1. Jonathan I. Israel, *The Dutch Republic: Its Rise, Greatness, and Fall, 1477–1806* (Oxford: Clarendon, 1995), 1059.

2. For a fuller discussion, see Ineke Phaf-Rheinberger, "The Contemporary Surinamese Novel," in *A History of Literature in the Caribbean,* vol. 2, ed. James Arnold, Vera Kutzinski, and Phaf-Rheinberger (Amsterdam: Benjamins, 2011), 527–41, especially 528–30.

3. Roelof Bijlsma, "David de Is. C. Nassy: Author of the *Essai historique sur Surinam,*" in *The Jewish Nation in Surinam: Historical Essays,* ed. Robert Cohen and Mazal Holocaust Collection (Amsterdam: S. Emmering, 1982), 66.

4. Bijlsma, "David de Is. C. Nassy," 67.

5. David Isaac de Cohen Nassy, *Essai historique sur la colonie de Surinam* (Amsterdam: S. Emmering, 1968), frontispiece. "Sa fondation, ses révolutions, ses progrès, depuis son origine jusqu'à nos jours, ainsi que les causes qui depuis quelques années ont arrêté le cours de sa prosperité; avec la description & l'état actuel de la Colonie, de même que ses revenus annuels, les charges & impôts qu'on y paye, comme aussi plusieurs autres objets civils & politiques; ainsi qu'un tableau des moeurs de ses habitans en général, AVEC l'Histoire de la Nation Juive Portugaise & Allemande y Etablie, leurs Privilèges immunités & franchises: leur Etat politique & moral, tant ancien que moderne: La part qu'ils ont eu dans la défense & dans les progrès de la Colonie."

6. R. A. J. van Lier, *Frontier Society: A Social Analysis of the History of Surinam* (The Hague: Martinus Nijhoff, 1971), 91–92.

7. Van Lier, *Frontier Society,* 91.
8. Van Lier, 90–91.
9. Robert Cohen, ed., *The Jewish Nation in Suriname: Historical Essays* (Amsterdam: S. Emmering, 1982), 181–250.
10. Nassy, *Essai historique,* 1, xix–xxiv.
11. Nassy, 2, 11–12. "On ne trouvera peut-être pas dans toute l'Amerique sans excepter aucune Colonie, des Plantations plus régulières, plus belles, & plus remplies de superbes bâtimens & de jardins d'une somptuosité beaucoup au-delà des bornes du pouvoir qu'a Surinam."
12. James E. McClellan III, *Colonialism and Science: Saint-Domingue in the Old Regime* (Baltimore: Johns Hopkins University Press, 1992), 19–20.
13. Moreau de Saint-Méry, Médéric-Louis-Elie, *A Civilization That Perished: The Last Years of White Colonial Rule in Haiti,* trans. Ivor D. Spencer (Lanham, MD: University Press of America, 1985), 37.
14. Nassy, *Essai historique,* 1, 109–10. "Qu'est-ce que veut dire encore ce privilège de contribuer à la nomination des Magistrats de la Colonie? Un Negre libre qui a une Baraque ou un morceau de terrain en propre, ne jouit-il pas du même droit? Cette espèce de liberté démocratique que le pouvoir législatif a cédé aux habitans d'une Colonie qui travaillent également, & pour leur bonheur & pour celui de la mère patrie, est-il susceptible d'observations aussi puériles qu'injustes? M. Hartsink, sans vouloir sentir la vérité de ce fait, entrainé peut-être par ses propres préjugés, dit 'que cette liberté donnée aux Juifs, blesse encore le coeur des autres habitans,' pourquoi n'y a-t-il pas ajouté le mot d'*injustement* pour montrer son impartialité?"
15. Israel, *Dutch Republic,* 1013.
16. Robert Cohen, *Jews in Another Environment: Surinam in the Second Half of the Eighteenth Century* (Leiden: E. J. Brill, 1991), 157.
17. Cynthia McLeod, *Elisabeth Samson: Een vrije, zwarte vrouw in het 18e-eeuwse Suriname* (Breda: Conserve, 1993).
18. Cohen, *Jews in Another Environment,* 159.
19. Nassy, *Essai historique,* 1, 156. "On leur parlait même avec arrogance, & plusieurs fois les Juifs ont éprouvé (a la condamnation Juridique près) ce qu'a dit Candide, lorsqu'il est venu à Suriname." This reference to Voltaire's *Candide* reveals Nassy's familiarity with the Enlightenment's critical discussions of social and scientific problems.
20. Voltaire, *Candide: Romans et contes* (1759), ed. H. Benac (Paris: Classiques Garnier, 1958), 182. "Nous sommes au bout de nos peines et au commencement de notre félicité."
21. Voltaire, *Candide,* 183. "La rage de soutenir que tout est bien quand on est mal."
22. Yoseh Kaplan, *Judíos nuevos en Amsterdam: Estudios sobre la historia social e intelectual del judaísmo sefardí en el siglo XVII* (Barcelona: Editorial Gedisa, 1996), 73–74.

23. Cohen, *Jews in Another Environment*, 167.
24. Cohen, 101.
25. Cohen, 102.
26. Cohen, 102.
27. Nassy, *Essai historique*, 1, 10. "Con el Hollandio en el Brasil ardiente / Se opone al Portugues la Nation santa. / Y este ane en buda al imperial quebrante, / Que la amenaça con furor ambiente." (Nassy himself gives a French translation of this passage on the same page: "Avec Jes Hollandais dans le Brésil brûlant, la sainte Nation s'opposa aux Portugais, & dérouta dans cette année la force impériale, qui vouloit subjuguer la République.")
28. Kaplan, *Judíos nuevos en Amsterdam*, frontispiece. "Con un Pueblo estás mal quisto/por lo que te apartas del,/otro no te juzga fiel/por lo que fingir te ha visto."

Henrik Hertz and Racial Imagination in the Nineteenth-Century Danish Caribbean

David Gantt Gurley

> I was born in the midst of Jews in the Danish island of St. Thomas. For years the next-door neighbours of my parents were Jews. I played with Jewish boys, and looked forward as eagerly as they did to the annual festivals and fasts of their church. I always went to the Synagogue on the solemn Day of Atonement—not inside. The Synagogue stood on the side of a hill and from a terrace immediately above it we Christian boys could look down upon the mysterious assembly, which we did in breathless silence, with an awe and a reverence. . . .
>
> After spending twelve years in Africa I returned to St. Thomas to visit my mother, and I remember how cordially I was received by my Jewish acquaintances. . . . Through the thoughtful hospitality of a Jewish neighbour living opposite, tea and other refreshments were sent in to give me a practical, and . . . a most grateful welcome.
>
> —Edward Blyden, *The Jewish Question*, 1898

THERE WERE TWO iconic synagogues built during the Danish Golden Age (1800–50).[1] In 1833 the Great Synagogue on Krystalgade in Copenhagen was completed.[2] It is a marvelous structure, built in an Egyptian style, standing in the middle of Copenhagen as "an alien, isolated phenomenon with a tradition instead pointing out to foreign lands and distant times."[3] That same year the Beracha Veshalom Vegmiluth Hasidim (more commonly known as the St. Thomas Synagogue) was built in the port city of Charlotte Amalie on the island of St. Thomas, then a territory of the Danish West Indies.[4] The St. Thomas Synagogue, reportedly the oldest in continuous use in what is now United States territory, is known for its mesmerizing floor, which is covered with fine sand, sometimes said to represent the ancient

Hebrews' journey over the sands of Egypt.[5] Others have speculated that the sand muffles the steps and voices of those who enter the synagogue so as to hide their presence during more precarious times. Whatever the meaning of its legendary floor, the St. Thomas Synagogue and its small but steadfast community have been a vital and dynamic model for Atlantic Judaism for nearly two hundred years.[6] To my mind, the success of this extraordinary community is due to the radical nature of the Copenhagen Jewish community during Denmark's Golden Age, and thus these two unique synagogues are linked not only by the year of their completion but as emblems of a Denmark becoming modern.[7]

Despite the fact that Jews under the Danish crown were not granted citizenship until nearly the middle of the nineteenth century, they were allowed to conduct business and enjoyed a superficial freedom under the law since the late eighteenth century. The Decree of 1814 gave Jews a so-called paper citizenship.[8] Although the majority of the Jews living on St. Thomas had not come from Denmark, the small community that had settled in the Danish Caribbean benefited from these very reforms being enacted in the homeland. The largely Sephardic population had begun arriving from Brazil at the end of the seventeenth century, and, soon after, from France, and then, later, from places like Curaçao, St. Croix, and St. Eustatius.[9] Judah M. Cohen states that Jews in the Danish West Indies had the same official rights as the Jews in Danish-controlled Altona during the early nineteenth century.[10]

This also meant that there were Jewish slave traders in the Danish West Indies before the trade was banned throughout the Kingdom of Denmark in 1802.[11] After 1802 it was still legal to own slaves and there were still Jewish slave owners in the Danish West Indies during the 1830s and 1840s.[12] Furthermore, when the new synagogue was being constructed on St. Thomas, several Jewish plantations hired out their slaves for its construction.[13] Nevertheless, there is at least anecdotal evidence that Jews and Caribbean slaves shared community space and memory in the Danish West Indies, as the Blyden epigraph with which I began this essay surely suggests. In fact, Blyden's portrait of shared community produces a strong series of elisions and substitutions that make the ethical parameters of this volume even possible. And does a complicated question not arise when looking at this unsavory period in Danish colonial history: Was there a particular Jewish response at home to the Crown's colonial ambitions during the Golden Age?

By 1830, the approximately two thousand Copenhagen Jews had created a successful and surging community that was becoming more and more assimilated into the Protestant culture of the north.[14] However, the 1830s also saw an increase in anti-Semitic organization.[15] This was reminiscent for many of the so-called Hep-Hep riots of 1819. The anti-Semitic violence began in Würzberg in late summer and spread from Bavaria up the Rhine and into Denmark by late fall.[16] Still in the early days of being a unified, political entity, Danish Jewry had taken advantage of the social reform that had shifted the structure of Danish culture since the late eighteenth century, especially in the trade guilds. Jewish presence in Danish politics, social institutions, and the arts was at an unprecedented level in the 1830s and 1840s, thanks to the reformist, mercantilist, and editor M. L. Nathanson (1780–1868).[17] Under Nathanson's watch Jewish law and culture resonated more with Danish models of *dannelse* or *Bildung*.[18] With A. A. Wolff's tenure as Copenhagen's Chief Rabbi, which ran from 1830 to 1890, the community began to establish a more cohesive identity intent on emancipation.[19]

No other figure was more provocative in this push toward constitutional equality than the writer and editor Meïr Aaron Goldschmidt (1819–1887). In his 1845 novel *A Jew*, Goldschmidt offers an interesting simile that draws parallels between the Scandinavian Jew and the African slave. While arguing with his friend Levy about the topic of assimilation, the protagonist of the novel, Jakob Bendixen, exclaims: "We are and will remain Jews, just as the Negro slave is and always will be black, even if they *emancipate* him. Like him we were emancipated into a freedom and equality that has poisoned us."[20] For Goldschmidt ethnicity, like pigmentation, was a rigid construct of identity—it was the absolute arbiter of difference. Goldschmidt's suggestion that Jews and African slaves were inexorably tied together carves out for us a shared identity of the oppressed. In making this comparison he presents a striking rhetorical possibility: that race can be read as a trope for ethnicity.[21]

On a faraway island, perhaps better known for Blackbeard's castle, stood two very different, but nevertheless intertwined, problematic institutions symptomatic of the hypocrisy of the Golden Age's enlightened call for freedom: Atlantic slavery and the synagogue. Both were also instrumental in the discussion of a new Denmark that was becoming vocalized in the 1830s and 1840s. With the new constitution of 1849, slavery was abolished and Danish Jews were finally granted full citizenship and constitutional equality. It is perhaps not very surprising that a Golden Age novella on this very problem of slavery and race in the Danish West Indies exists. What is interesting is that it was written by a Jewish writer who was not very well known to the public as a Jewish writer.[22]

This essay problematizes the literary reception of the Danish writer Henrik Hertz by reading his first novel, *De Frifarvede* (The free-colored, 1836), as a political elucidation. During the 1830s and 1840s there was a great debate in Danish politics concerning the Danish West Indies and the notion of slavery. Hertz's novel takes place in the Danish West Indies, first on St. Thomas and then on St. Croix, and focuses on the complex relationship between a white plantation owner's son and his biracial cousin. Despite its melodramatic style, the novel is a critique of colonialism and a scathing commentary on the Crown's policies regarding slavery. Read as a commentary on the emancipation of the European Jew and against the grain of Romantic exoticism, *De Frifarvede* opens up questions regarding Hertz's authorship and provides a theoretical framework for exploring both Goldschmidt's simile and the idyllic synthesis of Blyden's recollection.[23] Hertz's novel is a radical call for the abolition of slavery in the Danish West Indies, but it also points to the correlation between the West Indian slave and the Danish Jew. For Hertz as well as Goldschmidt this correlation was centered around the figure of Moses. This essay explores the allegorical fabric of Hertz's novella from within the context of the social and political debates of 1830s Denmark.[24]

Edward Blyden was a young boy on St. Thomas in the 1830s and 1840s.[25] His early recollection in *The Jewish Question* reinforces Goldschmidt's view that there was a certain fictive kinship between the Jewish and African slave population in the Danish West Indies. Perhaps Goldschmidt is guilty of a certain naivety, or perhaps his comparison between the African slave and the modern Jew is somewhat disingenuous. However, when read in tandem with the passage from Blyden, we see two narrative attempts from opposite shores of the Atlantic to connect these two communities: one written from the short side of emancipation and radically charged; the other on the heels of freedom, gracious and idyllically nostalgic. I suggest that Hertz too should be read within this constellation of kindred opposites and that his authorship serves as a connective strand between a discussion of early Danish Jewish fiction and Caribbean letters and art.

Henrik Hertz (1798–1870) was born in Copenhagen to a middle-class orthodox Jewish family.[26] His father was a baker and died when the young boy was barely two years old. His mother then took over the family business and ran it astutely until it was completely destroyed in the English bombardment of 1807. During the offensive, the family fled to a farm on the nearby island of Amager, where they witnessed the city ablaze. Hertz later commented on the burning city of his youth: "The

Bombardment seemed to have had a harrowing and yet fortifying influence on my nerves."[27]

After his mother's death in 1814, Hertz moved in with his cousin Esther, twenty years his elder. This was a great turn of fortune for the boy, as Esther was married to none other than M. L. Nathanson, the most instrumental force of reform in nineteenth-century Danish Jewry. Hertz excelled in his new environment and went on to win the University of Copenhagen's Gold Medallion in 1824 for law. Two years later, he won the prestigious award again, but this time for his work in aesthetics, particularly the effect of the nation on its poets.[28] Hertz was a strong proponent of poetic realism and introduced a complex psychological element to the Danish theatre. Hertz's first vaudeville play, *Mr. Burchardt and His Family,* was performed in 1826 and over the course of his career he saw forty-two plays produced in the Royal Theatre. By 1890 Hertz's plays had been performed 1,102 times in Copenhagen's most illustrious venue.[29] His poetry and vaudevilles mark a transition from earlier universal Romanticism.[30] His plays were not only ahead of their time but also seemed to set the aesthetic bar for performance at the Royal Theatre.

Although Hertz was born into an orthodox family with ties to other prominent Jewish families in Denmark, his writings contain barely any Jewish elements.[31] With his conversion to Christianity in 1832 and his penchant for writing in the light comic style so popular during the Danish Golden Age, Hertz has never been read specifically as a Jewish writer, although Hans Kyrre does highlight, and to some extent problematizes, the Jewish context of Hertz's early life.[32] Unlike Meïr Goldschmidt, the only other major Danish Jewish fiction writer of that era, Hertz never explicitly explored the contemporary identity of the European Jew in his published fiction, comedy, and poetry. In general, scholarship has presented Hertz as a convert who excluded his Jewish background from his works and politics in order to succeed in the national theater.[33] Given the anti-Semitic violence that Hertz had witnessed in his early twenties, its ugly resurgence in his early thirties, and the racist banter he surely must have endured in the inner circles of the Copenhagen literary elite, it is easy to imagine a conversion based on fear, as his son Poul has so clearly contended.[34] Perhaps we should extend to Hertz the benefit of the doubt and try to imagine his conversion as due to both a spiritual choice and a desire for social mobility.[35] In any event his conversion does not require a disavowal of his Jewish heritage nor an erasure of his Jewish learnedness.

Kyrre reports that the word "Jew" does not appear in any of Hertz's published works.[36] There exists one remark in a journal where he refers to "the most tactless and offensive words" that critics use against him because of his "Jewish descent."[37] Kyrre also identifies a poetic passage in Hertz's comedy "One Hundred Years," where Hertz celebrates the Decree of 1814 and criticizes the Norwegian Parliament's 1814 ban on Jews entering Norway.[38] He also wrote a poem during the uprisings of 1819 entitled "Trust—The Night of September 5, 1819, During the Pogrom," which is a meditation on the strength of God during the horrific event. Perhaps the most striking piece of evidence that Hertz might be claimed as a Jewish writer comes more than a decade after his conversion. Early in a notebook that dates between July 1844 and February 1848, we find the plans for a novella entitled *Der Jude*:

Der Jude:
Title of a novella that would be best written in German, about a violin virtuoso who disguises himself as a Jew from Belgium because at that time Jews had great renown for their musical genius. However, he was not a genius and this is the reason for his indifference at defamation against him as a Jew. (Quietly he confides to the one he ought to defy, and they become friends.) A young patrician girl falls in love with him, but a Jew is a horror for her parents; he entrusts his secret to the parents and betroths the girl. In the novella the position of the Jews in Germany as compared to the Christians must be derided—the bitter irony which lies in the fact that a Christian poses as a Jew. The intolerance is depicted. He must thus be of a humorous nature, so that he is not portrayed in a despicable light, raised above prejudice while mocking the world. It could also mock the journalists who he gets to write romantic reviews of his spectacular playing, his violin's song—and concerning his Israelite life's romantic soul. All this he makes fun of himself.[39]

The draft written at least twelve years after his conversion and at most five years before emancipation shows that the possibility of exploring contemporary Jewish identity and politics was not far from Hertz's mind. One can also see in this brief outline Hertz's great comic and theatrical side. In a period where he was writing copious amounts of lyrical poetry and such celebrated historical plays as *King René's Daughter* (1845) and *Ninon* (1848), we see that Hertz was searching for a way to satirize bigotry against Jews in novel form. The irony of the story is that the Jew on the surface of the text is not Jewish at all, and in fact he seems naively unaware of the criticism targeting his veneer of performed Jewishness. What is so alluring about this work is that it is potentially void of actual Jewish characters, leaving the most Jewish thing about the novella its Christian author.[40] Moreover, the plans illustrate for us that Hertz was invested in depicting the contemporary Jewish experience in Danish letters. This evidence and timeline position Hertz at odds with the nationalistic readings of his authorship and also justify the claim that he was an early pioneer of modern Jewish fiction.[41]

With these texts in mind, Hertz shows a certain kinship with such writers as Heinrich Heine (1797–1856), who, despite being a convert himself, began writing *The Rabbi of Bacharach* during a particular political situation in the 1820s and finished it during another in 1840.[42] Not only is there a general danger in totally deracinating a writer due to the surface of his or her fiction, but it seems to overlook an important historical movement. There was a telling phenomenon in northern European Jewry that caused a vast political reaction from different fiction writers in the 1830s and 1840s. The emancipation of Jews in northern European countries during this period led to a broad political reaction from different fiction writers. Although Hertz never turned his outline for *Der Jude* into an actual novella we do have something equally important and equally as biting: Hertz's novella about slavery and race in the Danish West Indies.

The historical contexts of *De Frifarvede* are numerous: the French Revolution in 1789; the Haitian Revolution, which began in 1791 and ended in 1804; the banning of the slave trade in the Danish West Indies in 1802; and the full legal rights given to persons of biracial descent in the Kingdom of Demark in 1834.[43] This novel, however, should be read not only as a commentary on the Danish West Indies, but also in conversation with the debate at home concerning the emancipation of the Danish Jews. Hertz's novel is a radical call for the abolition of slavery, but it also points to the connectivity between the West Indian slave and the Danish Jew that we saw from Goldschmidt's metonym above. But there is an even deeper narrative joining these two distinct peoples: Jews are connected to Africa though their own enslavement in Egypt.[44] While it lies beyond the scope of this essay, it is worth remarking here that Goldschmidt makes a strong correlation between the "Blackness" of Jews and their time in Africa, a place he radically viewed as a type of homeland. In fact, it was in ancient Egypt that Goldschmidt found the source of his Judaism.[45] Even without adopting the heretical parallelism found in Goldschmidt's writings, we are still left with a striking metonymical possibility in Hertz's work: that Jews too are "free-colored," half European and half African, but still not yet emancipated.

There is a tropological model that might help us talk about Jewish fiction that does not deal overtly with Jewish topoi or Jewish personae. I do not mean to suggest that there is something essential about ethnicity or religion that functions underneath the narratives Jews produce. Rather, that writing a text absent of a Jewish milieu or a Jewish figure does not mean that the text is free or clean of ethnic markers, especially when that text elicits themes of injustice, such as slavery, poverty, and social isolation based on class. Nor do I mean to invoke the powers of full allegory—for example, the idea that a text is not at all about the overt themes and content of its narrative. The social realism that is found in the fiction of many early Jewish writers does not speak to a fantasy of escape but rather evokes a pointed system of substitutions where gender, social class, and even race cluster underneath a glaze of normativity and nationality.

I suggest *alleotheta* might be helpful in looking at the alignment of race and ethnicity in a text such as *De Frifarvede,* not as a rhetorical vice or grammatical mistake but as the possibility of narrative function. Alleotheta comes from Greek *allothen* (from another place) and *theteuo* (to work for). It is a substitution of one grammatical case, gender, mood, number, or person for another. It is sometime called *alloeosis* and is a type of enallage. It is more prevalent in highly inflected languages (like Greek and Latin) where pronouns identify exact gender and case. The most common type of alleotheta in modern English concerns number. For example: "Each of the students should bring their own pencil for the exam." Here we see "their" substituted for either "his" or "her" as a way to express gender neutrality, regardless of number. A more provocative example of the trope is from Edgar Allen Poe's "Fifty Suggestions." Here, Poe shows us the possibility of misdirection in the substitution and answers the claim that alleotheta is purely vice: "Mr. A— is frequently spoken of as 'one of our most industrious writers;' and, in fact, when we consider how much he has written, we perceive, at once, that he *must* have been industrious, or he could never (like an honest woman as he is) have so thoroughly succeeded in keeping himself from being 'talked about.'"[46]

Here we see that the trope is not at all a mistake, but a type of derogatory insult. Despite Poe's obvious misogynistic tones, this substitution of gender is closer to what I am proposing. I suggest that alleotheta is the trope at play behind the converted, pseudonymous, and often unknown voices of many Jewish writers of the nineteenth century. There is no tradition of writing and publishing as a Jew in Denmark in the early nineteenth century. Therefore, the socioeconomic and socioreligious paradigms of the nation are substituted for the ethnic realism we see in more overt Jewish productions during this period, and Hertz is one of the masters of this ethnic elision.[47] With alleotheta, the social criticism and social isolation that we see on the surface of the narrative points to the Jewish voice behind the text. The monocultural or non-Jewish screen is used as an instrument for recovery of the minority voice, all guided under the illusion of monolinguistic assimilation.

This trope plays into a type of narrative hygienics. It turns out that the surface of the text itself is the perfect reflection for the good Jew.[48] However, my use of alleotheta requires that the veneer of the text—that which is most visible but not necessarily the most vivid—stand for the cleanness of the text at large. I do not mean to present alleotheta as a strategy by the writer to clean the stereotype of the Jew from notions of social negativity, but to use the projected image of the positive Jew in order to code the text into a contiguity of Jewish expression. The expectation is that the surface tension of the linguistic world is immune to substitution or deceit—that is, its normalcy as a "clean" text (Protestant text) is established by the image of the good Jew, an assimilated creature that does not draw lines demarcating himself from the notion of a monocultural world. In my reading of the alleotheta, the list of functional substitutions could include ethnicity, religion, social status, and race. Like Goldschmidt, Hertz may be being somewhat disingenuous with this substitution; however, it is important to realize that the rhetoric of alleotheta is a political act and aimed at putting emancipation and abolition in a mutual conversation.

De Frifarvede is Hertz's first published work of prose fiction. A novella, the text comprises seventy-two pages of Danish in the modern edition.[49] Because the text has never been translated into English, I will give a short introduction. *De Frifarvede* is narrated by an individual who grew up on St. Croix and knew the families whose story he is recounting.[50] He recalls these events of his childhood "from his oldest memories."[51] The novel opens with a metaphorical tapestry of Caribbean fantasy; there are inexhaustible goldmines, small boats with many sails, and porcelain dishes filled with "jam of a dark mystical color, like so many wonderful fairytales in *A Thousand and One Nights*."[52] In short, the opening reads like a typical colonial narrative where the legend of El Dorado is mixed with a lavish orientalism, resulting in a climate that produces the noblest of humans, "their golden complexions, and their fine English clothes."[53] This aesthetic is perfectly realized in an exquisite Danish that lulls the senses with its depiction of a paradisiacal vision of a far away island life.

Early in the novella, however, this colonial fantasy is disrupted when the narrator focuses on the relationship between "the white or *blancs* and the Negroes or the black slaves: the former in possession of freedom, culture, and all civil rights, the latter damned to slavery, drowning in ignorance, deprived of basic human rights let alone those of a citizen."[54] Hertz further focuses his attention on the category in between Black and white: "Those called *free coloured men, hommes de couleur* or free-colored, also at that time called Mulattos."[55] Even though they were free at the time Hertz is writing the story, the narrator makes a declaration strongly reminiscent of Goldschmidt's simile between Jews and slaves: "They are free, for certainly they are not slaves, but not free as far as they are excluded from enjoying the precious rights of the citizens."[56] Thinking of Goldschmidt's simile as a touchstone for Hertz's novella, we might extend the context of this statement to include the Jews of Denmark. Despite the novella's opening, which is full of Romantic tropes of the exotic Caribbean, there are definitive statements made about the hypocrisy of freedom in the colonies as well as in the Danish homeland. The narrative's setting in both St. Thomas and Denmark helps to bring these spaces into mutual critique.

The story is a tale of a family split between two brothers. In the novel's prehistory, the one brother, Richardt, was a brutal planter and slave owner who traded with "the Spanish colonies in South America."[57] The other, William, a rebel, married a biracial woman and became the target of his family's hate. This violence forced this branch of the family to move to America. At the end of the novella's prehistory the story focuses on the Graves, Dano-Norwegian plantation owners, and the Hoquevilles, the biracial offspring of William Graves and a slave woman. Both are residing on St. Croix when the story opens.

George Graves, the grandson of Richardt, is the protagonist of the story. After his father died, when he was twelve, he took over the plantation and ran it with his overbearing mother. He falls in love with his biracial cousin, Marguerite Hoqueville, and in secret from his mother the two lovers become engaged. Meanwhile, George's mother lures him to Norway, where he meets Miss Heloise Carstens. The meeting was secretively arranged by the two families, as Heloise's father was a rich lieutenant colonel with holdings in the West Indies.

Heloise is the opposite of Marguerite; she is a domineering "manly" figure whose life's passions are hunting and riding. Slowly Mrs. Graves's plan begins to work as "she observes with secret triumph his growing passion."[58] George finds himself split between his love for Marguerite and Heloise, and the text is often burdened with the justification and psychology of his temptation. It is ironic, though, that the foreignness of the Norwegian girl is what enraptures George. Since he has spent his whole life in the Caribbean, he becomes entranced by the exoticness of the simple Norwegian girl. The two become betrothed.

Soon after, George departs for Copenhagen and Heloise takes advantage of this time to hunt. One day while riding in an iconic birch forest she sees "a dark-colored, shapeless lump."[59] Moving closer to learn more of the strange object, she finds herself face to face with an aggressive bear. The bear moves in to attack. It is so close she can feel its breath. Just as it is about to bite her there is a loud shot. Both Heloise and the bear fall to the ground, with the bear mortally wounded. A strange man pulls her from the bear's grasp and finishes the animal off with a hunting knife. This stranger is one of the most beautiful men Heloise has ever seen. We are told that "the black, ardent eyes complimented his face's dark color. But it was clear that it was not the wind and weather of the Norwegian mountains that had browned these cheeks but rather a hotter climate."[60] His skin was too brown for him to be from Norway, and his broken Danish betrayed his foreign birth. He was an American. We see in Hertz that the Other is not only something infinitely substitutable but also something always displaced. Soon after this encounter Heloise runs to the stranger's room in the middle of the night and a torrid affair ensues. The pattern of exotic longing becomes reversed in the north. Here, the female, wild with desire, is the figure of the exotic and the initiator of the illicit encounter.

A few days later, George returns from Denmark. While attempting to follow Heloise on horseback, he ignorantly stumbles across the American freedom fighter. They speak about current politics in the West Indies and the stranger invites George to his nearby house for a short visit. There George sees "a Negro" in the corner with a basket. The stranger says, "This woman is my sister, Marguerite Hoqueville, your betrothed bride before both God and Conscience's court of law."[61] The American is revealed to be Arthur Hoqueville, Marguerite's long-lost brother, who had abandoned her and their mother on St. Thomas after the death of their father by his side in the Haitian revolt. Arthur's earlier words when he was first reunited with his pregnant sister in Port-au-Prince come to mind through George's actions, "Cruel, disgraceful race . . . they treat us like playthings for their desire and then cast us despicably away whenever they are bored of us."[62] George is shocked to recognize Marguerite and learns that the little boy in the basket is his own son. George breaks down, repents, and again decides to marry Marguerite. In a fit of false courage, he brings the infant to see his mother and to announce his intentions.

Mrs. Graves is, of course, outraged and rebukes George. He runs away in a tantrum, leaving the baby with his mother and Elsebeth, her slave.

After fighting off a moment of maternal instinct at the child's sweetness and innocence, Mrs. Graves returns to her vitriolic nature. Reconsidering the damage the bastard will do to her family reputation and estate, she instructs Elsebeth, "Lock the basket! Slide a cloth over it so that no one can see what you are carrying. Take the boy—he is a son of one of my negroes and a white—take him and set the basket in the river."[63] Elsebeth follows her directives and watches the child float toward a deadly waterfall. This is clearly the emotional center of the story, and I will return to it below.

As George continues to struggle between his loyalty to Marguerite and their son and his love for Heloise and his mother's will, the drama comes to a climax as George again meets up with Arthur. In this meeting he finds out that Arthur and Heloise have previously met and learns the heroic story of Arthur saving Heloise from the bear. He concludes correctly that they are in love. George becomes enraged and shoves Arthur off a cliffside, watching him fall to his death. George again runs away from the scene and flees to the safety of his mother, declaring, "I will. Tomorrow I will extend my hand to Miss Carstens."[64]

The next day in the little parish church George and Heloise gather with their families and friends to exchange vows. As the priest asks George to say "I do," George suddenly notices that "Arthur Hoqueville stood leaning against the wall, pale as a corpse."[65] Once again we see the melodrama of the situation crystallize into irony with Hertz's game of alleotheta. The dark and beautiful figure appears in the church "pale as a corpse." Despite the strange presence in the corner, George musters the strength to say, "I do!" The priest then turns to Heloise, and just as she goes to utter the nuptial vow Arthur steps forward and speaks: "Do not answer, Miss! Your 'I do' is null and void. This man's hand is no longer free." At this George loses consciousness, falling hard to the floor.

As George suffers from a fever caused by a contusion from the fall, we learn that the little child has been saved by the slave Dominique. Soon mother and son are reunited and Marguerite brings the child to visit George. She tells George what had transpired with George's mother and the child. George leaps out of bed and goes to confront his mother, but afterward the excitement proves to have been too much for him and he relapses into his fever.

In the ensuing days, Arthur, Marguerite, and the child move in with George, and Marguerite watches over him. Their love blossoms, but, soon after, George dies in Marguerite's arms. Heloise witnesses the strength of their love and gives them a substantial income to depart for Denmark.

Heloise eventually takes leave of Norway and meets Arthur and Marguerite in Copenhagen. She and Arthur rekindle their passion and are married. George and Marguerite's son builds a strong reputation for himself in later years in the Republican Chamber as someone vehemently opposed to the cultivators of slavery. He is adamant in his pursuit of justice and the narrator projects him as a social hero. The novella ends with an image of Mrs. Graves alone and demented, vexed by her family's fall.

The novella is a uniquely important work of early nineteenth-century Danish fiction, but it has received very little attention. On the surface, it has a sentimental and exotic atmosphere, but I would argue that it is a much more complicated text. The constant substitutions happening underneath the language of the text add to it a theater-like irony, with the plot constructed as a moral chiasmus. Although the novella begins with the rich white plantation owner taking advantage of the biracial female, in the end it is the biracial freedom fighter, the foreign bear-hunter, who marries the stereotypical Norwegian girl. It is George who is now pale as a corpse. The house of Graves, which stood strong in the Danish West Indies for at least four generations, is cursed by its hatred for human freedom and supplanted by the biracial line of the family as Arthur, and then, later, the rightful heir, the unnamed biracial son of George and Marguerite, inherits control of the family fortune.

The clustering of alleotheta throughout the text becomes even more layered when we begin to look at the possibility of Hertz's Jewishness. Most of the narrator's quotes and statements regarding race and slavery can be interpreted as comments on Danish Jewry by substituting "Jew" for "slave" or "free-colored" along the lines that Goldschmidt describes.[66] As Goldschmidt has suggested, these are reciprocal terms, politically, and introducing one brings the other to mind. The many nuanced and yet unstable descriptions of color and countenance also support this kind of tropological indexing. In short, this exoticness presented on the surface of the text is pure fantasy. It is the glaze that a contemporary Protestant audience expects to see in a Copenhagen text of the early 1830s, yet I am not of the opinion that this glossy veneer is the only text available or in itself the whole of the text, as many narrative substitutions occur through its use of biblical allusion.

I would now like to return to what is the most vivid and profound moment in *De Frifarvede:* Mrs. Graves ordering Elsebeth to set the young infant into the river. This scene and the one later describing the infant's rescue are pointed allusions to the story of baby Moses in Exodus 2:1–10. The connection between the biblical story and Hertz's novella is the break in the surface tension of the text, the place where alleotheta as possibility becomes unleashed. In Exodus, Moses's mother is unable to hide the child any longer from Pharaoh and sets him in the reeds of the river. When Pharaoh's daughter comes down to bathe in the river she sees the basket among the reeds and sends her slave girl to retrieve it. She recognizes the child is a Hebrew and summons a wet-nurse for it. This boy became a son to Pharaoh's daughter, and she called him Moses, "for from the water I drew him out."[67]

Hertz illustrates for us the technique of biblical inversion so pervasive in Goldschmidt and later writers like Franz Kafka. Instead of wanting to protect the infant, the grandmother wants to get rid of him. She is effectively reenacting Pharaoh's decree in Exodus to drown all male infants. Like Pharaoh, she, too, is doing this to protect her empire, and like Pharaoh her hatred of the Other is based on fear of their number and the political shift that their freedom would cause.[68]

Instead of Pharaoh's daughter discovering the young boy, the slave Dominique sees Elsebeth slinking about with a strange basket and follows her in secret to the river. There he sees her set the basket in the water. After she departs, Dominique, who is said to have "the faith of a hound," jumps into the river and draws the baby out of the current just before it would have gone over the waterfall.[69] Unlike baby Moses, the infant is sound asleep when Dominique gathers it. In jubilation he jumps up and dances before sneaking the infant back to his mother.

This scene, a hauntingly beautiful and sophisticated allusion to Exodus, is an instance of alleotheta creating a poetic connectivity between the adoption of Moses into Phaorah's house and the adoption of the unnamed infant into the Hoqueville side of the family. It also gives validity to the boy's later support for the letter of the law and his help in saving his people. But for Hertz this allusion also creates the possibility of substituting the political triumphs of the colonized in the Danish West Indies with the looming emancipation of Jews in Denmark. Just as Moses is both Hebrew and Egyptian, alleotheta allows for the boy drawn from the river to be both biracial and Jewish. It simultaneously substitutes into the cluster the fact that Hertz is both Christian and Jewish. Through the unnamed infant becoming the unnamed statesman, we have not only a precursor to Goldschmidt's, and later Freud's, notion of Moses as an Egyptian, but also a prefiguring of seminal twentieth-century icons like Aimé Césaire, Marcus Garvey, and Isaac Hayes, all of whom make correlative substitutions between the modern Caribbean slave and his descendants and the ancient Hebrew lawgiver.[70] Moreover, the historical reception of the slave trade in a postcolonial world has been dependent on the figure of the Black Moses to create an alleothetic fabric to incite a call for absolute freedom and justice.[71]

This scene and this type of radical midrash[72] suggest that *De Frifarvede* would be more productively read in continuity with Goldschmidt's *A Jew* rather than with something like Hans Christian Andersen's *The Mulatto* (1840), the usual and, I suppose, most obvious object of comparison.[73] This statement in and of itself goes against the nationalistic tide that asserts Hertz's position in Danish letters as a type of father figure. Let us not forget that, even though Hertz converted in the early thirties, he was not a full citizen of Denmark until 1849. Certainly, Hertz was consistently aware of this fact.

This essay has demonstrated one of the pitfalls of nationalistic readings of Jewish writers. Nineteenth-century Jewish writers are as native and as fluent in European vernacular as their citizen counterparts. Despite his legal and political status, Hertz's career illustrates for us how patriotic and well versed in the national aesthetic a Jewish artist could be.[74] However, at the same time, he proves capable of using that aesthetic as a glaze or veneer on the surface of his texts to create both a more complicated political dynamic and difference. What this first novel amounts to is an innovative system of alleotheta, where meaning in the narrative clusters around multiple substitutions between race and ethnicity, kingdom and colony, and pigmentation and appearance.

It is true that Hertz alternately concealed his Jewishness in private notebooks, in a Danish style highly concentrated in national aesthetics, or in the figure of the freed biracial in the Danish West Indies, but this should not ultimately mean that we cannot read him as a Jewish writer. Like Goldschmidt, Heine, and Freud, his Jewishness is forced to the surface of the text by the figure of Moses the Egyptian.[75] The displacement these writers experienced being in the center of a Germanic aesthetic is figured through pointing outward to the foreign sands of the Nile Delta. We must remember that muteness is not the absence of sound, only the attempted suppression of the projection of sound. The muted voice of conversion (itself alleotheta) functions like the fabled sand floor in the little synagogue on St. Thomas: it does not erase the members of the Jewish congregation inside, it only conceals them.

Notes

1. For an overview of the Danish Golden Age, see Bruce Kirmmse, *Kierkegaard in Golden-Age Denmark* (Bloomington: Indiana University Press, 1990), 1–258.

2. See Carol Herselle Krinsky, *Synagogues of Europe: Architecture, History, Meaning* (New York: Dover, 1996), 403–4. The Great Synagogue of Copenhagen was designed by G. F. Hetsch (1788–1864). The commissioning of Hetsch in 1829 signaled that authority of the archaic rabbinical elite was beginning to collapse, giving way to the rise of a congregation interested in contemporary aesthetics and culture.

3. Joachim Meyer, "The Danish Synagogues," in *Danish Jewish Art*, ed. Mirjam Gelfer-Jørgensen, trans. W. Glyn Jones (Copenhagen: Rhodos, 1999), 184. See also Krinsky, *Synagogues of Europe*, 403–45.

4. For a recent history on the Jews of St. Thomas, see Judah M. Cohen, *Through the Sands of Time: A History of the Jewish Community of St. Thomas, US Virgin Islands* (Lebanon, NH: Brandeis University Press, 2012); for the building of the St. Thomas Synagogue, see 53–57.

5. Besides the St. Thomas Synagogue, there are four other sand-floor synagogues that have upheld this vernacular tradition in modern times: the Kahal Kadosh Shaare Shalom Synagogue in Kingston, Jamaica (1912); the Portuguese Synagogue of Amsterdam (Esnoga in Ladino, 1675); the Snoa in Curaçao (1732); and Zedek ve Shalomin in Suriname (1735), which had a sand floor, but now its furnishings reside in the Mandel Wing for Jewish Art and Life of the Israel Museum. For a recent discussion of the phenomenon, see Barry Stiefel, *Jews and the Renaissance of Synagogue Architecture, 1450–1730* (London: Routledge, 2016), 121–24. Stiefel also suggests that the sand could have a more practical purpose, in that it helped clear the synagogue of mud and dirt from the shoes of the congregation.

6. Cohen, *Sands of Time*, 10–12. Cohen suggests that in 1802 there were less than two hundred Jews on St. Thomas (35).

7. For a recent discussion of the Copenhagen Jews during the late eighteenth and early nineteenth century, see Gantt Gurley, *Meïr Aaron Goldschmidt and the Poetics of Jewish Fiction* (Syracuse, NY: Syracuse University Press, 2016), 27–36.

8. Gurley, *Meïr Goldschmidt*, 34–35.

9. Cohen, *Sands of Time*, 34–35.

10. Cohen, 66.

11. Denmark was the first European nation to prohibit the slave trade, but not before ships flying the Danish flag had transported at least one hundred thousand slaves to the New World. See Erik Gøbel, *The Danish Slave Trade and Its Abolition* (Leiden: Brill, 2017), 15 and 183.

12. On the Jewish presence in the slave trade, see Eli Faber, *Jews, Slaves, and the Slave Trade: Setting the Record Straight* (New York: New York University Press, 1998).

13. Cohen, *Sands of Time*, 54; and Neville A. T. Hall, *Slave Society in the Danish West Indies, St. Thomas, St. John and St. Croix*, ed. B. W. Higman (Kingston, JA: University of the West Indies Press, 1992), 90–93.

14. Bent Blüdnikow, "Jews in Denmark: A Historical Review," in *Danish Jewish Art*, 36.

15. Bent Blüdnikow, "Jødeuroen i København 1830," *Historie: Jydske Samlinger* 14 (1981): 633–50.

16. Gurley, *Meïr Goldschmidt*, 36, 190n50, 190n53.

17. Gurley, 34.

18. German *Bildung* means both "education" in the formal sense and "artistic formation" within a national paradigm. Danish *dannelse* captures this semantic nuance. For a discussion of *Bildung* and its role in Ashkenazi Jewry, see Georg L. Mosse, *German Jews Beyond Judaism* (Bloomington: Indiana University Press, 1985), 3.

19. Bent Blüdnikow, "Jews in Denmark," 38.

20. Meïr Aaron Goldschmidt, *En Jøde* (A Jew), 7th ed. (Copenhagen: Gyldendal, 1927), 123. All translations in the essay are my own.

21. Gurley, *Meïr Goldschmidt*, 88.

22. As I have argued elsewhere, a nineteenth-century Jewish writer was one steeped "in Jewish textual and storytelling traditions, and whose reading habits had a great effect on his fiction." What I am arguing is that a veneer of Jewishness on the surface of a text is not what makes it a Jewish text nor a product of a Jewish writer. See Gurley, *Meïr Goldschmidt*, 8–9. From a different angle, Dan Miron has argued for a "positive contiguity" expounding on the contact either synchronic or diachronic that creates a reifying politic between writers "which the conventional critical imagination would never have dreamt were possible." See Dan Miron, *From Continuity to Contiguity: Toward a New Jewish Literary Thinking* (Stanford, CA: Stanford University Press, 2010), 307–8.

23. Goldschmidt was some twenty years younger than Hertz. The two writers were familiar with one another and knew each other's work intimately, but were not on intimate terms. Even though Goldschmidt was taken with the philosophical notion of nemesis in Hertz's play *Ninon* (1848), a letter from Hertz to his brother, Sylvester, dated September 24, 1839, suggest the relationship between the two was not amicable in the 1830s and 1840s. See Poul Hertz, *Breve Fra Og Til Henrik Hertz* (Copenhagen: n.p., 1895), 67–69.

24. Hertz never traveled to the Danish West Indies and there is little evidence that he was significantly acquainted with anyone from the West Indies or Africa. Since there does not appear to be any biographical condition for Hertz's interest in the Danish Caribbean, I am arguing that his interest is political and rhetorical. However, it should be noted that the more general motif of love and justice is commonly found in Hertz's oeuvre.

25. Blyden is specifically speaking about his childhood on St. Thomas, and much of Hertz's novel takes place on St. Croix. However, much of the early

narrative takes place on St. Thomas, and it is clear that any cultural distinction between the two islands was unknown by Hertz. Rather, I am using the Blyden quote to authoritatively mark an evocative juxtaposition of Danish and Caribbean Jewish spaces. This juxtaposition or elision is also performed exquisitely by Hertz's novel.

26. The only complete biography of Hertz is in Danish: Hans Kyrre, *Henrik Hertz: Liv og Digtning* (Copenhagen: Hagerup's Forlag, 1916).

27. Kyrre, *Hertz,* 22.

28. Kyrre, 54; and Jul Schiøtt, *Lyriske Digte: Med Portrætvignetter Af Nordiske Digtere* (Kjøbenhavn: n.p., 1891), 60.

29. Peter Vinten-Johansen, "Johan Ludvig Heiberg and his Audience in Nineteenth-Century Denmark," in *Kierkegaard and His Contemporaries: The Culture of Golden Age Denmark,* ed. Jon Stewart (New York: de Gruyter, 2003), 353f.

30. Sven Hakon Rossel, *A History of Danish literature* (Lincoln: University of Nebraska Press, 1992), 207–8.

31. Although Hertz converts to Christianity in 1832, he still kept close contact with many Jewish friends and family in the Jewish community, including his brother Sylvester and the Nathansons. After a visit to his boyhood love, Hanna Nathanson, in 1845, Hertz fell madly in love with her fifteen-year-old niece, Louise v. Halle, and the two were married in 1850. See Mogens Brøndsted, "Henrick Hertz," August 29, 2017, http://adl.dk/solr_documents/hertz-p. For a discussion of the national and political aesthetic in Hertz's writing, see Torben Hamman Hansen, "Patriotisk dannelse og biedermeier-idyl. Ved 200-året for Henrik Hertz's fødsel," in *Danske studier 1998* (Copenhagen: Reitzels Forlag, 1998), 152–62.

32. Kyrre, *Hertz,* 54–64 (although it should be noted Kyrre does not discuss *De Frifarvede* in his biography).

33. Sune Auken, Knud Michelsen, Marie-Louise Svane, Isak Winkel Holm, and Klaus P. Mortensen, *1800–1870,* vol. 2, *Dansk litteraturs historie* (Copenhagen: Gyldendal, 2008), 289–90; Rossel, *History of Danish Literature,* 207; and Jan Schwarz, "'Serving Up His Grandmother in a Spicy Sauce': Conflicting Views on Jewish Literature in Nineteenth-Century Denmark," in *Speaking Jewish—Jewish Speak: Multilingualism in Western Ashkenazic Culture,* ed. Shlomo Berger, Aubrey Tolerance, Andrea Schatz, and Emile Schrijver, Studia Rosenthaliana, vol. 36 (Leuven, BE: Peeters, 2003), 198.

34. P. Hertz, *Breve,* 246–48n5.

35. A similar movement can be seen in the fact that M. L. Nathanson, the quintessential Danish Jew, had all eight of his children baptized and their names changed to Nansen, a definitely Danish name. Andrew Buckser, *After the Rescue: Jewish Identity and Community in Contemporary Denmark* (New York: Palgrave Macmillan, 2003), 37.

36. There are also several letters where Hertz confirms he is intellectually and politically engaged in the Jewish community and current discussions of

emancipation. See especially the letter to his brother, Sylvester, dated September 25, 1838, where the topic is the public debate of the emancipation of Jews, in P. Hertz, *Breve*, 60–63.

37. Kyrre, *Hertz*, 62.
38. Kyrre, 63.
39. Kyrre, 50–51b.
40. This is not an unusual phenomenon for Jewish writers. In this regard we might compare the works of Heinrich Heine and Ragnhild Goldschmidt.
41. See Gurley, *Meïr Goldschmidt*, 9–13.
42. See Jonathan Skolnik, *Jewish Pasts, German Fictions: History, Memory, and Minority Culture in Germany, 1824–1955* (Stanford, CA: Stanford University Press, 2014), 45-66.
43. Anne Walboom and Eva Frellesvig, "Introduction," in Henrik Hertz, *De Frifarvede: Fra kjærligheds veie nytaarsgave 1836* (Årslev: Dansk Vistindisk Selskab and Herning: P. Kristensen, 1998), 5–8.
44. The Mosaic trope is employed in many slave narratives and negro spirituals, but it is interesting here to foreground its mirror opposite: Jewish writers using Moses's African heritage as a metonym from which to map their emancipation onto the plight of the Atlantic slave.
45. See Gurley, *Meïr Goldschmidt*, 12–15, 94–97.
46. Edgar Allen Poe, "Fifty Suggestions," 14:181, quoted in Brett Zimmerman, *Edgar Allan Poe: Rhetoric and Style* (Montreal: McGill-Queen's University Press, 2005), 116.
47. Two other Danish writers pertinent to this discussion of alleotheta are Johanne Luise Heiberg (1812–1890), who also converted to Christianity, and Ragnhild Goldschmidt (1828–1890), who wrote anonymously and with no specific Jewish markers or elements.
48. Gary Rosenshield, *The Ridiculous Jew: The Exploitation and Transformation of a Stereotype in Gogol, Turgenev, and Dostoevsky* (Stanford, CA: Stanford University Press, 2008), 10–11.
49. The only modern edition of the work is Henrik Hertz, *De Frifarvede: Fra kjærligheds veie nytaarsgave 1836* (Årslev: Dansk Vistindisk Selskab and Herning: P. Kristensen, 1998).
50. Mogens Brøndsted and Anne Walboom and Eva Frellesvig have speculated rather casually that something in Hertz's Jewish background could be behind the novella, but neither offer any solution to how this could be the case. See Brøndsted, "Henrick Hertz"; and Walboom and Frellesvig, "Introduction," 7–8.
51. Hertz, *De Frifarvede*, 9.
52. Hertz, 9.
53. Hertz, 10.
54. Hertz, 14.
55. Hertz, 14.
56. Hertz, 15.

57. Hertz, 12.
58. Hertz, 34.
59. Hertz, 38.
60. Hertz, 39.
61. Hertz, 49.
62. Hertz, 51.
63. Hertz, 60.
64. Hertz, 71. Note that George and Arthur are also cousins and there is a possible reading here of kin-killing and an allusion to the story of Cain and Abel from Genesis.
65. Hertz, *De Frifarvede*, 73.
66. Hertz was aware of Goldschmidt's novel and his journalism, although *A Jew* came out nine years after *De Frifarvede*. I am suggesting that Goldschmidt's simile is a touchstone for Hertz's politics in the novella.
67. *The Five Books of Moses*, trans. Robert Alter (New York: W. W. Norton, 2004), 312–13.
68. Exodus 1:9–10.
69. Hertz, *De Frifarvede*, 74.
70. Nick Nesbitt refers to Césaire as the Moses of Martinique. See Nesbitt, *Caribbean Critique: Antillean Critical Theory from Toussaint to Glissant* (Liverpool: Liverpool University Press, 2013), 120; and Edmund D. Cronon, *Black Moses: The Story of Marcus Garvey and the Universal Negro Improvement Association* (Madison: University of Winconsin Press, 1955). Isaac Hayes's album *Black Moses* was released in November 1971. The original LP could be unfolded into a cruciform image of Hayes dressed in robes by the shores of the sea.
71. There are numerous examples of this phenomenon, to spirituals such as "Go Down Moses" to Zora Neale Hurston's *Moses, Man of the Mountain* (1939). Also, see the recent, important documentary *The Black Moses* (2014) by Bahamian filmmaker Travolta Cooper.
72. The term is Robert Alter's. See Robert Alter, *Canon and Creativity* (New Haven, CT: Yale University Press, 2000), 66–67.
73. *The Mulatto* is a melodrama set in Martinique that deals with the passions of a biracial character who falls in love with a French countess. It is representative of Andersen's fascination with exotic figures and is one of the more sexually provocative works of the Golden Age. For a brief introduction and short translation of Andersen's work, see Werner Sollors, *An Anthology of Interracial Literature: Black-White Contacts in the Old World and the New* (New York: New York University Press, 2004), 292–99.
74. This is reminiscent of not only Heine but also L. A. Frankl, who composed patriotic ballads in German. See Edan Dekel and Gantt Gurley, "How the Golem Came to Prague," *Jewish Quarterly Review* 103 (2013): 248–49.
75. See Gurley, *Meïr Goldschmidt*, 13; and Jeffrey S. Librett, *Orientalism and the Figure of the Jew* (New York: Fordham University Press, 2015), 235–64.

Jamaican Jewish Tricksters
Philip Cohen Labatt's Literary Crossings

Heidi Kaufman

IN HIS INTRODUCTORY essay to *Selections from the Miscellaneous Posthumous Works of Philip Cohen Labatt,* published in 1855, I. Lawton describes his subject as "a man of letters" and "a valuable member of the Literary Society" in Jamaica.[1] At the time of his death in 1854 at the age of thirty-one, Labatt had established himself as a prolific writer and an accomplished editor. In addition to contributing to the first Jamaican Jewish literary periodical, *First Fruits of the West* (1844), Labatt produced and edited a literary journal of his own called *The Echo.*[2] Labatt's *Catechism of Jamaica: History and Geography of Jamaica* (1848), became a standard textbook in the Jamaican school system throughout the nineteenth century.[3] And from 1843 to 1850 Labatt served as editor of the *Daily Gleaner,* a periodical founded in 1834 by Jamaican Jewish brothers Joshua and Jacob DeCordova. Bertram W. Korn notes that in this period the *Daily Gleaner* was "probably the best-known newspaper in the entire Caribbean area."[4] Throughout his writing and editing career Labatt remained interested in the history and geography of Jamaica, English literature, Spanish and British colonialism, global Jewish culture, and slavery.

Despite this extensive range of literary accomplishments achieved during his short life, neither Labatt's personal history, which began in Kingston, Jamaica, nor his literary output are remembered today.[5] In one of the only scholarly discussions of his writing, Kenneth Ramchand cites Labatt as an important figure among Jamaican short-story writers, noting that, while "not consciously laying the foundations of a West Indian Literature," Labatt is noteworthy for making an "attempt to represent what we recognise as Creole languages in process of formation."[6] Ramchand's analysis continues with a curious dismissal, claiming that Labatt is among a group of writers who, "with some amusement at what they stigmatise as bad and pretentious English . . . notice the Black person's delight in big words and resounding phrases, without an inkling that this might have been less a striving after fine English than an attempt to incorporate African oratorical tradition. They register physical and cultural differences, although they write in ignorance, from the outside, and with a sense of cultural superiority."⁷ While Ramchand's claim may ring true for some of the writers he discusses in his essay, the charge that Labatt wrote "from the outside" and "in ignorance" or "with a sense of cultural superiority" about African oratorical traditions stands at odds with many of Labatt's publications.⁸ Admittedly, Labatt's work is frustratingly thorny, presenting race relations in Jamaica in confusing or perhaps contradictory ways. At times, for example, Labatt reproduces racist or racializing codes, even as he challenges those codes. Despite these difficulties, the following discussion suggests that categorizing Labatt as an insider or outsider, or, alternately, as an ignorant or well-informed Jamaican, are troubling and misleading categories that foreclose opportunities to recognize his complex position as a Jamaican Jewish writer responding to the violence of colonial power.

Ramchand's approach emerges from a scholarly moment engaged in the important project of recovering the unrecognized work of Afro-Caribbean writers. And he wisely notes that, typically, white or British writers were misinformed about the cultural nuances of Black Jamaican culture. As a result, their depictions bolstered or expanded racist lenses rendering Afro-Caribbean figures and culture as primitive or demonic in comparison to an imagined cultural superiority of the British. More recently Evelyn O'Callaghan has suggested that instead of focusing exclusively on registering these "demonizing homogenized racial categories" we should strive to "identify differences *within* these racially distinct groups, to investigate how race figures differently across cultural contexts and thus to advocate the extermination, interrogation, and, where necessary, contestation of these categories."⁹ Her concern, therefore, is "with social relationships in the Caribbean" and with the ways that "a careful reading of marginal texts . . . can open up meanings of whiteness by highlighting the differences within the category."¹⁰

The following discussion draws from this approach in an analysis of Labatt's discourse of trickery and tricksterism in his short story "Curgy's Funeral, or the Old Time Busha." I begin by recognizing the need to read beyond the assumption of stable racial boundaries, and by suggesting that Jamaican writers such as Labatt worked at the intersection of multiple storytelling practices and cultural perspectives. Labatt's oeuvre is noteworthy in part because of the manner in which he uses and challenges the racial stereotypes of his age. In several of his stories his critiques of Spanish and British colonialism lead to thoughtful, albeit complicated, presentations of slave rebellions. In other texts, Labatt explores the subtleties of tricksterism and acts of dissimulation among slaves engaging in resistance to colonial or plantation power. I'm interested in considering how these narrative traditions and political critiques are brought together in moments of cultural exchange and crossing that, as Ramchand puts it, demonstrate "Creole languages in process of formation." Indeed, Labatt's unusual methods of weaving together rhetorical and literary traditions register instances of Jamaican literary culture as simultaneously, and somewhat paradoxically, engaged in blending and reinscribing racial, religious, and literary differences.

Scholars have long sought to define Creole culture's parameters, character, and history. Kamau Brathwaite's seminal work *The Development of Creole Society in Jamaica, 1770–1820* carefully draws distinctions between African and British colonial culture in the formation of early Creole culture. Brathwaite's later work, *Contradictory Omens: Cultural Diversity and Integration in the Caribbean,* moves on to define Creole's emergence as a cultural expression "divided into two aspects of itself: ac/culturation, which is the yoking (by force and example, deriving from power/prestige) of one culture to another (in this case the enslaved/African to the European); and inter/culturation, which is an unplanned, unstructured but osmotic relationship proceeding from this yoke. The creolisation which results (and it is process not a product), becomes the tentative cultural norm of the society."[11] While Brathwaite has been emphatic about the African roots of Creole culture, later commentators have questioned his conclusions. In their work *In Praise of Creoleness,* Jean Bernabé, Raphael Confiant, and Patrick Chamoiseau define créolité as a kind of negation of Africanness, European culture, and Asian culture.[12] In contrast, Percy H. Hintzen emphasizes how ideas of creolization emerged through the constructed concepts of racial purity. Racial or cultural hybridity, after all, stand in contrast—falsely, Hintzen notes—to the notion of racial purity. Thus, "purity emerged as a boundary defining and maintaining principle separating Creole society from the external world. It is a central principle in the discourse of difference that separates the 'local' Creole White from the foreign 'pure' European."[13] More recently, in his *Introduction à une poétique du divers* (Introduction to a poetics of diversity), Édouard Glissant has defined "a creolizing world" as one in which "the cultures of the globe, [have been] placed in contact with one another." Those cultures do not remain static, nor do they weave together identifiable strands of discernable cultural patterns. Rather, Glissant continues, creolization leads cultural expressions into a "process of changing through their exchange."[14] How, then, might we place Labatt's literary output within the range of discussions concerned with the formation of Creole culture and racial categorizations and exclusions in nineteenth-century Jamaica? And how might we understand his literary crossings, or weaving together of multiple literary traditions, in light of his position as a Jewish writer and editor, dedicated to the production and promotion of literary and print culture throughout Jamaica in the 1840s and early 1850s?

While little is known of his short life, records indicate that Labatt identified with Jewish traditions and was socially and religiously aligned with Kingston's Jewish community. Labatt's father, Robert Labatt, appears on the historical register at the moment of his son's birth to an unnamed mother. Synagogue records are specific on this point: Philip Cohen Labatt was born "illegitimate" in Jamaica in 1823.[15] It's tempting to speculate. Possibly Philip Cohen Labatt's mother was white and Jewish, and she chose to rebel against social conventions by giving birth out of wedlock. It's also just as possible, and very much in keeping with 1820s Jamaican custom, that a white-skinned and Sephardi-descended Robert Labatt engaged in sexual liaisons with a nonwhite woman to produce an illegitimate son. Recently Stanley Mirvis has documented the prevalence of "emotional bonds that developed between Sephardi men, women of colour, and their children in late eighteenth-century Jamaica."[16] Very telling as well are the observations of the American journalist John Bigelow, who offered a first-hand account of Jamaican society during his 1850 visit to the island. His observations may help to contextualize Labatt's birth record:

> Kingston contains about forty thousand inhabitants at present, nine-tenths of whom, at least, are colored. . . . The whites are mostly English, or of English descent. The proportion of Jews of all colors is fearfully great. I had never seen a black Jew before, and I was astonished to find how little the expression of the Israelitish profile was effected [sic] by color. My imagination could never have combined the sharp and cunning features of Isaac with the thick lipped, careless, unthinking countenance of Cudjoe; but nature has done it perfectly, if that can be called a combination in which the negro furnishes the color and the Jew all the rest of the expression.[17]

These historical accounts indicate that a relationship between a white Jewish man (assuming Robert was white) and a Black woman (who may have identified as Jewish) was not an unusual occurrence in this period. Despite the dearth of biographical information about Labatt's parentage, the unnamed mother on the birth record, combined with the sting of his classification in the synagogue records as "illegitimate," raises the distinct possibility that Labatt could have been born a biracial Jamaican Jew.

Jews held a definitive social position in early nineteenth-century Jamaica. Jane Gerber recalls that it wasn't until 1831 that Jamaican Jews acquired full civil rights: "six months after the free blacks and three years before the general abolition of slavery."[18] Kay Dian Kriz notes that, in this period, "not only was the construction of Jamaican Jews . . . a separate racial category common in widely circulated writings, such as Edward Long's *History of Jamaica*, but it was institutionalized in the colony's laws and in the island's racially segregated militias in which Jews were required to participate: whites, Jews, free blacks, and mulattoes each had separate units with 'white' officers in charge."[19] Holly Snyder notes a similar account from *Maria, Lady Nugent's Diary*, written in 1803: "'Of all colours and descriptions' attending the Spanish Town theater in 1803, she distinguished four separate elements among the audience: 'blacks, browns, Jews and whites.'"[20] Snyder concludes that, "although Jews [in Jamaica] were nominally free [and were] of European origin and therefore experienced neither the utterly degraded position of the enslaved nor the undesirable condition of those who arrived under indenture of servitude, they were nonetheless stigmatized as non-white by the Anglo-Jamaican elite."[21]

If writers like Labatt were stigmatized as not completely white and not a slave or descendent of slaves by the Anglo-Jamaican elite, how do we approach his body of work that effectively integrates voices, perspectives, storytelling traditions, and experiences of Jamaican Jews, slaves, free Blacks, and Anglo elites from the 1830s through the mid-1850s? In Labatt's work we have an opportunity to consider the neglected question of the role of Jewish writers in Caribbean creolization in the decades following emancipation. I read Labatt's short story "Curgy's Funeral" as a Creole text produced at a key moment when such stories were beginning to be written down rather than passed exclusively through oral culture. Barbara Lalla and Jean D'Costa have offered impressive analyses of what they describe as an "external and internal language history of Jamaican Creole," paying close attention to "the nature and consequences of language contact."[22] I offer a parallel study, not of Creole language formation in this period, but of Labatt's participation in the emergence of a creolized literary form. In "Curgy's Funeral" Labatt not only blends the colonial short story and theatrical farce, but embeds the psychology of slave and master positions by drawing from Afro-Caribbean narrative and rhetorical traditions.[23] Therefore, "Curgy's Funeral" is best read not from a fixed place where the outsider Jew filters Afro-Jamaican storytelling practices through the tradition of the English or colonial short story, but as a literary production where multiple forms of cultural and narrative tactics collude, and where a Jamaican Jewish writer exhibits signs of aesthetic engagement with an emerging creolized literary culture.[24] Labatt's intricate handling of obeah and trickster figures in this story suggests a familiarity—indeed an intimacy—with narrative and rhetorical strategies used by slaves on Jamaican plantations. As the following discussion makes clear, "Curgy's Funeral" presents a form of literary creolization shaped by a Jewish writer's exploration of the psychology of enslavement. And while Labatt may never have been enslaved, his knowledge of the subtleties of slave resistance and tricksterism offer context for his use of racial stereotypes and his critique of the master's violence.

The Trickster Plot

The plot of "Curgy's Funeral" focuses on four main characters: Tom Moody, a plantation owner; Joe, the story's narrator, who relays events that occurred on his visit to the Moody plantation; Curgy, one of Tom Moody's slaves, who attempts to achieve freedom through feigned obeah practices; and a slave named Caesar, Curgy's foe, who successfully controls the master (Tom) through signifying acts.[25] The narrator therefore presents two common forms of slave resistance—obeah and signifying—while simultaneously critiquing the master's failed efforts to assert control over his slaves. During the period in which Labatt was writing, as Srinivas Aravamudan notes, "several aspects of obeah function[ed] as political resistance by enslaved persons to the economic and racial oppression they endured under the system of plantation slavery . . . Observers characterized the practice as a form of black magic, and its opponents took preemptive actions against what was seen as obeah's political agenda against the plantocracy." Dianne M. Stewart adds that obeah enabled slaves "to exercise control over other people and invisible forces, functioning thus as a form of social control and as a system for checking and balancing power and authority in enslaved African communities where personal disputes were censored."[26] Rather than depict a single obeah figure or group of figures, Labatt situates obeah alongside other forms of tricksterism and trickery. The effect is not to undermine the integrity of obeah, but to show how little slave holders understood its power as a method of resistance to the violence of the plantation system.

Although events in the story take place during the period of slavery, "Curgy's Funeral" is narrated in the postemancipation era; hence, the story frames slavery's violence through the lens of its inevitable end.[27] Joe begins by explaining that even though he "never knew a planter who took less advantage of his power over his human cattle than did Tom" the planter nevertheless would flog his slaves "to within an inch of their lives" if he found them guilty of deception.[28] These opening lines set up a pattern of exposing Tom Moody as both violent and, comparatively speaking, not so bad by Jamaican planter standards. Joe's presentation of Tom's leniency, however, becomes a difficult position to sustain as the plot unfolds. Joe continues by explaining that Tom viewed floggings as a form of "medicine" and hence "the stronger the dose the better for the patient."[29] These opening descriptions help to establish the use of medicine to explore the story's tense bonds among cure, punishment, and revenge.

Joe explains that Tom's favorite slave, Curgy, appears with "his head bound up with an old handkerchief and looking very ill and flurried."[30] Joe notes that Curgy "shuddered till his very teeth rattled against each other."[31] When asked about his appearance, Curgy shares a long story about why he believes he's about to die. Importantly, while Joe summarizes the other slave voices throughout the story, Curgy is the only slave whose speech is directly presented: "Ah! Massa," replied Curgy, "dats the ting sar: Curgy nearly dead, massa."[32] Joe continues, "And then he entered into a long rambling explanation, half of which was Greek to me, of his having seen the 'perit' of his 'grandy' and of his having been warned by it of his approaching death. The result of his lachrymose tale was a hearty roar of laughter from his master and myself, and an injunction from the former to go about his business, and to take care that he was after no tricks."[33] Mention of the word "tricks" invokes the central tension at the root of the story. While Labatt masterfully depicts trickster culture as a prominent mode of slave resistance on the Moody plantation, he simultaneously mocks the master's attempt to mimic his slave's trickster tactics.

Hours after their exchange, a nameless slave described as an old nurse approaches Tom to share news of Curgy's illness. Tom and Joe visit the slave quarters, find Curgy in bad shape, and set out to gather medicine. On their way they meet Caesar, a slave described as "Curgy's rival."[34] Speaking in a "low sly chuckle" Caesar exposes Curgy's feigned illness as an attempt to trick his master and to secure manumission papers through deception. In response, Tom explodes in a fit of rage. Joe notes, "I never saw Tom so much moved before. One fit of passion has [sic] scarcely subsided when he fell into another."[35] Caesar angers his master through trickery, an example that follows the pattern Henry Louis Gates lays out in *The Signifying Monkey*. Playing the part of the monkey, Caesar succeeds in angering the lion/master who turns his anger onto the elephant/Curgy. In Labatt's version of this triad the lion never takes revenge on the monkey, presumably because he neglects to realize the monkey has played him.[36] Thus, even though the lion—in this case, Tom—seeks revenge through forms of trickery, he is the brunt of Caesar's joke. Labatt's use of this formula suggests an intimate knowledge both of signifying and of the master's insecurity about his power on the plantation.

Joe, much like the author, is both an interloper and an accomplice; as narrator he's positioned in such a way that grants him access, as we shall see, to knowledge of the master's thinking (as witness), moral exemplar (as a critic of Tom's violence), as a complicit player (for enabling and abetting Tom's revenge), and as sympathetic storyteller (who presents Tom's victims compassionately). At the same time, Joe details the slaves' success in their resistance; Caesar holds the power to control his master's temper while Curgy, as we shall see, enacts a figurative scene of escape by appearing to trick the master. While he may initially seem neutral or in support of the master's violence, as the story continues it becomes clear that Joe is critical of Tom's abuse. In contrast, his depictions of slave resistance are presented without judgment, and in many cases with sympathy. Joe's perspective is therefore slippery both for its failure to fit neatly into the plantation world's social order and because it shifts continually as the story develops.

Following their encounter with Caesar, Tom returns to his house to gather a physic to help Curgy. He takes the medicine from a bottle bearing the label "Laudanum." Joe intervenes by accusing his friend of "cold-blooded and deliberate murder."[37] In what Joes describes as "the same quiet tone which had so much alarmed" him a few moments earlier, Tom states, "I intended no further harm to the ungrateful scoundrel, than to punish him that he shall remember, to the day of his death."[38] The bottle, in fact, is itself a trick. While Tom appears to offer laudanum to Curgy as punishment for his trickery, as the label suggests, he explains to Joe that it is filled with the emetic ipecacuanha wine.[39] Joe's lengthy description of the effect of this wine on

Curgy following its ingestion helps to emphasize the extent of the master's seething rage:

> In the course of a few minutes Curgy's body was as convulsed as it if had been under the action of a powerful galvanic machine: his eyes protruded from their sockets, and his mouth opened and shut with wonderful rapidity, while his hands grasped the scanty coverlet as if he were in the agonies of the death struggle. Not a muscle of Tom's countenance moved during all this time, but when Curgy started up . . . and the whole of the contents of his stomach were poured forth through his mouth, the face of his master bore that expression which we might suppose the countenance of the devil to wear when he regards the torments of the damned.[40]

While Curgy's torture is painful to read, just as unsettling is Tom's behavior. Initially he stands frozen, staring at Curgy's "death struggle" with a devilish gaze. Although Joe facilitated this scene of violence, neglecting to stop Tom from administering the wine, here Joe seems to distance himself through his critique of the master's sadistic attack. This distancing is short lived, albeit noteworthy.

Despite Curgy's suffering, Tom's desire for revenge remains unfulfilled. He subsequently instructs the slave nurse to prepare for an early-morning funeral. Just before leaving the torture scene, Tom enacts further revenge on Curgy by composing a false manumission letter that reads, "My black scoundrel Lycurgus, otherwise called Curgy, has it in contemplation, as I have been informed, to obtain his freedom from me by means of a trick. Should he succeed in his attempt, this is to request the friends of the undersigned to lodge the rascal in the nearest house of correction until he is sent for."[41] Unable to read the letter, Curgy is unaware of Tom's trickery—of mislabeled bottles, false efforts to heal his slave, and fake manumission papers, all of which are designed specifically to torture and humiliate Curgy for his efforts to secure his freedom through his feigned illness and allusions to obeah.

Labatt's linking of poison and obeah is not original in colonial accounts and discourse. Edward Long's *History of Jamaica* (1774) offers a more famous example.[42] According to Long's account, "The most sensible among them [slaves] fear the supernatural powers of the African obeah-men, or pretended conjurers; often ascribing those mortal effects to magic, which are only the natural operation of some poisonous juice, or preparation, dexterously administered by these villains. But the Creoles imagine, that the virtues of baptism, or making them Christians, render their art wholly ineffectual; and, for this reason only, many of them have desired to be baptized, that they might be secured from Obeah."[43] Long's account helps to explain both why obeah held such power within the plantation system, and why Curgy believed his master's medicine may have helped him pull off his plan to secure manumission papers. Long continues,

> The lure hung out was, that every Negroe, initiated into the myal society, would be invulnerable by the white men; and, although they might in appearance be slain, the obeah-man could, at his pleasure, restore the body to life. The method, by which this trick was carried out, was by a cold infusion of the herb branched colalue; which, after the agitation of dancing, threw the party into a profound sleep. In this state he continued, to all appearance lifeless, no pulse, nor motion of the heart, being perceptible; till, on being rubbed with another infusion (as yet unknown to the Whites), the effects of the colalue gradually went off, the body resumed its motions, and the party, on whom the experiment had been tried, awoke as from a trance, entirely ignorant of any thing that had pass'ed since he left off dancing.[44]

It's possible that Labatt's use of western medicine may have been influenced by Long's well-known account. Alternately, Labatt's story of feigned obeah matched by medicinal sleight-of-hand might stem from a widespread fear of poisonings on the plantation. According to John Savage, "The wave of poisonings that struck during the early years of the Restoration era (1815–1830) in Martinique were ... understood by most planters to be interrelated, the product of a concerted effort undertaken by an underground network of African sorcerers or black magicians, sometimes described as obis."[45] Savage adds that the role of the giver of medicine, or the "sorcerer," was "seen as the root of his power among the wider slave population. 'Those people who call themselves poison doctors,' as another planter put it, take advantage of the knowledge they have of herbs and harmful substances ... in order to gain experience and make themselves feared and sought after by all the other blacks."[46] While it may be difficult to trace Labatt's source, it is clear that his presentation of both obeah and Western medicine as forms of trickery had roots in Caribbean plantation culture. Within this context, Tom's use of herbs to poison his slave stands as both a form of mimicry of obeah practitioners and as a sign of Western medicinal power. In this sense, he's not exclusively representing white medicine; he's also mimicking and mocking expressions of slave resistance. We might also read Tom's use of ipecacuanha wine as a way to underscore how Western forms of domination played upon slave culture. In both readings, Labatt presents plantation life as a stage where English and African expressions of power square off, illuminating in the process the master's cruel punishing acts as an inverse echo of the agency of slave tactics—of their strategic cunning and their will to assert power. In the process, Labatt presents forms of slave resistance alongside the very forces that prompt their resistance—that is, the cruel master who is clearly threatened by his slaves' power to deceive.

Following the scene of Curgy's poisoning, Joe observes that "the punishment which poor Curgy had already suffered did not seem to satisfy his master. A horrible idea had entered his head."[47] Once again escalating his punishment, Tom prepares for the burial. The next morning Curgy appears to feign death, as the "well-tutored" slaves "appeared not to take any notice of his having stirred." Joe adds, "I had donned an old gray dressing gown, and with a Johnson's dictionary in my hand, stood ready to act the part of the parson."[48] Although Curgy does not move, the other participants in the drama know he's alive. It's not until after Curgy is placed in the coffin, at the moment when nails are attached, that he fights back. Joe explains, "He yelled, he shrieked, cursed, swore, tore the grave-clothes, and struggled so manfully, that it was with the utmost difficulty he was forced down into the coffin" so that the nails could be reinserted.[49] The proceedings continue, with Caesar parading around as "chief mourner" while "grinning until every one of his white teeth was seen—gums and all."[50] Caesar's self-satisfied smile suggests that his play has succeeded in turning the master's attention against the beloved Curgy. With the sound of the first shoveling of dirt, Curgy kicks off the coffin lid, "and fled away as if the devil was at his heels" while "the whole troop of negroes following helter skelter after him."[51] Ultimately, Curgy is recaptured by the terms of his letter and is returned to Moody's plantation to work in the demoted status as field slave. Caesar moves into the role of favored, trusted slave—signaling that he has succeeded in outwitting and controlling the master. Yet Curgy is not entirely unsuccessful. His performance effectively disrupts plantation life. Just like Caesar, Curgy succeeds in using a form of tricksterism (obeah) to control the master's emotions and to incite his master to action.

Joe concludes the narrative on a strange note: "Poor Tom Moody! It is now twenty years since *we acted together the farce* I have just set down. What changes have taken place during that period! Curgy, if he be alive, is now a free man—and thou, Tom, art numbered with the dead."[52] The significance of the story turns on this last line, on the larger system of violence that underwrites Tom's trickery, and the fact of emancipation that helps to construct that violence as farce. Humor fails, of course, when we recall the subsequent violence imposed by the system of apprenticeship that followed slavery's violence and oppression. Still, it's worth pausing on Joe's mention of farce—a form of dramatic humor used to tell a story about the intersection of different forms of trickery—signifying, medicinal tomfoolery, and feigned obeah practices. The story's conclusion leans toward a hope for justice by rendering the master powerless (because he is dead) and by suggesting the possibility that Curgy finds his freedom in the postemancipation era. Yet, while the ending offers some closure, the narrator's position in relation to other characters remains a disquieting feature of the story.

Throughout "Curgy's Funeral" Tom gradually loses the ability to control his temper, while the narrator grows increasingly critical of his friend's sadistic behavior. He challenges Tom's threat of laudanum, and expresses dismay at Tom's rising anger. And yet, despite his censure of Tom's actions, Joe continues to participate in Tom's violent antics. Thus, he chooses to dress as a man of the cloth and to carry a copy of *Johnson's Dictionary*—acts that implicate Joe as well as English language and culture in Tom's violence. Joe's costume uncomfortably pokes fun at a malicious scenario of abuse while simultaneously reminding readers of the performance of power on the plantation.

As neither master nor slave, Joe occupies an in-between status on the plantation, much like Labatt. He seems to have some understanding of the emotional triggers and strategies of both groups. Yet, at the same time, his choice to write a story based on earlier events—a story that emphasizes the failure of written texts to convey meaning accurately—draws attention to his paradoxical position as both an abettor and a plantation visitor. For example, at several points in the story Joe refers to pieces of writing—the manumission letter; *Johnson's Dictionary;* the medicine bottle containing an incorrect label; and the story itself, which he identifies as a farce—all of which are deployed as unstable texts, or faulty signifiers taken out of context that ultimately fail to stand for the concepts they allegedly hold or represent.[53] Labatt's characterization of his story as farce therefore points directly to the untrustworthy nature of the written English word, which clearly raises more problems than it solves in his story.

Indeed, in calling the story a farce—a popular form of English drama in the period—"Curgy's Funeral" can be read as a kind of literary trickery in its own right. Robert B. Heilman explains that farce operates as "a generator of materials that can be utilized and even transformed by other modes—by comedy, of course, but even by romantic and tragic styles."[54] Heilman adds, "Farce is primarily physical. It is strenuous and tireless; all resources go into bodily activity. This is because no energy goes into real thought. No energy goes into real feeling, though stereotyped emotional responses may be screamed at us. No energy goes into moral concern, though moral fervor is often simulated. A good deal of the time, no energy goes into acts of will; action is then an automatic result of banana-peel incidents. Things happen to people more often than people make things happen."[55] While the story clearly draws from physical bodily activities—particularly in the lengthy passages describing Curgy's vomiting—inclusions of the master's growing sinister anger prevents these moments from functioning as light, banana-peel humor. Thus, Labatt avoids the risk of trivializing Tom's violence. Yet readers are faced with the difficulty of determining the object of our laughter or the butt of Joe's farcical jokes. We are also left with the challenge of categorizing a form of writing that integrates so many cultural and literary expressions in a way that resists disentanglement. Labatt draws traits from the farce, and at the same time "Curgy's Funeral" moves physical humor into a critique of the way of life represented in the story. In these ways, Labatt transforms literary motifs in a creolizing process that emerges through psychological strategies of subversion and resistance that thrived in Jamaican plantation life. It is in this very transformation, I argue, where we witness Labatt's creolizing literary practices.

In "Curgy's Funeral," Labatt does more than blend genres and styles; he reconstructs those genres in response to the demands of his story's historically situated content and contexts. Heilman's point that in farce "things happen to people more often than people make things happen" helps to locate Labatt's staunchest critique of slavery. The story's depiction of slavery is horrific and violent, signaled by the slave master's devil-like punishing acts and Curgy's suffering. In fact, there's nothing funny about this story. Labatt's blending of tricksterism, signifying, and farce work together to expose the master's insecurity, his inability to control his slaves *and* his temper, and his awareness of his vulnerable authority on the plantation. Similarly, despite his knowledge of obeah and the master's letter-writing power, Curgy fails to make his escape from slavery. He can prompt the writing of a manumission letter, but only British law can call an end to his enslaved status. In writing a farce Labatt suggests that while master and slave have some agency, both are acted upon and remain imprisoned within an ineffective, sick world where forms of medicine—Western and obeah alike—emerge as agents of power and control rather than as healing practices.

Trickster Crossings

In recent years scholars have recovered histories of intellectual and cultural crossings throughout the Atlantic world. David Armitage, for example, refers to a "Circum-Atlantic history" to address "the history of the Atlantic as a particular zone of exchange and interchange, circulation and transmission."[56] Adam Mendelsohn has focused on the role of print culture in shaping Atlantic Jewish experiences and identity. He explains, "The books, periodicals, poetry, tracts, and newspapers that poured from the presses diffused the values of Victorian Jewish culture across the Anglophone sphere."[57] And Arthur Kiron has traced histories of Atlantic Jews who "formed networks of commerce, communication, kinship and community."[58] Kiron adds that Atlantic Jewish communities—particularly those from port cities—created a "distinctive situation of early modern Jewish 'betweenness'—as 'middle-men' and women, merchants and cultural brokers, prosperous and poor, who lived between toleration and citizenship, on the outer edges of empires . . . and whose legal status and religious identity were often in flux."[59] Certainly, Labatt stands within these worlds of betweenness, as cultural and intellectual broker of multiple literary traditions, for "Curgy's Funeral," as well as his other published work, draws as much from the English farce as it does from literary accounts of plantation life in the Atlantic world. Moreover, as we see with "Curgy's Funeral," the author's position as a Jamaican Jew finds expression through narrators or characters who stand between, or at the margins of, social categories created by a colonial society—as neither slave, master, nor colonial administrator.

These studies are important for their recovery of Jewish writers and print cultures engaged with distant Jewish community practice and correspondence throughout the Atlantic. "Curgy's Funeral" reminds us, however, that Atlantic Jewish literary culture wasn't just a product of intercultural mixing among Caribbean, European, and Jewish American cultures. As I have tried to suggest, writers like Labatt were also deeply engaged with the cultures in which they lived and wrote. The subjects of Labatt's body of work suggest that he was well informed about global history and culture in addition to British literature. But as we see in "Curgy's Funeral," his writing was also an agent of a creolization process taking place in his native Jamaica, a form of writing that infused, translated, integrated, adapted, and appropriated Afro-Caribbean literary cultures. This process didn't begin with Labatt or his generation. For, as Sarah Phillips Casteel recalls, "in the aftermath of 1492 and the displacement of multiple populations that ensued, Black and Jewish diaspora histories became entangled with one another across the Caribbean region."[60] Thus, while Labatt's work clearly draws from English farce, *Johnson's Dictionary* project, and other references to colonial power, his simultaneous focus on the psychology of enslavement and his knowledge of the subtleties of signifying suggest that he is also deliberately drawing from Afro-Caribbean culture.

Part of the challenge of reading Labatt as a Jamaican Jewish writer stems from his choice not to address Jamaican Jewish subjects in his fiction, a common feature among Jewish writers, as we see with David Gantt Gurley's essay in this collection. Just as the narrator, Joe, occupies a position within and outside of the story he narrates, Labatt similarly writes from an ambivalent position. Indeed, "Curgy's Funeral," like all of Labatt's fiction, presents interpretive challenges, in part because of its blending of literary cultures and perspectives. "Curgy's Funeral" leaves readers wondering if his stereotypes are meant to be read as surface lies challenged or undone by Joe's descriptions of Caesar's and Curgy's intelligence, or if the use of these stereotypes implicate the narrator as not fully cognizant of the world he narrates. If the latter is true, then Labatt's use of an unreliable narrator may be understood as another kind of farce, critiquing the narrator, and perhaps also Jamaican readers, who make the choice to observe rather than obstruct plantocracy violence. Labatt's creation of a contradictory text that operates by forging a criticism of slavery while simultaneously drawing from the racial stereotypes as the grounds of that critique is difficult to decipher and might even be read as a sign of his own trickster tactics.

In his formative years Labatt witnessed dramatic changes in Jamaica—he would have been nine years old during the Baptist War (1831–32); he was in his teens when slavery officially came to a close; and he died in 1854, long before the Morant Bay rebellion in 1865. In this very short life Labatt witnessed slavery, the abolition of slavery, the decline of the plantocracy, and the rise of the apprenticeship system. In stories that explore the psychology of resistance alongside the stubbornness of colonial greed and violence, Labatt's writing reflects an important moment in literary culture's interest in colonialism and slavery read through the lens of a Jamaican Jewish writer.[61] As I have suggested, Joe's symbolic role as a narrator straddling multiple worlds might be read as an emblem for Labatt's unknown position as either a Jamaican Jew, a non–slave holding white man, or possibly a biracial Jew. Our lack of understanding of the perspective from which the story of slavery is drawn and narrated points to Labatt's interpolated position as a writer engaging within multiple narrative and cultural traditions. Regardless of where we place the author on the spectrum of identities, Labatt's writing testifies to the existence of a Jamaican Jewish Creole culture that emerged as much through its affiliation with the Jewish Atlantic and British Atlantic worlds as from its own island cultural matrix that actively blended colonial and diaspora literary histories and rhetorical traditions. Our inability to individuate a Jewish strand from Jamaican culture in this period does not negate its presence. Nineteenth-century Caribbean Jewish writers and editors, like Labatt, clearly drew from and reworked intersecting literary and cultural strands as they imagined new narrative forms whose rhetoric and aesthetics participated in and invigorated a creolizing process.

Notes

I would like to thank Sarah Phillips Casteel for helpful and insightful comments on earlier drafts of this essay. I would also like to thank Barbara Lalla and Jean DaCosta for their generosity in answering my questions about Creole literature and language. Finally, I wish to thank Ainsley Henriques, Marina Delfos, and Edgar Samuel for their assistance tracking down Labatt family history in England and Jamaica.

    1. I. Lawton, "Introductory," in *Selections from The Miscellaneous Posthumous Works of Philip Cohen Labatt; In Prose and Verse* (Kingston, JA: R. J. DeCordova, 1855), vii.

    2. David Cesarani notes that *Allgemeine Zeitung des Judentums* was "arguably the first proper Jewish newspaper" and "launched on 15 March 1837 in Leipzig by Ludwig Philippson (1811–1889). It promoted the ideology of emancipation and transmitted the social values of Bildung—education, self-improvement and civic betterment. The paper was also a vehicle for enabling Jews to keep in touch with one another and debate their mutual interests" (Cesarani 4). This mode and medium of debate continued in many of the Jewish periodicals that followed. In London the first Jewish periodical was the *Hebrew Intelligencer* (1823). Cesarani adds that "the paper ran for only three issues before it was obliged to cease publication" (4). The *Hebrew Intelligencer* was followed by other Jewish publications that fostered dialogue across national boundaries. The *Voice of Jacob* (London) appeared in 1841, the *Occident and American Jewish Advocate* (Philadelphia) in 1843, and the *First Fruits of the West* (Kingston) in 1844. Articles and editorials fostered transatlantic dialogue in all of these papers. Labatt was clearly interested in every aspect of literary and print culture, including the Jewish and Jamaican periodical press. In addition to producing literary works for the *First Fruits of the West*, he also served as editor of the Jamaican paper the *Daily Gleaner*. The editors of the *First Fruits* were ex-patriots. According to Hurwitz and Hurwitz, the editors were Reverend M. N. Nathan, a rabbi from London, and Dr. Lewis

Ashenheim, an Edinburgh physician who arrived in Kingston by way of London. Samuel J. Hurwitz and Edith Hurwitz, "A Beacon for Judaism: *The First Fruits of the West*," *American Jewish Historical Quarterly* 56, no. 1 (September 1966): 4–5. The editors of the *First Fruits* attempted to use the periodical press as an educational outlet. As Hurwitz and Hurwitz note, "Like *The Voice of Jacob* and *The Occident*, *The First Fruits* attempted to fill the gaps in the community's general knowledge of Jewish history and religion. To this end, the editors crammed every issue with simply written articles on every phase of Jewish life and letters. Articles and poems translated from Hebrew, French, and German were included" (9). Labatt's contributions were poems adapting events included in Hebrew Scriptures.

3. According to Mordechai Arbell, Labatt's *Catechism of The History of Jamaica*, published in 1848, "became a textbook used in the schools" in Jamaica (58). See Mordechai Arbell, *The Portuguese Jews of Jamaica* (Kingston, JA: University of the West Indies Press, 2000), 58.

4. Bertram W. Korn, "The Haham DeCordova of Jamaica," *American Jewish Archives* (November 1966): 141–54, 145.

5. Labatt married Judith DeCordova, daughter of Joshua DeCordova who cofounded the prominent Jamaican newspaper the *Daily Gleaner*, with his brother Jacob DeCordova. Philip Labatt and Judith DeCordova married on February 21, 1848, in Jamaica. They had two children: Ernest Labatt (1848–1850) and Lillian Labatt (1854–1913).

6. Kenneth Ramchand, "The West Indian Short Story," *Journal of Caribbean Literatures* 1, no. 1 (Spring 1997): 23. Hyacinth M. Simpson places Labatt's work squarely within Jamaican Jewish cultural production, particularly the "word paintings" produced by Jamaican Jewish artist I. M. Belisario from 1837–38. She notes, "Belisario's work grew into the sketches of Jamaican characters and life [that appear] in Philip Cohen Labatt's *Selections From the Miscellaneous Posthumous Works of Philip Cohen Labatt; in prose and verse* (1855)" (3). Simpson adds that Labatt's short fiction is relies upon "a careful selection and sequencing of detail for their 'storyness' and less on the aesthetic formalism of plot championed by late nineteenth-century American and British short fiction writers." Hyacinth M. Simpson, "Patterns and Periods: Oral Aesthetics and a Century of Jamaican Short Story Writing," *Journal of West Indian Literature* 12, nos. 1–2 (2004): 3. Belisario and Labatt lived in Kingston during the same period.

7. Ramchand, "The West Indian Short Story," 23.

8. Barbara Lalla adds that "much eighteenth- and nineteenth-century Jamaican discourse that includes Creole is naïve with regard to any viewpoint but British adventuring and exploratory perspective: clueless voyeur or reporter types of writing, in which Creole exoticizes the literature." Barbara Lalla, "Black Wholes: Phases in the Development of Jamaican Literary Discourse," in *Caribbean Literary Discourse: Voice and Cultural Identity in the Anglophone Caribbean*, ed. Barbara Lalla, Jean D'Costa, and Velma Pollard (Tuscaloosa: University of Alabama Press, 2014), 45. Lalla adds that, typically, "Creole speech in nineteenth-century

literary discourse continues to be represented by the nonspeaker. Indeed, apart from the local and perhaps colored Henry Murray, there is little evidence of local literary discourse that includes Creole" (46).

9. Evelyn O'Callaghan, "'The Unhomely Moment': Frieda Cassin's Nineteenth-Century Antiguan Novel and the Construction of the White Creole," *Small Axe* 13, no. 2 (2009): 95–106, 96.

10. O'Callaghan, "The Unhomely Moment," 99.

11. Kamau Braithwaite, *Contradictory Omens: Cultural Diversity and Integration in the Caribbean* (Mona, JA: Savacou, 1974), 6.

12. Jean Bernabé, Patrick Chamoiseau, Raphaël Confiant, and Mohamed B. Taleb Khyar, "In Praise of Creoleness," *Callaloo* 13, no. 4 (Autumn 1990): 886–909, 886. This text was first published in French under the title of *Éloge de la Créolité* in 1989.

13. Percy C. Hintzen, "Race and Creole Ethnicity in the Caribbean," in *Questioning Creole: Creolisation Discourses in Caribbean Culture,* ed. Verene A. Shepherd and Glen L. Richards (Kingston, JA: Ian Randle, 2002), 92–110, 95.

14. Reprinted in Chris Bongie, *Islands and Exiles: The Creole Identities of Post/Colonial Literature* (Stanford, CA: Stanford University Press, 1998), 3.

15. Labatt's name appears on several extant synagogue records. He was buried in the Jewish Orange Street Cemetery, and he wrote poetry advocating for global Jewish causes or that explored Jewish biblical stories. Labatt is part of a community of Caribbean Jews whose ancestors arrived in the years following their expulsion from Spain in 1492 and Portugal in 1497. By the eighteenth century, Ashkenazim, or Jews from central Europe also began finding their way to Jamaica. According to Arthur Kiron, by 1840 Jamaica "was home to approximately 1,500–2,000 Jews, roughly ten percent of London's perhaps 20,000 Jewish inhabitants, but perhaps more comparable to approximately the same number (1,500 Jews) thought to have been living in Philadelphia in that year." Arthur Kiron, "An Atlantic Jewish Republic of Letters?" *Jewish History* 20, no. 2 (2006): 182. In his introduction to Labatt's writing, I. Lawton makes it clear that Labatt was born in Jamaica and considered that to be his mother land. It's possible that his father had ties to the Sephardi Jewish community in London's East End, particularly Bevis Marks Synagogue.

16. Stanley Mirvis, "Sexuality and Sentiment: Concubinage and the Sephardi Family in Late Eighteenth-Century Jamaica," in *The Jews in the Caribbean,* ed. Jane S. Gerber (Oxford: Littman Library of Jewish Civilization, 2014), 224. In this work Mirvis engages in a study of wills and manumission papers that attest to the existence of "devotion on the part of Sephardi men to their illegitimate children and their mistresses, regardless of Jewish identity" (224). He concludes, "Children of mixed ancestry occupied a decisively more favourable social position among colonial Jamaican Jews, who, echoing colonial patterns more generally, treated their black slaves with the same accumulative ethos as non-Jews" (230).

17. John Bigelow, ed., *Jamaica in 1850: Or, the Effects of Sixteen Years of Freedom on a Slave Colony*, with an introduction by Robert J. Scholnick (Urbana: University of Illinois Press, 2006), 15.

18. Jane S. Gerber, "Introduction," in *The Jews in the Caribbean*, ed. Jane S. Gerber (Oxford: Littman Library of Jewish Civilization, 2014), 11.

19. Kay Dian Kriz, "Belisario's 'Kingston's Cried' and he Refinement of Jewish Identity in the Late 1830s," in *Art and Emancipation in Jamaica: Isaac Mendes Belisario and His Worlds*, ed. Tim Barringer, Gillian Forrester, and Barbara Martinez-Ruiz (New Haven, CT: Yale University Press, 2007), 163–78, 165.

20. Holly Snyder, "Customs of an Unruly Race: The Political Context of Jamaican Jewry, 1670–1831," in *Art and Emancipation in Jamaica*, 151–62, 151. Kriz adds that "it was Jews, however, rather than blacks or non-Jewish whites, who were most closely associated with the Kingston Theatre and its stage in the early nineteenth century" (72). This may explain Labatt's interest in farce and his one remaining play, which also happens to be a farce.

21. Snyder, "Customs of an Unruly Race," 151.

22. Barbara Lalla and Jean D'Costa, *Language in Exile: Three Hundred Years of Jamaican Creole* (Tuscaloosa: University of Alabama Press, 1990), xiv. Lalla and D'Costa offer an important observation: "Because Jamaican Creole [languages] grew out of folk usage and was thus an oral language, those who spoke it rarely wrote it down. Instead, most of its chroniclers were educated Britons who wrote in the metropolitan English of their times, employing a variety of genres, styles, and registers. In literary usage, JC can play an important part in dialogue, characterization, and setting" (37). Labatt's story follows this pattern. The narrator speaks with a metropolitan English dialect. Yet Labatt includes dialogue, characterization, and setting that attempts to represent Jamaican Creole culture. His depictions of both Curgy's interest in obeah and the white mens' inability to understand Curgy's dialect and narrative underscores the fact that while Creole might have been common enough for Labatt to include spoken dialect, it was not understood by all those who made contact with Creole speakers.

23. Tim Barringer and Gillian Forrester have helpfully noted that the term "Creole" was also used "to refer more specifically to people of mixed race heritage—for whom other terms, such as 'brown' and 'mulatto,' were also used." Barringer and Forrester identify distinctions within Creole society between "Afro-Creole" and "Euro-Creole" cultures to destabilize binaries of whiteness and blackness. Tim Barringer and Gillian Forrester, "Introduction," in *Art and Emancipation in Jamaica*, 3.

24. "Curgy's Funeral" in particular blends the English farce and the trickster figure to stage a critique of Tom Moody's trickery upon his slave Curgy; of the slave Caesar's trickery upon his Master which attempts to undermine the fellow slave, Curgy; and of Curgy's resistance to his master and the system of slavery.

25. For a detailed analysis of signifying, see Henry Louis Gates's *The Signifying Monkey*. In this work Gates explains that "tales of the Signifying Monkey

seem to have their origin in slavery. Hundreds of these have been recorded since the early twentieth century" (51–52). Gates explores the origins, history, and role of signifying in American slavery. Labatt's choice to include a character who follows this pattern provides examples of the way signifying worked outside of the United States in this period. One wonders if Labatt was knowledgeable of American literary representations of signifying during the period in which he wrote "Curgy's Funeral," or sometime between 1838 and 1854.

26. Srinivas Aravamudan, introduction to *Obi, or, The History of Three-Fingered Jack* by William Earle (Peterborough, ON: Broadview Editions, 2005), 9; Dianne M. Stewart, *Three Eyes for the Journey: African Dimensions of the Jamaican Religious Experience* (Oxford: Oxford University Press, 2005), 42. Labatt oeuvre suggests that he had a longstanding interest in writing about obeah. Several of his short stories focus on obeah practices or practitioners. Typically, Europeans depicted obeah without fully understanding its nuance or function; rather, they dismissed it as a sign of simplistic superstition. Maarit Forde and Diana Paton have noted, for example, that "writers such as Long, Edwards, and Moreau not only drew on but also reinforced European 'knowledge' that Africans (or 'Negroes') had no religion but instead worshipped 'fetishes'" (14). In this way, they add, "they characterized enslaved people's religious practice as magic or witchcraft rather than religion." Forde and Paton, "Introduction," 14. John Savage rightly notes that obeah was never a unified or fixed form in Jamaican culture. He explains that it was frequently used "as a vessel to contain all sorts of different content" (150). John Savage, "Slave Poison/Slave Medicine: The Persistence of Obeah in Early Nineteenth-Century Martinique," in *Obeah and Other Powers: The Politics of Caribbean Religion and Healing*, ed. Diana Paton and Maarit Forde (Durham, NC: Duke University Press, 2012), 150, 149–71. While obeah stood as a serious and powerful belief system and set of practices, in "Curgy's Funeral" Labatt uses it as a cover for tricksterism. Read within the context of his other work, Labatt suggests that part of obeah's power stemmed from its ability to empower slaves to rebel. Janelle Rodrigues has noted that "while obeah was of course 'knowable' to its practitioners and adherents, this form of knowledge was antithetical to the colonial project of 'rationalisation'. In observing and recording encounters with obeah, colonists repeatedly found that their 'facts' were not necessarily 'reality.'" Janelle Rodrigues, "Obeah(Man) as Trickster in Cynric Williams' *Hamel, the Obeah Man*," *Atlantic Studies* 12, no. 2 (2015): 220–21.

27. It's possible that Labatt based this story on actual events. The British Slave Database (http://www.ucl.ac.uk/lbs/claim/view/15256) lists a Thomas Moody as the owner of Southfield Plantation in the parish of St. George. Claim #215 identified thirty-eight slaves owned by Moody between 1811 and 1839.

28. Philip Cohen Labatt, "Curgy's Funeral, or the Old Time Busha," in *Selections from the Miscellaneous Posthumous Works of Philip Cohen Labatt; In Prose and Verse* (Kingston, JA: R. J. DeCordova, 1855), 30.

29. Labatt, "Curgy's Funeral," 30.

30. Labatt, 31.

31. Labatt, 31.
32. Labatt, 31.
33. Labatt, 31.
34. Labatt, 31. Labatt may have drawn the name "Caesar" from Maria Edgeworth's well-known story "The Grateful Negro." Aravamudan explains that, in Edgeworth's tale, Caesar, the "grateful Negro" of Edgeworth's title, exposes the obeah-inspired plot involving his fellow-slaves Hector and Esther and helps vindicate the paternalistic slave-owning practices of the "good" master Edwards, named in tribute to the Caribbean historian Bryan Edwards. Caesar's switch of loyalty from his obeah-practicing fellow-slaves is motivated by his gratitude toward Edwards, his new master, who brought him to keep him from being separated from his wide and sent to Mexico to pay his previous owner's debts. Caesar's gratitude triumphs over all previous obligations an all desires for revenge against slaveowners and overseers (Aravamudan, "Introduction," 44). Yet it's also possible that Labatt's choice to name this character Caesar comes from newspaper accounts of the 1780s describing the Three-Fingered Jack depicting accounts of a gang of dangerous runaway slaves who threaten to "kill every Mulatto and Creole Negro they can catch" (10). While their leader was known as the Three-finger'd Jack, this group's second in command was named Caesar.
35. Labatt, "Curgy's Funeral," 31–32.
36. According to Gates, "The Signifying Monkey invariably repeats to his friend, the Lion, some insult purportedly generated by their mutual friend, the Elephant. The Monkey, however, speaks figuratively. The Lion, indignant and outraged, demands an apology of the Elephant, who refuses and then trounces the Lion. The Lion, realizing that his mistake was to take the Monkey literally, returns to trounce the Monkey. It is this relationship between the literal and the figurative, and the dire consequences of their confusion, which is the most striking repeated element of these tales. The Monkey's trick depends on the Lion's inability to mediate between these two poles of signification, of meaning." Gates, *The Signifying Monkey*, 55.
37. Labatt, "Curgy's Funeral," 32.
38. Labatt, 32.
39. For a related discussion of poisoning in colonial Martinique, see John Savage, "Slave Poison/Slave Medicine: The Persistence of Obeah in Early Nineteenth-Century Martinique," in *Obeah and Other Powers*, 149–71.
40. Labatt, "Curgy's Funeral," 33.
41. Labatt, 35.
42. Edward Long, *The History of Jamaica*, 3 vols. (London: T. Lowndes, 1774).
43. Long, *The History of Jamaica*, vol. 2, 416.
44. Long, 417–18.
45. Savage, "Slave Poison/Slave Medicine," 151.

46. Savage, 153. Aravamudan has argued persuasively that "Obeah is about demonstration of metaphysical and technological mastery as much as it is about the purported hoodwinking of the naïve and the gullible" (26). Moreover, Aravamudan adds, that it was Tackey's Rebellion in 1760 that "brought the existence of obeah into the colonial consciousness" ("Introduction," 29).

47. Labatt, "Curgy's Funeral," 33.

48. Labatt, 34. In this passage Labatt has not italicized the title of this book. I have therefore left this reference in unitalicized form. References to *Johnson's Dictionary* in my own discussion (not a direct quote from Labatt's story) follow standard rules of italicizing book titles.

49. Labatt, "Curgy's Funeral," 35.

50. Labatt, 35. It's worth noting that the nurse, Curgy's caretaker, is the one to note her master's mistake by pointing out that Curgy is not dead. Tom placates her by explaining that Curgy *is* dead but has been possessed by "the jumbi of his grandy," (35) who "had entered his body and was playing such tricks" (35). The narrator's response betrays the story's emphasis on trickery as a mode of manipulation. The narrator explains: "The old woman believed this probable explanation, and was immediately quieted" (35). We are left wondering precisely what part of the explanation she believes—that the spirit of Curgy's grandfather had entered his body, or that the memory of his dead grandfather was playing a trick?

51. Labatt, "Curgy's Funeral," 35.

52. Labatt, 35, emphasis added.

53. Gates has explored the use of this tactic in texts that point to the tension between "surfaces in the double-voiced discourse." Gates, *The Signifying Monkey*, 21.

54. Robert B. Heilman, "Farce Transformed: Plautus, Shakespeare, and Unamuno," *Comparative Literature* 21, no. 2 (Spring 1979): 113.

55. Heilman, "Farce Transformed," 114. Irving Howe adds, "Farce does not compromise, neither is it kind. It hits below the belt. It flattens out the refinements that sensitive people value. It is a sort of fart among genres. It levels us all to an ultimate equality: man on his ass. There are few metaphysical consolations or ennobling ends in farce, certainly nothing like those we impute to comedy; there is only the putdown or the social demolition which gleefully levels the world (the Marx brothers)" (5). Irving Howe, "Farce and Fiction," *Threepenny Review* 43 (Autumn 1990): 5–6.

56. David Armitage, "Three Concepts of Atlantic History," in *The British Atlantic World, 1500–1800*, ed. David Armitage and Michael J. Braddick (New York: Palgrave Macmillan, 2002), 11–27, 16–18.

57. Adam Mendelsohn, "Tongue Ties: The Emergence of the Anglophone Jewish Diaspora in the Mid-Nineteenth Century," *American Jewish History* 93, no. 2 (June 2007): 177– 209, 192.

58. Arthur Kiron, "An Atlantic Jewish Republic of Letters?" *Jewish History* 20, no. 2 (2006): 171–211; 171.

59. Kiron, "Atlantic Jewish Republic," 172.

60. Sarah Phillips Casteel, *Calypso Jews: Jewishness in the Caribbean Literary Imagination* (New York: Columbia University Press, 2016), 4.

61. Labatt made a more prominent pronouncement on this front in his poem "The Rhyme of the Ancient Planter. Altered from Coleridge." In this poetic adaptation of Samuel Taylor Coleridge's "The Rime of the Ancient Mariner," the speaker describes a planter at a dinner party who is compelled to "stoppeth one of three." The unsympathetic narrator cries,

> Cheap Sugar, cried the British *child,*
>   Cheap sugar I must buy—
> What care I if whole seas of blood
> Be shed if by that crimson flood,
>   My wish I gratify!
>
> Ruin, ruin every where
>   And every heart did sink;
> Ruin, ruin every where;
>   When Britain blood did drink.

Labatt, "The Rhyme of the Ancient Planter," *Selections from the Miscellaneous Posthumous Works of Philip Cohen Labatt In Prose and Verse* (Kingston, JA: R. J. DeCordova, 1855), 80–83, 81.

Translating Cuba

Language, Race, and Homeland in Cuban-Yiddish Poetry of the 1930s

Rachel Rubinstein

WHILE CUBA IS identified as the source of a significant immigrant population in the United States, it is rarely considered by Americans to be itself another "nation of immigrants." But, in 1940, Cuban sociologist and founding figure in Afro-Cuban studies Fernando Ortiz coined the term "transculturation" to describe the dynamic and often traumatic interchange of cultures and the creation of new cultures that he argued were constitutive of Cuba more than any other nation in the Americas.[1] The Indigenous presence in Cuba, he notes, had been quickly decimated, necessitating the importation of a "complete new population, both masters and servants." The resulting waves of slaves and immigrants, including "Indians from the mainland, Jews, Portuguese, Anglo-Saxons, French, North Americans, even yellow Mongoloids"—each "torn from his native moorings, faced with the problem of disadjustment and readjustment, of deculturation and acculturation"—produced the "real history of Cuba . . . history of its intermeshed transculturations."[2] "This is one of the strange features of Cuba," he concludes, "that since the sixteenth century all its classes, races and cultures, coming in by will or by force, have all been exogenous and have all been torn from their places of origin, suffering the shock of this first uprooting and a harsh transplantation."[3]

Writing half a century later, Cuban-American literary scholar Gustavo Perez Firmat, building upon Ortiz's transformative idea of cultural exchange, argued that Cuban literature has also always been constitutively shaped by literary and linguistic transactions, and, most fundamentally, by acts of translation. If Cuban culture is defined by its "mutability and uprootedness," then a "translation sensibility" permeates much of its national literature. "Cuban culture," he argues, "subsists in and through translation."[4] The example he begins with is a Jewish one: he recounts attending a Cuban-Jewish wedding in Miami, during which the Cuban band played a rendition of "Hava-Nagila" with a Cuban Latin beat (Perez Firmat calls it "Havana-gilah"). "There was something peculiarly Cuban," he writes, "in that irreverent, creole translation of this Hebrew song. Like [that] performance, Cuban culture results from the importation, and even the smuggling, of foreign goods."[5]

Perez Firmat's characterization of Cuban literature resounds with accounts of Yiddish literature as constitutively translational rather than foundational. Yiddish, based in Middle High German, written in Hebrew characters, and infused with Aramaic and Hebrew, as well as with the Romance and Slavic vocabularies picked up by its speakers in their migrations across Europe, was the major European Jewish vernacular for nearly a millennium. Yiddish literature first emerged in the early modern period in an effort to translate, explain, and adapt religious texts, which were in Hebrew, to Jewish readers who were not educated in Hebrew and frequently described in such texts as "women and uneducated men."[6] The earliest secular Yiddish literature consisted of adaptations and translations of popular European tales, such as Elye Bokher's *Bovo D'Antona,* often called the *Bovo-Bukh* (composed in 1507), a Yiddish adaptation of the popular Italian chivalric romance *Buova D'Antona,* itself an adaptation of the Anglo-Norman romance Bevis of Hampton.[7] Benjamin Harshav characterized Yiddish as a "uniquely open language," a fusion language "radically more open" than even English in the time of Chaucer, because it "lived among or close to its stock languages and was constantly reminded of their full extent and contemporary, casual or 'correct' form."[8] Yiddish speakers were nearly always multilingual and could therefore absorb new vocabularies into Yiddish with ease or shift spoken registers based on geographical or cultural context.[9]

Thus, as Anita Norich has noted, "of necessity, then, Yiddish has always been permeable, open to other literary influences, looking to other languages and traditions, in dialogue with them." And, she concludes, "this multilingual cultural exchange may make Yiddish literature peculiarly adaptive to translation."[10] Translation and adaptation into Yiddish of texts in non-Jewish, coterritorial languages continued to figure significantly in the emergence of a self-consciously modern, secular Yiddish literature under the influence of the Enlightenment, and in the global Yiddish dispersions of the late nineteenth and twentieth centuries. Frequently these translations and adaptations played with Yiddish's mongrel status in relation to major European literary traditions, thus domesticating, deflating, and undermining the original. Many Yiddish speakers (and scholars) retell the joke of American Yiddish performances of Shakespeare, impudently billed as "fartaytsht un farbesert" ("translated and improved"), which, as Naomi Seidman observes, "rests precisely on an understanding of languages as unequal in status: on the one hand, the exalted language of Shakespeare; on the other, the *zhargon* of the unwashed Jewish masses."[11] As Yiddish writers migrated to the Americas and confronted the legacy of New World colonialism and settlement, translations and adaptations of national narratives or mythologies became a way to assert *both* belonging and outsiderness, often, after Homi Bhabha's characterization of translation by postcolonial subjects, as "a way of imitating, but in a mischievous, displacing sense."[12] Certainly translation and translators have a fraught history in the colonial history of the Americas in facilitating conquest; translation is always, Seidman reminds us, a political negotiation that "appears in a variety of relational modes: translation as colonialist, imperialist, or missionary appropriation, *but also* translation as risk, as assimilation, as treason, as dislocation, as survival" (9, my italics).[13] In the United States, Yiddish writers translated Harriet Beecher Stowe's *Uncle Tom's Cabin,* Walt Whitman's poetry, and Native American chants;[14] in Mexico, Yankev (Jacobo or Yaakov) Glantz composed an epic poem titled *Kristobal Kolon,* published, like the Yiddish poems I examine here, in the 1930s.[15] What was unique, however, about the Yiddish writers in Cuba described in this essay is the degree to which they received attention and interest from non-Jewish Cuban writers attuned to instances of syncretism and hybridity, and who thus authenticated and affirmed their transculturated visions of Cuban citizenship.

This essay offers reflections on two encounters between Cuban and Yiddish literary cultures: the 1931 poem *Hatuey* by Oskar Pinis (also known as Asher Penn) and the 1932 poem *Maceo* by Eliezer Aronowsky, both epic poems with popular Indigenous and Afro-Cuban revolutionary subjects. Both writers were participating in important Cuban nationalist literary rituals by writing about Hatuey, the martyred sixteenth-century Taíno Indian and protorevolutionary who became a popular subject in Cuban drama and poetry from the nineteenth century on, and Maceo, the so-called "bronze titan" of Cuba's nineteenth-century struggles for independence. Both Hatuey and Maceo were contested figures in 1930s Cuba. Further, both poems were translated almost immediately into Spanish by a non-Jewish, nonimmigrant Cuban poet, Andrés de Piedra-Bueno, who celebrated and publicized these poems' Jewish origins. What is more,

Hatuey continues to have a significant afterlife, as currently klezmer avant-gardist Frank London and librettist Elise Thoron have adapted the poem into an opera, performed in English, Spanish, Yiddish, and Taíno.

Cuba's history as a place of refuge for Eastern European Yiddish-speaking refugees between World War I and II is part of a broader and more complex history of migration to and within the Americas that complicate the United States' exceptionalist myths about immigration and national identity. In particular, looking at Yiddish literary production in the geographical "margins" of the Americas challenges our still very bordered notions of what defines American, Latin American, and Jewish/Yiddish literatures. Even now, when scholars of Jewish and Jewish American literatures are paying renewed attention to Latin America and the Caribbean, much work remains to be done in Yiddish literary production. In response, this essay will consider how dominant nation-building narratives may be transformed through practices of translation into and out of Yiddish. I aim to not only revive and rehabilitate texts from the cultural and geographic margins, especially in the context of a Yiddish literary canon that has always been particularly unsettled and in flux, but also to resituate Yiddish cultural production in the context of a linguistically diverse Caribbean where multiple Creole/Patois languages have likewise been considered "lesser" linguistic forms.[16]

The Jews of Cuba

"The atmosphere of post–World War I Cuba," writes historian Robert Levine, "was unique: blacks and mulattos, immigrants from Jamaica and Haiti, Chinese, and Jews served a dual elite of Creoles and the largest foreign expatriate business community in the Americas. Immigrant Jews competed for the same jobs and chances to make a living as other immigrant groups, most directly with newcomers from Spain and, to a lesser degree, with the descendants of the Chinese coolies brought to Cuba in the mid-nineteenth century as laborers."[17] Spain had authorized Jews to enter its Cuban colony in 1881,[18] and until the US occupation of Cuba in 1902 the Jewish population of Cuba was comprised of a tiny group of mostly Sephardic families, whose family networks spread across the Caribbean. Many of them were intermarried and raised their children as Catholics.[19] José Martí, Cuba's national hero of independence, successfully raised funds among American Jews for the Republican cause.[20] Several dozens of Jews participated in the US campaign in Cuba, and many American Jews remained in Cuba during and after the US occupation as part of an expatriate business community attracted by economic opportunities. This community of "American Jews," even though some of its early members were Yiddish speaking, continued to conduct its affairs in English for decades, and remained distinct from the Sephardic, then Eastern European, then German waves of Jewish migration to Cuba.[21]

Indeed, as Levine notes, one of the "major characteristics" of Cuban Jewish life and in contrast to the United States, was that Jews sought to preserve their identities as Jews, while remaining in separate linguistic and cultural enclaves from one another. Judeo-Spanish and French-speaking Sephardic Jews from the Ottoman Empire and North Africa, and Yiddish-speaking eastern European Jews began to arrive in greater numbers after 1902, but maintained distinct boundaries from one another. By 1919, there were about 2,000 Jews estimated to be residing in Cuba.[22] The Yiddish-speaking population was especially mobile, with many only staying for a year or so until departing for other destinations, primarily the United States and sometimes Mexico.[23] The early 1920s were a period of intense migration, with 7,000 Jewish immigrants entering per year between 1921 and 1923 alone. Between 1925 and 1935, when the United States passed the Johnson Act, establishing restrictive immigration quotas and effectively halting eastern and southern European immigration, the Jewish population of Cuba stabilized at about 8,000 or so, roughly 2700 of whom were Sephardic.[24]

Margalit Bejarano observes that "Cuba did not extend a warm welcome to its transit passengers."[25] She describes the culture shock ("the language was strange, the heat was unbearable"), and the poverty of the new immigrants. Many did not have the thirty dollars required by the Cuban government to enter the country, and so were detained in the Tiscornia Camp (Cuba's Ellis Island). Many could not find jobs during the economic crises of the 1920s, and, unable to afford even the cheapest rents, slept in the parks. Nevertheless, even as Yiddish speaking immigrants waited to receive "the visa they had yearned for so long," they established a *Yidishe Kulturgrupe* in the 1920s, holding debates, lectures, literary salons, Yiddish theater performances, and, eventually, a school.[26] In 1927 the organization, now renamed the Centro Israelita, began to publish a regular Yiddish periodical, *Oyfgang,* in which the following short poem, "Oyfn Inzele" (On the island) by M. Gutshteyn, meant to be sung to the tune of "Oyfn Pripitchik," was published in 1928:

Oyfn inzele, vos heyst kuba
Di zun brent do heys

Geyen pedlerlakh mit di kestelakh
Oysgeveykt in shveys

Fargest in yurop mit amerike
Az ir zent in kuba do
Muzt ir onfangen, nebekh onfangen
Fun kometz alef—"o."

Ven ir vet kinderlakh, azoy zikh oppedlen
A tsvey, dray, fir yor
Vet ir im yirtsey hashem, zayn balabosim'lakh
Aleyn fun a stor

To pedler, kinderlakh, mit groys kheyshek
Itzt iz ayer tsayt
Ver fun aykh es pedlt beser
Der vet zayn "Al-rayt."

(On this island called Cuba
The sun burns so hot
Peddlers go with their bundles
Soaked in sweat
Forget Europe with America
You're in Cuba now
You must begin from the beginning, poor things,
Kometz-Alef: "O"
When you are children, so you peddle
Two, three, four years
Then, with God's help, you'll be *balabosim*
With your own store
So peddle, children, with passion
Now is your time
He who peddles best
Will be "all right")[27]

Alongside this tongue-in-cheek piece, however, the Yiddish press urged its readers to "become Cubanized" and to "love their adopted land."[28] This tension is illustrative of immigrants' certainly ironic and often ambivalent attitude toward their new home.

Oyfgang was joined in 1932 by *Havaner Lebn* (later also called *La Vida Habanera*), which was coedited by Penn and Aronowsky.[29] The two editors formed the nucleus of a group of writers who dubbed themselves *Yung Kuba,* a title reminiscent of the avant-garde Yiddish poetic movements of New York (*Di yunge*) and Poland-Lithuania (*Yunge Vilne*).[30] Asher Tshutshinsky, a member of *Yung Kuba*, later termed their collective voice a "nusekh Kuba": the product of the "mix of Spanish-European and African cultures," shaped by the "tropical climate, endless summer and atmosphere of freedom," in contrast to the cold, poverty, and terror of eastern Europe.[31] Alan Astro describes the literary production of these Cuban-Yiddish writers as "un sincretismo judeoafrocubano," ("a judeoafrocuban syncretism") exemplified by the stories of Avrom Yosef Dubelman and Pinkhas Berniker, which often described encounters between Jewish peddlers and merchants and the Afro-Cubans of the interior. Dubelman, Berniker, and Aronowsky, whose early collections included *Kubaner lider* (Cuban poems, 1928) and *Tropishe Likht: Lider un Poemen fun Kuba* (Tropical light: Songs and poems from Cuba, 1930), constitute, according to Reinaldo Sanchez Porro, "una triada representativa de la literature Yiddish en Cuba, en plena transculturación" (a representative triad of Yiddish literature in Cuba, in full transculturation).[32]

And yet, despite their identification with Cuba, and, unlike those in Latin American Yiddish-speaking communities, many Yiddish writers emigrated to the United States after only a few years. David Korman, for example, who had immigrated to Cuba in 1926 from Poland, published one book of poetry in Havana, *Af Inzlsher Erd* (On island ground, 1927), before departing for New York in 1928. Oskar Pinis arrived in Cuba in 1924, published *Hatuey* (1931) and a book of stories titled *Der goldener fontan* (The golden fountain, 1934) in Havana, and then immigrated to the United States in 1935, taking on the name Asher Penn. Dubelman, who immigrated to Cuba from Poland in 1925, wrote regularly for *Havaner Lebn* and contributed to Yiddish journals in New York, and published his first collection of short stories, *Af Kubaner Erd* (On Cuban ground) in 1935, and continued to live and publish in Havana until leaving for Miami in 1961, like many Cuban Jews after the revolution.[33] But Berniker, the third member of the "triad" who immigrated to Cuba in 1925 from Belorus, left for the United States in 1931.[34] He wrote at the time that while receiving his visa "was the realization of a sweet dream he had cherished for six years," since coming true, the dream had "lost its sweetness."[35] Had he then come to feel at home in Cuba after all?

Other Yiddish writers, like Leyzer Ran and Aaron Zeitlin, though not associated with Yung Kuba, spent significant amounts of time there. Zeitlin, an important poet in both Yiddish and Hebrew, spent some months stranded in Cuba at the outbreak of World War II and wrote several poems in Yiddish on Cuban themes, including "Der Gayego," in which a gallego (what Cubans called the rural Galician Spanish laborers who comprised the largest immigrant population in Cuba) confesses his crypto-Jewish ancestry, and "Karmensita, oder di Doyres-kayt," about an Afro-Cuban performer with crypto-Jewish heritage who sings the "Al kheyt" melody in a nightclub.[36] Yiddish bibliographer and historian Leyzer Ran spent several years in Cuba after World War II and in 1952 published what is considered to be a major archive of Yiddish Cuba, *Hemshekh oyf Kubaner Erd,* on the occasion of the twenty-fifth anniversary of the Centro Israelita.[37]

While we might read the entire Cuban-Yiddish literary corpus as an act of what Bhabha has termed cultural translation, Aronowsky, who immigrated to Cuba from Poland in 1924, also engaged in the literal textual translation of several poems by Cuban poet Andrés de Piedra-Bueno from Spanish into Yiddish, which Piedra-Bueno proudly included in his *Obras Completas* in 1939. Piedra-Bueno, a poet and scholar associated with El Grupo Indice, a collective of writers and intellectuals based in Matanzas, also included in his *Obras Completas* his own Spanish translations of Pinis's *Hatuey,* Aronowsky's *Maceo,* and a glowing introduction to Aronowsky, whom he praised as a "trailblazer in Cuban letters" ("Eliezer Aronowsky abre una senda en las letras cubanas").[38]

Piedra-Bueno describes Cuba's role as a place of sanctuary for the post–World War I Jewish refugees of Europe, asserting that Cuba, in turn, has been enriched by this influx of immigrants:

> La isla—imán atlántico, brazo geológico—atrajo la emigración hebrea . . . La caravan de la post-guerra abrió la tienda en esta tierra joven. El éxodo israelita—inercia secular—fecunda todos los surcos de la humanidad. Cuba! La proa bíblica cortó la ola antillana. Y crea, crea. Y trae su música de atávica novedad.
>
> (The island—an Atlantic magnet, a geological arm—drew and beckoned the Hebrew migrants . . . The post-war caravan opened its store—set up its tent—in this young land. The Israelite exodus—inexorable—fertilizes all the furrows of humankind. Cuba! The biblical prow cut the Antillean wave. And it created, created. And brought its modern music with its ancient roots.) (my translation)[39]

Were these new Yiddish-speaking arrivals immigrants or refugees? Were they ready to make Cuba their home or did they consider it a temporary stopping place on their way to the United States? Were they instruments in the efforts of the ruling elite to "whiten" Cuba after World War I, or were they identified with other undesirable foreigners like those from Haiti and Jamaica, in the increasingly xenophobic and racist atmosphere of the 1930s?[40] All of these characterizations emerge in discussions of this period and this community, and exist in tension with Piedra-Bueno's strenuous claims to these Yiddish writers' Cubanness. I read a highly self-conscious and unsettled sense of Cuban-Yiddish identity across the work of both Pinis and Aronowski. In writing Yiddish versions of *Hatuey* and *Maceo* in the early 1930s that developed a discourse of Jewish *indigenismo*, Penn and Aronowski translated and revived important nationalist revolutionary tropes as a way to speak to Cuba's political and racial struggles in their present. Thus, they participated in Cuba's continuing effort, three decades after independence, to define the racial and cultural terms of its national character.

Hatuey, Maceo, and Cuban History in Translation

El Indio Hatuey first emerged in the writing of sixteenth-century priest and reformer Bartolomé de las Casas. Other early accounts of Hatuey's rebellion and martyrdom followed, with similar outlines. In the early 1500s, Hatuey, a Taíno leader from Hispañola (today's Dominican Republic and Haiti), set sail to Cuba with four hundred followers ahead of Diego Velasquez, to warn them of impending Spanish invasion. Most Hatuey narratives feature his famous speech to the Indians of Cuba denouncing the Spaniards' rapacious and violent desire for gold. In many versions Hatuey is unsuccessful in persuading others to join him; he then wages a guerrilla war against the Spanish with a very few followers. Captured and sentenced to burning at the stake (in many versions, betrayed by one of his own), Hatuey makes his second famous speech. Offered the choice to be baptized by a priest so he can go to heaven, Hatuey asks if there are other Christian Spaniards in heaven. Assured there are, he announces that he would rather go to hell.[41]

According to Larry Backer, Hatuey's story, "with significant Christological overtones of ministry, journey, betrayal, torture, sacrifice, and transfiguration, becomes a pivotal moment in Cuban history and Spanish literary tradition. Hatuey dies a great leader of indigenous rebellion against European conquest. He is reborn centuries later as the first great patriot and martyr of a reconfigured indigenous people of Cuba within which Indians play a marginal role."[42] Backer argues that this ideal of a Cuban *indigenismo* that did not rely upon any actual Indigenous presence, was first articulated by José Martí, the Cuban nationalist in the later nineteenth century, who identified the struggle against Spain for independence with Hatuey's rebellion. All Cuban nationalists, in Marti's formulation, were therefore Indians. Francisco Sellén, a Cuban intellectual and revolutionary exiled to the United States in the late nineteenth century for his anti-Spanish activities, wrote his poetic drama *Hatuey* in 1891, intending his play to be the "first national drama of Cuba."[43] Bonifacio Byrne, another exiled revolutionary and Cuban poet, in his collection *Efigies* (1896), wrote poems about Maceo, Hatuey, Céspedes, and Martí, all of whom had become heroes of the revolution. Andrés de Piedra-Bueno collected and edited a selection of Byrne's poems in 1942, calling *Efigies* "su magnífica colección de sonetos patrióticos" (his magnificent collection of patriotic sonnets).[44] In the Cuban fight for independence there was in fact an Indian regiment that was named the Hatuey Regiment.[45]

In the 1920s and 1930s, Hatuey's meanings shifted. That period in Cuba saw the development of Afro-Cubanismo, a powerful arts movement that sought to affirm the African foundations of Cuban culture. The "most aggressively avant-garde publication" of the Minoristas (a group of artists and intellectuals who promoted the new Afro-Cuban cultural nationalism), first published in 1927, was called *Atuei*.[46] Invoking Hatuey could gesture toward revolutionary, nationalist, and Afro-Cuban modernist mythologies, thus illustrating his malleability as a signifier.

In 1927 and 1928, a writer named Yaakov Shponka serialized biographies of Hatuey, Maceo, and Martí in *Oyfgang*, articles explicitly framed to educate new arrivals about Cuban history. Shponka calls Hatuey "the first Cuban freedom-fighter" as well as the first Cuban victim of the Inquisition, a fate that would have resonated with Yiddish readers and fellow writers, who often addressed crypto-Jewish themes in their fictions.[47] Given Hatuey's ubiquity, it is quite surprising that in 1935, an advertisement for Piedra-Bueno's Spanish translation of Pinis's *Hatuey* in *Havaner Lebn* (*Vida Habanera*) claimed, "This is a great work, to which Cuban critics who have seen the manuscript have already responded enthusiastically. Hatuey, the great Siboney hero, has up until now not broken into the Cuban literature."[48]

Pinis's Hatuey follows the general contours of popular Hatuey legend, but is reframed within the poet's own narrative of migration and adoption:

> Hatuey un di zun—iz ot do a farglaykh. Beyde ineynem balaykhtn zey dem mentshlikhn veg in kuba.

Un shteyendik af ot dem kubaner zunikn veg, af der erd, vos hot azoy brayt
mikh ufgenumen un vos iz in mayn yugnt mayn tsveytn heym gevorn, trog
ikh tsu mayn baytrag—dos gezang tsu Hatueyen.[49]

Hatuey y el sol son la misma cosa en Cuba.
Los dos alumbran el camino humano.
Y yo, en este sendero solar, en la tierra que
Me ha abierto su corazón y que ya es mi segunda
patria, ofrezco este homenaje: el poema de
Hatuey.[50]

(Hatuey and the sun: they are the same here. Both illuminate the human way in Cuba. Standing here on this bright Cuban path, in this land that has opened its heart to me and became in my youth my second home, I bring my gift—this song of Hatuey.) (my translation)[51]

Pinis's Hatuey has a vision of the freedom fighters who will succeed him—this is a national hero self-conscious of his legacy: "Er veyst, az es veln nokh fray zayn di erdn/ vayl nit er iz der letzter vos vil es zayn fray" (He knows that the earth will be free, that he is not the last to desire freedom).[52] In the Spanish translation, Hatuey's martyrdom is even more explicit: Hatuey "sabe que el sacrificio de su vida no sera/ el último que se ofrezca/por amar la libertad!" ([Hatuey] knows that the sacrifice of his life will not be the last offered for the love of liberty!)[53] Pinis's Hatuey concludes with a glossary of Native terms—like *areito*, *cacique*, and *yucca*, used in the Yiddish text, foreign terms to Yiddish that are not glossed in the Spanish translation—thus reifying the "translation sensibility" that animates the poem, marking its distance from its subject even as its author claims identification and intimacy.

De Piedra-Bueno's 1935 Spanish translation argues for the sympathies between Pinis, Cuba, and Hatuey. Piedra-Bueno's translation includes a biographical note reprinted from a 1933 survey of Cuban literature that included an entry on Penn:

Su primer libro fué una exquisita e interesante aportación a la poesía épica cubana, a través de un ardiente temperamento hebreo, que sintió vibrar en su alma el espíritu rebelde del glorioso indio Hatuey y se extremeció ante la crueldad hispana de la horrible hoguera. Desde los primeros sorbos de historia cubana, Pinis empezó por cantar al Hatuey enemigo de los opresores, del oro, Dios de los blancos.[54]

([Penn's Hatuey] was an exquisite and fascinating contribution to Cuban epic poetry, by way of an ardent Hebrew temperament, that felt vibrating in its soul the rebellious spirit of the glorious Indian Hatuey, and shuddered before the cruel, terrible bonfire of the Spanish. From his first tastes of Cuban history, Pinis began to sing of Hatuey, enemy of the oppressors and of gold, the god of the whites.) (my translation)

Both the Hebrew and Indian "spirits" are passionate, rebellious, anti-imperialist, and anticapitalist—a subtle but politicized recasting of Pinis and his attraction to Hatuey's rebellion in the era of Machado's regime. From his manipulated reelection in 1928 through his ouster in 1933, Machado maintained martial law and increasingly targeted Jewish organizations and individuals, primarily labor organizers and Communists.[55] The Jewish Telegraphic Agency reported in 1932, for instance, that Eliezer Aronowsky and three other Cuban Jews had been arrested "on charges of expressing opposition to the present government"; one of the group was the former editor of the Yiddish paper *Dos Yidishe Velt*.[56] Piedra-Bueno's 1935 translation can also be read as a response to the tumult of 1934, which had just seen a popular and progressive uprising against Machado, a short-lived reformist government, and the installation of the first Batista-controlled government: a "dictatorship," Levine terms it, "in democratic clothing."[57]

Antonio Maceo was likewise a contested figure in 1930s Cuba, signifying for Euro-Cubans an idealized postracial Cuban identity, and working in Afro-Cuban memory as a symbol of the patriotism and contributions of Black Cubans to Cuban history.[58] Shponka's biography of Maceo in *Oyfgang* is notably in the latter camp in that he emphasizes Maceo's roots in slavery: he describes Maceo's childhood as one of unremitting hard labor during which his father's tales of his great-grandfather's kidnapping from Africa and enslavement by the conquistadores awaken the boy's racial consciousness.[59] Shponka suggests that Maceo joined the revolutionary effort of 1868 as much to liberate Cuba's slaves as to create an independent Cuban republic ("the brown and black sons of Oriente, bound to their forced slavish labor, take up rifles and cry: 'Freedom? Freedom? Wait for the setting of the sun? No!'").[60] In conclusion, Shponka describes the sculpture of Maceo on his horse in Havana, erected in 1912, as "the most beautiful monument in Havana," and notes that Maceo is an important figure for all Cubans, but particularly for Black Cubans, "who especially love him."[61]

Like Pinis's *Hatuey,* and likely influenced by Shponka's biography, Aronowsky's *Maceo* should be read as at once conventionally patriotic verse and political resistance. Again like *Hatuey,* Aronowsky includes a glossary with *Maceo,* in which he explains place names (Oriente, Pinar del Rio) as well as the Indigenous or local words (*machete, bodega*) that are feathered throughout the poem.[62] In Piedra-Bueno's 1939 re-publication of his Spanish translation of Aronowsky's *Maceo,* Piedra Bueno reminds his readers that the poem was originally published in both Yiddish and Spanish in 1932, during Machado's increasingly despotic regime: "días," he writes, "de tiranía y barbarie. Toda allusión política se refiere, pues, a esa época" (days of tyranny and barbarism. All political allusions refer, therefore, to that period).[63] Both Yiddish poems thus mediate not only between languages and cultures, but between the violence and revolutions of Cuba's past and the repressions of its present.

Aronowsky's poem begins with Maceo's birth and follows him through the first battle for independence, his exile, the second war of independence and his heroic sacrifice. Where Shponka is explicit about Maceo's race consciousness, Aronowsky is more oblique. He writes of Maceo's birth: "Hot an oreme muter a kind oyf der velt itst gebrakht,—/vos er vet tsureysn di keytn fun shklafishe hent" (A poor mother has now brought a child into the world/who will break the chains from enslaved hands). Aronowsky's socialist leanings are apparent here, where Piedra-Bueno's nationalist translation renders Aronowsky's references to enslavement a metaphor for Cuba's colonial condition: the young Maceo "desatará todas las manos esclavas" (will untie all chained hands), and as he grows up he apprehends "la tristeza de la patria," the despair of the nation,[64] whereas Aronowsky's Maceo sees "toyznter shklafn far a shtikele trukene broyt; / dem vey in di hertser, trogn zey yokhedik shtum!" (thousands of slaves for a crust of bread; / carry the despair in their hearts in silent bondage).[65]

The last section of the poem, "Di shtim fun Maceo" (La Voz de Maceo/The voice of Maceo) takes up the present and its unfulfilled promises of liberty. In a striking echo of Shponka's essay in *Oyfgang,* Aronowsky also concludes with Maceo's monument in Havana. He describes children playing at the foot of Maceo's statue within which the spirit of Maceo lives. The children are deaf to the statue's efforts to speak, and Maceo continues to suffer for his country:

Bafrayt iz gevorn dos land, fun finstern, shpanishn yokh . . .
Avek zaynen tsendliker yorn, fun yener heroisher tsayt,

Tsurik iz dos folk haynt faroremt, in hunger un noyt . . .
Dos land hot fun shpanye—oyf yenke gemakht nor a bayt.
Nor s'hobn di zeydes, di zomen, in di kinder farzayt.[66]

In Piedra-Bueno's translation, "Se ha libertado por fin/la patria del yugo viejo . . . pero en realidad, la patria/sólo ha cambiado de dueño."[67] Translated from the Yiddish: "The land has become free of the dark Spanish yoke . . . but years have passed since that heroic time/the people are back in poverty, hunger, and want . . ./the land, moaning, has only made a trade." Piedra-Bueno is even more pointed: "In reality, the nation has only changed its landlord" (my translation).

In a moving final image, at night the animated statue of Maceo gallops on his horse through the silent, impoverished neighborhoods of Cerro, Luyano, and Regla, as he weeps. The sea silently witnesses his suffering and waits for "stormier times" when it will once again swell with the blood of Cuba.[68] The revolutionary race consciousness of Shponka's Maceo is here subordinated to a revolutionary *class* consciousness, exemplified by Piedra-Bueno as he adds that Maceo suffers "con la miseria del proletariado."[69] The resulting dialectic between Shponka, Aronowsky, and Piedra-Bueno thus aligns multiple Maceos, from the "official" memory of Maceo as revolutionary war hero and patriot, to the revisionist memory of the Afro-Cuban Maceo emerging in the 1930s as a "symbol of the unfinished project of racial equality," to the prophet and symbol of the class struggle.[70] Both Hatuey and Maceo functioned therefore as flexible signifiers who allowed Cuban writers across languages to imbricate and analogize multiple histories of oppression and struggles for liberation in ways that both participated in and challenged nationalist myth-making.

Memories of Fire: Translating Yiddish Cuba

Contemporary interpreters identify an additional subtext for Pinis's *Hatuey*, about which both Piedra-Bueno and Pinis himself were silent. As Alan Astro writes, in addition to sympathizing with victims of the Inquisition now that they found themselves living in its former territories, Yiddish speaking immigrants, many involved in leftist causes in their countries of origin, had also fled pogroms and state-fomented violence, "no menos cruel que el Santo Oficio" (no less cruel than the Santo Oficio).[71] Where Cuban readers of the 1930s might have easily seen parallels between the violence and persecutions of the Inquisition, the modern struggle for liberation from Spain, and the repressions of Machado's regime (not to mention the struggle against the fascists in Spain), Yiddish readers in particular might have additionally identified the violent anti-Semitism of the Inquisition with that of twentieth-century Eastern Europe.

In 1927 Pinis authored a three-part narrative in *Oyfgang*, "*In a finsterer tsayt (tsum shvartsn andeynkung fun petlyoren)*" (In a dark time: the Black legacy of Petliura), that describes a pogrom in his town that he and a group of Jewish families survive by hiding in a Christian neighbor's barn.[72] They hide for hours, listening to gunshots and screams outside. When night falls, the neighbor decides he cannot hide them anymore. The tale ends as the desperate families leave the barn for an unknown fate.[73] Pinis was only eighteen or nineteen years old when he published the piece; he had been in Cuba for three years.

In *Hatuey*'s current iteration as a multilingual opera for a contemporary American, and now Cuban, audience, Pinis's childhood trauma of witnessing and surviving a pogrom has emerged as an explicit theme, as has the violence of Machado's regime. Frank London and Elise Thoron's opera is set in a Havana nightclub in 1931, where young Ukrainian poet and refugee Oscar falls in love with Tinima, a singer of Taíno descent, and is drawn into her revolutionary activities against the Machado regime. All the while Oscar is writing his poem *Hatuey*, telling the story of Cuba's first Indigenous freedom fighter, who dies at the stake resisting the Spanish in 1511. The two stories intertwine and inform each other, as characters shift in time and place from Havana club in 1931 (sung in Spanish), to the world of Oscar's poem in Maisi, 1511, (sung in Yiddish) where his hero Hatuey encounters Velasquez and the Spanish.[74]

In a striking example of what we might term judeoafrocuban *indigenismo,* the opera, like the work of the Cuban-Yiddish writers who serve as its inspiration, imbricates histories—Spanish conquest, the Inquisition, slavery, Ukrainian pogroms, Machado's dictatorship—languages, and identities, through the interpolation of a new frame that features an intercultural, interracial romance. London's score likewise fuses Afro-Cuban, avant-garde jazz and klezmer genres. Thoron writes of translation that

> translation is at the root of performance: life to theater, page to stage, word to movement, poem to song—all are modes of translation. Most often we think of translating one language to another, and it is desirable for this translation to be seamless and unnoticed. "Good" translation gives the illusion that all is commutable, a comfortable flow, from one culture to another—like travelling Business class. The opposite is often true: translation is painful, wrenching, an

impossible dare-devil leap to bridge a gap. But this is where the most exciting, jagged, dramatic aspects of translation occur. In cross cultural work the bumps and obstacles in understanding lead to the biggest discoveries. Our common humanity in the end trumps all, but we are vastly different; it is from those differences that we learn about ourselves and others. So engaging in modes of translation that allow those gaps and differences to emerge on stage is very dramatic and exciting, for an audience as well as performers.[75]

Indeed, the opera *Hatuey: Memory of Fire* has been, and continues to be, in an ongoing and dynamic state of translation. London and Theron began developing the opera in 2014, imagining an Anglophone audience and commissioning English translations of both the Spanish and Yiddish versions of *Hatuey*, though the libretto would be in multiple languages, including Yiddish, Spanish, and some Taíno. But in 2016, when they were offered the opportunity to bring the opera to Havana to be performed by Ópera de la Calle, they determined that they needed to translate the opera back into Spanish. Ultimately, the opera was performed in Havana in Spanish, with Yiddish and Taíno words. Multiple translators, many proficient in both Yiddish and Spanish, have worked on the libretto as it has moved between and among English, Yiddish, Spanish, and Taíno. As one translator of the libretto, Judith Lang Hilgartner, writes, "Throughout the opera, the code-switching of languages is held together by London's operatic jazzy-klezmery-cubano fusion."[76]

Perhaps because of the United States' new openness to Cuba, and Cuba's renewed visibility in American culture, the curiosity of a Cuban-Yiddish poem making its way back to Havana as an opera inspired a great deal of coverage in the American, Jewish American, and Cuban press, the former usually foregrounding Pinis as a Ukrainian Jewish refugee who fled to Cuba and adopted the literary themes of his new country, with the latter seeing the opera as an important symbol of contemporary Cuban-US artistic collaboration.[77] The meanings of *Hatuey* have thus undergone further transformations through these acts of cultural translation and exchange: from revolution to nationhood to commercial appropriation (these days, most know *Hatuey* as the name of a beer—a fact that plays an important narrative role in the opera *Hatuey*), from avant-gardist Afro-Cuban modernism to linguistic extinction and revival, from the possibility of a new homeland and new future to a reminder of a traumatic and violent past, and more recently from a harbinger of renewed diplomatic relations between two estranged nations under Obama, to an act of resistance against the current administration that threatens to close the door once again, not only to Cuba but to the rest of the world.

The journey of *Hatuey* in particular, from Spanish to Yiddish to Spanish; from Spanish to English; and now again from Spanish into Yiddish, Spanish, English, and Taíno, embodies the multidirectional relationships Yiddish in the Americas could and did develop with other languages. Yiddish immigrant audiences in the Americas engaged with national myths—including and perhaps especially those that produced racialized understandings of people and nationhood—in and through translation. The continuing afterlife of Penn's *Hatuey* demonstrates to us how Yiddish literary texts circulated and continue to circulate among non-Yiddish readers in the Americas through translation and thus continue to engage with, challenge, and transform national narratives.

Notes

A *hartsikn gedank* to Alan Astro, Ruth Behar, Marty Ehrlich, Itzik Gottesman, Michele Hardesty, Rosa Perelmutter, Rabbi Jim Ponet, Michael Posnick, Raanan Rein, Elise Theron, and Miriam Udel for their introductions, answers, and insights into Hatuey, Maceo, Cuba, Yiddish Cuba, the opera *Hatuey: Memory of Fire*, and Jewish Latin America, to Halina Rubinstein for her invaluable aid with translation, and to the editors of this volume for their attentive, generous comments on this essay in draft form.

    1. Fernando Ortiz, *Cuban Counterpoint: Tobacco and Sugar*, trans. Harriet de Onis (Durham, NC: Duke University Press, [1940] 1995).

    2. Ortiz, *Cuban Counterpoint*, 98.

    3. Ortiz, 100.

    4. Gustavo Perez Firmat, *The Cuban Condition* (Cambridge: Cambridge University Press, 1989).

    5. Firmat, *Cuban Condition*, 1.

    6. Naomi Seidman, *A Marriage Made in Heaven: The Sexual Politics of Hebrew and Yiddish* (Berkeley: University of California Press, 1997), 16.

    7. See Claudia Rosenzweig, *Bovo D'Antona by Elye Bokher, A Yiddish Romance: A Critical Edition with Commentary* (Leiden: E. J. Brill, 2016).

    8. Benjamin Harshav, *The Meaning of Yiddish* (Berkeley: University of California Press, 1990), 61.

    9. See Harshav, *The Meaning of Yiddish*, 61–73.

    10. Exchange between Kathryn Hellerstein, Laurence Rosenwald, and Anita Norich, *Prooftexts* 20, nos. 1–2 (2000): 213–14.

    11. Naomi Seidman, *Faithful Renderings: Jewish-Christian Difference and the Politics of Translation* (Chicago: University of Chicago Press, 2006), 9.

12. Jonathan Rutherford, "The Third Space, Interview with Homi Bhabha," in *Identity: Community, Culture, Difference* (London: Lawrence & Wishart, 1990), 210.

13. Also see Joel Berkowitz, *Shakespeare on the American Yiddish Stage* (Iowa City: University of Iowa Press, 2002).

14. For a discussion of *Uncle Tom's Cabin* in Yiddish and the politics of translation, see Rubinstein, "'Strange Rendering': *Uncle Tom's Cabin* in Yiddish," *American Jewish History* (Spring 2017): 35–55. For discussions of Whitman, Native chant, and other "Indigenous" writers translated into Yiddish, see Rubinstein, "Going Native, Becoming Modern," in *Members of the Tribe: Native America in the Jewish Imagination* (Detroit: Wayne State University Press, 2010), as well as the chapter "From Heine to Whitman: The Yiddish Poets Come to America," in Julian Levinson, *Exiles on Main Street: Jewish American Writers and American Literary Culture* (Bloomington: Indiana University Press, 2008).

15. Yaakov Glantz, *Kristobal Kolon* (Tel Aviv: Farlag Y. L. Peretz, [1939] 1980).

16. My thanks to Sarah Casteel for her insight into the parallels between Yiddish as jargon or mongrel language and the emergence and status of Caribbean creole and patois languages.

17. Robert M. Levine, *Tropical Diaspora: The Jewish Experience in Cuba* (Gainesville: University Press of Florida, 1993), 16. See also Boris Sapir, *The Jewish Community of Cuba: Settlement and Growth*, trans. Simon Wolin (New York City: JTSP University Press, 1948).

18. There were likely conversos in Havana from the moment of European contact. The Inquisition was established in Havana in 1519 and regularly accused conversos of secretly practicing Judaism (Levine, *Tropical Diaspora*, 9).

19. Levine, 2.

20. Levine, 3.

21. Levine, 3.

22. Levine, 307.

23. See Margalit Bejarano, "Cuba as America's Back Door: The Case of Jewish Immigration," *Proceedings of the World Congress of Jewish Studies*, Division B, vol. 2, 1989, 481–88.

24. Levine, 307; Rosa Perelmutter, "Yiddish in Cuba: A Love Story," *Hispanófila* 157: (December 2009): 134, citing Jay Levinson, *Jewish Community of Cuba. The Golden Age 1906–1958* (Nashville: Westview, 2006), 60.

25. Bejarano, "Cuba as America's Back Door," 483.

26. Bejarano, 483.

27. M. Gutshteyn, "Oyfn Inzele," *Oyfgang* 11, January 15, 1928.

28. Perelmutter, "Yiddish in Cuba," 134.

29. Alan Astro, "La literatura yidish de Cuba," *Cuadernos Americanos* 96 (2002): 195.

30. Astro, "La literatura yidish de Cuba," 195, quoting Sol Liptzin, *A History of Yiddish Literature* (Middle Village, NY: Jonathan David, [1972] 1985), 406–9.

31. Asher Tshutshinski, "Yidishe literarishe shafungen oyfn indzl kuba," in *Antologye: Meksikanish, Urugvayish, Kubanish*, ed. Shmuel Rozhanski (Buenos Aires: Literatur-gezelshaft baym/Argentina: YIVO, 1982), 319. Also quoted in Astro, 207.

32. Reinaldo Sanchez Porro, "Tradición y Modernidad: Los judíos en La Habana," *Cuadernos de Historia Contemporanea*, no. 18, Servicio de Publicaciones (Madrid: Universidad Complutense, 1996), 180.

33. Alan Astro, ed. *Yiddish South of the Border: An Anthology of Latin American Yiddish Writing* (Albuquerque: University of New Mexico Press, 2003), 148. See Astro's translation of Dubelman's short story "Der Kurandero" (The Faith Healer), 148–55.

34. See Alan Astro's translation of and introduction to Pinkhas Berniker's short story "Jesús," in *Hopscotch: A Cultural Review* 2, no. 4 (2001): 134–45.

35. Quoted in Bejarano, "Cuba as America's Back Door," 484.

36. See Alan Astro, "Aaron Zeitlin's Cuban Exile," *Judaica Latinoamericana: Estudios Historico-Sociales* 4 (2001): 451–64.

37. Leyzer Ran, *Hemshekh oyf kubaner erd: zamlbukh tsum finf un tsyantsik yorikn yoyvul fun Yidishn tsenṭer in Ḳuba, 1925–1950* (Havana: Centro Israelita de Cuba, 1952).

38. Andres de Piedra-Bueno, *Obras Completas* (La Habana: P. Fernandez y Cia, 1939), 133. In translating *Maceo*, Piedra-Bueno worked from a literal translation by David Haimovitz, "'diletantti' de las belleza—yo ha escrito el romance. La voz es de Aronowsky. Y el mérito" (133).

39. Piedra-Bueno, *Obras Completas*, 133.

40. See Levine, *Tropical Diaspora*, and Margalit Bejarano, "Antisemitism in Cuba under Democratic, Military, and Revolutionary Regimes 1944–63," *Patterns of Prejudice* 24, no. 1 (1990): 32–46.

41. Larry Catá Backer, "From Hatuey to Che: Indigenous Cuba Without Indians and the UN Declaration on the Rights of Indigenous Peoples," *American Indian Law Review* 33, no. 1 (2009): 199–236; Bartolome De Las Casas, *The Devastation of the Indies: A Brief Account (1642)*, trans. Herma Briffault (New York: Continuum, 1974).

42. Backer, "From Hatuey to Che," 202.

43. Nicolas Kanellos et. al., eds., *Herencia: The Anthology of Hispanic Literature of the United States* (Oxford: Oxford University Press, 2002), 566.

44. Bonifacio Byrne, *Selección poética*, con "Prisma en siete notas" de Andrés de Piedra-Bueno, Cuadernos de cultura (La Habana: Publicaciones del Ministerio de Educación, Dirección de Cultura, 1942), 10.

45. Backer, "From Hatuey to Che," 216.

46. Robin Moore, *Nationalizing Blackness: Afrocubanismo and Artistic Revolution in Havana 1920–1940* (Pittsburgh: University of Pittsburgh, 1997), 197, 269n14. Atuei is an alternative spelling for Hatuey. Moore writes that this "represents yet another example of the appropriation of indigenous symbolism in the twentieth century" (269n14).

47. Yaakov Shponka, "Hatuey: Der ershter frayhayt-kemfer in Kuba," *Oyfgang*, December 12, 1927. Alan Astro observes that for Yiddish writers in Cuba the Spanish Inquisition was in fact an "obsession" (Astro, "La literature yídish de Cuba"), 196. For discussions of crypto-Jewish themes in Cuban and Caribbean literary fiction, see chapters in this volume by Leonard Stein, and Linda Weinhouse and Efraim Sicher.

48. Anonymous, *Havaner Lebn*, no. 129, April 26, 1935, 1.

49. Y. A. Pinis, *Hatuey* (Havana: Yidisher Kultur Gezelshaft, 1931), 6.

50. Oscar U. Pinis, *"Hatuey: Poema," Version de Andres de Piedra-Bueno* (Havana: La Habana, 1935),10.

51. English translations from Yiddish and Spanish versions of *Hatuey* are my own.

52. Pinis, *"Hatuey,"* 126.

53. Pinis, *"Hatuey,"* 96.

54. Pinis, 99–100. Biographical note reprinted from Gerardo Castellanos G., *Panorama Historico: ensayo de cronologia Cubana que comprende desde 1492 hasta 1933* (Habana: Ucar Garcia), 1934.

55. See Levine, *Tropical Diaspora*, 51–52.

56. *Jewish Telegraphic Agency*, December 22, 1932, http://www.jta.org/archive.

57. Levine, *Tropical Diaspora*, 58.

58. See Moore on the "vogue" of Afro-Cubanismo, and how the celebration of the African presence in Cuba could often serve to obscure continuing racial inequity (145–46). Also see Robert C. Nathan, "Imagining Antonio Maceo: Memory, Mythology and Nation in Cuba, 1896–1959," MA thesis, University of North Carolina, 2007.

59. Y. Shponka, "Antonio Maceo," *Oyfgang* no. 20 December 31, 1928, 7 (my translation).

60. Shponka, "Antonio Maceo," 7.

61. Shponka, 8.

62. Eliezer Aronowsky, "Maceo," in *Tropishe Likht: Lider un Poemen fun Kuba* (Havana: Oyfgang, 1930), 223–24.

63. Andrés de Piedra-Bueno, "Maceo" (Version castellana del poema MACEO, en idish, del poeta Eliezer Aronowsky) in *Obras Completas*, vol. 2 (La Habana, Impresores: P. Fernández y cía), 133. It is unclear if Aronowsky's arrest in 1932 was connected to the publication of *Maceo*.

64. De Piedra-Bueno, *Obras Completas*, vol. 2, 135.

65. Aronowsky, "Maceo," 205.

66. Aronowsky, 205.
67. De Piedra-Bueno, *Obras Completas,* vol. 2, 143.
68. Aronowsky, "Maceo," 220.
69. Aronowsky, 144.
70. Robert C. Nathan, *Imagining Antonio Maceo: Memory, Mythology, and Nation in Cuba, 1896–1959,* MA thesis, University of North Carolina at Chapel Hill, 2007, 53.
71. Astro, "La literatura yídish de Cuba," 195–96.
72. Symon Petliura was a Ukrainian nationalist whose role in fomenting the anti-Jewish violence that swept across Ukraine in 1919 is controversial to this day. Pinis's childhood town of Gysin was one of those affected by the violence.
73. Y. Pinis, "In a finsterer tsayt," *Oyfgang* November 4, 1927, continued in two subsequent issues.
74. http://www.elisethoron.com/hatuey.html.
75. http://www.elisethoron.com/works/translateworks.html.
76. See https://www.elon.edu/e-net/Article/145227 and http://ladinolives.squarespace.com/research-1/ for a full list of contributors.
77. See http://www.elisethoron.com/Hatuey/hatueypoetry.html for links to American and Cuban media coverage.

PART II

Revisiting the Inquisition and the Sephardic Caribbean

David Dabydeen's Hogarth
Blacks, Jews, and Postcolonial Ekphrasis

Sarah Phillips Casteel

[*Johnson's Dictionary*] is my seventh novel, and it is the last novel I will write on the colonial or postcolonial condition. I've finished that now; no more Jews, no more blacks, no more Indians, no more masters.
—David Dabydeen, interview, 2014

WHILE OTHER POSTCOLONIAL authors have "written back" to Shakespeare and Charlotte Brontë, it is William Hogarth who figures most centrally in David Dabydeen's creative as well as academic writing. In particular, plate 2 of Hogarth's 1732 series *A Harlot's Progress* is a key site of the Guyanese writer's creative engagement with the eighteenth-century English artist. In the 1980s, Dabydeen's academic studies *Hogarth's Blacks: Images of Blacks in Eighteenth Century English Art* (1985) and *Hogarth, Walpole, and Commercial Britain* (1987) drew attention to the persistent but neglected presence of Blacks in Hogarth's corpus.[1] More recently, Dabydeen's fiction has reappropriated those Black subjects in a complex and ambivalent act of postcolonial ekphrasis that combines homage and critique. In an interview, Dabydeen describes Hogarth as a "friend" to whom he owes a debt, but provocatively suggests that the eighteenth-century satirist is in turn indebted to Dabydeen, who "brought out his black people which nobody before had done. . . . So we have also rescued him from being dead. And he, in return, has given my imagination characters who become live on the page: it's a mutuality."[2] This reciprocal relationship is powerfully expressed in Dabydeen's novels *A Harlot's Progress* (1999) and *Johnson's Dictionary* (2013), which bring to life the figures of the slave boy, harlot, and Jew who make up the central grouping in Hogarth's plate 2. Strikingly, then, Dabydeen populates his Hogarth novels not only with Hogarth's Blacks, but also with Hogarth's Jews.

Why does Dabydeen return repeatedly—one might say obsessively—to plate 2 of Hogarth's *A Harlot's Progress* and to the figure of the Jew in particular? Why is it that for him, as notably indicated in the epigraph to this essay, to write about the colonial or postcolonial condition *is* to write about Jews? Dabydeen is part of a generation of Caribbean and Caribbean diaspora writers that has tended to advance a sympathetic reading of Jewishness. In contrast to the dynamic of interethnic competition that shapes the discourse surrounding Black-Jewish relations in the United States, invocations of Jewishness and Jewish historical experience in postwar Caribbean literature are generally identificatory in their orientation, as reflects the impact of the Holocaust on these writers, as well as their awareness of the deep historical presence of Jews in the Caribbean since the seventeenth century. For the generation of Caribbean and Caribbean diaspora writers who came of age in the early postwar period, when a public discourse about slavery was not available, Jewish historical trauma has often served as a surrogate site of identification and memorialization.

The most prominent example of this pattern of cross-cultural identification with Jewishness in Caribbean diaspora writing is that of St. Kitts–born British writer Caryl Phillips. Phillips's Holocaust novel *The Nature of Blood* (1997) and his essays on Anne Frank and the Venice ghetto are frequently cited as unique instances of Caribbean Jewish intersectionality. Yet Jewish themes can also be traced in the work of a number of other Caribbean writers. Dabydeen's engagement with Jewishness, for example, is as sustained and worthy of analysis as is that of Phillips. Moreover, unlike Phillips, Dabydeen addresses Jewishness, not primarily in the context of the Holocaust, but instead against the more distant historical landscape of eighteenth-century Britain and its colonial possessions, thereby recalling the significant presence of Sephardic port and plantation Jews in Caribbean colonies such as Suriname, Curaçao, Barbados, and Jamaica. Dabydeen's Hogarth novels thus extend the dialogue between postcolonial and Jewish studies beyond the question of Holocaust memory that has been the focus of such discussions, as well as beyond narrative and into the visual realm. The secondary literature has understood Dabydeen's concern with Jewishness in terms of Holocaust/slavery analogies, and in interviews Dabydeen himself has pointed to the influence of the Holocaust on his work.[3] His novels and scholarship, however, reveal a more multifaceted and historically informed interest in "the Jew" as a sign of difference in eighteenth-century European textual and visual discourses, as well as in the relationship between Sephardic Jews and the colonial economy.

As I have argued elsewhere, although an analysis of the global circulation of Holocaust memory offers one important means of effecting a rapprochement between postcolonial and Jewish studies, another such avenue is the phenomenon of Caribbean literary *sephardism,* or the invocation in Caribbean literature of the Sephardic Caribbean diaspora and Sephardic historical experiences of expulsion and conversion.[4] Dabydeen is among a number of Caribbean writers, including Maryse Condé, Derek Walcott, and Cynthia McLeod, who recall the Sephardic communities established in the Caribbean in the seventeenth century in the aftermath of the Iberian expulsion that built some of the oldest synagogues and Jewish cemeteries in the hemisphere.[5] The fiction and poetry of these writers complements the emerging historiography of the Jewish Atlantic, which has drawn attention to the widespread presence of Sephardic trade networks in the Atlantic world—a presence also highlighted by a 2015 exhibition on Dutch Caribbean Jewry at the Jewish Historical Museum in Amsterdam.[6] Although Dabydeen is not alone among Caribbean writers in invoking the Sephardic Caribbean, what distinguishes his postcolonial engagement with Jewishness is its visual dimension.[7] His Hogarth novels challenge racialized representations of Jewish difference by establishing discrepant relationships between word and image.[8]

Postcolonial Ekphrasis

One of the hallmarks of Dabydeen's fiction and poetry are their intermedial reworking of visual intertexts. Reconfiguring artworks in literary form, Dabydeen develops a specifically postcolonial form of ekphrasis.[9] Preeminently in his poem *Turner* (1995), he resuscitates the drowned slave in J. M. W. Turner's 1840 painting *Slave Ship* in a corrective strategy that refocuses the eye to ensure that what had been relegated to a footnote in John Ruskin's famous defense of the painting now becomes central to our understanding of the work. In his preface to *Turner,* Dabydeen explains that he "focuses on the submerged head of the African in the foreground of Turner's painting. It has been drowned in Turner's (and other artists') sea for centuries. When it awakens, it can only partially recall the sources of its life, so it invents a body, a biography, and peoples an imagined landscape."[10] In this way, as Mary Lou Emery observes, Dabydeen's *Turner* redefines ekphrasis as a verbal account "of what cannot be fully seen in the painting, but only imaginatively envisioned through words."[11] Similarly, Dabydeen's Hogarth novels supplement Hogarth's graphic art by inventively restoring life to its Black figures. In this regard, the images came first and the text second, for as Dabydeen explains, "Before I even wrote [*Johnson's Dictionary*] I had the illustrations in mind, the figures in mind." Deeply familiar to Dabydeen after decades of study, Hogarth's Blacks are "like my neighbours, or members of my family": "So you just bring the family together and let them get on with it and let them talk and just write about it."[12] Perhaps less expectedly, in the course of refashioning Hogarth's graphic art into text, Dabydeen also rescues the figure of the cuckolded Jewish merchant from plate 2 of *A Harlot's Progress*. Dabydeen's postcolonial revision of Hogarth thus entails a comparative analysis of the construction of Black and Jewish Others in eighteenth-century British and colonial cultures.

In plate 2 of Hogarth's series of six engravings (originally paintings) about a young country woman who falls into prostitution in London, the harlot Moll has become the mistress of a Jewish merchant, whom she is deceiving with a secret lover, who escapes in the background. Moll is situated in between the figure of the cuckolded Jewish merchant and a turbaned slave boy. The Jew and the slave boy, who stare at each other across a table and tea service that is in the midst of being overturned, wear matching expressions of surprise that are echoed in the monkey's visage in the bottom left corner of the engraving. While elsewhere in Hogarth's work bearded and swarthy Jewish peddler and musician figures are relegated to the margins of the image, in plate 2 the Jewish merchant is positioned at the center.[13] Meanwhile, the orientalized, turbaned slave boy is situated off to the side, serving as the shocked spectator who observes the debauched behavior of the Europeans. The slave boy thus functions much like other Black figures in Hogarth's art in which, as Peter Wagner observes, "the satirical frame contrasts alleged African primitiveness with real English behavior that can hardly be distinguished from that of animals."[14] In the case of plate 2, the behavior in question is the prostitute's duplicity as well as the materialism that is signaled by the overturned tea set, an emblem of colonial wealth. Also targeted by Hogarth's satire in plate 2—anticipating the debates surrounding the Jewish Naturalization Bill of 1753—is the unsuccessful assimilation of the clean-shaven Jew, whose fashionable dress and ill-fitting wig fail to disguise his decidedly un-English physical features.[15]

Dabydeen's eponymous novel takes up both the figure of the slave boy and that of the Jewish merchant, recontextualizing them to highlight the discursive traditions and colonial power structures that govern Hogarth's racialized caricatures. In Dabydeen's *A Harlot's Progress*, the slave boy from Hogarth's engraving becomes the protagonist Mungo, the author

A Harlot's Progress, plate 2, William Hogarth, 1732. (Courtesy of the National Gallery of Art, Washington, DC, Rosenwald Collection)

of an eighteenth-century slave narrative who narrates the story of his enslavement to the abolitionist Thomas Pringle (a character inspired by the editor of Mary Prince's slave narrative). Meanwhile, Hogarth's Jewish merchant becomes Sampson Gideon, a name Dabydeen borrows from the prominent eighteenth-century Sephardic English banker who may have inspired Hogarth's caricature. In Dabydeen's rendering, Sampson is not a financier but a quack doctor who encounters Mungo at the house of his master, Lord Montague. A visual detail from one of the engravings in *A Harlot's Progress* introduces each section of the novel, thereby inviting the reader to reconsider the meaning of particular figures and creating a new sequencing of images that responds to Hogarth's original series.

In his more recent novel *Johnson's Dictionary*, Dabydeen adopts a different visual strategy, inserting plate 2 in its entirety as part of a sequence of eleven works of European art, including a number by Hogarth, as well as by Albrecht Dürer, William Blake, and others. Like Dabydeen's first Hogarth novel, *Johnson's Dictionary* is populated largely by figures pulled from Hogarth's engravings—in particular, slaves, harlots, and Jews.

Moving back and forth between the colony of Demerara and eighteenth-century London, the novel follows the harlot Elizabeth as she journeys to the colonies, seduces a Scottish doctor, and reinvents herself as a woman "of elevated character."[16] Resisting linear plotlines and traditional characterization, *Johnson's Dictionary* presents us with a variety of Black and Jewish figures who speak back to Hogarth's pictorial representations. Word-image correspondence is established through the periodic insertion into the novel of European artworks, among them a number of Hogarth's most significant portrayals of Blacks. As with his introduction of visual details in *A Harlot's Progress,* Dabydeen's sequencing of artworks in *Johnson's Dictionary* can be understood as a play on the seriality for which Hogarth is known. Hogarth's narrative, theatrical approach to his graphic art brings word and image closer together and encourages the intermedial approach of Dabydeen's novels. Wagner has described Hogarth's engravings as iconotexts, "work[s] of art made up of visual and verbal signs . . . in which text and image form a whole (or union) that cannot be dissolved."[17] Dabydeen's fiction, in which the textual becomes inextricably bound up with the visual, echoes this interpenetration of word and image in Hogarth's work.

But why Hogarth rather than, for instance, the Italian and French painters that have inspired some of Walcott's poetry? Hogarth's works are resonant for Dabydeen in part because their status as iconotexts makes them an especially rich site for a consideration of racial stereotypes as they are articulated through the interplay of word and image. The satirical mode that Hogarth favored and the more accessible medium of engraving that he helped to popularize express these racial stereotypes in a heightened fashion and point to the role of print culture in their dissemination. In *Hogarth's Blacks,* Dabydeen suggests that in exploiting racialized myths for satirical purposes, Hogarth risked validating and perpetuating them, particularly among those consumers who may not have been sophisticated enough to register their satirical intent. Yet he also maintains (in a rather charitable account) that sympathy underlies Hogarth's caricatures, arguing that "compassion for the fate of the common people . . . is the distinguishing feature of his art."[18] More broadly, then, Hogarth is significant for Dabydeen as a visual artist who portrayed ordinary people who had seldom been illustrated. Among those subjects Hogarth deemed worthy of representation are Blacks, whose longstanding presence in England Hogarth's art documents. Crucial for Dabydeen's purposes is the way in which Hogarth, as Wagner notes, "draw[s] our attention to the stereotyped depiction of Africans while boosting their seemingly peripheral role in art and life."[19]

If Hogarth is important to Dabydeen thematically, he is equally important to the Guyanese writer in formal terms. Hogarth's highly intricate graphic art requires the viewer to read on multiple levels simultaneously. His crowded scenes are puzzles for the viewer to decipher; almost always his images present not a single story but multiple stories and backstories unfolding. Thus, Dabydeen describes how "Hogarth himself challenges us to speculate and to indulge in a hectic chase after meaning. He invites us to unlock his narrative puzzles and sees this as providing essential intellectual fun for the interpreter of his work."[20] Somewhat paradoxically, Hogarth's sequential, realist art helps to inspire Dabydeen's departure from realism and the linear emplotment favored by the slave narrative:

> Within one frame of a picture you get stories that multiply and teem, and other stories; every detail triggers off a story that then connects up with another detail, which then connects up to another story. . . . It seems to be some kind of social realism, but then it can be endlessly complicated in terms of being a narrative that changes upon itself, turns upon itself, sets up other narratives, etc., within the one frame. So what I tried to do in *A Harlot's Progress* was also to destroy the surface realism of a story by complicating it, by making it almost unreadable—in a sense replicating what Hogarth was doing in terms of endless, complex narratives.[21]

Dabydeen's unsettling, often bewildering postmodern slavery fiction makes significant demands on the reader to decipher the text and interpret the relationship between word and image. Even more so than Hogarth's engravings, Dabydeen's Hogarth novels are digressive, excessive, and multilayered. Especially in *Johnson's Dictionary*, the insertion of images disrupts the linear progression of the narrative and distracts the reader from the text. The visual elements in both novels function somewhat like the paintings that hang in the background of Hogarth's works, offering the reader clues regarding how to interpret what is unfolding in the narrative foreground. Dabydeen's Hogarth-inspired strategy of interrupting his novels with visual works that bear a sometimes oblique relationship to the plot ultimately encourages the reader to reflect on the nature of representation and, in particular, racial representation.[22]

Also important from a hermeneutic perspective is the way in which Hogarth's graphic art encourages a relational understanding of difference by presenting a system of signs that are defined against one another. Bernadette Fort and Angela Rosenthal observe in their introduction to *The Other Hogarth: Aesthetics of Difference* that Hogarth's scenes work by establishing a series of relationships among the figures represented: "The identities in this picture do not exist prior to representation, nor do they emerge *sui generis;* rather, they are brought into being through a complex iconographic orchestration based on alterity. The interlacing of references and meaningful juxtapositions make sense within a system of differences. Not marked as fixed, unchanging, or essential, this assortment of peculiar characters and the objects that scaffold their virtual space come into being through complex visual markings that work with and against one another, producing significance."[23] Strikingly, whereas Fort and Rosenthal's collection gives little attention to how Jewish difference contributes to the production of meaning in Hogarth's work, Dabydeen understands Jewishness as central to Hogarth's "aesthetics of difference."[24] Thus he resists both the tendency Michael Galchinsky identifies to isolate the Jewish question from a larger "discourse of marginality" and the tendency of postcolonial studies to neglect Jewishness altogether.[25]

In his scholarship and fiction, Dabydeen shows himself to be acutely conscious of the literary and visual traditions of depicting the Jew's physical and moral character that Hogarth both drew upon and consolidated.[26] In the eighteenth century, the figure of "the Jew" carried a range of associations including materialism, untrustworthiness, and deicide[27] as well as sexual perversion, boorishness, and criminality.[28] In *Hogarth, Walpole, and Commercial Britain,* Dabydeen argues that Hogarth's Jewish merchant in plate 2 needs to be situated more specifically with respect to portrayals of Jews in the South Sea Bubble prints, poetry, and drama of the 1720s. Dabydeen points to the trope of the "stockjobbing Jew" and the dandified, deceived Jewish merchant as rooted in this tradition of associating Jews with stock-market speculation and a questionable colonial trade. As part of his larger argument for a political rather than moral reading of Hogarth's series, Dabydeen discusses contemporary literary, visual, and journalistic discourses about Jews, who had only recently been allowed to return to England:

> Jews were a traditional target of Christian hostility and their situation had not altered much in eighteenth century Britain in so far as they were still liable to be bashed about by the mob at the slightest excuse. Hogarth is shamelessly and greedily capitalizing on popular prejudice against the Jew by depicting him in a contemptuous light: he is the type of image that would boost sales among the

populace, both among its hooligan as well as its respectable classes. The situation of the Jew and his Christian mistress in Plate 2 of *A Harlot's Progress* is an immediately recognisable one to the spectator accustomed to reading saucy literature about English courtesans bubbling their Jewish keepers. There was a popular belief that Jews were licentious creatures much addicted to patronage of Christian whores whom they attracted by their ready commercial wealth, although there was an anti-semite law expressedly prohibiting such contact.[29]

As Dabydeen is aware, Hogarth's Jewish merchant simultaneously drew on the popular iconography of the Jew and distilled it, inspiring the emergence of a new stage Jew, "Beau Mordecai." Variations on this new Jewish type, a more unequivocally negative rendering of the oversexed, wealthy Jewish dandy who patronizes brothels and exploits naive country girls, appeared in such plays as Theophilus Cibber's *Harlot's Progress* (1733), Henry Fielding's *Miss Lucy in Town* (1742), and Charles Macklin's *Love à la Mode* (1759).[30] By writing a novel that carries the same name as Hogarth's series, Dabydeen extends this tradition of textual adaptation of Hogarth. Yet, unlike the eighteenth-century dramatists, rather than intensifying Hogarth's caricatured portrayal of the cuckolded, lecherous Jew, Dabydeen's novels challenge it as part of his larger critique of colonial regimes of representation.

A Harlot's Progress

Dabydeen's *A Harlot's Progress* advances a corrective reading of the Jew along with other elements from Hogarth's series by generating discordant relationships between word and image. Late in the novel, we learn that Hogarth's inspiration for his engraving had come from a visit made to a London clinic for harlots where the slave Mungo assists the Jewish quack doctor, Sampson Gideon. Hogarth's misrepresentation in plate 2 of the individuals he encounters at the clinic parallels the abolitionist Thomas Pringle's misrepresentation of the slave Mungo, whose life story Pringle invents. In a circular fashion characteristic of the novel, Pringle's fabricated narrative of Mungo's life proves to be itself inspired by Hogarth's engraving. Just as the falseness of plate 2 is exposed in part through Hogarth's mischaracterization of the Jewish doctor as a corrupter of harlots, the falseness of the slave narrative that Pringle constructs is revealed through his persistent casting of Jews as a threat to "the moral intactness of the nation."[31] In a scene that thematizes the intermedial adaptation and shaping influence of Hogarth's engraving on subsequent literary productions about the Jew, Pringle invents for Mungo's biography a figure he identifies as "the notorious Jewish trickster Mr Gideon."[32] Dabydeen's slavery novel problematizes the editorial function of abolitionists such as Pringle in part by suggesting that his antislavery campaign is motivated by anti-Jewish (as well as anti-French and anti-Catholic) xenophobia: "Jews and Jacobites and Papists and their spies are everywhere, threatening the stability of England. . . . They're all thieves together, great and small, their joint actions eroding the foundation of the country. True, the Jew is worse, his money-making scheme being part of a conspiracy with Papists and Jacobites to create chaos. He finances their plots to overthrow King and Parliament and the commercial system on which the security of the nation depends. The Jew will profit from England's demise, buying up enterprises cheaply and stripping them of their assets."[33] Taking control of Mungo's narrative, Pringle infuses it with virulent anti-Jewish rhetoric that Mungo in turn inculcates, so that the slave later recalls: "From the time I land in England all I hear is curse, but after a while I too believe: vile Jew, rich Jew, rob-and-cheat Jew, Jew carpenter who shave and plane the wood into Christ's Cross, then charge extra for the nails."[34] Part 5 of the novel is replete with references to the Jew as foreign contaminant, as lecherous, as exploiting Christian girls. Orientalist imagery also features in the washerwoman Betty's account of the Jew as a seductive, dangerous, and untrustworthy foreigner who is "dark, fine-boned, exotic in manner."[35] Thus in part 5, Dabydeen presents the reader with an invented Jew or "the Jew" as sign.

When Dabydeen subsequently introduces an actual Jew into the novel, he upsets the correspondence of word and image by presenting him not as a Hogarthian Jew but as a sympathetic ally of the slave and harlot. Part 7 of the novel is prefaced by a detail from plate 2 showing the Jewish merchant, signaling to the reader that we should now focus our eye on the Jew at the center of Hogarth's engraving and reconsider the meaning of this figure. In this section of the novel, Lord Montague has purchased Mungo to replace Lady Montague's dead monkey. Here Mungo becomes the figure of the turbaned slave boy who features not only in plate 2 but also (as Dabydeen shows in *Hogarth's Blacks*) repeatedly in European painting as a foil to the European subjects whose superiority and civility the slave contrastively highlights. Displaced from London to the Montague household, Mungo (now renamed Perseus) embodies the alienation and humiliation that Dabydeen suggests slaves used for such decorative purposes must have experienced.[36] Mungo's isolation is eventually alleviated, however, by the arrival of the Jewish doctor, Sampson Gideon, who ministers to Lady Montague's ailing health with his "Amazing Eastern Cordial."[37] The expressions of surprise worn by the Jew and slave boy in plate 2 are recast in a scene in which Mungo/Perseus answers the Montagues' door to Sampson: "Perseus opens the door expecting to find a crooked-back and bearded Jew, hook-nosed, darkly complexioned, his hands worn by a lifetime of counting money. . . . Instead, he is confronted by a fresh-faced man, dark-haired, handsome, in his mid-twenties. He beholds Perseus with momentary alarm, as if the door had opened to an inevitable fate. Recovering his composure, he attempts a benign smile and announces himself modestly as Mr Sampson Gideon. He waits politely for Perseus to stop gaping."[38] As fellow aliens, the Black slave and the Jewish doctor quickly become aligned, vilified as coconspirators by Lady Montague's servants and by Lady Montague herself as parasites who feed on her decay. Initially evoking associations with sexual perversion, disease, and degeneration, Sampson instead emerges in part 7 as a gentle, gracious, and sympathetic figure who facilitates Mungo's escape from slavery. When Mungo absconds from the Montague household and joins Sampson in London, Sampson is cast in an exaggeratedly positive light as the slave's savior, as well as that of the prostitutes to whom he tends. Some ambiguity remains, however, as Mungo experiences lingering doubts regarding the Jew's character.

As Lars Eckstein comments, Dabydeen's Jew in *A Harlot's Progress* is perhaps the most pronounced example of how his "free imaginative transformation" of visual models challenges the xenophobic popular stereotypes to which Hogarth's engravings appealed.[39] In this respect, it is useful to consider James Heffernan's account of how ekphrasis "stages a contest between rival modes of representation" and "evokes the power of the silent image even as it subjects that power to the rival authority of language."[40] Heffernan's account illuminates Dabydeen's novel, which simultaneously draws attention to the potency of Hogarth's images and seeks to displace them through alternative textual representations. Dramatizing the contest between word and image is a scene in which the harlot Moll violently disfigures a painting and damages a bust that Mungo had stolen from the Montagues. Yet the novel also suggests that Dabydeen's art may be no match for Hogarth's. Toward the end of the novel, Mungo abandons his narrative of Moll's decline, saying: "Go to Mr Hogarth's prints on Moll to sate your curiosity, for he has fixed her for all time on the point of his burin. How can my halting feeble art release her from such agony?"[41] Frank Felsenstein has noted the lasting impact of Hogarth's Jewish merchant, who, with his sharp features, prominent nose, goggle eyes and dark complexion, was "the earliest widely known graphic representation of the Jew."[42] Moreover, another Jewish type established by Hogarth was that of the bearded, swarthy Jewish peddler who appears in his *Election* series in *Canvassing for Votes* (1757) and that remained culturally entrenched until at least the mid-nineteenth century.[43] Hogarth thus popularized not one but two enduring pictorial Jewish types. Mungo is right, then, to worry that he "will forever be associated with the indecencies of merchants and whores, for Mr Hogarth's prints will last forever."[44] The power of Hogarth's popular series seems inescapable to Mungo, for the prints "sold uncommonly well, spreading the message of me throughout the realm."[45]

Johnson's Dictionary

In *Johnson's Dictionary,* Dabydeen deepens his engagement with Jewishness and with the ekphrastic strategy of his first Hogarth novel by situating the Jew (as well as Hogarth himself) not only in the European metropole but also in the colonial West Indies and by integrating the visual still more extensively into the text. In Dabydeen's *A Harlot's Progress,* Jews are briefly linked to the colonies through the figure of a Jewish slave ship doctor who is thrown overboard alongside a number of slaves in an incident that recalls the *Zong* massacre. This alignment of Jews and slaves as fellow victims of one of the most notorious incidents in the history of the Atlantic slave trade contrasts with the association of Jewishness with the forces of enslavement and corrupt colonial wealth that Hogarth's original engraving and the South Sea Bubble cards promoted. Dabydeen notes that Hogarth's Jewish merchant "who patronises whores does so from wealth derived from colonial trade (the black boy with his tea-kettle, the monkey, and the mahogany table indicate this much)." Thus, in Dabydeen's analysis of plate 2, "The Jewish merchant is a slave dealer in two ways: he is the polite keeper of courtesans like Moll who are slaves to his pleasure, and he also deals in Africans, who are slaves for his profit, either shipping them to the colonies for sale or working them in his West Indian plantations or trading in the products of their labour (tobacco, sugar, rum, brandy, tea, *et cetera*)."[46]

In his novel *A Harlot's Progress,* Dabydeen hints at this association between Jews and an unsavory colonial trade by naming his Jewish protagonist after a Sephardic Jewish banker whose father, Rowland Gideon (né Rehiel Abundiente), was a merchant from a Portuguese *Converso* family and who lived, in classic port Jew fashion, in Barbados, Boston,

Nevis, and London.⁴⁷ In *Johnson's Dictionary,* Dabydeen makes this historical connection between Sephardic Jews and the colonial Caribbean more explicit by locating his key Jewish protagonist, Theodore, in the colony of Demerara, where he works as the accountant on a plantation. Accordingly, Theodore is also a more ambivalent figure than is *A Harlot's Progress*'s Sampson Gideon. I would argue, however, that this ambivalence speaks less to a historical argument that Dabydeen wants to make about the role of Jews in the colonial economy than to his interest in "the Jew" as an overdetermined sign that problematizes the truth claims of realist representations of racialized Others.

In *Johnson's Dictionary,* colonial and metropolitan spaces become still more deeply imbricated than in Dabydeen's first Hogarth novel, and, by extension, British art becomes more deeply implicated in colonial relations. Dabydeen's insertion into his novel of a series of works of European art, including a number by Hogarth, serves to resituate these works against the background of colonial-metropolitan relations. Having made a brief appearance in *A Harlot's Progress,* in *Johnson's Dictionary* Hogarth now resurfaces in the colonies, where he is the master of the slave Cato and the "Official Artist of the Colony of Demerara and Contiguous Territories." Hogarth is thus triply present in the novel as a protagonist, as the primary inspiration for the novel's characters, and as the creator of artworks periodically inserted into the text. In Dabydeen's unflattering portrayal, Hogarth is a drunken artist whose task as part of the machinery of empire is to "make record of the factories and the fields and the whitefolk who run the colony."⁴⁸ As in *A Harlot's Progress,* here Hogarth's art is exposed as misrepresentation: "Oh so much more pretty to see your life in paint, because Massa don't bother to put in the Negro sweat and the hate. Canvas is a special cloth: you can't spoil it with too much real life. Canvas is Christ's miracle. On canvas the lame walk, the hungry get fish and loaves, water turn into wine, work make a man free."⁴⁹ In *Johnson's Dictionary,* Dabydeen dramatizes the power of painting genres such as the colonial picturesque to distort and excise "real life." Underscoring the political nature of painting as an expression of colonial power, the slave Cato "dream[s] that the paintbrush in my hand is a torch that will burn down canefield and factory."⁵⁰ Driving home the connection between European art and the brutally exploitative conditions of the plantation that supports its production, Cato at one point rubs sugar directly into one of his master's canvases.

If resituating Hogarth in Demerara exposes the ideological underpinnings of European art, relocating the Jew to the Caribbean colony would appear to implicate the Jew in the plantation economy. In part 2 of *Johnson's Dictionary*, which takes place in London, we are presented once again with the triangulation of harlot, Jew, and slave boy that structures plate 2 of Hogarth's original series. The first image of the Jew that confronts the reader in the novel is that of the Jew as patron of prostitutes. We are told that the harlot Elizabeth "specialized in Jews, liking the brushstroke of their beards which she plucked, voided her rheum into, play-acting a child's anger at the lewd assaults. Afterwards they paid her a shilling more than the normal rate and hobbled off to be purified in their special home-wells."[51] Quickly, however, we move from this pictorial image of generalized Jews (underlined by the reference to the "brushstroke of their beards") to an individual Jewish figure who overturns the first image. Employing a similar strategy of inversion to that of his first Hogarth novel, Dabydeen here presents his London Jew as the harlot's benefactor rather than seducer: "Folk said all Jews were mean, hoarding their lot, but their Jew seemed to be bent not on saving but on salvation."[52] The unnamed London Jew of part 2 is a parodically benevolent figure who, like Sampson Gideon in *A Harlot's Progress*, has made it his life's mission to provide sanctuary to harlots: "'I am here to protect her and you. I have wandered the earth, guided by the light of stars and comets, and my journey has brought me here,' the Jew said."[53] With his elevated, poetic language and messianic tone, the London Jew seems drawn from the Scriptures. Accordingly, seeking to solve the mystery of the Jew's true motives, Elizabeth searches for clues in a painting of the golden calf that features a bearded Jew, whom she mistakes to be "a portrait of their Jew when he was young."[54] This ekphrastic passage suggests the difficulty of disentangling contemporary Jews from biblical Jews as well as individuals from typological graphic representations.

Soon tiring of the Jew's benevolence, Elizabeth flees and becomes associated with a Black man, Francis, thereby completing Hogarth's triangle of Jew, harlot, and slave. As in Hogarth's engraving, in *Johnson's Dictionary* Black and Jew are paralleled with each other. Both Francis and the London Jew are mysterious figures who inexplicably single out Elizabeth and whose dialogue, actions, and sense of mission echo one another. Elizabeth's affiliation with Francis anticipates her eventual move to the colony of Demerara, where she seduces a hapless Scottish doctor and acquires a plantation. In the colony, Elizabeth makes the acquaintance of a still more intriguing Jew, Theodore, who appears in part 3 as a guest in her salon.

In both of his Hogarth novels, Dabydeen resists linear emplotment and conventional characterization by generating proliferating versions of a given narrative thread or figure. Thus, between the two novels, we are confronted with multiple incarnations of the harlot, the slave, and the Jew. Alongside Sampson Gideon in *A Harlot's Progress* and the London Jew who appears in part 2 of *Johnson's Dictionary*, Theodore represents yet another reworking of Hogarth's Jewish merchant. Significantly, Theodore's appearance follows closely after the insertion into the novel of plate 2, which is recontextualized through its enfolding within the narrative of the harlot Elizabeth's rise (or "progress") in the colonial society of Demerara. As in Dabydeen's first Hogarth novel, here the relationship between image and text is an ambivalent one. Plate 2 both helps to inspire the novel and at the same time disrupts the flow of the narrative in a manner that threatens to supplant it. The visual image of Hogarth's Jew introduces a set of powerful associations that will overdetermine Theodore and make it difficult to discern his true nature.

Working as an accountant for the Catholic overseer Mr. Basnett on a plantation with three hundred slaves, Theodore manifests a series of recognizably "Jewish" traits. As with the unnamed London Jew in part 2 of the novel, he is a shadowy figure of mysterious origins: "Theodore divulged nothing of his past to Mr Basnett (me being his sole confessor). Mr Basnett took him to be English, but a hint of darkness of skin and accent suggested some foreign infusion, possibly from Portugal."[55] Repeatedly linked to the idea of impure blood, Theodore's Jewishness connotes foreignness as well as miscegenation, in keeping with the fear of sexual contact between Jews and gentiles expressed in Hogarth's plate 2.[56] Although some details of Theodore's biography, including his Portuguese appearance, the fact that he is Dutch speaking, and his movement from Holland to France and Demerara, strongly suggest a Sephardic lineage, the slave Francis later discovers that Theodore "was from Eastern Europe, a scion of privilege, a relative of the Czar no less, his family owning several estates in Russia and Poland."[57] Theodore represents a peculiar conflation of the Sephardic and Ashkenazi diasporas that dispersed across the Caribbean, a composite of these histories.[58]

Conforming to the image of the crafty Jew that appears in one of the South Sea Bubble cards that Dabydeen reproduces in *Hogarth, Walpole*,[59] Theodore is a trickster, possessed of linguistic skills as well as the "dexterity of a cardsharp."[60] Like Hogarth's Jewish merchant, Theodore affects the "refined manners" of a gentleman: "He was versed in all the arts of refinement, an accomplished gambler, violinist, fencer, equestrian and linguist."[61] He is also a libertine and a rake, envisaged at one point as lasciviously clutching Elizabeth in a "gross clasp" that recalls the clawlike hand of Hogarth's Jew.[62] Associated with sexual corruption and lechery, Theodore is equally perceived as a force of economic corruption who "sow[s] and reap[s] figures" rather than sugarcane.[63] Depicted as "poring over the ledger books," he appears obsessed with figures and calculations.[64] The moral and economic danger that Theodore represents is manifested in his "thin and wily-looking" physiognomy.[65]

As with his other Jewish protagonists, however, Dabydeen soon undermines these stereotypes and breaks the word-image correspondence between the novel and plate 2 by disclosing Theodore's motivation to be one of reforming rather than profiting from the plantation. Theodore uses his gift for trickery to confound the overseer Basnett and to impose various reforms to benefit the slaves including longer lunch breaks, improved diet, payment of a monthly bonus, additional holidays, and reading lessons. "So you are an abolitionist at heart; is that your dirty secret?" charges Basnett. "A foreigner with dark complexion, a tincture of the Jew in him."[66] Theodore is revealed to be the redeemer of slaves rather than the enslaver of Hogarth's engraving, just as Sampson Gideon and the London Jew are the redeemers of prostitutes.

Profoundly enigmatic and mysterious, Dabydeen's Jews in *A Harlot's Progress* and especially *Johnson's Dictionary* are figures of questionable loyalty. Yet, in Dabydeen's fiction, the untrustworthiness traditionally ascribed to the Jew raises concerns not so much about the Jew's moral character as about the reliability of representation itself. The contest between word and image that Dabydeen's Hogarth novels stage, in which the visual stereotypes threaten to overwhelm his textual revisions, points to the difficulty of escaping the discursive traditions that surround racialized Others. Dabydeen's Jews are enigmatic not because Jews are deceitful, treacherous creatures but because "the Jew" as a sign is so overdetermined that the reader cannot escape its excessive signification, its profusion of meanings, to uncover a "real Jew" underneath. Moreover, by encouraging the reader to understand his Jewish protagonists not as characters but as discursively produced visual and textual signs, Dabydeen draws attention to the related status of "the slave" as a widely disseminated emblem in eighteenth-century England. Accordingly, the London scenes in *Johnson's Dictionary* present the metropole as saturated by shop-sign images of Blacks: "The painted Negroes held up sheaves of tobacco, bottles of liquor, sugar loaves and other goods shipped from across the seas. They grinned stupidly; most were half-naked."[67]

More broadly, then, Dabydeen's enigmatic, ambivalent Jewish figures serve to foreground and problematize colonial symbolic economies.

Eckstein observes of Dabydeen's *A Harlot's Progress* that "the novel hardly ever proposes any valid, alternative accounts. Instead of claiming 'truth,' it continually contradicts itself, sheds doubt on its own narrative postulations, and suggests an inevitable plurality of meaning."[68] My argument is that, in his postmodern Hogarth novels, Dabydeen resists the truth claims of realist forms such as the slave narrative in part by exploiting the excessive and contradictory quality of figure of the Jew, or what Bryan Cheyette refers to as "the protean instability of 'the Jew' as signifier."[69] Proposing an understanding of "the Jew" not as a fixed, unchanging stereotype but as an expression of ambivalence and incoherence, Cheyette maintains that "it is the very slipperiness and indeterminacy of 'the Jew' . . . that enables an uncertain literary text to explore the limits of its own foundations."[70] It is precisely this questioning of the text's foundations—in particular the colonial text's—that is Dabydeen's project in his Hogarth novels.

As Cheyette points out, "In a post-modern context, 'semitic confusion' is not only a virtue but a prototype for the lack of fixity in language as a whole."[71] He cautions, however, against a dehistoricized embrace of this emblematic reading of Jewishness that fails to confront the "particular European cultural history" that generated a semitic discourse.[72] In his scholarship and fiction, Dabydeen avoids such a danger by pursuing a detailed and penetrating analysis of eighteenth-century constructions of the Jew. As I have suggested, this historicizing drive in Dabydeen's writing usefully opens up alternative channels for thinking about the relationship between Jewishness and postcolonial writing. In particular, by returning us to the eighteenth century, Dabydeen recalls the presence of Sephardic port Jews such as Sampson Gideon's father in the colonial Caribbean, one that has recently been recovered by historians of the Jewish Atlantic such as Jonathan Schorsch, Aviva Ben-Ur, and Natalie Zemon Davis.[73] This is not to suggest that the Holocaust does not also contribute to Dabydeen's interest in Jewishness, but rather that Holocaust memory and sephardism often become intertwined in Caribbean invocations of Jewishness.

The relational and intermedial reading of representations of slaves and Jews that Dabydeen develops in his Hogarth novels generates a more complex, historically nuanced understanding of the relevance of Jewishness to Black historical experience than is captured by the more familiar Holocaust/slavery analogies. Jonathan Boyarin has identified a tendency in postcolonial studies to neglect Jews because their travails as Europe's internal Others significantly predated the age of imperialism.[74] Dabydeen's historical fiction redresses this lacuna in postcolonial studies by revisiting a period of English history in which Jews occupied a subaltern position. By addressing graphic representations of both Jewish and Black bodies, he is able to analyze more fully how racial signs operate, are disseminated, and build on and play off of one another. Dabydeen's Hogarth novels are doubly comparative, engaging both Blacks and Jews, text and image. His ekphrastic fiction thus suggests how a postcolonial critique of regimes of representation can be deepened through a comparative engagement with a variety of racialized and religious Others and through an examination of multiple struggles for emancipation.

Notes

I am grateful to Heidi Kaufman and Mark Phillips for their comments on an earlier draft of this essay.

1. David Bindman observes that "since the publication of David Dabydeen's *Hogarth's Blacks* . . . it has been impossible to ignore the fact that Africans . . . are a substantial presence in Hogarth's paintings and satirical prints." Bindman, "'A Voluptuous Alliance between Africa and Europe': Hogarth's Africans," in *The Other Hogarth: Aesthetics of Difference,* ed. Bernardette Fort and Angela Rosenthal (Princeton, NJ: Princeton University Press, 2001), 260.

2. "'Word People': A Conversation with David Dabydeen," interview with Abigail Ward, *Atlantic Studies* 11, no. 1 (2014): 39.

3. See Jutta Schamp, "Transfiguring Black and Jewish Relations: From Ignatius Sancho's *Letters* and Olaudah Equiano's *Interesting Narrative* to David Dabydeen's *A Harlot's Progress,*" *Ariel* 10, no. 4 (2009): 30–31, as well as David Dabydeen, "Getting Back to the Idea of Art as Art—an Interview with David Dabydeen," interview with Lars Eckstein, *World Literature Written in English* 39, no. 1 (2001): 30.

4. Sarah Phillips Casteel, *Calypso Jews: Jewishness in the Caribbean Literary Imagination* (New York: Columbia University Press, 2016).

5. See Condé's *I, Tituba, Black Witch of Salem,* trans. Richard Philcox (New York: Random House, 1992); Walcott's *Tiepolo's Hound* (New York: Farrar, Straus & Giroux, 2000); and McLeod's *The Cost of Sugar,* trans. Gerald R. Mettam (Paramaribo, SR: Waterfront, 2010). As I argue elsewhere (Casteel, 2016), for some of these writers, repositioning Jewishness in the context of Atlantic slavery helps to prevent the slave narrative from becoming ossified in its well-established generic conventions.

6. The exhibition, entitled *Joden in de Cariben* (Jews in the Caribbean), ran from January to June 2015.

7. Perhaps the only other Caribbean writer to address in a sustained fashion the Sephardic Caribbean in the context of European art history is Walcott (see his *Tiepolo's Hound*).

8. Jewishness notoriously blurs distinctions among racial, ethnic, religious, and national differences. Accordingly, there will be some slippage among these terms in my discussion, but I emphasize racial definitions of Jewishness in particular to reflect the eighteenth-century historical setting that Dabydeen addresses and the links that he makes between the construction of Jews and Blacks during this period.

9. For a broader discussion of ekphrasis as it is employed by Caribbean writers, see Mary Lou Emery, *Modernism, the Visual, and Caribbean Literature* (Cambridge: Cambridge University Press, 2007), chap. 4.

10. David Dabydeen, "Preface," *Turner* (Leeds: Peepal Tree, 2010), 7.

11. Dabydeen, "Preface," 31.

12. Dabydeen, "Word People," 34.

13. The figures of the Jewish peddler and fiddler appear in plates 2 and 4 respectively of Hogarth's *Election* series (1757–58). David Solkin notes that the Jewish merchant in plate 2 of *A Harlot's Progress* "is the only secondary character who has the centre of a composition all to himself." Solkin, "The Excessive Jew in *A Harlot's Progress*," in *Hogarth: Representing Nature's Machines*, ed. Frederic Ogée, David Bindman, and Peter Wagner (Manchester: Manchester University Press, 2001), 228.

14. Peter Wagner, "Hogarth and the Other," *Word and Image in Colonial and Postcolonial Literatures and Cultures*, ed. Michael Meyer (Amsterdam: Rodopi, 2009), 32.

15. See Heidi Kaufman, who argues that Hogarth's depiction of the Jew as a poor mimic of Englishness speaks to contemporary anxieties surrounding not only Jewish assimilation and economic power but also "the racial implications of extending citizenship rights to Jewish immigrants." Kaufman, *English Origins, Jewish Discourse, and the Nineteenth-Century British Novel: Reflections on a Nested Nation* (University Park, PA: Penn State University Press, 2009), 12–13.

16. David Dabydeen, *Johnson's Dictionary* (Leeds: Peepal Tree, 2013), 98.

17. Peter Wagner, "Introduction: Ekphrasis, Iconotexts, and Intermediality—the State(s) of the Art(s)," in *Icons-Texts-Iconotexts: Essay on Ekphrasis and Intermediality* (Berlin: Walter de Gruyter, 1996), 15.

18. David Dabydeen, *Hogarth's Blacks: Images of Blacks in Eighteenth Century English Art* (Athens, GA: University of Georgia Press, [1985] 1987), 11. Disagreeing with Dabydeen, Bindman questions whether Hogarth had a special sympathy for Blacks, which "would have put him in the minority in his own time, place, and circumstances" (Bindman, 260).

19. Wagner, "Hogarth and the Other," 25.

20. David Dabydeen, *Hogarth, Walpole, and Commercial Britain* (London: Hansib, 1987), 12.

21. Dabydeen, "Getting Back," 29.

22. Emery comments that "in representing, through words, another representational language—that of the visual—ekphrasis represents representation itself" (Emery, *Modernism*, 182).

23. Bernadette Fort and Angela Rosenthal, "The Analysis of Difference," in *The Other Hogarth: Aesthetics of Difference,* ed. Bernadette Forte and Angela Rosenthal (Princeton, NJ: Princeton University Press, 2001), 3. Relatedly, Mark Hallett remarks how *A Harlot's Progress* "encourages the viewer to compare each man to the other, and to satirically appreciate the continuities and correspondences between these seemingly diverse individuals." Hallett, *Hogarth* (London: Phaidon, 2000), 93.

24. Solkin notes that although Hogarth scholars have been hesitant to discuss the Jewish figure in *A Harlot's Progress* and its relationship to popular images of the Jew, Dabydeen is an exception (Solkin, "The Excessive Jew," 219–20).

25. Michael Galchinsky, "Africans, Indians, Arabs, and Scots: Jewish and Other Questions in the Age of Empire," *Jewish Culture and History* 6, no. 1 (2003): 47.

26. As Solkin observes, "Hogarth's Jew was hardly an original creation; he, too, was already known to his audience, if not from a single prototype, then from a multiplicity of sources rooted in a tradition of English representations of Jewishness going back centuries." Solkin, "The Excessive Jew," 220.

27. Isaac Land, "Jewishness and Britishness in the Eighteenth Century," *History Compass* 3 (2005): 4–5.

28. Constance Harris, *The Way Jews Lived: Five Hundred Years of Printed Words and Images* (Jefferson, NC: McFarland, 2008), 119–25.

29. Dabydeen, *Hogarth, Walpole,* 109. Dabydeen's interpretation would be rejected by Paulson, who in a 2001 collection engages in a polemic with Solkin regarding whether Hogarth opportunistically exploits popular anti-Jewish prejudice (as Solkin maintains) or in fact humanizes the Jew, any anti-Semitism being "incidental" to his real purpose of parodying Dürer's New Testament scenes (as Paulson would have it). See Solkin, "The Excessive Jew," and Ronald Paulson, "Some Thoughts on Hogarth's Jew: Issues in Current Hogarth Scholarship," in *Hogarth: Representing Nature's Machines,* ed. Frederic Ogée, David Bindman, and Peter Wagner (Manchester: Manchester University Press, 2001), 236–63.

30. See Frank Felsenstein, *Anti-Semitic Stereotypes: A Paradigm of Otherness in English Popular Culture, 1660–1830* (Baltimore: Johns Hopkins University Press, 1995), 54–55; and Montagu Frank Modder, *The Jew in the Literature of England* (New York: Meridian, 1960), 66–68. Accordingly, Felsenstein discusses the "extraordinary cultural influence" of plate 2, which "served as a graphic prototype . . . in the reactivation of the Jew-figure in the popular imagination" (55). See also Solkin's contention that Hogarth's merchant is the most influential image of the Jew in early eighteenth-century British culture (221).

31. David Dabydeen, *A Harlot's Progress* (London: Vintage, 2000), 143.

32. Dabydeen, *Harlot's Progress,* 3.

33. Dabydeen, 143.

34. Dabydeen, 250–51. Thus, as Schamp observes, the novel suggests how anti-Jewish stereotypes cross both class and racial barriers (31–32).
35. Dabydeen, *Harlot's Progress*,145.
36. Dabydeen, 21.
37. Dabyden, 227.
38. Dabydeen, 227.
39. Lars Eckstein, *Re-Membering the Black Atlantic: On the Poetics and Politics of Literary Memory* (Amsterdam: Rodopi, 2006), 139.
40. James Heffernan, *Museum of Words: The Poetics of Ekphrasis from Homer to Ashbery* (Chicago: University of Chicago Press, 1993), 6. For Heffernan, "Ekphrasis . . . is a literary mode that turns on the antagonism . . . between verbal and visual representation . . . and often reveals a profound ambivalence toward visual art, a fusion . . . of veneration and anxiety" (7).
41. Dabydeen, *Harlot's Progress*, 271.
42. Dabydeen, 53.
43. Felsenstein, *Anti-Semitic Stereotypes*, 57.
44. Dabydeen, *Harlot's Progress*, 273.
45. Dabydeen, 273. See Hallett, *Hogarth* (94–95) on the commercial success of Hogarth's series.
46. Dabydeen, *Hogarth's Blacks*, 108; 114.
47. My thanks to Michael Hoberman for supplying additional information about Rowland Gideon.
48. Dabydeen, *Johnson's Dictionary*, 21.
49. Dabydeen, 23–24.
50. Dabydeen, 26.
51. Dabydeen, 32.
52. Dabydeen, 36.
53. Dabydeen, 33.
54. Dabydeen, 34.
55. Dabydeen, 117.
56. See also Dabydeen, *Johnson's Dictionary*, 117: "Mr Basnett was pleased that Theodore appeared to have Portuguese in him, albeit only to the degree of an octoroon."
57. Dabydeen, 118.
58. I am indebted to Heidi Kaufman for sharing this observation with me.
59. See Dabydeen, *Hogarth, Walpole*, 26.
60. Dabydeen, *Johnson's Dictionary*, 120.
61. Dabydeen, 118.
62. Dabydeen, 176.
63. Dabydeen, 122.
64. Dabydeen, 119.
65. Dabydeen, 116.
66. Dabydeen, 144.

67. Dabydeen, 40.

68. Eckstein, *Re-membering the Black Atlantic,* 139.

69. Bryan Cheyette, *Constructions of "the Jew" in English Literature and Society: Racial Representations, 1875–1945* (Cambridge: Cambridge University Press, 1995), 8. See also Linda Nochlin's discussion of the "Jew's representational instability" in "Starting with the Self: Jewish Identity and Its Representation," in *The Jew in the Text: Modernity and the Construction of Identity,* ed. Linda Nochlin and Tamar Garb (London: Thames & Hudson, 1995), 13, as well as Solkin's suggestion that images of the Jew stand apart from other stereotypes by virtue of being "unusually rich in meaning" (220).

70. Nochlin, *Jew in the Text,* 11.

71. Nochlin, 274.

72. Nochlin, 275.

73. See Jonathan Schorsch, *Jews and Blacks in the Early Modern World* (Cambridge: Cambridge University Press, 2004); Aviva Ben-Ur, "A Matriarchal Matter: Slavery, Conversion, and Upward Mobility in Suriname's Jewish Community," in *Atlantic Diasporas: Jews, Conversos, and Crypto-Jews in the Age of Mercantilism, 1500–1800,* ed. Richard L. Kagan and Philip D. Morgan (Baltimore: Johns Hopkins University Press, 2009), 152–69; and Natalie Zemon Davis, "David Nassy's 'Furlough' and the Slave Mattheus," in *New Essays in American Jewish History* (Cincinnati: American Jewish Archives, 2010), 79–94.

74. Jonathan Boyarin, *Storm from Paradise: The Politics of Jewish Memory* (Minneapolis: University of Minnesota Press, 1992), 81–82.

Jubanidad and the Literary Transmission of Cuban Crypto-Judaism

Leonard Stein

De su religión, los hebreos como los polacos, hacen patria. ¡Otros la hacen de un amor, y muerto él, van por la tierra como desterrados! ¡Otros la hacen de un sueño!

(From their religion, the Hebrews, like the Poles, make a homeland. Others make it from love, and if that dies, they go through the land as exiles! Others make it from a dream!)
—José Martí, "Nueva York, 24 de diciembre de 1881"

ALTHOUGH JEWS HAVE made up only a tiny fraction of the general Cuban population throughout the twentieth century, dwindling to just over a thousand following the revolution, the history of Cuban literature reveals a considerable interest toward Jewish experiences on the island. Before Jews could even legally live in colonial Cuba, imagined stereotypes of them in Cuban abolitionist literature of the nineteenth century were used, as Hispanist Stephen Silverstein has demonstrated, "as a psychological stabilizing force."[1] Following the Cuban War of Independence in 1898, American Jews and those emigrating from the Ottoman territories were the first to bring a multiethnic Jewish presence to Cuba, but it had been Ashkenazi Jews leaving their hostile conditions of Eastern Europe during the 1920s who introduced a vibrant, non-Spanish literature to Cuba. As Rachel Rubinstein discusses in the present volume, poets like Pinkhas Berniker and editor Oscar Pinis contributed to a growing Yiddish press during the 1930s. Temporary and immigrated Jews would continue to publish in Cuba up to the end of the revolution in 1959. Like other Cuban-Americans, Jewish Cubans such as the modern poet José Kozer, who blends nostalgic life on the island with Jewish themes, would continue writing in Spanish in the diaspora. Today, the experience of Cuban Jews continues to inspire the work of inland Cuban writers. Leonardo Padura's 2013 Mario Conde detective novel, *Herejes* (*Heretics*), for example, includes long narrative stretches through Cuba's modern history in search of a Jewish family's heirloom painting.

To understand this nexus between Jews, Cuba, and the literary production that ties them together, it is perhaps useful to travel back to the winter of 1881, when, writing about the significance of Hanukkah for the Caracas newspaper *La Opinión Nacional*, the Cuban poet, intellectual, and revolutionist José Martí identified with the plight and spirit of a wandering people he had come to befriend in his American travels. For Martí, an exile in New York pining for an independent Cuba, triumph over tyranny and the brief reclamation of the Judean temple provided an aspirational model for a contemporary crisis. And, like the Jewish people, who survived by preserving their history and ancestral language "con pasión," Martí would ensure his poems and ideas lived in posterity with the collection and publication of all of his works.[2] Martí's confluence of a homeland and the preserved past engenders a more accurate translation of that Latinate word *patria*, similar to what the French moralist Joseph Joubert once dismissed as that "paternal land," what the "ancients" claimed out of old attachments connecting them to their land, be it temples, tombs, or ancestors.[3] Like Martí's revolutionary rhetoric, Cuban Jewish literature written in America articulates a complex identity through a spatiotemporal framework, negotiated by a patria of both homeland and memory, exile and the sacred attachments to the past.

The anthropologist and fellow contributor to this volume Ruth Behar first theorized the temporal contours of what she referred to as being *Juban,* her self-identifying notion for complex Cuban, American, and Jewish hybridity. Borrowing from Salman Rushdie's thoughts on exile, Behar imagines a *Juba* built "from both family stories and my own struggle to reclaim all the forgotten villages of my mestiza identity."[4] Behar has since documented this personal quest to understand *Juban* identity through various creative outlets, including a documentary, poetry, a memoir, juvenile fiction, and her primary academic research in anthropology. In *An Island Called Home* in particular, Behar merges her family history with ethnographic fieldwork on the remaining Jews living in present-day Cuba. Photographs taken by Humberto Mayol accompany each account, in which Cuban Jews pose with precious photographs from their family's past as they reveal what Behar claims as "the relationship people had with the Jewish past and the fierce ways they were holding on to this past, which they had made their own through conversion or the belated recuperation of their heritage."[5] Caroline Bettinger-López, Behar's former student, has expanded upon the study of this minority by conducting fieldwork from the other side of the straits in Miami. Labeling Cuban Jewishness as *Jubanidad,* an offshoot of the familiar and multiethnic term *cubanidad,* Bettinger-López refers to the "double diaspora" of Cuban Jews living in America, guiding their assimilation as Latinos and Jews through an imagined constellation that incorporates a spiritual homeland of Israel and a geographic homeland of Cuba.[6] Like Behar, Bettinger-López underscores the role of memory, particularly those parental memories from the island passed on to second-generation *Jewbans* born and raised in Miami.[7]

Drawing from Behar and Bettinger-López's emphasis on memory, I wish to consider how assertions of a fraught family heritage and exiled life, notions underlying Jubanidad, are reinforced in creative literature. Unlike anthropologists or historians, however, creative writers offer an access point to their family's elusive past by imaginatively writing them into existence. This essay explores Cuba's link to crypto-Judaism, a development rooted in the presumed history of the island that, as Martí suggests, implicates the search of a patria as a recovery of a ruptured homeland with a ruptured past. Achy Obejas's semiautobiographical novel *Days of Awe* (2001), as well as a memoir, *My 15 Grandmothers,* by Cuban-American Genie Milgrom (2012), depict experiences imagined and real related to the sense of a minority identity shifting over time and space. I refer to this process of understanding Jewishness as one of *transmission,* a term that evokes a range of meanings: the conveyance of preserved information, genetic or constructed, through intimate relationships with others; the passage of history through unspoken traditions; and the transference and dissemination of the hidden to the revealed. Like Bettinger-López and Behar, these writers offer personal narratives of a Jewish Cuba negotiated by text and memory, while creatively recovering the apertures of a particular subset of Jewish identity defined by concealment.

A Brief History of Cuban Crypto-Judaism

Historical research on the Jewish presence in Cuba preceding the twentieth century remains understandably challenging. To claim a Jewish history in colonial Cuba during the Spanish Inquisition, which lasted until 1824, requires the historian to sift through fragments of an intentionally self-effacing community while assessing archived records of Inquisitors who labeled as *Judaizing* various forms of aberrant behavior. Nevertheless, a pre-Independence crypto-Jewish narrative of the history of Cuba, from which Obejas conjures her novel, offers a foundation story of the island on the heels of Spain's Jewish expulsion. Traveling with other presumed *Conversos* along Columbus's accidental voyage to the Americas, it was Luis de Torres—the interpreter who, as Bartolomé de las Casas noted, "had been a Jew, and knew . . . Hebrew and Chaldean [Aramaic] and even a bit of Arabic"—who on November 2, 1492, explored the island's Indigenous people called *Colba*.[8] A decade later, Spanish and then Portuguese Jewish converts to Catholicism, referred to as New Christians, joined other Spanish colonists inhabiting the land, a phenomenon large enough to frustrate newly arrived bishops. As Spanish archives reveal, with a Holy Office soon established in Havana, paranoid authorities searching for a proliferation of secret Jews on the Catholic territory produced various sentences and autos-da-fé (public burnings) during the sixteenth and seventeenth centuries.[9] Whatever the actual degree of practicing Jews, Behar claims that Cuban crypto-Judaism disappeared because "Jewish traditions couldn't be passed on openly."[10] By contrast, the exponentially larger population of Spanish-colonized Yoruba slaves syncretized African religious traditions with Catholicism in what became known as Santería, still popularly practiced on the island today.

By the early twentieth century, signs of a previous era of crypto-Judaism only appear in the penumbra of tales told by Eastern European and Sephardic Jewish immigrants, who saw in the island a refuge and passageway toward the United States or elsewhere. Margalit Bejarano's oral history of Jews in Cuba, for example, reveals what would ordinarily elude the printed page. David Ilan (Olinsky), a Lithuanian Jew who briefly lived in Cuba, shares with Bejarano a curious incident that occurred around 1933–34 in Havana. He explains that, after fulfilling an invitation to personally deliver a suit at the house of a customer,

> I encountered a table already set and the gentleman from the morning came in and invited me in and told me: "I am the mayor of Havana. It was not in vain that I purchased the suit and that I asked you to bring it over. I have some things here that I want you to explain to me." He pulled out a very beautiful Bible, bound in leather with gilded edges. He opened it up and I saw that there was a genealogy book inside, the roots of which went as far back as the year 1492. He came from a family of *conversos*. He pulled out a *mezuzah* [doorpost

scroll] and something which I don't recall and he asked me to explain to him what they were. He told me: "This came down to me from my father who had received it from my grandfather, etc. There is a list here, but I do not understand what it's all about." I remained there for over two hours, giving him the explanation, although I did not speak Spanish very well.[11]

The recorded interview presents a motif that will recur throughout the following discussion of the crypto-Jewish transmission of identity typifying Jubanidad. The mayor possesses precious objects that signify his Jewish identity, yet they are indecipherable to him. After generations on the island, the memory of his family's *Converso* traditions have been limited to a list of names, a rupture with the past the mayor seeks to repair. The disjuncture of translation between the old *Converso* and the new immigrant Jew impedes necessary signification, paralleling the ways in which the presentation of the story itself represents the challenge of relaying crypto-Jewish history. Over the decades, Ilan has forgotten crucial details of his account, even the mayor's name.[12] The memory of the story, however, has been textually preserved as part of an elemental narrative in Bejarano's oral history of Jewish Cuba, decades after it originally occurred and in a foreign land.

Cuban Crypto-Jewish Writing

The urge to reclaim a Cuban crypto-Jewish heritage has only recently surfaced in printed literature, with Cuban Americans documenting their personal journeys into their ancestral past. In his article "Documentary Sources for Cuban and Latin American Anusim Genealogical Research," for example, Cuban American Eugene A. Alonso lists names and cases of Judaizing during the Cuban Inquisition to "help elucidate the past for those who seek to find more about their own familial ties . . . a point of departure for many people on the island and around the Caribbean to make those links."[13] Similarly, having served as president of the Society for Crypto-Judaic Studies and various other Jewish community organizations, Cuban American Genie Milgrom has been one of the most sedulous advocates for crypto-Jewish genealogical research, as articulated in her self-published and relatively obscure memoir *My 15 Grandmothers*.

Milgrom's memoir charts her journey to recover her Jewish identity, from her memories of growing up in Cuba in an affluent Catholic family to her emigration to Miami and conversion to Judaism and the painstaking process of searching for her family's secret Jewish heritage. Milgrom locates her Jubanidad by going beyond Cuba, searching through countless Spanish and Portuguese Inquisitorial archives and the small Spanish village of Fermoselle to eventually pinpoint the origins of her crypto-Jewish genealogy. The search, as the memoir's title suggests, ultimately leads her to discover a remarkable and unbroken chain of *Converso* women in her maternal line that goes back to before the Spanish expulsion of 1492. Milgrom describes the cathartic implications of such a discovery: "I had grown up with a strong sense of not fitting in, then feeling the Jewish connection in my soul, finally converting to Judaism, then living as a convert while being an integral part of the Jewish people and only afterwards finding out I was Jewish all along. I had come full circle."[14] Instead of passed-down stories and photographs that typically mark family history, Milgrom yearns for the records that document names—not on the back of a family bible, but ironically archived by institutions responsible for suppressing her family from identifying as Jews. The weight of a recovered genealogy supersedes her conversion, as it reaffirms her immutable Jewish identity while proving the key to her family's ancient home; knowing an ancestral name allows Milgrom to travel and precisely locate the house still standing in Fermoselle, bridging five centuries of a circuitous exile from Spain to Miami.

The memoir emphatically serves as a guidepost for others who seek to connect to a crypto-Jewish past. Milgrom admits, upon walking through her ancestor's village, that her "story has to be told so that other descendants of the B'nai Anusim [children of crypto-Jews] would feel comfortable in coming forward and reclaiming their ancestral religion."[15] Accordingly, Milgrom has published an accompanying manual in Spanish and English, *How I Found My 15 Grandmothers,* outlining all of her archival steps in order to help others with their genealogical questions.

Buried History

Translating the motif of a secret family past into fiction, in her novel *Days of Awe* Achy Obejas creatively imagines the idea of fragmented memory and the recovery of history from the locus of Cuba. Centered on Alejandra San José, Obejas's semiautobiographical narrator, the novel recounts a personal history of the Cuban revolution that caused the San José family to immigrate to Chicago, a displacement from both homeland and the past that she seeks to recover. As a Cuban American interpreter with close ties to communist Cuba, Alejandra visits her hometown to discover her crypto-Jewish father's traumatic history, one which transplants the historical plight of the Iberian Inquisitions onto a modern landscape. Exemplifying the sense of patria in Jubanidad, Alejandra's journey into Cuba and into her father's memory conflate in order to understand the meaning of her heritage as a Cuban and a Jew.

If documentary evidence and oral history can only hint at a crypto-Jewish presence in colonial Cuba, Achy Obejas's fiction emphatically affirms the inextricable relationship between Jews and modern Cuba by framing the San José family history within the actual history of modern Cuba, stretching from independence to the contemporary. Alejandra is born on the day of the Triumph of the Revolution, her father shares a birthday with Fidel Castro, her great-grandfather patriotically fights in the War of Independence, and the Sephardic family friend Moisés Menach obdurately believes in Cuba's failing communist project as a Jewish value. Furthermore, Alejandra narrates that her family had been "on the island from the very beginning"[16] and later attests to the apparent crypto-Jewish origins of Fidel Castro, positioning Jews "at the foundations of Cuban history itself."[17] Efforts to uncover information about the lost history of crypto-Judaism in Cuba correspond to the novel's blurring of historical record with fiction. Obejas records factual history about Jews in Cuba throughout her novel, spanning Columbus's journey to the island; the 1914 founding of the Sephardic *Chevet Ahim* synagogue; the tragic lingering on Havana's shore of the *St. Louis* ocean liner carrying Jews escaping Nazi Germany; and contemporary dilapidations of Jewish sites.

As Alejandra concedes that "what documentation exists there [about crypto-Jews] is as scarce as it is dubious," Obejas's fictionalization of the San José family gestures toward a replacement of an official historical record.[18] In Alejandra's account of her father, "being a Jew was something tangible . . . the void between Cuba and Spain, between him and everybody else": in other words, an occlusion of information that emblematizes the grander lacuna of Cuban historicization of Otherness in the form of the crypto-Jew.[19] The lack of an official record of Jewish Cuba and the transmission of an imagined history recall the work of anthropologist Marie Theresa Hernández, who has studied the "buried" history of *Conversos* in contemporary Nuevo León, Mexico. Hernández claims that when narratives "have been displaced by the Scriptural Economy" (a concept drawn from Michel de Certeau's *The Practice of Everyday Life*, regarding the hegemonic force of official texts), those narratives become "fiction and ancient legends."[20] These legends, even those confirmed as specious, reveal darker aspects of history (i.e., Mexican or Cuban Inquisitions) repressed from a collective memory. The writing of Obejas, a novelist, similarly engages with the lack of official Cuban crypto-Jewish history by offering a text, albeit fictional, that alludes to its void.

Depicting the spatiotemporality of Jubanidad common to Behar and Bettinger-López's anthropology of Jewish Cuba, Alejandra's access to Jewish memory is paralleled with her access to the island of Cuba itself. In Chicago, her romantic relationships with Seth and Leni, both secular Jewish Americans, allow for a minimal projection of an identity she cannot reproduce, considering the pattern of erasure entrenched within her family history. Similarly, the island of Cuba, whose voice in the form of sea waves she recurrently hears in dreams and who she believes, after an unidentified telephone call, has reached out to her as a "young woman in some sort of panic," appears to her personified as another kind of lover, elusive and somehow Jewish.[21] Most explicitly, Alejandra refers to the anti-Semitic sobriquet—common among some Latin Americans—that Cubans are the "Jews of the Caribbean."[22] More than just a derogatory stereotype about Cuban greed, the term establishes a linkage between Jewish and Cuban culture and history:

> Cubans and Jews both had families in which people had peculiar accents, both cooked funny foods, both were obsessed with a country in the Third World, both lived lives in the subjunctive, and both, quite frankly, thought they were the chosen people. . . . When I was older, I discovered that Cubans have a Masada, too. Like the Jewish story—which is never mentioned in the Torah or Talmud—the Cuban legend is also outside the official history books. . . . Unable to imagine continuing to live in such misery, the Indians decided to kill themselves by eating dirt, poisoning their bodies with the very ashes and bones of their ancestors.[23]

Alejandra's final point of comparison between Jews and Cubans aptly applies to the legend of the crypto-Jews in Cuba as well. As in Hernández's discussion of buried history, official narratives of Cuban colonialism erase the unprinted voices of Indigenous and *Converso* people, both marginalized and often conflated by the Cuban Inquisition for their heresy.[24] The account of Indigenous deracination through ashes and bones, however, requires a fatalistic union with the victim's ancestral past; Alejandra's search to understand her family heritage through memory—such as when she seeks meaning in a photograph inherited from her father—illustrates the access to a crypto-Jewish past as ameliorative. The ruptured transmission of history, Kelli Lyon Johnson notes in her analysis of *Days of Awe*, signals the impairment of "collective remembering and . . . those signposts of untranslatability that hinder the transmutation of the experience of exile—for Jews and Cubans—from one culture to another."²⁵ In other words, without the preservation of unwritten stories drawn upon through memory, Alejandra cannot construct her own sense of Jubanidad, as she resides in an exile from her homeland and a father's past.

Marking Crypto-Jewishness

The recurring problem of transmitting identity in *Days of Awe* reflects the historical experience of fifteenth- and sixteenth-century crypto-Jews who had struggled to preserve a generational chain of Jewish continuity. The novel illustrates a problematic process, depicted in instructions, confessions, and purported genetic characteristics that inform characters of their Jewishness—problematic, since, unlike Milgrom, Obejas marks crypto-Jewish identity as fluid and fragmentary. The value of secrecy, central to the crypto-Jewish experience, challenges the concept that identity itself can be discovered, appropriated, or affirmed. Historian David Gitlitz has shown that the survival of postexpulsion crypto-Judaism rested on close family members passing information that became increasingly sparse with each successive generation. Marks betraying Jewishness, such as doorpost *mezuzot,* were hidden until symbolically remembered by their absence. The scarcity of objects and prayers exemplifying post-Inquisition *Converso* life echoes the journey of Alejandra, who must sift through a paucity of material objects and family stories in order to understand how they relate to her.

Mirroring historical crypto-Judaism in fiction, then, allows Obejas to explore how hidden texts, signifying a generational chain of retained Jewish memory, eventually disintegrate. Encrypted information not only secures safety from inquisitors, but also destabilizes the source sustained by its inheritors. As Seth Kunin argues in his anthropological research on contemporary crypto-Judaism in the American Southwest, an individual's self-understanding of her identity constitutes the most significant evidence for the historical transmission of crypto-Judaism, since this self-understanding often occurs in a rite of passage where a family member tells an adolescent, "Somos judíos."²⁶

The instability of oral history, as fluid and fading evidence, obscures generational memories and generally typifies the fragility of crypto-Jewish identity. The voices of elders haunt Obejas's crypto-Jewish characters, not only adolescents hearing their Jewishness uncovered, but the future children of those inheritors further removed from that transmission. Alejandra, for example, can only imagine how a relative must have told her father, "You are a child of Abraham, of Moses and the patriarchs," since her father has withheld even this limited information from her.[27] This shadow of transmission, the presumed inheritance of an identity undiscerned, develops into a kind of crypto-Jewish tradition in Alejandra's family, starting with her grandfather Luis, who, "like the distortions inherent in a child's game of whispers . . . had no real understanding of Hebrew. . . . He knew he was a Jew, but he wasn't altogether sure he really understood, or cared, what that meant."[28] Family transmission, imagined or fragmentary, emphasizes the deconstruction of a stable identity as a Cuban crypto-Jewish experience.

As in Bejarano's oral history of a *habanero* mayor, the identity of crypto-Jews in *Days of Awe* is revealed in the bibles they conceal, where, "on the inside pages next to the elaborate family trees, each dating back to 1492," methods for performing circumcisions and other rituals have been scrawled.[29] The mark of circumcision, which physically identifies a new Jewish boy, has been reduced to the metonym of its instructions, *marked* in the Book. For crypto-Jews who could not receive a circumcision, the marginal notes on the protected pages of a book demonstrate the identity of its owners. Interestingly, the shift from ritual circumcision to written instruction astutely suggests an interchangeable equivalence between body and text, as the Hebrew word for "circumcision," *milah*, is homonymous with the term for "word." The eventual destruction of these words thus suggests a rupture of inherited identity in the body of the individual, while heightening the importance of words themselves responsible for creating narratives.

As Alejandra learns, her father Enrique's Jewish story began after his grandfather Ytzak kidnapped him, traveling through the Cuban countryside to Santiago in order to give Enrique a proper circumcision. The crypto-Jewish family reacts furiously to news of the kidnapping, provoking Enrique's father Luis to throw Ytzak's family bibles down the Mayarí River, where they "spilled their rare ink into the waters, and with it our family history."[30] The loss of texts in the San José family indicate the impossibility of transmitting Jewish knowledge as a crypto-Jewish experience, doubly emphasized by the destruction of family bibles that contain this transmitting information. Unlike concealable or destructible family bibles, which can render family history inaccessible, Enrique's body comprises the transmission of the family's secret by its ability to reveal Jewishness. When a young Fidel Castro—of all people—discovers Enrique naked by the river and asks about his circumcised penis, Enrique admits to being a Jew, "the only time in his life he would ever volunteer that."[31]

The knowledge of Jewishness, symbolically lost with the cutting of the foreskin, reflects Enrique's incessant struggle to conceal what is most elemental to him, while foreshadowing the family's intolerable conditions in Castro's Cuba. Where books cannot ultimately protect secrets, the body stores and inscribes what can only be shared in privacy.

As seen in the representation of circumcision as written instructions, the physical body of a crypto-Jew marks the ephemerality of identity transmission. When her father, Enrique, dies, Alejandra follows written instructions to have his body cremated and his ashes scattered along the Havana bay. What has defined his relationship with his daughter during his life—the inaccessibility of his Jewishness and her need to communicate with him—continues even after his death.[32] With his ashes scattered on the water, Enrique removes the possibility of leaving any physical mark for his daughter to access, a final disconnect that signifies the impossibility of transmitting the Jewish identity of a crypto-Jewish father. Instead, he returns to the island he has never publicly acknowledged as his home. Enrique's openly Jewish grandfather Ytzak, by contrast, with a Star of David and Jewish name appearing on his headstone, dies with an identity indelibly marked for his relatives and the public to see. When Alejandra visits the grave in Guanabacoa, Cuba, she places a few pebbles on the headstone, a Jewish tradition in contradistinction to her subsequent act of scattering her father's ashes. Her involvement in both sites of death charts the legacy of crypto-Jewish history as a vanishing heritage. Whereas Alejandra symbolically *adds* to the memory of her Jewish great-grandfather by physically placing a mark on his grave, she *removes* her father's presence from Cuba and from her life by scattering his remains. The parallel between Enrique's repression of his past Jewish life in Cuba and his body's erasure in Cuba underscore an elusive patria uneasily retained by text or body.

Inheriting Identity

The novel's theme of establishing a generational chain of memory through the trope of a written or oral confession also challenges notions of identity as essentialist and biological. The idea of Jewish identity as a racial marker is most clearly challenged by Alejandra's mother, Nena, whose lineage "is as clear as stitches, as irrefutable as forensic bands of DNA."[33] With genealogical charts going back to pre-Inquisition Seville, and a surname—Abravanel—to which the protagonist attributes a claim of Sephardic nobility, Nena ironically affirms none of the historical Jewish roots that her crypto-Jewish husband desperately seeks and that are celebrated in Milgrom's memoir. She shows no interest in her family history, does not suffer from the "feverish kind of racial memory that compels [Alejandra and her father] to constantly glance backward," and practices an Afro-Caribbean religion estranged from that of her *Converso* Sephardic ancestors.[34] As opposed to her crypto-Jewish husband, Enrique, who attempts to recover an erased Spanish Jewish heritage in his profession as a Spanish translator, Nena's clear lineage does not indicate a genetic transmission of Jewish identity.

Furthermore, despite her proximity to a crypto-Jewish father actively engaged in Jewish rituals, Alejandra learns nothing from him about her family's Jewish heritage. Any information about Enrique's religious convictions and background comes from an openly Jewish family friend still living in Cuba, Moisés, who shares bits of the San José family's Cuban history in the letters he occasionally sends to Alejandra; despite her exile, Alejandra becomes dependent on her active link with Cuba to understand what she cannot receive in Chicago. As previously discussed regarding texts recovering memory, the device of transmitting textual knowledge signals crypto-Judaism as a nonessentialist form of identification, learned from elders and in fragments. When Alejandra, as a child, discovers her father praying while wearing *tefillin* (phylacteries), "she was able to recognize the practice as something sacred, both extraordinary and clandestine," although she cannot, like her grandfather's illiteracy, understand the meaning of those black boxes.[35] Furthermore, her attempts to wear her father's *tefillin* in a synagogue after his death, which quickly ends after the protest of male coreligionists, suggests that Alejandra cannot inherit the religion of her father, nor can she translate its expressions from the private to the public sphere. Nevertheless, like Moisés's daughter Deborah, whose tattoo of the letter *aleph* on her hand proves that she "will wear the legacy" of Jewishness, Alejandra's and her father's commitment to wearing *tefillin* offers symbolic propinquity toward identification.[36] Housing parchments with portions from the Torah about commandments for loving God, the commandment to remember the exodus, and the duty to teach children the Torah, the *tefillin* here represent Alejandra's urge to be inscribed by Hebrew text, the act of placing them on her body symbolically recovering the words of Torah and family history lost to the Mayarí generations ago.

Nevertheless, Alejandra does inherit and reinterpret some Jewish rituals and holidays. Every year, for example, she attends a Passover seder that her friends conduct in her parents' neighborhood. For Alejandra, the holiday signifies "that rather obvious topic" of exile already familiar to her as a Cuban American; her reading of Psalm 137, which relates the Jewish exile in Babylon, and the participation of refugees from Iraq, Yemen, Argentina, and Brazil during the seders, highlight the holiday's association with exile.[37] Interestingly, Alejandra does not seem to recognize how, aside from celebrating the Jewish exodus, Passover and the rituals surrounding the seder primarily emphasize the commandment for parents to transmit to their children an ancestral Jewish history; her parents encourage her participation, but offer no active way to inform Alejandra of her Jewish roots (and one that, as discussed, parallels the Cuban exile experience). As a result, Alejandra can only nourish the "need for connection . . . felt so feverishly" by witnessing the seder as a guest, illustrating the perpetuated displacement from her father's religious identity.[38]

Although Obejas eschews the Passover holiday's framework of transmitting Jewish identity, she indirectly engages in other forms of Jewish tradition, particularly the spiritual journey underscored by the title of the novel. The Days of Awe are an introspective ten-day period from Rosh Hashanah to Yom Kippur aimed toward repentance of the past and purification for the Jewish New Year. In the novel, this period delineates the Jewish- and Cuban-inflected parameters of the plot, since, as others have observed, the novel's forty chapters (reflecting the biblical period for journeys), start with Alejandra's birth on New Year's Day, 1959 (i.e., the beginning of communist Cuba), and end on Yom Kippur in Havana, a time frame that marks the beginning of Alejandra's exile and her presumed return through a conflation of Jewish and Cuban calendars.[39]

Additionally, the Days of Awe capture Alejandra's spiritual journey, which attempts to transmit her family's history as a renewal of her own sense of Jubanidad. Obejas does not refer to the popular, though apocryphal, legend that the *Kol Nidre,* a declaration for the absolution of past and future vows recited at the beginning of Yom Kippur, derives from *Conversos* during the Spanish Inquisition who sought to exculpate their conversions. The *Kol Nidre*'s declaration imagines a relationship between crypto-Jews, the challenge of inheriting the past, and the period in the Jewish New Year so symbolically central to the novel. In her analysis of *Days of Awe,* Dara Goldman considers the novel's title as signaling Alejandra's self-understanding. Since the beginning of the Jewish year involves "formal rituals of self-examination, contrition and spiritual cleansing," Alejandra's narrative "traces the process of inscription and renewal that . . . is mobilized as part of a (trans)cultural self-affirmation."[40] In other words, Alejandra's identity formation involves not only an inheritance of family knowledge and ritual, but also a reinterpretation of that information, so that "it is not preservation of an unchanged tradition, but adaptation to reality that becomes crucial."[41] Alejandra's religious practice, whether reciting a poem in place of the *kaddish* prayer or leaving an offering for her mother's idol—nonnormative practices in either traditional Judaism or Catholicism—*inscribes* and *renews* her family's past as a process that significantly parallels the fluid complexity of crypto-Judaism, itself a quasi-religion of developed rituals supplanting its erased Jewish precedents.

In her analysis of the novel, Bridget Kevane considers Alejandra "immersed in her family's broken history of Judaism," constantly trying to piece together the fragments of information available to her.[42] When Alejandra declares her Jewishness to a Christian proselytizer, for example, she realizes that she has momentarily "avenged the injustices of five hundred years ago,"[43] making her declaration "an act of redemption and recovery" so that she "will finally be able to translate the secret and celebrate the future."[44] Like the *Kol Nidre,* the performative speech act of declaring "I'm a Jew" allows Alejandra to confront her past and reshape it. Similarly, when at the end of the novel Alejandra scatters her father's ashes in Havana on Yom Kippur—a blatantly antinomian act considering the Jewish prohibition on cremation—she *renews* the *kaddish* traditionally recited by a Jewish mourner, reciting lines from the Spanish Jewish poet Judah Halevi in place of the foreign Aramaic words. Kevane argues that the poetry becomes Alejandra's "way of celebrating her father's return, in death, to Judaism, and her beginning of a new Jewish life as a woman."[45] In my reading, the feminist affirmation of Kevane's assertion is not fully evidenced by Obejas's novel, as Alejandra's religious identification appears calculatedly more ambiguous than Kevane suggests. Nevertheless, the recitation of the Halevi poem does establish a link between Alejandra and her Sephardic origins by imagining a recovery of the past through a text, signifying a transmission of family heritage.

Writing as Recovery

In depicting various forms of attempted transmission, Obejas resists simple, stable, or inherent concepts of identity. The construction of an identity depends upon external forces, such as learning a ritual or hearing a father's confession, but Obejas's characters consistently miss out on reviving familial ties to Judaism, or they appropriate them as their own.

Alejandra's journey in self-identification is defined by her break from the paradigms of a crypto-Jewish father and openly Jewish ancestors, a break that illustrates another paradox central to the Cuban Jewish experience: the yearning for a chain of memory that has long been ruptured.

Obejas's interest in Cuban crypto-Jewish identity arose after the issue was brought to her attention by inquiring readers, interested in her seemingly crypto-Jewish surname; in the novel, the narrating Alejandra alludes to this discovery, noting that, since her ancestors "seemed to convert easily, we were spared the usual torments and the odious subterfuge of having to rechristen ourselves with the names of places, plants, or animals: Torres, Flores, *Oveja*."[46] Like the metatextual citations of Spanish poetry found throughout the novel (i.e., "Translation by A. O."), Obejas writes herself into the text by supplementing an interview with Ilan Stavans at the end of the book.[47] The interview comments on the thematic issues and motivations of her writing, including the fact that her father's reticence to discuss her family's crypto-Jewish heritage initiated her research into the history of crypto-Judaism. This research led to the semiautobiographical plot of her novel, exploring what was denied to her outside the page and, as previously mentioned, blurring the distinction between literature and history. Furthermore, *Days of Awe* as a creative product illustrates how the process of searching for crypto-Jewish identity through writing transmits into the public sphere: "Ordinary life is filled with all sorts of clues about *anusim* [crypto-Jews] in Cuba and throughout Latin America, but the signs have been corrupted and often coopted, so it's not easy. The story's sweet and brave and tragic, and I wanted to tell it—to retell it, and to imagine it aloud, and to name it so others can come along and do something else, take it a step further, enrich it."[48] By narrativizing the religious revitalization of the remaining thousand Jews in Cuba, Obejas's semiautobiographical novel parallels Behar's *An Island Called Home*, written by an exiled Cuban Jew whose self-declared role is "to carry these memories back and forth."[49] Although Obejas invents a Cuban narrative that reflects her personal experience as a lesbian Cuban American translator with crypto-Jewish roots, her declaration as a storyteller reifying Cuban crypto-Judaism and passing on its story for others to "enrich it" reshapes her novel into an act of transmission. The objective of such fiction resembles Bettinger-López's description of the Miami Cuban Jewish community's written accounts of its history, in which "the written word signifies that which is chosen to be remembered collectively and passed through the generations."[50] And, like Hernández's anthropology of recalling buried history, Obejas's writing fills a lacuna of information by preserving in print the stories and histories previously limited to an exclusive community.

To consider this instructive role of the novel requires us to view the text as material culture, concretized in ink and largely imagined, similar to the physical pieces of evidence of identity claimed by crypto-Jewish descendants. Obejas's supplemental interview about *Days of Awe* makes the novel seem like an artifact of the author's family history, as photographs of Cuban Jews posing alongside old photographs did in Behar's *An Island Called Home*. Obejas's artifact, however, goes further than simply reestablishing a family heritage; it attempts to recover a grander historical scope of broken transmission in Cuba. Texts obviously do not serve as impartial evidence for a crypto-Jew's unbroken lineage, nor should they. As Seth Kunin writes in his anthropological study, the discourse on contemporary claims to crypto-Judaism focuses too narrowly on the academic's judgment of historical authenticity. Cultural authenticity, however, which emphasizes "the issue of identity and self-identification," focuses on the subjective practices and beliefs of individuals.[51] To value how individuals define themselves and their heritage, as Kunin implores us to do, means to also recognize the role that creatively written literature plays in assigning crypto-Jewish cultural authenticity. As previously mentioned, the novel bridges the dichotomy between written historical fiction and oral personal confession to re-create the edifying experience of the author conveying her identity onto the reader. By asserting her family identity in this novel, Obejas redefines the agency of the crypto-Jew by changing the trajectory of crypto-Judaism's resistance to erasure. Instead of recapitulating a colonialist Cuban history of a minority's oblivion, Obejas celebrates the potential for recovered memory in the fragmentation and temporal displacement of *Juba,* transmitting a countermetanarrative that reconciles a history of concealment with a renewal of published text.

The shift from an anthropological study of Jubanidad to the fiction and creative nonfiction discussed in this essay does not aim to neatly equate one with the other, especially since the phenomenon of crypto-Judaism departs historically and experientially from openly Jewish hybrid identities. Although Jews in Cuba and *Jewbans* in America might confront similar issues of displacement and preservation, depictions of crypto-Jewish identity consider the dream of a patria, in which connection to a homeland and a family heritage appear inaccessible. The priority of memory, whether transmitted through the generations or constructed by the individual, abate the geographic and spiritual exiles common to both. Finally, it is worth considering the plethora of historical, anthropological, and literary studies on the overtly practicing Jews of Cuba (a portion of which has been cited in this essay), despite the small scale of this minority. If I may contribute to this academic interest, it is though yet another act of transmission, one which throws into relief a subset of Cuban Jewry that has largely escaped the printed page.

Notes

1. Stephen Silverstein, *The Merchant of Havana: The Jew in the Cuban Abolitionist Archive* (Nashville: Vanderbilt University Press, 2016), 13.

2. José Martí, "Nueva York, 24 de diciembre de 1881," in *En los Estados Unidos: Escenas Norteamericanas*, vol. 9, *Obras Completas* (La Habana: Editorial de Ciencias Sociales, 1991), 205, my translation.

3. Joseph Joubert, *Pensées, Essais, et Maximes de J. Joubert*, ed. Paul Raynal (Paris: Didier, 1861), 395, my translation.

4. Ruth Behar, "Juban América," *Poetics Today* 16, no. 1 (1995): 165.

5. Ruth Behar, *An Island Called Home: Returning to Jewish Cuba* (New Brunswick, NJ: Rutgers University Press, 2007), 34.

6. Caroline Bettinger-López, *Cuban-Jewish Journeys: Searching for Identity, Home, and History in Miami* (Knoxville: University of Tennessee Press, 2000), 159.

7. Bettinger-López, *Cuban-Jewish Journeys*, 163.

8. Christopher Columbus, *The Diario of Cristopher Columbus's First Voyage to America, 1492–1493*, abstracted by Fray Bartolomé de las Casas, trans. Oliver Dunn and James A. Kelley Jr. (Norman: University of Oklahoma Press, 1988), 129.

9. Eugene A. Alonso, "Documentary Sources for Cuban and Latin American Anusim Geneological Research," *Journal of Spanish, Portuguese, and Italian Crypto Jews* 8 (2016): 21; Seymour B. Liebman, "Cuban Jewish Community in South Florida," in *American Jewish Year Book*, vol. 70, ed. Morris Fine and Milton Himmelfarb (American Jewish Committee and Jewish Publication Society of America, 1969), 228–29; Robert M. Levine, *Tropical Diaspora: The Jewish Experience in Cuba* (Gainesville: University Press of Florida, 1993), 1–16; Sender Kaplan, Raul Moncarz, and Julio Steinberg, "Jewish Emigrants to Cuba: 1898–1960," *International Migration* 28, no. 3 (1990): 295.

10. Behar, *An Island Called Home*, 4.

11. Margalit Bejarano, *The Jewish Community of Cuba: Memory and History*, ed. Haim Avni, trans. Susan Avni (Jerusalem: Magnes, 2014), 60.

12. If authentic, Ilan might be referring to Dr. Alejandro Vergara Leonard, Rafael Trejo Loredo, or Miguel Mariano Gómez Arias.

13. Alonso, "Documentary Sources," 27.

14. Genie Milgrom, *My 15 Grandmothers* (Createspace Independent Publishing Platform, 2012), 140.

15. Milgrom, *15 Grandmothers,* 146.

16. Achy Obejas, *Days of Awe* (New York: Ballantine, 2001), 35.

17. Dalia Kandiyoti, "Sephardism in Latina Literature," in *Sephardism: Spanish Jewish History and the Modern Literary Imagination,* ed. Yael Halevi-Wise (Stanford, CA: Stanford University Press, 2012), 243.

18. Obejas, *Days of Awe,* 35.

19. Obejas, 119.

20. Marie Theresa Hernández, *Delirio: The Fantastic, the Demonic, and the Réel: The Buried History of Nuevo León* (Austin: University of Texas Press, 2010), 5. I thank Dalia Kandiyoti in her critical treatment on the subject for first bringing Hernández's work on *converso* history to my attention.

21. Obejas, *Days of Awe,* 203.

22. Obejas, 103. For an example of the derogatory term, see, Jorge Duany, "Two Wings of the Same Bird? Contemporary Puerto Rican Attitudes toward Cuban Immigrants," *Cuban Studies* 30 (2000): 29–31.

23. Obejas, *Days of Awe,* 104–5.

24. Alonso, "Documentary Sources," 21. Alonso points out that Juan Muñoz, for example, was the first person in the Americas to die by the Inquisition's auto-da-fé, condemned by the Bishop of Cuba in 1518 for being a "Judaizing Indian."

25. Kelli Lyon Johnson, "Lost in *El Olvido*: Translation and Collective Memory in Achy Obejas's *Days of Awe,*" *Bilingual Review/La Revista Bilingüe* 27, no. 1 (2003): 38.

26. Seth D. Kunin, *Juggling Identities: Identity and Authenticity Among the Crypto-Jews* (New York: Columbia University Press, 2009), 91, 218.

27. Obejas, *Days of Awe,* 191.

28. Obejas, 116.

29. Obejas, 125.

30. Obejas, 125.

31. Obejas, 136.

32. Obejas, 191.

33. Obejas, 39.

34. Obejas, 39.

35. Dara E. Goldman, "Next Year in the Diaspora: The Uneasy Articulation of Transcultural Positionality in Achy Obejas's *Days of Awe,*" *Arizona Journal of Hispanic Cultural Studies* 8 (2004): 73n6.

36. Obejas, *Days of Awe,* 323.

37. Obejas, 264.

38. Obejas, 284.

39. Kevane, "Secret Jew," 108; Socoloksky, "Deconstructing," 247.

40. Goldman, "Next Year," 68.
41. Carolyn Wolfenzon, "*Days of Awe* and the Jewish Experience of a Cuban Exile: The Case of Achy Obejas," in *Hispanic Caribbean Literature of Migration*, ed. Vanessa Pérez Rosario (New York: Palgrave Macmillan, 2010), 114.
42. Kevane, "Secret Jew," 117.
43. Obejas, *Days of Awe*, 273.
44. Kevane, "Secret Jew," 114–15.
45. Kevane, 117.
46. Obejas, *Days of Awe*, 36, italics mine.
47. Obejas, 285.
48. Obejas, *Days of Awe*, 366–67.
49. Behar, *Island Called Home*, 34.
50. Bettinger-López, *Cuban-Jewish Journeys*, 82.
51. Kunin, *Juggling Identities*, 213.

Diaspora and Hybridity
Jewish American Women Write the Caribbean

Linda Weinhouse and Efraim Sicher

THIS ESSAY EXAMINES how two Jewish American writers, Achy Obejas and Alice Hoffman, use the Sephardic Caribbean experience to construct subversive postcolonial and diasporic identities. We will focus in particular on how they romanticize Sephardic history in the Caribbean and ask to what extent this opens fixed categories and engages with postcolonial narratives. Obejas and Hoffman raise issues that are common to Caribbean literature, such as creolization and hybridity, and they uncover passions and family secrets from the past that subvert myths of lineage and heritage. Like Caribbean writers including the émigré Marie Vieux-Chauvet in *Love, Anger, Madness: A Haitian Trilogy* (1968), they look at a fictionalized family history of repressed desire and secrets that connects gender, class, and race in a society that has been slow to emerge from the rule of patrimony and racialization.[1] The mixed racial, sexual, and religious identities of Jewish or crypto-Jewish protagonists offer these contemporary American Jewish women writers the opportunity to work through topical issues of multiethnic identities and feminism. Their strong female protagonists search for their roots and their ancestors, reflecting a need, born of displacement and a feeling of loss of the past, to return to "imaginary homelands." In his well-known essay "Imaginary Homelands," Salman Rushdie tells us he can only return to his native India vicariously or as a stranger, knowing the provisional nature of all truths, including truths about place.[2] In the novels to be discussed in this essay, these homelands are never the original homes of ancestors, in Spain or the ancient Jewish homeland in the land of Israel, but, rather, the diaspora countries to which their ancestors fled and found temporary havens.

In American Cuban writer Achy Obejas's *Days of Awe* (2001), also discussed by Leonard Stein in the present volume, Alejandra returns to Cuba in body and imagination to discover (like Rushdie) the discontinuity between who she is and who she might have been. She is a foreigner coming home, but she constantly repositions herself with regard to history and family secrets.³ Similarly, in *The Marriage of Opposites* (2015), the popular American author Alice Hoffman's novel about a nineteenth-century Jewish woman's life in the Caribbean, Rachel, in her "return" to France (a country she never previously visited), writes herself into history as the mother of the Caribbean-born Impressionist painter Camille Pissarro.⁴ In both novels, a woman with a *Converso* or crypto-Jewish background imagines a return to a land where she lived vicariously before actually going there. While the perspective of American Cuban lesbian writer Obejas differs from that of the American popular novelist Hoffman, both address multiple Jewish identities in the context of a burgeoning multiethnic and transnational American literature that bridges English and Spanish and crosses ethnic and gender boundaries.⁵

Obejas and Hoffman seem to be unconsciously following in their imagination intrepid early modern Jewish women who tackled on their own terms the challenges of evading the Inquisition in a dangerous world of intrigue and pirates, such as the legendary Beatrice de la Luna (better known as Doña Gracia Nasi Mendes), a Portuguese *Conversa* woman who managed trade and escape routes for Jews in the sixteenth century. Her contemporary counterparts in the two novels discussed in this essay take control of their lives despite cultural and religious pressure to conform to societal or communal expectations. Their journeys engage with the postcolonial issues of migration, hybridity, and diaspora and posit transitional spaces as surrogate lost homelands, presenting de-essentialized or multiple identities within a globalized network of ethnic, racial, and sexual identities. Their appropriation of the Sephardic past, or, more precisely, Sephardism, the use of Spanish Jewish history in the modern literary imagination and in cultural discourse, conjures up associations of the double identities of Jewish *Conversos,* who converted to Christianity but practiced Jewish or crypto-Judaic rituals in secret.⁶ Since the nineteenth century, Sephardism has carried with it the romance of martyrdom and noble birth (far superior to the poverty of east European Jewish peddlers and moneylenders), but also an idealized multicultural symbiosis in medieval Al-Andalus. This may explain the themes in the works we will discuss of transmission of a mystical religion and hidden identities. The trend of historical novels by women (e.g., Naomi Ragen and Rachel Kadish) to romanticize Sephardi Jewish history imagines empowered females in times of upheaval and migration who act out a wish for intellectual or sexual empowerment in contemporary Judaism. While referencing a real historical past of Jews in the Caribbean, both Obejas and Hoffman embellish it with fantasy and resist the familiar narrative of the return of the Jewish people to its homeland in Israel, preferring the postcolonial story of a diasporic people in global migration that settles in various lands where it adopts hybrid identities. The allure of Sephardism in the narratives of uprootedness and exile opens up (rather than collapses) diverse ethnic, gender, and sexual heterogeneity that are characteristic of diaspora Jewishness, but also of postmodern and postcolonial multiple or hybrid identities. Moreover, shifting the familiar Eurocentric axis of Jewish history to the Atlantic gives a different perspective on the identities of Caribbean and Latin American Jews and on their roles in the local as well as global economy and culture.[7]

The notion of diaspora in its Caribbean setting has been defined by sociologist Stuart Hall as a metaphorical term for cultural identity that does not depend on a fixed notion of return or on exclusionary claims to place. For Hall, this is quite different from a more conservative notion of diaspora and ethnicity that he associates with Zionism. Diaspora, for Hall, begins with the construction of Caribbean cultural identity, along with the African and French presence, in the terra incognita of the Americas. Diaspora is defined here by a "recognition of a necessary heterogeneity and diversity; by a conception of 'identity' which lives with and through, not despite, difference; by *hybridity*."[8] Because Caribbeans creolized the dominant colonial and African languages and cultures, constantly transforming and mixing hybrid identities, the Caribbean became a site of a narrative of displacement, rather than one of belonging, and therefore, as Hall explains, "gives rise to a certain imaginary plenitude, recreating an endless desire to return to 'lost origins,' an unrequited and unfulfillable desire (like the imaginary in Lacan) to return to the mother or nostalgia for some beginning, and thus the infinitely renewable source of memory and desire, search and discovery."[9] Sarah Phillips Casteel, in her study *Calypso Jews: Jewishness in the Caribbean Literary Imagination* (2016), has attempted, for her part, to show that Jewish history in the Caribbean demonstrates parallels and cultural intersections between Hispanics, Blacks, and Jews that question whether lost origins can ever be found.[10]

Imagined Embodied and Spiritual Homelands

The *Conversos* who fled Spain and Portugal found that the Inquisition caught up with them in the New World; some managed to escape from discriminatory regulations to the relatively benign colonial rule of the Dutch, British, or Danish in the Caribbean, where they were welcome as entrepreneurs, middlemen, and even plantation owners.¹¹ In Cuba, Jews who arrived at the turn of the twentieth century or in the 1920s, after the gates closed in the United States, fled again, many to Miami, when communism threatened their livelihoods. Alejandra, the narrator of Obejas's *Days of Awe*, was born in Cuba on the day of Castro's takeover in 1959, so that she is quite literally a child of the revolution, yet for her revolution means the will to fulfill insatiable desires so that it is always ongoing and can never be completed. Whisked away to the States by her parents when she was only two, she yearns for the island of her birth beyond the barrier of the US embargo and finds a way to return to Cuba by working as an interpreter. Her hopes in the revolution—or, rather, in revolution as such—remain undeterred by the daily hardships suffered by Cubans under the communist regime. Growing up in Chicago, she dreams of her former home in Cuba, and when she visits the island she sees for the first time the places that had such a strong hold on her imagination. As we will see, the return to the imagined homeland is coupled with the complex hybridity of Alejandra's ethnic and sexual identities, which are never stable or exactly what they seem. In her writing, Obejas often aligns multiple ethnic and sexual identities with global migration and with the revelation of hidden origins, as in her novel *Ruins* (2009), about a Cuban man with secret crypto-Jewish lineage. We cannot disconnect either ethnicity or sexuality from history. The bodily contiguity of Alejandra's sexuality with Cuban history repeats itself throughout *Days of Awe*. In one example, when staying at a Caribbean tourist hotel, she has sex with Roberto, her Cuban lover, who fancies himself as something of a stud, then mounts him in a scene that merges with the image on the TV screen of the mass exodus from Cuba during the Special Period in 1994. She rides him as if she too were navigating an unsteady boat among the sea of swimming brown bodies fleeing Havana, reenacting her family's escape with Johnny to Miami, but also reimmersing herself in the body of Cuba: "Then I tugged at him hard, as if he were an unreliable, rebellious sloop while, on the TV screen behind my back, Havana continued to flow into the sea."¹²

In her fragmented narrative Alejandra hears stories about her family from others, mingled with her own imaginings, and discovers a number of secrets about her crypto-Jewish father. In her description of her struggle for life after a difficult birth, she imagines him whispering a Hebrew incantation, "the candle of God is the soul of man," a verse from Proverbs (20:27) referring to the memorial candle lit for the dead, while (in typical *Converso* fashion) he mouths a Catholic prayer, whereas her mother lights a candle to her pantheon of pagan and Catholic idols.¹³ Her father Enrique

San José's family memory of the Spanish Inquisition, which persecuted the *Conversos* who had fled to the Americas, has ingrained in him instinctive habits of fear and concealment. He is embarrassed when he is forced to admit he is Jewish and, until he is on his deathbed, only acknowledges the fact to Alejandra furtively or indirectly. He has nevertheless been initiated into Judaism by his grandfather Ytzak Garazi, who ran away with him to Havana and brought him to the city's Chevet Ajim synagogue. His parents Luis and Sima, however, were (according to Alejandra) "more secret assimilationists than clandestine Jews," who wanted to be Cuban, not to be believing Catholics, but to be like everyone else, to speak Spanish and forget they ever knew Ladino or Hebrew, to be rooted in the land in which their family lived for four hundred years.[14] They were horrified by Ytzak's open performance of Jewish rituals and his pride in Jewish history, but trapped by their fears, they were forced into secrecy about the Jewishness from which they were alienated.[15]

Enrique defies Nazi sympathizers, sustaining physical blows, and is ashamed that on another occasion he denied his Jewish identity when, out of fear, he raised his arm in a Heil Hitler salute. He nevertheless wishes to abnegate his Jewish heritage because it brought nothing but persecution and disaster, yet he had to admit he was a Jew when he met the young Fidel Castro, then a wealthy factory-owner's son, who examined his circumcised penis with curiosity.[16] Concealment, therefore, resulted from the embarrassment and pain of revealing who he really was. In revealing his concealment, Alejandra's narration reveals her own concealed identities.

Jewishness in Obejas's novel is a somatic marker of suffering and martyrdom, in a romanticization of Sephardim that was common in the nineteenth century and was associated with a hidden but noble lineage.[17] Enrique's hidden Jewish identity is defiantly Sephardic, and when, on his deathbed, Enrique asks Alejandra to wrap him in his phylacteries (*tefilin*), he abjures the Ashkenazic rituals. Her mother is more of an "open book" and brings a priest to administer the last rites, much to Alejandra's dismay and resentment as the one to whom Enrique symbolically transmitted his hidden Jewishness. The Marrano, whose many disguises and habitual concealment of split identities makes him postmodern avant la lettre, becomes a trope for fluid definitions of "Jewishness," including the proposition that Cubans themselves are vicarious "Jews." The idea that Cubans are somehow themselves "Jews" is one that Alejandra takes up in her definition of indigeneity. She postulates one theory that the original natives of Cuba and the Americas were descendants of Israel's lost tribes, who were rooted to the earth and the spirits, living in harmony with nature, in an idyllic Garden of Eden.[18] This theory of the Judaic origins of primitive tribes, popular in the Enlightenment, asserted that colonized peoples were either latent Christians or ripe for conversion because of their innate spirituality. Here the remnants of a fossilized Judaism serve to support a New Age bricolage of deities and spirits. Enrique's friend Moisés, who never left the island, still lives there with his wife, Ester, his son, Ernesto, his daughter, Angela, and her husband, Orlando; he believes that, given the intermingling of blood, every Cuban is an unwitting Jew, part of a divine plan of redemption, which he understands in terms of a Marxist revolution (a variation on the popular idea that Jewishness is embodied in revolution, above all in Cuba).[19]

A second theory, to which Deborah, Orlando's artist daughter, subscribes, goes back to the converted Jews (*anusim*) who fled Spain with Columbus and settled in the New World, sowing a seed of resistance through the generations in the preservation of their clandestine traditions. Deborah has tattooed the Hebrew letter *aleph* on her hand as a mark of her bodily shame as well as the perversity of her origins. This too fits Alejandra's theory of revolution as a persistent resistance to the reigning dogmas and could be understood figuratively in the sense that a *Converso* status represents a form of otherness, even after crypto-Jews have come out openly as Jews, as Ytzak and Sima do when they proudly attend synagogue. According to this logic, Castro himself is something of a Jew because he is not baptized and is a rebel.

A third theory, more common and less romantic, has it that Jews came to Cuba in the nineteenth century with the wave of immigrants from Europe, poor and desperate Ashkenazim, but among them descendants of *Conversos,* such as, purportedly, Castro's paternal grandfather.[20] The first two theories of origins help explain Alejandra's instinctive yearning for the island of her birth as a place of primal origins that preserves its Jewish roots through miscegenation and through the repressed Indigenous culture, in which Alejandra finds affinities with Jewish practice.[21] Racial mixing is one more element in the hybrid mixture of cultures, religions, and languages in Alejandra's postmodern makeup. But it also gives support to the affinity of Cubans with Jews. The Cubans of Miami Beach are in fact called by other Latin Americans (with anti-Semitic intent) the "Jews of the Caribbean" because, like Jews, their business acumen is perceived as greedy and covetous, a badge Cubans wear with pride.[22]

Alejandra's exploration of Cuba, real and imagined, reveals not just her father's secret religious practices, but also her own sexual and gender orientations. In a series of mirrored scenes of voyeurism, Alejandra peeps at the beautiful Celina enjoying oral sex with Orlando, and she is also watched having sex with Seth by Félix after she arouses him by telling him about Celina, with whom she is infatuated; later she has sex with Orlando. Her bisexuality opens up possibilities for her de-essentialized sense of Jewishness in the fluidity of her identities: she states she can be anything and anyone she wants, man or woman.[23] Yet, at one point, when challenged by missionaries at an airport, she declares she is a Jew—a statement of identification with her persecuted people rather than a description of her observance of the traditions of Judaism, with which she is barely familiar beyond the annual gathering of friends at the seder table (never at her family's house). "Who am I in all this?" Alejandra asks, answering that she is "a stranger, out of place as a whale whimpering on a shore, a lute, a hairless native pretending to live free," heir to her father's legacy of exodus and mystery, but also to her mother's veneration of the Madonna.[24] She cannot be sure she shares her father's faith in the hidden God to whom he prays clandestinely on Friday evenings. She thinks of herself naked of identity, as in "The Emperor's New Clothes," wondering who will love her now.[25] Her exposure of who she might be reveals a tangle of contradictions of her hybrid selves.[26]

Growing up in America, Alejandra walks around with a map of Cuba in her head, but when she arrives in her native country she feels "nothing, absolutely nothing, but the slightest shiver of an echo from a bottomless pit."[27] Her job as an interpreter for an American delegation of political activists gives her the advantages of the outsider, yet it puts her in the situation of being invisible, with no words of her own in her country of origin.[28] Nevertheless, unlike English, Spanish has a subjunctive voice that allows Alejandra to dream herself into the possibilities of what might have been and to enter the homes of her parents' close friends as one of the family, although she has never met them before. Now she hears for the first time the stories of which her parents are a part. Her pilgrimage ought to be a journey of self-discovery, but, as Dara E. Goldman argues, the paradoxical narrative strategies create instead a series of displacements, beginning with the displacement of language in translation itself.[29] Translation from Spanish is for Enrique a "spiritual return" to Spain, although he has never been there, and he dreams of the Spanish heaven (*cielo*) as a linguistic as well as cultural homeland that can never be properly translated or converted into English.[30] Alejandra imagines him being drawn to Ladino or to the Hebrew verse of the medieval Spanish-Jewish Hebrew poet Yehuda Halevi as a way of living out the state of exile, always dreaming of returning to a land (an "imaginary homeland") one has never visited. Significantly, Enrique hands over his translation project of an erotic Cuban novel to Alejandra, who has hitherto only taken on the job of interpreter. Alejandra discovers that as an interpreter she can observe local life as an outsider, which allows her to play out her fantasies and explore her desires without the risks of being involved emotionally or politically. As a translator, however, she has to convert one culture into another and face her own position as mediator.

Alejandra's rebelliousness crosses boundaries of gender and sexuality, but also blurs ethnic categories. Compared with her lesbian partner, Leni, she thinks she is more authentically "Jewish" because she does not deny the contradictions in her multiple identities. Then again, Alejandra can be caught in a dubious and ambivalent position, as when she shares the predatory gaze of the youths abusing her own father, who is praying in his *tefilin,* unaware of being seen. Alejandra finds herself on the wrong side of the divide between a cruel, hostile world and the hiding place of the secret Jew, feeling in her body all the pain and blood of the vulnerable victim as she observes the glass from the window smashed by her friend shattering onto her father.[31]

These tensions play out in the climax of Alejandra's last visit to Havana, when she comes to some kind of closure by scattering her father's ashes in Cuban waters (his own "Zion"). Her recitation of a poem by Yehuda Halevi, "On the Sea," serves as a surrogate *kaddish* and offers a revisionist rereading of Halevi, as if the spirit of exile and wandering the sea was the essence of diasporic Judaism. Halevi's yearning for Zion, it should be remembered, was realized by his departure from Spain for the Holy Land, although he apparently never reached his destination. Indeed, Alejandra expresses the wish of her grandparents Luis and Sima to feel settled in Havana, not a paradisiacal Seville, by substituting Halevi, whose feet were in Spain and whose heart was in Jerusalem, with Cuban national hero and poet José Martí.[32] On this visit Alejandra stays with Moisés's family for the Jewish New Year and Day of Atonement (Yom Kippur)—the Days of Awe, or *yamim noraim* of the book's title. Obejas translates awe (reverent fear) as wonder and mistakenly ascribes the term to the Days of Penitence between the New Year and Day of Atonement, thus perversely reinterpreting the meaning in Judaism of the phrase for the days of judgment and self-reckoning: "But in Cuba all element of wonder is erased, giving way to fatalism and error. In Cuba, the holiest days in the Jewish calendar are called *los días terribles*—the terrible days."[33] The translation into Spanish converts Judaic concepts into local conditions of unending and unredemptive survival on a daily basis, which corresponds to Alejandra's own perseverance in attempting to realize her insatiable desires. Staying up late (*trasnochar*) in the feverish heat, wishing the beautiful Celina would come to her and listening to lovers copulating, Alejandra feels in her overheated and aroused daze at one with the night life of her country: "In my country the sidereal clock is backward," she observes and quotes José Martí's lines about Cuba and the night being his two homelands.[34] This is when Alejandra learns about the nonconformist Deborah's protest performance of descending from the cathedral roof draped only in a Cuban flag, which she dropped to expose her naked body, thus challenging the institutionalization of national identity in monuments and fixed categories (reminding us of the Cuban performance artist Ana Mendieta). This brings us back to Hall's notion of diaspora as state of mind, not a return to an ancestral homeland, but which here characterizes the hybrid identity of a figurative "Maranno," whose identity is always concealed in order to be revealed. That diasporist vision looks to hybrid sexual, religious, and ethnic identities in the Caribbean.

Returning to Imaginary Homelands

In Hoffman's historical novel *The Marriage of Opposites,* Rachel seems just as willful and rebellious as Alejandra in *Days of Awe*. Rachel has been brought up by her father, Moses Monsanto Pomié, a wealthy Sephardi Jewish businessman, on the Caribbean island of St. Thomas (in the Danish West Indies, now the US Virgin Islands), to read and take interest in business matters, to go beyond the domestic duties of a middle-class European woman in the early nineteenth century. Rachel proclaims that from her childhood, "I rarely did as I was told."[35] Her father says she thinks like a man.[36] She departs from the expectations for young women of the Jewish community of the island, but cannot escape her life as a nineteenth-century woman without legal rights. When widowed and free she is more trapped than ever. She defies laws and strict morality, furious that she is powerless as a woman, and refuses to stick to her needlework and childcare while the world makes decisions about her life. When her father dies, Rachel takes up a shovel to participate in covering the coffin with earth, a ritual usually only performed by men, and comments, "In so many ways I was my father's son."[37] She identifies with her father rather than her strict, overbearing mother and receives her education in her father's library, where he teaches her Spanish, Hebrew, and Danish, in addition to the French she speaks with a Creole accent.

Rachel is nevertheless expected to marry a man of her father's choice, Isaac Petit, a trading partner with whom an alliance is a matter of commercial considerations. Thinking that she can manage him, she agrees to marry Monsieur Petit, a widower with children, who is much older than she is. However, she cannot make any decisions against her husband's wishes, and the business acumen she has picked up from her father's ledgers is to no avail when her husband dies and both her father's inheritance and her own family's assets pass to her husband's relatives in France, leaving her helpless with seven children to support, a situation that was not unusual for this time. We can see this predicament in real life in the personal correspondence of Grace Cardoze, who lived on St. Thomas in the second half of the nineteenth century, which testifies to the trials and tribulations of a woman managing a family on her own and facing financial setbacks as well as bereavement, but never losing her faith, despite her husband's infidelity.[38] Unlike Grace, however, Rachel makes her own choice of partner when she remarries, ignoring rules and laws.

Hoffman's narrative of descendants of *Conversos* imaginatively retells the life of Rachel Monsanto Pomié Petit Pizzarro, the mother of Camille Pissarro. Hoffman picks up the story where the family has escaped from a slave revolt inspired by the French Revolution on another island and her father's life has been saved by a devoted slave, whom he frees as a reward. Rachel harbors thoughts of revolt against the strict marriage rules of both her society and her tiny Jewish community. Similar to Alejandra, Rachel is consumed by unnamable longings: she is drawn to the Indigenous spirits and exotic landscape of the tropical island, yet wants to go to France. She dreams of waking up in a bed in rainy Paris, although she never previously visited France, her family's first country of residence after fleeing the Spanish Inquisition, a country which she knew about only from fashion catalogs and her father's books.

Although *The Marriage of Opposites,* in common with *Days of Awe,* reveals concealed family secrets, it deconstructs the standard narrative of the journey toward uncovering a Jewish past. The Jewish characters in *The Marriage of Opposites* do not hide their *Converso* heritage: they are proud of it and determined to maintain their Jewish identities whatever disaster and distress may threaten them in their centuries-long persecution and wandering. There are, however, interracial couplings in the novel that are known but not talked about. In reality, illicit relationships in the Caribbean (e.g., in Jamaica and Barbados) between Sephardim (mostly men) with local women (mostly but not only Black) were well known, and the illicit offspring were sometimes acknowledged in wills and manumission documents (some were baptized, others brought up as Jews).[39] Hoffman pursues a multiethnic agenda when Rachel thinks of members of her community who are said to have fathered children with local Black women (like Nathan Levy), little suspecting how close to her life such secrets might come. The "marriage of opposites"—a term in alchemy—joins together disparate elements and produces a new, hybrid culture, but leaves traces in the illegitimate children nobody wishes to talk about.

Rachel herself defies the leaders of the Jewish community to marry her late husband's nephew, Frédéric Pizzarro, the representative of Isaac Petit's family who comes from France to take over the business and her property after her husband's death. Their marriage is refused sanctification on the grounds that it is incestuous, and Rachel is condemned for seducing a younger man, but the couple ignores the universal disapproval of their family and community. Only much later are they reconciled with the synagogue and its members.[40] When Rachel steals into the synagogue to inscribe her son's name in the official records, she discovers the deletions and cover-ups in the birth registry that reveal the hypocrisy of the community. Rachel is treated as a whore and loses her faith out of bitterness and anger at the injustice she now sees all around her. When Frédéric, a proud Sephardic Jew also of *Converso* origins, prays in the garden or on the synagogue doorstep, this is because for so long the community ostracized him, not because of any fear of persecution.[41] Yet Rachel herself pleads with her son Camille (who much later changes the spelling of his family name to Pissarro) not to marry a Catholic because, she says, "our people have struggled in order to survive, that is why we band together and why it is a sin to marry outside our faith."[42]

As in Obejas's novel, the sense of Jewishness as a survivalist creed is bound to a history of suffering, but Jewish identity is shown through the revelations of miscegenation in *The Marriage of Opposites* to be a social construct of dubious origins. In the general population of the island, the rules forbidding interracial relationships are honored mostly in the breach, for many of the islanders "didn't have fathers, or at least not the ones they knew. Those of mixed blood who had white fathers were given their freedom, even when a man was not cited by name, and people of mixed race accounted for more than half the population of color."[43]

What is revealed in *The Marriage of Opposites* is not any crypto-Jewish ritual or double identity, but interracial mixing among prominent members of the Jewish community. In the course of the novel, Rachel discovers that Jestine, the daughter of their African maid, Adelle, who is her closest friend and soulmate, is also most likely her half-sister, the daughter of a hidden liaison between her beloved father and Adelle, to whom Rachel's father secretly sent monthly stipends. Another example in her own home is Rachel's cousin Aaron, who was raised in her household and is not allowed to marry Jestine, with whom he fathers a child, but whom he spurns when he returns (after the death of Rachel's father) with his French Jewish wife, Elise, a spoiled wealthy beauty. Elise abducts and forcibly adopts Aaron's child, and we are told that this behavior is what local Blacks expect from Jews, who are whites slightly lower in the social pecking order than Europeans, with fewer rights but perceived as part of the established hierarchy: Jestine tells Rachel, "You people always get what you want."[44] Jestine and Rachel can do nothing to prevent the childless Elise from having her way. Bringing up one's husband's illegitimate Caribbean child is not shameful, but simply not spoken of. Aaron himself is revealed to be the child of Mrs. Halevy's daughter and an African sailor. Ironically, throughout her life Mrs. Halevy is the staunchest enforcer of the rules of the Jewish community and Rachel's nemesis. Rachel thus forms her identity against a backdrop of widespread mixing of the races and faiths that evolve into hybrid identities.

Creolization among Caribbean Jews is shown to arise not just from racial mixing but also from cultural contact. Rachel gravitates toward Adelle, who is "known for having the gift of sight" and collects the folk stories and superstitions of the women in the market in a notebook that she keeps hidden from her mother.[45] She regularly runs down to the beach with Jestine to look for the legendary women-turtles, creatures that might seem to the modern reader emblematic of women trapped in their shells, like Rachel. Female sea-turtles do migrate across oceans and return to the same beach to nest and give birth. In Hoffman's imagination they are seductive, empowered females divided between the human and submarine worlds, driven by the urge to return to the sea. Hoffman seems to be echoing the spiritual hybridity of New Age religions of the twenty-first century that look back to Caribbean and African spiritualism when she has Rachel declare, "I chanted the prayers of my own faith, but I remained interested in the spirit world. I knew that our people once believed in seers and signs."[46] This misperception of Judaism as an occult belief system reveals Rachel's affinity with local religions which creolized Christianity and mixed Catholicism with a potent pantheism of gods and spirits (particularly Santería), in recognition of a deity so powerful, as Stuart Hall notes, that it could be found in a proliferation of manifestations in the natural and social world.⁴⁷ Although as a member of a privileged family she does not need to do menial tasks, Rachel willingly undertakes the slaughter of the chickens for the Sabbath meal, feeling the quivering heart of the living creature and thrilled by its blood, which recalls the rite of slaughtering a chicken (*kaparot*) on the eve of the Day of Atonement, considered by locals in *Days of Awe* as a Santería rite.⁴⁸

Not only is Rachel attracted to African diaspora religions, but she identifies her Jewishness with the hybrid history of the island. She describes the way in which Jews are viewed as "mysterious beings," and some Christians whispered they were like "shadows, able to slip through a net like fish," just as in *Days of Awe* Jews are likened to flightless birds, always wandering but never settling for longer than they feel safe, though here this sense of a precarious existence is given a spiritual dimension.⁴⁹ The religious life of the Jewish community on St. Thomas is bound up with its history of wandering. When they rebuild the synagogue after several fires, they build it fireproof and hurricane-proof, but they maintain a tradition of sand floors to "remind the congregation of the sand floors that had muffled steps when they prayed in secret."⁵⁰ This popular tradition explains the practice (kept in only five synagogues, one in Amsterdam and four others in the Caribbean, including the one on St. Thomas) as a sign of the perpetual fear of discovery and the need for secrecy, even when Jews could later pray openly.⁵¹ The Jews' diasporic existence is not only marked by a collective memory of wandering and persecution, but by hybridization, as Jews carried with them the cultures and cuisine of the countries their ancestors had lived in: "We were called Creoles, Europeans who had never been in Europe. Jews who hadn't stopped running from persecution until we came here. Yet we still cooked our food in the French way; we added olives and chives and caperberries, in the old Spanish style. We carried our pasts with us. Perhaps that was what made us appear to be shadows, the burden carried with us, the other lives we might have led."⁵²

In a parallel to Obejas's ascribing Indigenous roots to Cuban Jews, Rachel sees the wanderings of the Jews as analogous to the Caribs' beliefs about their own origins: "The native people, called the Caribs, believed their ancestors journeyed to this island from the moon; having seen the dull earth they'd come to give it light. . . . But the Caribs' ancestors were trapped here by storms and had no choice but to stay in a place where they never belonged."⁵³ Though Rachel is born on the island, like the Caribs, who believe they came from elsewhere and were trapped on the island, she never views it as her real home. She too feels trapped on the island, "much like the people who had come across the sky and could do nothing more than stare at the moon through the vast distance."⁵⁴ The heat of the island makes Rachel want to step out of her clothes "and dive into another life, one where there were linden trees and green lawns, where women wore black silk dresses and crinolines that rustled when they walked, a country where the moon rose like a silver disc into a cold, clear sky."⁵⁵ Rachel is thus a kind of wandering spirit herself: in the opening chapter, "We Followed the Turtles," whose title refers to the migration of sea-turtles and Jews, she relates the history of the Jews expelled from Spain on the Ninth of Av "the worst day in the history of our people," and of those who converted and came to Latin America.⁵⁶ Yet, in seeking her imaginary homeland, she turns her back on the ancient homeland of the Jewish people where the Temple stood, as well as other countries where the *Conversos* fled, such as Mexico, Brazil, and Saint-Domingue. She identifies with France, a land of refuge where her grandparents sojourned only briefly and in which her father never lived. She memorizes maps of Paris she finds in her father's library and comes to believe that it is the place where "everything beautiful began and ended."⁵⁷ Nonetheless, the France she creates in her mind turns out later to be an illusion, for Haussmann's reconstruction of Paris from 1853 under Napoleon III made the city "a mystery, replacing my father's maps with a new and gorgeous vision."⁵⁸

A central symbol in *The Marriage of Opposites* is the apple tree transported from France, where Rachel's ancestors had gone after leaving Spain and Portugal, seeking an elusive freedom that sent them and their apple seedling to the paradise of St. Thomas. The apple becomes for Rachel a talisman, a charm that accompanies her in her struggle with grief and suffering. Yet, although Rachel's father declares he will never travel again after reaching St. Thomas, Rachel dreams throughout the narrative of returning to the temporary refuge her grandparents found in France, home of the apple from which her family got its name, Pomié. The apple tree transplants the knowledge of mixed origins, for it turns out to have been a gift from Rachel's father to Adelle. It is also a symbol of displacement, as it is a tree that does not grow well in the tropics and never grows large in the ceramic pot in the courtyard. For Rachel, it is a fruit from the paradise she imagines for herself, where she truly belongs; throughout her life she dreams "of another country and another life, the yearning that unsettled you and made your waking existence difficult to get through."⁵⁹ Yet, predictably, once in France, Rachel sometimes "longed for the brilliant sunlight" she had always despised.⁶⁰ When her husband dies in France she dreams that she could go back in time: "The place I'd always hated, I longed for desperately now."⁶¹

Rachel is never fully reconciled to her son Camille's relationship with a Catholic servant girl, Julie, but the fruit in the apple orchard beside Julie's house, she believes, is a gift from God. In thinking of those apples whose taste evoked France for her and sent her seeking a new home, Rachel reveals the ways in which she remains tied to her people and the home in which she was raised: "Her God, I did not say out loud, not ours. The God that chased our people into hiding, from one country to another, in the case of my husband's family, for nearly three hundred years. I thought of the tree we had left behind in St. Thomas, the one my father had loved . . . with its twisted bark and bitter fruit, our namesake. I wondered if I had cursed myself for not bringing it with us to France. Perhaps it was fate that out of all the girls I might have hired, I chose the one who could bring me apples from Dijon."[62] The story ends shortly after the US Civil War and the abolition of slavery, concluding with an account of Camille Pissarro's defiance against established conventions of religion, class, and art: "He did not believe in our faith or God or in any God it seemed. . . . He was an anarchist and a leader of his fellow painters. . . . He grew more radical, faithful to the best interests of the workingman. . . . The established painters did not care for his work, or his politics."[63] This streak in Camille's character is seen in his affinity with working people, which is a counterpart to Rachel's own willfulness and instinctive identification with the working-class islanders. Camille rather likes the idea of growing up as an outcast, which, though he is an unbeliever, makes him feel sympathy for Jesus, whom he heard about at his missionary school. Like his mother, he does as he pleases and has a visionary eye for what lies below the surface of things. He loves his native island, but is driven by a desire to travel, and, to his surprise, he is able to fulfill his mother's dream of traveling to Paris sooner and with greater ease than she, when one day he receives the ticket that proves to be his ticket to freedom.

Camille tracks down Jestine's daughter Lydia in Paris and arranges for her to be given his painting of Jestine's house on stilts, which reawakens her dream vision of her origins and which she now realizes is her home on St. Thomas—the island from which Camille would like to escape. Thus, her imaginary homeland is the inverse of his wish to return to France, for her the land of the real, for him the land of his dreams, where he wishes to become a painter. Lydia and Camille each resist the attempts of a hypocritical society to make them something different from the Other that they are, and in both cases their outsider status grants them a visionary gift of exotic lands elsewhere. In the end, Camille Pissarro rejects the religion of his forebears, marries his mother's Catholic maid, and together with Degas and Cassat inaugurates a new revolutionary style of painting that would come to be known as Impressionism. Rachel never accepts Camille's wife, Julie, but Rachel herself all along goes against the grain in her ideas about gender and sexuality, above all in her belief that love (as Adelle tells her when she agrees to an arranged marriage) determines one's fate, not the rules of religion and society, which, in the Caribbean Jewish context, are shown to conceal hidden truths.

The Destiny of Love

The Marriage of Opposites closes with a woman-turtle landing in Paris and walking the streets, a kind of homecoming of Rachel's Caribbean spirit that signals a decision to choose the human and the destiny of love, with all its losses and a woman's struggle for survival. Throughout Hoffman's novel, this embrace of the destiny of love is linked with a belief in spirits and in hybrid religious practices, which returns us to the question with which we started: how fixed categories are opened up to hybrid identities and beliefs. Shortly before Rachel's father tells her that she will need to marry for convenience to safeguard their failing finances, Adelle tells her that nonetheless she will eventually fall in love and have many children, a prediction she repeats on her deathbed.[64] She is drawing here on the spiritualism of the "old religions" of her Christian forebears, whom she shortly joins in the African cemetery. The Indigenous belief in spirits of ancestors is assimilated to New Age spirituality, just as in *Days of Awe* native spiritualism is assimilated to multiculturalism and eroticism. Like Alejandra's scattering of her father's remains in *Days of Awe*, the spirits of the dead return to their source in nature, though they live on in dreams.

In their erotic relationships, the protagonists live out their nostalgia for a dream world or an imaginary homeland that is nevertheless real. Obejas and Hoffman opt for a cosmopolitan rootlessness that absolves Jews of any charge of essentialism or suspicion of Zionism and brings them into line with the ideological discourse of postcolonialism. The female protagonist in each of these novels embraces fluidity instead of fixed or constructed identities and rejects patriarchal norms and gender roles, while embracing a "diaspora of the mind."[65] Franz Rosenzweig, in *Der Stern der Erlösung (Star of Redemption,* 1921), saw in the extraterritoriality of the Jewish diaspora a negation of the blood ties of other nations that linked indigeneity with land and wrote that "the land is in the deepest sense its own only as land of longing, as holy land."[66] In a rather different sense, each of these novels imagines a land of longing and privileges a diasporic existence, preferring Babylon to Zion (as Obejas puts it) or dreaming of rainy Paris in *The Marriage of Opposites*.[67] Far from any wish to return to Zion, these fictional descendants of *Conversos* yearn for the unfulfillable, for desire itself.

Notes

1. On contemporary Caribbean women's writing, see Caroline Rody, *The Daughter's Return: African-American and Caribbean Women's Fictions of History* (Oxford: Oxford University Press, 2001); and Jennifer Browdy de Hernández, ed., *Women Writing Resistance: Essays on Latin America and the Caribbean* (Cambridge, MA: South End, 2003).

2. Salman Rushdie, "Imaginary Homelands," in *Imaginary Homelands: Essays and Criticism, 1981–1991* (New York: Penguin, 1992), 12–13.

3. Achy Obejas, *Days of Awe* (New York: Ballantine, 2002).

4. Alice Hoffman, *The Marriage of Opposites* (New York: Simon & Schuster, 2015). A previous fictional biography of Camille Pissarro—Irving Stone's *Depths of Glory: A Biographical Novel of Camille Pissarro* (New York: Doubleday, 1985)—does not describe Pissarro's life in the Caribbean but takes up the story with Pissarro's move to join the family in Paris. For a discussion of the significance of Pissarro's Caribbean upbringing and especially the creolized culture of Caribbean Jews, as well as for an understanding of diaspora Jewishness in his painting, see Nicholas Mirzoeff, "Pissarro's Passage: The Sensation of Caribbean Jewishness in Diaspora," in *Diaspora and Visual Culture: Representing Africans and Jews*, ed. Nicholas Mirzoeff (London: Routledge, 2000), 57–75. See also Derek Walcott's poetic biography of Pissarro, *Tiepolo's Hound* (2000).

5. On Obejas's use of Spanish, see Hana Wirth-Nesher, "'Who Put the Shma in Shmattas?': Multilingual Jewish American Writing," *MELUS* 37, no. 2 (2012): 54–56.

6. Yael Halevi Wise, ed., *Sephardism: Spanish Jewish History and the Modern Literary Imagination* (Stanford, CA: Stanford University Press, 2012).

7. See Richard L. Kagan and Philip D. Morgan, eds., *Atlantic Diasporas: Jews, Conversos, and Crypto-Jews in the Age of Mercantilism, 1500–1800* (Baltimore: Johns Hopkins University Press, 2009).

8. Stuart Hall, "Cultural Identity and Diaspora," in *Identity: Community, Culture, Difference*, ed. Jonathan Rutherford (London: Lawrence & Wishart, 1990), 235.

9. Hall, "Cultural Identity and Diaspora," 236.

10. Sarah Phillips Casteel, *Calypso Jews: Jewishness in the Caribbean Literary Imagination* (New York: Columbia University Press, 2016), 72–75, 282n6. For Casteel's application of "sephardism" to the Caribbean, see *Calypso Jews*, 35–39.

11. See *The Jews in the Caribbean,* ed. Jane S. Gerber (Oxford: Littman Library of Jewish Civilization, 2014); and Zvi Loker, *Jews in the Caribbean: Evidence on the History of the Jews in the Caribbean Zone in Colonial Times* (Jerusalem: Misgav Yerushalayim, 1991).

12. Obejas, *Days,* 230. See the chapter by Leonard Stein above in the present volume.

13. Obejas, 3–4.

14. Obejas, 119–20.

15. Obejas, 120.

16. Obejas, 136.

17. On the idealization of the Sephardic past, see Ismar Schorsch, "The Myth of Sephardic Supremacy in Nineteenth-Century Germany," in Wise, *Sephardism,* 35–57; and John M. Efron, *German Jewry and the Allure of the Sephardic* (Princeton, NJ: Princeton University Press, 2016).

18. Obejas, *Days,* 332.

19. Obejas, 332–33.

20. Obejas, 333–34.

21. Obejas, 104.

22. Obejas, 105.

23. Obejas, 237.

24. Obejas, 192.

25. Obejas, 193.

26. On Obejas's mixed feelings about her search for her Jewish roots and her use of this novel to demonstrate her inability to commit in a simple or straightforward way, see Bridget A. Kevane, *Profane and Sacred: Latino/a American Writers Reveal the Interplay of the Secular and the Religious* (Lanham, MD: Rowman & Littlefield, 2008), 105–19. See also Carolyn Wolfenzon, "*Days of Awe* and the Jewish Experience of a Cuban Exile: The Case of Achy Obejas," in *Hispanic Caribbean Literature of Migration: Narratives of Displacement,* ed. Vanessa Pérez Rosario (New York: Palgrave Macmillan, 2010), 105–18.

27. Obejas, *Days,* 75.

28. Obejas, 76. On the significance of translations and translating in the novel, see Kelli L. Johnson, "Lost in *El Olvido:* Translation and Collective Memory in Achy Obejas's *Days of Awe,*" *Bilingual Review* 27, no.1 (2003): 34–44. On translation as religious and cultural conversion, see also Maya Socolovsky, "Deconstructing a Secret History: Trace, Translation, and Crypto-Judaism in Achy Obejas' *Days of Awe,*" *Contemporary Literature* 44, no 2 (2003): 225–49.

29. Dara E. Goldman, "Next Year in the Diaspora: The Uneasy Articulation of Transcultural Positionality in Achy Obejas's *Days of Awe,*" *Arizona Journal of Hispanic Cultural Studies* 8 (2004): 63.

30. Obejas, *Days,* 91, 93.

31. Obejas, 108–9.

32. Obejas, 120.

33. Obejas, 319.
34. Obejas, 320.
35. Hoffman, *Marriage*, 1.
36. Hoffman, 162.
37. Hoffman, 74.
38. See Josette Capriles Goldish, "'My heart is grieved': Grace Cardoze—A Life Revealed Through Letters," in *The Jews of the Caribbean*, 329–39.
39. See Karl Watson, "Shifting Identities: Religion, Race, and Creolization among the Sephardi Jews of Barbados, 1654–1900," in *The Jews of the Caribbean*, 195–222; and Stanley Mirvis, "Sexuality and Sentiment: Concubinage and the Sephardi Family in Late Eighteenth-Century Jamaica," in *The Jews of the Caribbean*, 223–40.
40. Apparently, the marriage was not sanctified because the couple had bypassed the local Hebrew congregation and applied directly to the King of Denmark for a marriage license. Rachel was six months pregnant at the time, though the Danish Chief Rabbinate later confirmed the union and all the children from this relationship were entered in the synagogue birth register; there is no evidence the incident affected the family's relationship with the congregation. Moreover, cousin marriage is not considered incestuous among religious Jews and was common among the Sephardim of the Caribbean. This is one example out of many of inaccuracies or use of poetic license in this novel. See Judah M. Cohen, *Through the Sands of Time: A History of the Jewish Community of St. Thomas Virgin Islands* (Hanover, NH: University Press of New England, 2004), 39–40; and Bradd H. Boxman, *A Short History of the Hebrew Congregation of St. Thomas* (Charlotte Amalie: Hebrew Congregation of St. Thomas, 1983), 25.
41. Hoffman, *Marriage*, 169, 189, 210.
42. Hoffman, 341.
43. Hoffman, 19.
44. Hoffman, 90.
45. Hoffman, 23.
46. Hoffman, 23.
47. Hall, "Cultural Identity and Diaspora," 227.
48. Hoffman, *Marriage*, 17; *Days*, 117–18.
49. Hoffman, 16.
50. Hoffman, 78–79.
51. The reason for the sand-covered tiled floor is disputed; on the 1831 rebuilding of the synagogue, see Cohen, *Through the Sands*, 43–50.
52. Hoffman, *Marriage*, 16.
53. Hoffman, 4.
54. Hoffman, 4.
55. Hoffman, 2.
56. Hoffman, 2.
57. Hoffman, 5.

58. Hoffman, 331.
59. Hoffman, 296.
60. Hoffman, 344.
61. Hoffman, 344.
62. Hoffman, 337.
63. Hoffman, 343–53.
64. Hoffman, 24.
65. See Bryan Cheyette, *Diasporas of the Mind: Jewish and Postcolonial Writing and the Nightmare of History* (New Haven, CT: Yale University Press, 2013).
66. Franz Rosenzweig, *The Star of Redemption,* trans. Barbara E. Galli (Madison: University of Wisconsin Press, 2005), 319.
67. Obejas, *Days,* 93.

PART III

Colonialism and Caribbean Holocaust Memory

Splattering the Object
Césaire, Nazi Racism, and the Colonial

Ben Ratskoff

IN MAY 1943, Martinican writer and poet Suzanne Césaire performed a seemingly innocuous task: she requested a paper ration from Martinique's wartime Vichy regime in order to print the next issue of *Tropiques*. Founded in 1941 by Suzanne Césaire, her husband Aimé Césaire, and the pioneering Black surrealist-Marxist René Ménil, the *Tropiques* review served as a vehicle for Black surrealist poetics and anticolonial politics in Martinique until its dissolution in 1945. As European surrealists fled the continent during the years of Nazi interdiction, *Tropiques* became a central space of surrealist activity at large; and, as the implied heir of the 1932 journal *Légitime Défense,* it explored the emancipatory possibilities of surrealism for the working, colonized, and Indigenous classes. But, following the pattern of suppression that Nazi occupiers enacted against surrealist and Marxist groups across Europe, Martinique's Nazi-collaborationist governance soon collided with the dissenting Black writers and artists of *Tropiques*.[1] Lieutenant de Vaisseau Bayle, a naval officer and Vichy's chief of information services in Martinique, responded to Suzanne Césaire's request by withholding paper for publishing. He cited his "serious objections to a revolutionary, racial, and sectarian journal."[2] The Nazi occupation of hexagonal, or metropolitan, France advanced to Martinique through the very geographic circuits paved by the French colonial empire. In addition to landing scores of racist white French soldiers on the Caribbean colony, the Vichy state evidently trafficked fascist policies of censorship to it.

This episode of censorship in Martinique—withholding the very paper upon which the cohort would produce a revolutionary Black surrealist Marxism—functions as a momentary representation of the material, rather than merely conceptual, articulation of Nazism with colonialism.[3] In other words, beyond highlighting analogous practices and ideologies *between* Nazi Germany and various colonial governments, this episode shows how Nazi policy vis-à-vis political and creative dissent effected the restriction of material resources from Black writers and artists in the Caribbean. In doing so, it unearths the circuits of exploitation that sustain a *global* system of white supremacy while underscoring the colonized Caribbean as a crucial site for redressing the absence of Jews from postcolonial theory. While many scholars have done considerable work since Bryan Cheyette suggested postcolonial theory's need to incorporate "Jewish history or the history of antisemitism into an understanding of colonising Western modernity," the possibilities implied in *Tropiques,* and largely in Aimé Césaire's *Discourse on Colonialism,* advise a turn to the anticolonial and antiracist writing that anticipates postcolonial theory.[4]

In his *Multidirectional Memory,* Michael Rothberg has compellingly argued that Martinique "was by no means 'marginal' to the dramas of world history and culture in this era; rather, it offered the potential of a privileged perspective on the crosscutting events of war and colonialism."[5] This privileged perspective emerges from the geography of French empire building that, perhaps unwittingly, stages an encounter in the Caribbean between a transmuted Nazism and a formerly enslaved, colonized Black population. From their unique Antillean gaze, as Rothberg describes it, the *Tropiques* writers delivered a sardonic defense to de Vaisseau Bayle a mere two days after he expressed his objection: "We have received your indictment of Tropiques . . . 'Racists,' yes. The racism of Toussaint L'Ouverture, of Claude McKay, and of Langston Hughes—against that of Drumont and Hitler."[6] The *Tropiques* cohort comically poses the vindicationist politics and poetics of L'Ouverture, McKay, and Hughes against the violent supremacies of Édouard Drumont and Adolf Hitler.[7] In doing so, they expose how de Vaisseau Bayle, in his denunciation of the "revolutionary, racial, and sectarian journal," absurdly dislocates race from any existing structures of governance and inequality. Instead, he reduces the "racial" to a totally abstract ethnocentrism, enough to fully indict it. However, the *Tropiques* writers' rebuttal, referring to Drumont and Hitler, contextualizes racism within a contemporaneous web of colonialism, anti-Semitism, and white supremacy.

Seven years later, Aimé Césaire would publish the first version of his *Discourse on Colonialism.* An extraordinarily incisive and devastating critique of European civilization, *Discourse* radically (re)conceptualizes racism by highlighting the relation between Nazism internal to Europe and Europe's colonial projects abroad (and also by expanding upon the latent implications of the earlier confrontation with Bayle).[8] The manifesto stands out in Césaire's largely poetic and dramatic oeuvre while also recalling his earlier polemical writing for the Paris-based student journal *L'Etudiant noir*. Born in 1913 to a working-class family in Basse-Pointe, Martinique, Césaire excelled in school and, after graduating from the prestigious Lycée Schœlcher in Fort-de-France, embarked on an eight-year stay in Paris. He moved through various Black diasporic circles there, most famously with Senegalese poet Léopold Senghor and French Guyanese poet Léon Damas, before returning to Martinique in 1939 and working as a schoolteacher. By 1950, when *Discourse* was first published, Césaire had for five years been a leader in Martinique's Communist Party. While Rothberg demonstrates Césaire's interventions in the fields of memory, genocide, and trauma studies, this essay will build upon what Rothberg terms the "colonial turn in Holocaust studies" by foregrounding *Discourse*'s implications for the concept of racism.[9]

Other than Rothberg's analysis, most texts associated with this "colonial turn" do not reference Césaire, and the rare ones that do lack sustained critical engagement with *Discourse*.[10] At the same time, in postcolonial studies, Césaire's text has largely been eclipsed by those of his student Frantz Fanon, which are routinely credited with providing postcolonial theory with its origins. But *Discourse*'s particular surrealist style, based in Césaire's personal theory of poetics, along with its rhetorical figures of the *choc-en-retour* and the horticultural graft, make critical interventions in both the aforementioned fields of Holocaust and postcolonial studies by (re)aligning Nazi racism well within the scope of European colonialism. Césaire's polemical centering of European colonialism produces a conceptual model of racism informed by the modern world-system's historical coloniality yet still inclusive of Nazism; furthermore—and in contrast to the conventional discourse on racism—Césaire reads Nazism as continuous with, rather than deviant from, Western humanism and (its) coloniality.[11] In turn, he deexceptionalizes the Jewish experience of Nazism as racism's urtext while suggesting the incorporation of European Jewish history into anticolonial critique.

The Backsplash of Antinomies; the Contradictions of the Racism Concept

Césaire delivers his argument in the form of a "splattering of the object." Important for contextualizing Césaire's surrealist mode in *Discourse*, the phrase "splattering of the object" appears in a rare lecture, "Poésie et connaissance," delivered by Césaire in September 1944 at the Congress of Philosophy in Port-au-Prince, Haiti: "La connaissance poétique est celle où l'homme éclabousse l'objet de toutes ses richesses mobilisées" (Poetic knowledge is characterized by humankind splattering the object with all its mobilized richness).[12] Césaire argues that poetry accesses a knowledge external to the regime of "reflection, observation, and experiment," posing "poetic knowledge" as this alternative to the alienation and instrumentalization inherent to empirical science.[13] Poetic knowledge centers the relation between the knowing subject and the web of phenomena surrounding and intercepting him. Alienated from this networked landscape of existence, "scientific knowledge is a lion without antelopes and without zebras. It is gnawed from within. Gnawed by hunger, the hunger of feeling, the hunger of life."[14] Césaire's metaphor here emphasizes scientific knowledge's simultaneously self-constituting and self-destructive distance from the multilayered world that nourishes it.

Césaire's characterization of poetic knowledge as "humankind splattering [*éclabousse*] the object" appears as the third in the lecture's concluding list of summations. The list's concise and condensed language, reducing Césaire's winding assertions to a series of final directives, makes it difficult to decipher this third summation's practical meaning. Nonetheless, it does attempt to offer some methodological criterion for the production of poetic knowledge: that it emerges when the poet exposes and discharges the fertile depth of the object, the unities and contradictions between self, object, and world—"all its mobilized richness." Ronnie Scharfman, commenting on another comparable expression in the essay, argues that Césaire "wants to convince us that true poetry only is capable of saying both self and world, of sounding the bitter absurdity of the world, the irrationality of life, the richness of the universe, the injustice of colonial history, and the suffering of a people formerly enslaved."[15] *Éclabousser* seems an unusual verb to describe this poetic capability, suggesting a chaotic multidirectionality—to echo Rothberg's term—that exceeds any traceable, linear intention. By conjuring the complex relations between object and world and splashing them back onto the object, poetic knowledge emerges as the unpredictable backsplash of antinomies, the staining spray that results when a poet mobilizes his object's buried contradictions.

In *Discourse on Colonialism,* Césaire performs a poetic "splattering" that, in choosing European civilization as its object, enacts a politics of anticolonialism.[16] While *Discourse* does not, strictly speaking, operate in the mode of Césaire's French poetry, its fabulous rhetoric, marvelous language, and unruly structure suggest how his surrealist style bleeds across genres. Robin Kelley has labeled the *Discourse* a "poetics of anticolonialism," suggesting "it should be read as . . . perhaps even an unintended synthesis of Césaire's understanding of poetry (via Rimbaud) as revolt and his re-vision of historical materialism."[17] At a more textual level, Rothberg has demonstrated how Césaire's frequent inclusion of colonial tropes before actual citations of colonialist philosophers and administrators works as a rhetorical mimicry of peripheral colonialism's return to the metropolis.[18] In other words, Césaire stylistically performs his own argument, critiquing Western civilization by mobilizing its buried contradictions and splattering them back onto it from the position of the colonized, from the Antillean gaze. His abundant invocations of colonialist language—including extensive, direct quotations—illustrate this formal strategy by ultimately exposing the colonial rot at the core of Nazism:

> I have talked a good deal about Hitler . . .
> I cannot help thinking of one of [Hitler's] statements: "We aspire not to equality but to domination. The country of a foreign race must become once again a country of serfs, of agricultural laborers, or industrial workers." . . .
> Who is speaking? I am ashamed to say it: it is the Western *humanist*, the "idealist" philosopher. That his name is Renan is an accident.[19]

Césaire deliberately confuses the reader here, attributing a quote to the German Hitler before ironically explaining that the speaker's *actual* name is Renan. The effect displaces Hitler as the sui generis site of racist language; at the same time, Césaire calls into question the German "megalomaniac's" vaunted difference from the French "scholar" by foregrounding their sameness. Césaire's mockery comes from a (poetic) understanding of Hitler and Renan's closeness, following his specification in "Poésie et Connaissance" that "in poetic emotion nothing is ever closer to its [apparent] opposite."[20] It is Césaire's poetic knowledge, then, that here in *Discourse* exposes how France's disavowal of racism contradicts its own practices of racial domination.

Césaire's critique of the French disavowal of a pejoratively *German* racism points to the very genealogy of the racism concept, as well as French amnesia of it. For it is in France that *racism* first emerges as a conceptual term, near the turn of the twentieth century. Briefly reviewing this genealogy will help illuminate Césaire's departure from it. As the pseudo-science of race and reactionary anti-Semitism proliferated in national discourse, the concept valorized those public French intellectuals who advocated on behalf of a discrete and pure French race.[21] But, with the rise of Nazism, the French racism concept morphed into a discursive tool used to distinguish Germany's fascist nationalism from France's enlightened, liberal variety. Designating a pathological Aryan supremacy, the racism concept, as Barnor Hesse explains, "emerged and coalesced around a stigmatizing critique of Nazi Germany's racially hierarchical distinctions," and "thematically central to these analytical engagements was the contested status of race science in its idioms of Aryanism, Nordicism, and antisemitism."[22] Hesse's critical essay, "Racism's Alterity: The After-Life of Black Sociology" (2014), describes how the French racism concept transformed into a self-fashioning, nationalist imputation leveled against the nonuniversal, irrational—and thus non-French—German enemy. Notably, within this French discourse, the non-European victims of Europe's long-standing racial discourse remain outside the conceptual frame.

More specifically, this racism concept remains indifferent to the colonial subjugation of nonwhite and non-Christian populations since "the emergence of the Atlantic commercial circuit."[23] Hesse refers to these colonial histories preceding and coinciding with Nazism as "the racism concept's alterity," an erasure produced by the Western liberal definition of racism.[24] For even the early conceptualizations in Magnus Hirschfeld's *Rassismus* (1933/4) and Marie de Roux's "Le Nationalisme français" (1937) emerged as exclusive critiques of illiberal ideology and white psychology. Therefore, rather than including the colonial histories preceding and coinciding with Nazism in a global concept of white supremacy, the Western liberal definition of racism instead served to erase these histories.[25] At the same time, this definition framed an exclusive ideological play between (supposedly nonracist) liberalism and (racist) fascism within Europe. By 1942, Franz Boas's student Ruth Benedict would explicitly define racism as a dogma, to which, tellingly, African American sociologist Oliver Cox would object.[26] By the 1950s, as David Theo Goldberg explains, "Racism was formatively understood . . . as a prejudice, as an irrational premodern bias."[27] If Nazism figures as a deviant, irrational dogma in the progressive teleology of enlightened, liberal humanism, then the colonial practices of domination strikingly apposite to Nazi violence and fortified by this very humanism remain sheltered from critique. This racism concept thus prevents colonialism abroad from presenting any conceptual challenge to the liberal march of progress while at the same time segregating European Jewish victims of Nazism from any meaningful articulation with the non-European victims of Western violence. However, Césaire's Antillean gaze, determined by the Nazi occupation of a French-occupied Martinique, underscores Martinique's, and perhaps the broader Caribbean's, privileged position in unearthing the intersections of European Jewish and colonial histories.

Césaire's Jewish Question and the *Choc en Retour*

Césaire, in contrast to this conventional discourse, reads Nazism as continuous with, rather than deviant from, the historical elaboration of coloniality. He opens with a sharp accusation: "The so-called European civilization—'Western' civilization—as it has been shaped by two centuries of bourgeois rule, is incapable of solving the two major problems to which its existence has given rise: the problem of the proletariat and the colonial problem."[28] Césaire identifies here the capitalist administration shaping Western civilization—in Mignolo's terms, coloniality—as constituting these two problems. Haunting Césaire's language of problems and solutions is the Jewish problem and its (attempted) final solution; he invokes a well-worn, Euro-Christian heuristic for "handling" social difference. Noticeably, Césaire does not directly mention this most notorious Jewish problem and solution and barely seems to mention Jews in *Discourse* if at all. However, bookending this apparent silence is on the one hand Césaire's earlier reference, as part of the *Tropiques* cohort, to the quite specifically anti-Semitic Drumont and Hitler, and on the other Césaire's 1955 addition to the *Discourse* of an unequivocal comment on the "bonfires" that exterminated the Jews.[29] Rothberg suggests that one understand the 1955 addition within the context of Césaire's increasing alienation from the French Communist Party since the *Discourse*'s first publication in 1950; he shifts from the party's overwhelming universalism, subsuming historical difference, to a more multidirectional and comparatively perceptive framework for reading Western violence and genocide.[30]

Thus bookended by such references to Jews, even if marginal and indirect—and in light of the exceptional uniqueness routinely attributed to the Jewish genocide—Césaire's elision of a "Jewish problem" in *Discourse* can be read *productively*.[31] In other words, we might today read the elision as a recalibration of the Jewish genocide's predominance, a creative subordination of European Jewish history to narratives of colonialism. Certainly, the incontrovertible scope of the violence, plunder, and murder of European Jewry, as well as Césaire's earlier references to anti-Semitism and his sustained fixation on Hitler, prevent us from simply passing over Césaire's elision without pause. Likewise, by appropriating the Euro-Christian heuristic of problems and solutions and inverting it, Césaire frames Western civilization in the inquisitorial crosshairs normatively focused on Jews. Precisely through the elision of a "Jewish problem" from his accusation, Césaire implicitly assimilates

Euro-Christian anti-Judaism (and its attendant anti-Semitism and Nazism) to either the *problème du proletariat* or the *problème colonial,* or both.

How might Césaire's implicit assimilation of Euro-Christian anti-Judaism into capitalism and colonialism, or his structuring of the *problème du proletariat* and the *problème colonial* within the terms of Euro-Christian anti-Judaism, reframe Nazi racism? Césaire proposes that colonialism in Africa and Asia produces a *choc en retour,* a backlash, in which the methodical violence of the colonies returns forcefully to Europe: "Et alors, un beau jour, la bourgeoisie est réveillée par un formidable choc en retour: les gestapos s'affairent, les prisons s'emplissent, les tortionnaires inventent, raffinent, discutent autour des chevalets" (And then one fine day the bourgeoisie is awakened by a terrific boomerang effect: the gestapos are busy, the prisons fill up, the torturers standing around the racks invent, refine, discuss).[32] One cannot overlook Pinkham's peculiar translation of *choc en retour* into Hannah Arendt's terminology of "boomerang effect." When not overshadowing him entirely, Arendt's *Origins of Totalitarianism*—and, in particular, her notion of the boomerang effect—figures as a frequent companion to Césaire in discussions of race, colonialism, and Nazism.[33] But, by deploying Arendt's term, Pinkham not only forces Césaire to speak *through* Arendt but also dismisses the particular contours of Césaire's *choc en retour.*

Arendt's boomerang effect describes the journey of racist "behaviors" and "attitudes" away from their colonial site of origin: "There were, however, real and immediate boomerang effects of South Africa's race society on the behavior of European peoples: since cheap Indian and Chinese labor had been madly imported to South Africa whenever her interior supply was temporarily halted, a change of attitude toward colored people was felt immediately in Asia where, for the first time, people were treated in almost the same way as those African savages who had frightened Europeans literally out of their wits."[34] Arendt naturalizes the European treatment of "African savages," her possible irony notwithstanding; the European treatment only becomes problematic when applied to (nonsavage?) Asians. The problem, for Arendt, seems to be a confusion of racial categories rather than the categories themselves. Furthermore, Arendt admires "a sharp line between colonial methods and normal domestic policies" that, in the British case, avoided "the feared boomerang effect of imperialism upon the homeland."[35] Arendt's boomerang effect thus comes to reify a distinction between the violence of colonial subjugation and that within domestic Europe, underscoring "race society's" transgressive movement (*not* return) from the colony, through the Empire, and eventually to the metropole. If only it could be contained.

Unlike Arendt's boomerang effect, Césaire's *choc en retour* suggests less a journey through time and space than an inadvertent implosion caused by the shock of colonialism itself. It is not colonialism's sudden arrival in Europe that is problematic, as Arendt has it, but the practice of colonialism tout court. Also lost in Pinkham's translation is *choc en retour*'s suggestive allusion to a lightning bolt's return shock, the delayed electrocution of a previously charged object itself distant from the actual site of the lightning bolt's discharge.[36] It is as if the colonial violence peripheral to Europe chaotically induces the submerged violence of the European core, transforming previous anti-Judaisms and anti-Semitisms into the ordered logic of Nazism. As colonial violence suddenly ricochets, Nazi violence becomes *symptomatic* of—rather than merely comparable to—colonialism; the phenomenon of Nazi violence in Europe evidences the racial violence of the colonies, for Hitler "applied to Europe colonialist procedures which until then had been reserved exclusively for the Arabs of Algeria, the 'coolies' of India, and 'niggers' of Africa."[37] Rather than an extreme intolerance aberrant to Western liberalism, Nazism emerges seamlessly at the end of the liberal West's colonialism.

But Nazism is also present at its constitution. Interrupting European progress, Césaire frames Eurocentrism, capitalism, and liberalism—European colonialism's explosive cocktail—as Nazism's homologous antecedents: "Au bout du cul-de-sac Europe . . . il y a Hitler. Au bout du capitalisme . . . il y a Hitler. Au bout de l'humanisme formel et du renoncement philosophique, il y a Hitler" (At the end of the blind alley that is Europe . . . there is Hitler. At the end of capitalism . . . there is Hitler. At the end of formal humanism and philosophic renunciation: there is Hitler).[38] Whereas Pinkham's translation to "blind alley" illustrates an (Arendtian) unidirectional movement to Europe from the colonies, Césaire's figure of the cul-de-sac works to position Europe, rather than the colonies of "savage Africa," as the site of colonial violence. Colonialist practice external to the European continent becomes the *mediating* ground of Nazi racism, an external site of violence shocked by European colonialism but not the origin of the shock itself.

In turn, Césaire asks us to reevaluate Nazi racism's relationship to colonial governance. Addressing the transformative nexus between precolonial power relations and modernity/coloniality, Césaire describes European colonialism's production of a hybridized structure: "L'Europe colonisatrice a enté l'abus moderne sur l'antique injustice; l'odieux racisme sur la vieille inégalité" (Colonialist Europe has grafted modern abuse onto ancient injustice, hateful racism onto old inequality).[39] Césaire proposes that European colonialism grafted (*enté*) racism onto preexisting inequality. The horticultural term describes the cultivation of racism as a process of transplanting extant imbalances of power and organizations of difference. Césaire's parallel phrasing—"l'abus moderne sur l'antique injustice ; l'odieux racisme sur la vieille inégalité"—presents modern abuse and odious racism as analogous within European colonialism. This parallel suggests a conception of racism based in particularly modern forms of exploitation, refusing to reduce racism to structural inequality or ethnocentrism in an eternal sense; such a reduction would, like Arendt, naturalize the European "response" to dark Africans as merely one in a long historical list of antagonistic "encounters." Césaire reads Nazism as an iteration of colonial governance, itself a grafted structure built, perhaps, from Europe's ancient anti-Jewish animus.

Grafting Colonialism and Nazism

In order to understand Nazism's iteration of colonial governance, it becomes necessary to decipher the particularly modern forms of exploitation that define colonialism and the particular relations that colonialism enacts. Césaire discloses his association of modernity with production when he later describes—albeit in a hopeful, revolutionary tone—"the productive power of modern times."[40] However, before directing a spectral gaze toward the proletarian ownership of production, Césaire provides a detailed answer to the more fundamental question of how to describe colonial relations: "Between colonizer and colonized there is room only for forced labor, intimidation, pressure, the police, taxation, theft, rape, compulsory crops, contempt, mistrust, arrogance, self-complacency, swinishness, brainless elites, degraded masses. No human contact, but relations of domination and submission which turn the colonizing man into a classroom monitor, an army sergeant, a prison guard, a slave driver, and the indigenous man into an instrument of production."[41] If, as Césaire claims, at the end of capitalism there is Hitler, then the colonial relations of commodification too achieve a certain apotheosis in Nazism.

Returning to Césaire's horticultural figure, the relations of domination and submission that reduce the colonized to an instrument of production—"l'abus moderne," "l'odieux racisme"—graft onto "ancient injustice" and "old inequality." As a graft, Césaire describes a point of both differentiation and linkage between preexisting inequality and the modern emergence of colonial exploitation.[42] The most straightforward suggestion for the preexisting inequality seems to be class inequality, in which the exploitation of the European peasantry provided a model for new forms of exploitation in the colonized world. However, in light of our productive reading of Césaire's silences, one can also suggest colonial exploitation's relationship to another ancient injustice: Christian Europe's historical hostility to Jews. Within such a framework, the graft provides a pathway for the shock of colonial violence to induce anti-Jewish violence *in* Europe, returning to the mother plant. Nazism iterates colonial governance, but only because colonial governance is already grafted from anti-Jewish oppression.

Attention again to Pinkham's translation practice reveals how she obscures this nascent notion of articulation and its currency for theorizing the relationship between Nazism and colonialism. By translating "l'odieux racisme" as "hateful racism," Pinkham translates Césaire's condemnation—"l'odieux"—to an indictment specifically addressed to attitudes and pathologies ("hateful"). Pinkham situates Césaire safely within the conventional discourse that condemns Nazism as irrational dogma. This subtle move of refocusing the psychology of the white colonizer occurs more than once: first, when Pinkham translates colonialism's "odieuses solutions" as "hateful solutions," and, again, when she translates Césaire's description of European complicity from "tous haïssables" to "all hateful," instead of the more accurate "all detestable."[43] This latter difference in translation is nothing less than a shift from the *colonized's* indictment of "detestable" Western bourgeois society (in Césaire) to the *colonizer's* "hateful" intolerance of the colonized (in Pinkham).

A correction of Pinkham's translation underscores Césaire's actual deviation from the conventional discourse. Césaire clearly rejects the impulse to explain racism as (white) pathology. Césaire advises, "Do not seek to know whether personally these gentlemen are in good or bad faith, whether personally they have good or bad intentions. Whether personally—that is, in the private conscience of Peter or Paul—they are or are not colonialists, because the essential thing is that their highly problematical subjective good faith is entirely irrelevant to the objective social implications of the evil work they perform as watchdogs of colonialism."[44] To conceptualize racism as a set of personal, malintentioned prejudices recklessly prescribes self-control and humanist transcendence as correctives without addressing the "objective social implications" of colonial subjugation.

Césaire therefore argues that centering subjective conscience effectively ignores colonialism's primary constitution in practice and its ideological justification a posteriori. After offering his grafting metaphor, Césaire exclaims, "If I am attacked on the grounds of intent, I maintain that colonialist Europe is dishonest in trying to justify its colonizing activity *a posteriori* by the obvious material progress that has been achieved in certain fields under the colonial regime."[45] Plunder, not progress, provided the subjective field for colonial adventure, and ascribing good intent a posteriori only serves as an antihistorical deception. Characterizing this justification as dishonest, Césaire highlights the mistaken assumption of a static and an ahistorical Africa waiting for the engines of Europe. The concern for Peter or Paul's intent and the emphasis on material progress also erase continued exploitation and inequality. Attacking the characterization of Africa (and Asia) as inert, and pointing to persistent inequalities, Césaire writes, "The proof is that at present it is the indigenous peoples of Africa and Asia who are demanding schools, and colonialist Europe which refuses them; that it is the African who is asking for ports and roads, and colonialist Europe which is niggardly on this score; that it is the colonized man who wants to move forward, and the colonizer who holds things back."[46] While Césaire falls back on Eurocentric temporalities of progress and regression, as Rothberg shows, he does so polemically, as a corrective.

Césaire offers an indictment alternative to the castigation of conscience and dogma. The European bourgeois scandalized by Nazism, by the *choc en retour* of colonial violence to European shores, cannot be left to charge Europe for its crimes. Rather, Europe is charged "on a world scale, by tens and tens of millions of men who, from the depths of slavery, set themselves up as judges."[47] For the condemnation heard from the European bourgeois blindly treats Nazism (internal to Europe) as the supreme terror while simultaneously buttressing European colonialism (external to Europe). In perhaps the most important passage for reframing Nazi racism, Césaire charges, "It would be worthwhile to study clinically . . . and to reveal to the very distinguished, very humanistic, very Christian bourgeois of the twentieth century that without his being aware of it, he has a Hitler inside him, that Hitler *inhabits* him, that Hitler is his *demon*, that if he rails against him, he is being inconsistent and that, at bottom, what he cannot forgive Hitler for is the not *the crime* in itself, *the crime against man,* it is not *the humiliation of man as such,* it is the crime against the white man, the humiliation of the white man."[48] Césaire locates the origin of Hitlerian practices and ideologies within the humanist, Christian, bourgeois subject, refusing to locate their origin in the imperial "encounter" external to Europe. One can attribute the blame for Hitler neither to the frenzied violence of imperial "contact" nor the unique pathology of decidedly *German* actors. Rather, in a splattering of the object (Europe) that mobilizes its internal contradictions, Césaire shows a Hitler immanent to humanist, Christian, bourgeois Europe *in toto.*

Césaire's continual centering of Europe does not contradict his attention to colonial violence; rather, the *choc en retour* exposes the backlash, the inadvertent implosion at the site *from which* the humanist, Christian bourgeois launched his shock of colonial violence—Europe. Césaire seethes "that before [white Europeans] were its victims, they were its accomplices; that they tolerated Nazism before it was inflicted on them, that they absolved it, shut their eyes to it, legitimized it, because, until then, it had been applied only to non-European peoples; that they have cultivated Nazism, that they are responsible for it, and that before engulfing the whole edifice of Western, Christian civilization in its reddened waters, it oozes, seeps, and trickles from every crack."[49] The poison injected into the colonized world chaotically travels back through the syringe to the metropolitan heart of the colonial world-system. Césaire illustrates not merely the error but the *investment* in fixating on pathologized Aryanism, for such a fixation leaves the entire colonialist edifice out of focus and maintains the West's superior moral stance.

Still, regardless of our *productive* reading of the absence of Jews from Césaire's text, his total collapse here of Nazism's European Jewish victims into a homogenous category of white bourgeois Europeans seems to subvert his earlier intimations of a grafted articulation between Euro-Christian anti-Judaism and colonial exploitation. While this conflation remains problematic, Césaire's language claiming Europeans "have *cultivated* Nazism" (emphasis added) at the same time recalls his grafting metaphor, illustrating how the poison's backflow travels precisely by way of this cultivated articulation. Furthermore, the 1955 addition of a reference to the particularly *Jewish* extermination provides further nuance to his indictment. After burning the world over and then itself, Europe concludes—in the words of then UNESCO administrator Roger Caillois—that, on moral grounds, "no one should be exterminated." Césaire comments (in the 1955 text), "With [Caillois], the Negroes are sure that they will not be lynched; the Jews, that they will not need new bonfires. There is just one thing . . . the Negroes, Jews, and Australians owe this tolerance not to their respective merits, but to the magnanimity of M. Caillois . . . to a decree of M. Caillois's conscience."[50] The advanced morality of Europe will henceforth *tolerate* difference—Black, Jewish, and Aboriginal difference. But Europe will also once again accord itself the supreme responsibility to govern.

Whither Racism?

Weaving a surrealist web of coloniality, Césaire playfully flaunts the contradictions inherent to Western humanism, bewilderingly invokes (and conflates) colonialist and Nazi characters, and meanders fantastically between the unconscious of the bourgeois, humanist psyche and the material practices of Western geopolitics—a splattering of the object indeed. This surrealist mode in turn points to the production and circulation of Nazism internal to material colonialism as well as the European intellectual tradition. Ultimately, then, in Césaire's text, we perhaps face less a concept of racism than a network of colonial structures and practices whose violent excess enabled the chaotic backlash of Nazism, and whose own structures and practices replicate historic inequalities internal to Europe. Césaire's polemical conflation of Hitler and Renan, to take just one example, invokes a sweeping frame of modernity/coloniality inclusive of European humanism and Nazi racism. Where the concept of racism does emerge, we find a compelling theoretical model that links the colonial exploitation of modernity to older structures of domination and inequality. The metaphor of grafting suggests how old topographies of (anti-Jewish) violence and domination induced colonialism's backlash to metropolitan Europe. This conceptual model of *l'odieux racism*, informed by the material practice of colonialism rather than Nazi dogma, demonstrates Nazism's symptomatic relationship with European colonial subjugation. And Césaire's *choc en retour* clarifies how this relationship is not one of neat causality but a violent, multidirectional backlash that responds to the *choc*—the abrupt practices of domination and exploitation—launched against Africa and Asia from the heart of Europe. Nazism appears no longer aberrant to modernity/coloniality but determined by it.

While Césaire ultimately revealed a certain bankruptcy of the racism concept, accusations and designations of racism continue to flourish in both scholarly and popular discourse. This continuity coincides with a present resurgence of white nationalist politics globally, and the continued deployment today of an imputed "racism" charge recalls de Vaisseau Bayle's original indictment of *Tropiques*. The high irony of de Vaisseau Bayle's accusatory designation, a white objection to the very "invocation of race," resonates disturbingly in our present moment.[51] For one representative analogue in the contemporary French context, the Ligue Internationale Contre le Racisme et L'antisémitisme (LICRA) in May 2017 denounced Paris's militant, Afrofeminist festival Nyansapo for reserving certain festival spaces exclusively for Black women, provocatively tweeting, "#RosaParks doit se retourner dans sa tombe" (#RosaParks must be turning in her grave), and Paris mayor Anne Hidalgo threatened to ban this "festival 'interdit aux blancs'" (festival "forbidden to whites"), quoting Licra's original post. It is not coincidental that the origin of both Licra's and Hidalgo's indictments is a press release from then–Front National treasurer Wallerand de Saint-Just. De Saint-Just questioned the use of municipal buildings for an event "mettant en avant une conception ouvertement racialiste et antirépublicaine de la société" (putting forth an overtly racialist and antirepublican conception of society).[52] Captain Bayle's designation of *Tropiques* as racial and sectarian echoes alarmingly in de Saint-Just's statement.[53]

Césaire's *Discourse* thus seems, sadly, more urgent than ever. The current global revitalization of white nationalism, largely through a decentralized network of reactionary movements and internet cultures, coincides with renewed traffic in conventional Euro-Christian attacks on Jews. Surreptitious media influence, backdoor manipulation of global finance, urban-cosmopolitan degeneracy—these are well-developed tropes that are now weaponized to target Black and Brown folks, queers, immigrants, Muslims, and women. The weapon has remained the same, but the scope has widened, revealing the persistence of a submerged anti-Judaism/Semitism waiting for catalysis. Beyond theoretical or imaginative links across time and space that might read, for example, purity of blood laws, restrictive ghettoization, legal emancipation, and the expropriation of Jewish wealth by Euro-Christian regimes within the context of colonialist law, exploitation, and violence, the relatively compressed field of the French Caribbean between 1943 and 1955 provides rather literal links from which the intimacies of Jewish history and "colonising Western modernity," as Bryan Cheyette termed it, cannot be ignored.[54] In *Discourse*, Césaire's splattering of his object—l'Europe colonisatrice—exposes a colonialism immanent to anti-Jewish violence and suggests a history of anti-Judaism immanent to colonialism.

Notes

Many thanks to Barnor Hesse, Michelle Wright, Michael Rothberg, and Robin Kelley, as well as the participants of the 2017 Max and Hilde Kochmann Summer School in European-Jewish History and Culture, for the conversations, comments, and insights that have influenced this essay.

    1. David Macey describes the implications of France's defeat for the Caribbean colonies, writing, "When the Vichy government in France signed an armistice with Germany, [Admiral Georges Robert] effectively staged a coup in Martinique and established a tropical equivalent to Pétain's collaborationist regime. Wary of the possible implications of this, the United States used its naval forces to blockade the island, and at one point drew up contingency plans to invade it. Robert was obliged to disarm his ships and planes and to base his men on shore. Martinique and Fort-de-France were quite accustomed to dealing with sailors on brief periods of shore leave, but not with thousands of men based indefinitely on shore. . . . Elected black mayors and council members were removed from office and replaced by white appointees. The sailors cast off their masks and behaved, Fanon was to recall in 1955, like 'authentic racists'. Martinique had effectively been occupied, but it had been occupied by France." See David Macey, "Frantz Fanon, or the Difficulty of Being Martinican," *History Workshop Journal* 58 (August 2004): 211–23, 214. See also Kristen Stromberg Childers, "The Second World War as a Watershed in the French Caribbean," *Atlantic Studies* 9, no. 4 (2012): 409–30.

    2. Lieutenant de Vaisseau Bayle, "Lettre du Lieutenant de Vaisseau Bayle, chef du service d'information, au directeur de la revue *Tropiques*," in *Tropiques 1941–1945: Collection Complète* (Paris: Éditions Jean-Michel Place, 1978), xxxvii, my translation.

    3. Robin Kelley writes of this episode, "The official policy of the regime to censor *Tropiques* and interdict the publication when it was deemed subversive also hastened the group's radicalization. . . . The essays and poems [*Tropiques*] published by the Césaires, René Menil, and others reveal the evolution of a sophisticated anticolonial stance as well as a vision of a postcolonial future. Theirs was a conception of freedom that drew on modernism and a deep appreciation for precolonial African modes of thought and practice; it drew on surrealism as the strategy of revolution of the mind and Marxism as revolution of the productive forces." See Kelley, *Freedom Dreams: The Black Radical Imagination* (Boston: Beacon, 2002), 168–69. See also Katerina Gonzalez Seligmann, "Poetic Productions of Cultural Combat in Tropiques," *South Atlantic Quarterly* 115, no. 3 (July 2016): 495–512. My identification of the journal's Black Marxism should not refer to a harmonious relationship between the Black writers and artists of *Tropiques* and, either, the official organs of the Communist Party or Marxist thought. Rather, in the spirit of Cedric Robinson, the term reflects "the encounter of Marxism and Black radicalism, two programs for revolutionary change." See

Robinson, *Black Marxism: The Making of the Black Radical Tradition* (Chapel Hill: University of North Carolina Press, 2000), 1.

4. Bryan Cheyette, "Venetian Spaces: Old-New Literatures and the Ambivalent Uses of Jewish History," in *Reading the "New" Literatures in a Post-Colonial Era*, ed. Susheila Nasta (Cambridge: Boydell & Brewer, 2000), 53–54. Cheyette has done important work himself in this regard with respect to Fanon's oeuvre, demonstrating how Fanon "bring[s] together diasporic Jewry and the history of antisemitism with the colonial struggle and anti-Black racism." See Cheyette, "Frantz Fanon and the Black-Jewish imaginary," in *Frantz Fanon's Black Skin, White Masks: New Interdisciplinary Essays*, ed. Max Silverman (Manchester: Manchester University Press, 2005), 75.

5. Michael Rothberg, *Multidirectional Memory: Remembering the Holocaust in the Age of Decolonization* (Stanford, CA: Stanford University Press, 2009), 72.

6. Rothberg, *Multidirectional Memory*, 71; Aimé Césaire et al, "Réponse de *Tropiques*," in *Tropiques 1941–1945: Collection Complète* (Paris: Éditions Jean-Michel Place, 1978), xxxix, my translation.

7. African American scholar St. Clair Drake used the term "vindicationism" to describe a clear tradition in black writing that seeks to counter racist depictions, histories, and narratives of black people and black life while stressing black contributions to civilization. See Drake, *The Redemption of Africa and Black Religion* (Chicago: Third World, 1971).

8. Césaire was not the only black thinker exploring links between European colonialism and Nazism. Robin Kelley notes that *Discourse*'s argument was "echoed or repeated by several black intellectuals who witnessed fascism first hand, including Du Bois, C. L. R. James, George Padmore, and Oliver Cox. . . . They viewed fascism as a blood relative of slavery and imperialism, global systems rooted not only in capitalist political economy but racist ideologies that were already in place at the dawn of modernity." See Kelley, "Césaire's Lessons for the New Empire," *Black Renaissance/Renaissance Noire* 5, no. 3 (2004): 162–66. A year after Césaire first published his text, Hannah Arendt published her *Origins of Totalitarianism*, offering a comparable but certainly not identical analysis, one aspect of which will be addressed later. Arendt's own racist/colonialist assumptions, however, cloud over the work—as they would in "Reflections on Little Rock" (1959) and, peripherally, in *Eichmann in Jerusalem* (1963)—and prevent her from contributing to a concept of racism that makes room for both victims of Nazism and colonialism. See Rothberg's critique of Arendt's Eurocentrism in *Multidirectional Memory*, 39–40.

9. Rothberg, 70.

10. See, for example, A. Dirk Moses's "Empire, Colony, Genocide: Keywords and the Philosophy of History," in *Empire, Colony, Genocide: Conquest, Occupation, and Subaltern Resistance in World History*, ed. A. Dirk Moses (New York: Berghahn, 2008).

11. The concept of coloniality refers to Walter Mignolo's assertion that "colonialism is a concept that inscribes colonialism as a derivative of modernity . . . the colonial period implies that, in the Americas, colonialism ended toward the first quarter of the nineteenth century. Instead coloniality assumes, first, that coloniality constitutes modernity. As a consequence, we are still living under the same regime." Earlier, "the emergence of the commercial Atlantic circuit in the sixteenth century was the crucial moment in which modernity, coloniality, and capitalism, as we know them today, came together. Modernity/coloniality is the moment of Western history linked to the Atlantic commercial circuit, the transformation of capitalism . . . and the foundation of the modern/colonial world-system." *Coloniality*'s particular relevance here is its ability to include within its theoretical frame systems of power and social classification that technically may exceed formal colonialism's spatial and temporal limits—for example, Nazism. See Walter D. Mignolo, "The Geopolitics of Knowledge and the Colonial Difference," in *Coloniality at Large: Latin America and the Postcolonial Debate*, ed. Mabel Moraña, Enrique Dussel, and Carlos A. Jáuregui (Durham, NC: Duke University Press, 2008), 248–49. Previous to Mignolo, however, Jacques Derrida, in his *Le monolinguisme de l'autre: ou la prothèse d'origine* (1996), argued, "'Colonialism' and 'colonization' are only high points [*reliefs*] . . . the jealous rage of an essential *coloniality* and *culture*, as shown by the two names. A coloniality of culture." He later particularizes this culture, admitting, "The paths and strategies that I have had to follow in this work or passion also follow the dictates of some structures and therefore of some assignations that are internal to the Graeco-Latino-Christiano-Gallic culture to which my monolingualism forever confines me." Derrida's writing is significant here in light of Robert Young's demonstration that many of Derrida's concepts, later taken up by postcolonial theory, emerge from his minority status as an Algerian Jew. See Jacques Derrida, *Monolingualism of the Other; or, The Prosthesis of Origin*, trans. Patrick Mensah (Stanford, CA: Stanford University Press, 1998), 24, 71; and Robert J. C. Young, *Postcolonialism: An Historical Introduction* (Oxford: Blackwell, 2001), 421.

12. Aimé Césaire, "Poésie et Connaissance," in *Tropiques 1941–1945: Collection Complète* (Paris: Éditions Jean-Michel Place, 1978), 170. English translations from Aimé Césaire, "Poetry and Knowledge," trans. A. James Arnold, in *Lyric and Dramatic Poetry, 1946–82*, by Aimé Césaire, trans. Clayton Eshleman and Annette Smith (Charlottesville: University Press of Virginia, 1990), xlii–lvi.

13. Césaire, "Poésie et Connaissance," 157.

14. Césaire, 158. This assertion interprets a passage from Aldous Huxley's "One and Many."

15. Ronnie Scharfman, "Aimé Césaire: Poetry is/and Knowledge," *Research in African Literatures* 41, no. 1 (Spring 2010): 109–20, 115.

16. The importance of Césaire's style in *Discourse* cannot be overstated. As A. James Arnold has provocatively pointed out, "At exactly this time Gabriel

Marcel was writing *Man against Mass Society*, in which he dwelt on what he called the 'techniques of degradation' recently employed by the Nazis. The measured prose of the Catholic essayist could offend no right-thinking individual. Mutatis mutandis, Césaire's thesis that the exploitation of colonialism degrades the colonizer was practically identical, and it was shocking. The difference lies not in the truth of the proposition . . . but in the style." See Arnold, *Modernism and Negritude: The Politics and Poetics of Aimé Césaire* (Cambridge, MA: Harvard University Press, 1981), 177.

17. Robin D. G. Kelley, "Introduction," in *Discourse on Colonialism*, by Aimé Césaire, trans. Joan Pinkham (New York: Monthly Review, 2000), 7.

18. Rothberg, *Multidirectional Memory*, 75.

19. Césaire, *Discourse*, 37.

20. Césaire, "Poetry and Knowledge," l.

21. Pierre-André Taguieff marks this origin in his *Force of Prejudice: On Racism and Its Doubles*, trans. Hassan Melehy (Minneapolis: University of Minnesota Press, 2001).

22. Barnor Hesse, "Racism's Alterity: The After-Life of Black Sociology," in *Racism and Sociology*, ed. Wulf D. Hund and Alana Lentin (Berlin: Lit Verlag, 2014), 146.

23. Mignolo, "Geopolitics of Knowledge," 228.

24. Hesse, "Racism's Alterity," 145. Hesse clarifies, "The European political constitution of racism as an object of critique was motivated by the challenge to exempt white populations in Europe from the Nazi version of socially ordered colonial regulation, the effect of which was to sustain the normalization of western liberal-colonial forms of white domination." See Hesse, "Racism's Alterity," 150.

25. See also the appendix to George M. Frederickson's *Racism: A Short History*, which probes the historiography of white supremacy and anti-Semitism, respectively. American paradigms in sociology paralleled Hirschfeld and de Roux when their focus on "race relations" aimed at displacing the *biological* validity of racism without troubling practices and structures of colonialism abroad or at home; instead, (mostly white) academics argued over how to manage race through regulated patterns of assimilation. In other words, the notion of race as *social* construction was more a suggested shift in analytical focus rather than a critique of race itself. Robert E. Park, founder of the Chicago school of sociology, created the dominant race-relations model based on his analysis of African American migration to Chicago. For the history of this model's reproduction and transformation in the twentieth century, see Stephen Steinberg, *Race Relations: A Critique* (Stanford, CA: Stanford Social Sciences, 2007).

26. Hesse, "Racism's Alterity," 150–53.

27. David Theo Goldberg, *Racial Subjects: Writing on Race in America* (New York: Routledge, 1997), 19.

28. Césaire, *Discourse*, 31.

29. Aimé Césaire, *Discours sur le colonialisme* (Paris: Présence Africaine: 2004), 66; Césaire, *Discourse*, 72. See Rothberg, *Multidirectional Memory*, 100.

30. Rothberg, 99–100.

31. For a brief discussion of this exceptionalism as it appears in the works of Elie Wiesel, Claude Lanzmann, and Steven Katz, see Rothberg, 8.

32. Césaire, *Discours,* 13; Césaire, *Discourse,* 36.

33. Moses's article is a case in point.

34. Hannah Arendt, *The Origins of Totalitarianism* (Orlando, FL: Harcourt, 1994), 206.

35. Arendt, *Origins,* 155.

36. *Le Grand Robert de la langue français,* "choc," https://gr.bvdep.com/robert.asp (accessed June 4, 2017). Interestingly, the dictionary offers as a citation for *choc en retour* the following passage of Simone de Beauvoir's: "La plupart des gens nouveaux que j'ai rencontrés m'ont écrit parce qu'ils aimaient mes livres : les relations qui se sont créées entre nous, c'est moi qui les ai provoquées par une sorte de choc en retour." Striking in de Beauvoir's example and relevant for Césaire's usage is how *choc en retour* clearly focuses on the subject shocking—"c'est moi qui les ai provoquées"—rather than the victim shocked. In Césaire's case, Europe!

37. Césaire, *Discourse,* 36.

38. Césaire, *Discours,* 14; Césaire, *Discourse,* 37.

39. Césaire, *Discours,* 27; Césaire, *Discourse,* 45.

40. Césaire, *Discourse,* 52.

41. Césaire, 42.

42. He appears to anticipate Stuart Hall's discussion of the articulation of different modes of production and structures of dominance. See Stuart Hall, "Race, Articulation, and Societies Structured in Dominance," in *Sociological Theories: Race and Colonialism* (Paris: UNESCO, 1980), 305–45. See also Brent Hayes Edwards, *The Practice of Diaspora: Literature, Translation, and the Rise of Black Internationalism* (Cambridge, MA: Harvard University Press, 2003), 14–15. Césaire's friend and colleague Léopold Sédar Senghor also invoked the horticultural graft when describing the intrusion of French civilization into tribal governments in colonized Africa, labeling the "modification" of the "organisation politique et sociale du Négro-africain" as "LA GREFFE FRANÇAISE." See Senghor, *Liberté 1: Négritude et humanisme* (Paris: Seuil 1964), 54.

43. Literally, "hate-able." Césaire, *Discours,* 9, 39; Césaire, *Discourse,* 32, 55. Ironically, the *Grand Robert de la langue française* suggests "odieux" as a synonym for "haïssable." *Le Grand Robert de la langue français,* "haïssable," https://gr.bvdep.com/robert.asp (accessed June 4, 2017).

44. Césaire, *Discourse,* 55.

45. Césaire, 45.

46. Césaire, 46.

47. Césaire, 32.

48. Césaire, 36.

49. Césaire, 36.
50. Césaire, 72.
51. Hesse, "Racism's Alterity," 144.
52. For a summation of the tweetstorm, see Frantz Durupt, "Aux origines de la polémique sur le festival afroféministe Nyansapo," *Libération*, May 28, 2017, http://www.liberation.fr/france/2017/05/28/aux-origines-de-la-polemique-sur-le-festival-afrofeministe-nyansapo_1572874 (accessed June 1, 2017).

53. This sort of accusation of racism is hardly the exclusive property of the nationalist far-right. In April 2018, 80 prominent intellectuals published a letter in *Le Point* magazine frantically denouncing the slow influence of "decolonial thought" in French universities by circling the wagons in defense of French Republican universalism: "While presenting themselves as progressives (anti-racists, decolonizers, feminists), these [decolonial] movements have for many years diverted the struggles for individual emancipation and liberty towards objectives that oppose them and that directly attack Republican universalism: racialism, differentialism, segregationism (according to skin color, sex, and religious practice) . . . Our cultural, university, and scientific institutions (not counting our very much affected high schools) are henceforth targeted by attacks that, under the pretext of denouncing discriminations of 'colonial' origin, seek to undermine the principals of free expression and universality inherited from the Enlightenment. Conferences, exhibitions, shows, films, and 'decolonial' books that reactivate the idea of 'race' continue to exploit the guilt of some and exacerbate the resentment of others, nourishing interethnic hate and division." Those engaged in decolonial movements in France could have easily replied by resurrecting the *Tropiques* cohort's retort from nearly 80 years previous: "'Racists,' yes. The racism of Toussaint L'Ouverture, of Claude McKay, and of Langston Hughes—against that of Drumont and Hitler." See "Le 'décolonialisme,' une stratégie hégémonique : l'appel de 80 intellectuels," *Le Point*, April 12, 2018, https://www.lepoint.fr/politique/le-decolonialisme-une-strategie-hegemonique-l-appel-de-80-intellectuels-28-11-2018-2275104_20.php.

54. Cheyette, "Venetian Spaces," 54.

From Shtetl to Settler Colony and Back
André Schwarz-Bart's *The Morning Star*

Kathleen Gyssels

> Blot me from the book you have written.
> —Moses, Exodus 32:32, quoted in *The Morning Star*

IN THIS ESSAY I focus on French Jewish author André Schwarz-Bart's wanderings, which ultimately unsettled and cast adrift this bridge builder. Alongside and in tandem with his geographical and cultural migrations, André Schwarz-Bart and his Guadeloupean wife and coauthor Simone Schwarz-Bart envisioned a transnational, cross-cultural, and transatlantic literature in which the Caribbean postcolonial universe mirrored slaves' settlement zones and subsequent dispersion. While slaves should not be confused with Eastern European Jewry, in his writing Schwarz-Bart, an amateur anthropologist and etymologist, implicitly plays on the common etymology between *esclave* (French for slave) and *slav*, an ethnic marker for people who live in Eastern Europe and share the same geographic space as Jews who faced centuries of discrimination and oppression.

Schwarz-Bart's posthumously published novel *L'Etoile du matin* (2009), translated into English in 2011 as *The Morning Star*, may confuse readers because of its fragmented form and content.[1] In fact, it is hard to imagine how *The Morning Star* could differ more from Schwarz-Bart's Goncourt prize-winning novel *Le Dernier des justes* (*The Last of the Just*), which was published exactly half a century earlier, in 1959. *The Morning Star*'s fractured narrative structure emulates the displacement felt by an author torn between here and there, then and now, and between himself and his dybbuks, or the ghosts of the many friends and relatives he lost in the Holocaust and its aftermath. *The Last of the Just* pays tribute to the (just) men who helped Schwarz-Bart become a voice for the voiceless and a witness for those who disappeared in one of the most unforgettable and indescribable calamities of humankind. In contrast, *The Morning Star* exposes its author's troubled relationship with Jewishness and search for a place to call home. In these ways, *The Morning Star* operates as a kind of "circumfession," a journal of religious struggles like the one Jacques Derrida kept during the period when his mother was dying.[2]

Prominent Holocaust scholars such as Joyce Block-Lazarus have focused on Schwarz-Bart's "manipulation of time, both as a theme and a structural principle" while neglecting the spatial dimensions of his work.[3] Indeed, Bluma Finkelstein has convincingly demonstrated that spatial movements, inherent in narratives of migration and exile and lived by transitional figures in the wake of the new millennium, tend to be overlooked in scholarly conversations.[4] Building on the "spatial turn in Jewish Studies"[5] advanced by scholars like Elisheva Charlotte Fonrobert, my essay will highlight the significance of three places mentioned in *The Morning Star*: the place of Schwarz-Bart's origin, the Polish shtetl of his youth; the plantation universe in Guadeloupe; and his homeland in Israel.[6] In this fictional autobiography, or what Serge Doubrovsky calls "autofiction,"[7] Schwarz-Bart relentlessly searches for "espaces vécus," or inhabited spaces.[8] His posthumous work reads like a travelogue, moving among Jewish places associated with death and remembrance, memorials and museums, voids and relicts.[9] Even when Schwarz-Bart's protagonist Haïm Schuster dwells among living Jews in the Marais (a Parisian Jewish neighborhood) and Israel, he remains haunted by the past, and by his feelings of doubt, which render memories of the past unbearable.[10] The following analysis will explore Schwarz-Bart's engagement in *The Morning Star* with the meaning of place and the impossibility of a homecoming after the Shoah.

The Islands as Refuge

André Schwarz-Bart's writing effectively fuses cultures and traditions that are emblematic of creolization and métissage, as his authorship became enhanced through his literary collaborations with his wife, Simone. Bridging the dual worlds of cultural displacement and forced deportation in Europe and the Caribbean, the Schwarz-Bart collaborations produced a series of novels dealing with the intermingling and intersecting tragedies of African and Jewish history. Their Antillean novels resonate with depictions of Auschwitz. Similarly, in novels set in Poland or plays set in Guadeloupe, the Other's suffering lingers. As a reader of Martin Buber and Emmanuel Levinas, André Schwarz-Bart raises questions both of guilt and forgiveness as well as shame and responsibility.

With the aim of writing a series of novels that would bring Jews and Blacks together, André Schwarz-Bart begins his 1972 novel *A Woman Named Solitude* as follows: "Il était une fois, sur une planète étrange, une petite négresse nommée Bayangumay . . . Mais les habitants de ce lieu n'avaient pas d'Olympe, de Walhalla ou de Jérusalem céleste, ils n'aimaient pas se perdre dans les nuées" (Once upon a time, on a strange planet, there was a little Black girl named Bayangumay. . . . But the inhabitants of this place did not have an Olympus, a Walhalla or a heavenly Jerusalem; they did not like losing themselves in the clouds).[11] Read from the perspective of Michael Rothberg's "knotted" approach to such moments, this passage suggests the West Indies as a place of forced migration for both Africans and Jews who fled the Inquisition.[12]

Pierre Pluchon's *Nègres et Juifs au XVIIIe siècle: le racisme au siècle des Lumières* documents how the island of Saint-Domingue (today's Haiti) and the French Antilles were places for banned Jews to start over again. Even progressive thinkers like Hume, Montesquieu, Voltaire, Condorcet, and the Abbé Grégoire perceived both Blacks and Jews as "Other." In a more recent moment of Caribbean Jewish intersection, the West Indies welcomed a limited number of Jews well before the outbreak of World War II. Relatedly, in Schwarz-Bart's Holocaust novel *The Last of the Just*, the Levy family engages in desperate discussions about where to flee: "There's no border, Benjamin said, there's only the ocean—ocean or no ocean, where can we go if we have to leave—down to the bottom of the sea with the little fishes?"[13] Later on in the novel, Schwarz-Bart references the odyssey of the nine hundred Jews who left Hamburg in 1939 on the SS St. Louis for Cuba, a country from which they were ultimately expelled.[14] At one point, Haïm also hears about Hitler's plan to banish Jews to Madagascar.[15]

André Schwarz-Bart's own move to the island of Guadeloupe was prompted by his marriage to Simone. In *A Woman Named Solitude* he depicted islands as places of imprisonment, but now an island would provide a safe *kumbla* (Creole for womb) for his own career as a writer. Thus, at the same time as being a hell to which millions of Africans were shipped, Guadeloupe paradoxically becomes the space where the novelist set up a home in a vast, typical Caribbean mansion where he kept most of his library and an impressive book collection, and where he established his *atelier d'écriture* (writer's studio). Like other Jews in the Caribbean archipelago, Schwarz-Bart was part of a "diaspora in a diaspora," and he welcomed this place of retreat in which he could continue to write.

Simone stresses that, once her husband fled the French capital for the colony of Guadeloupe, he felt *"pleinement antillais"* (completely Antillean); at home with the landscape and village life of Goyave where he was very productive, writing novels, plays, poetry, and more.[16] He nonetheless always felt saddened that he was neglected by his fellow Caribbean-based writers (Ernest Pépin and Daniel Maximin were notable exceptions). The bestselling novel *The Last of the Just* (1959) made André Schwarz-Bart famous as a European Jewish writer.[17] With Simone, whom he convinced to become an author in her own right, Schwarz-Bart went on to publish a series of novels dealing with the intermingling and intersecting tragedies of African and Jewish history—works produced by those living in the dual worlds of displacement and cultures branded by forced deportation. Despite attracting a growing number of readers, André Schwarz-Bart remains less well known in the context of Caribbean literature. Simone recounts that she was embarrassed to receive the Carbet Prize in 2008 for their joint literary output because she believed her husband should have received this honor during his lifetime. The Schwarz-Barts had to contend with disappointment in their efforts to overcome the fragile feeling of being "strangers in the land," sojourners in their respective countries.[18]

The Morning Star: Return to the Shtetl, the Holocaust, and the Problem of Surviving

Published posthumously, *The Morning Star* reveals Schwarz-Bart's sense of identity as an uprooted traveler moving relentlessly back and forth between places of origin and settlement, and his subsequent feelings of belonging and unbelonging. In *Sauve-toi, la vie t'appelle* (Run away, life is calling you), neuropsychiatrist and Holocaust survivor Boris Cyrulnik points to Schwarz-Bart as an example of someone who, through fiction, runs away from his scattered childhood and traumatic wartime memories in order to retain his sanity and to be able to "envisager l'impensable" (envisage the unthinkable).[19] Yet this work raises the question of whether Schwarz-Bart ever found a place to call home. Indeed, moving between former places of origin (the shtetl) and new places of postwar migration—the Caribbean, the French capital, Indonesia, Senegal, Switzerland, French Guiana—in *The Morning Star* he describes the experience of failing to develop permanent roots and a sense of belonging to any of the three locations central to his life: Poland, Guadeloupe, and Israel.

Posthumous publications require scrupulous editing and often a team effort. *The Morning Star* raises and partly answers this question of the usefulness of publishing from notebooks and unfinished manuscripts left by an author too scrupulous and anxious to publish an original narrative that resonates with his earlier work. In her introduction to *The Morning Star*, Simone speaks about the challenges associated with such a project in terms of clarity and carrying out the author's wishes. She talks of their endless conversations, the help of their son, Jacques, and the assistance of loyal friends (all mentioned in a short acknowledgment) in preparing the heterogeneous autofiction for publication. Thus, her introduction deals in part with this question of the usefulness of publishing from notebooks and the misgivings associated with such a project.

The introduction to *The Morning Star*, which echoes passages from Simone's classic novel *Pluie et vent sur Télumée Miracle* (*The Bridge of Beyond*, 1972), is followed by an unsigned prologue that clearly bears André Schwarz-Bart's mark. The prologue demonstrates that, as a Holocaust writer, Schwarz-Bart kept coming back to this unnamable and major disaster. The prologue constructs an alternate history, set in the year 3000 after a nuclear catastrophe that makes human life on earth impossible. This catastrophe is so powerful that it destroys even Israel's Holocaust memorial Yad Vashem. Yet a manuscript is found in the subterranean ruins of the museum and monument for the victims of the Holocaust. It has a tag with Simone Schwarz-Bart's surname, Linemarie. In other words, the topos of the rediscovered manuscript explains the very existence of the book we are preparing to read—yet, as a simulacrum, readers encounter a conflation of voices. Indeed, Simone revealed herself as "Linemarie" in the introduction, hence underscoring the mission imposed on her by her late husband. The introduction also reveals that André struggled with the premonition that he would die before finishing his manuscript. Thus, we find two key elements: one is the framing narrative contained in the prologue that makes the internal story believable as a finished product; the other is the novel itself, created from different internal narrative strands and told through the third person of Haïm Lebke (in sections of the novel set before the war) and Haïm Schuster (in sections of the novel set after the war). The latter character, Haïm Schuster, who is clearly a stand-in for the author himself, identifies in chapter 2 of book 2 as "a Caribbean author" who had published "two or three" books.[20] The text's disjunctive structure notwithstanding, it remains without a doubt a sincere confession of the feelings of loss, mourning, and doubt about the ways the Holocaust must be remembered.

The prologue is followed by book 1, "KADDISH," written in capital letters in the text, followed by book 2, "UN CHANT DE VIE (SONG OF LIFE)," also in capital letters. Finally, *The Morning Star* concludes with a section entitled "Notes on a Book in the Making" that contains excerpts from Schwarz-Bart's own poetry, the Jewish Bible, and other sources. Adrift and afraid to revisit their parents' homeland (Poland), the author's two fictional doubles (Haïm Lebke before the Holocaust; Haïm Schuster after) must confront, as Derrida puts it, the "work of mourning" in the wake of his tragedy.[21] Haïm Lebke and Haïm Schüster, readers come to understand, represent two halves of André Schwarz-Bart's fragmented identity.

Like its predecessor, *A Woman Named Solitude*, *The Morning Star* begins in fairy-tale mode: "Once upon a time, a long, long time ago, there was a desperately merry Jew. He was called Haïm, son of Yaacov, son of Herschekele the book peddler, and the name of the humble native village was Podhoretz."[22] As with three giants of the Yiddishophone tradition, I. L. Peretz, Sholem Aleichem, and M. Mendele Sforim, the narrator leads us on a voyage to Yiddishland. He launches his reader on a journey through mythological time, which rapidly disintegrates under the threat of modernity and the invasion of the enemies' armies: "In those days, around the middle of the nineteenth century, Podhoretz was just an ordinary Jewish town lost among Count Potocki's estates."[23] In other words, André Schwarz-Bart recovers a folkloric and oral tradition of Jewish storytelling corresponding to the Creole folk tradition in his Caribbean works. Hence, *The Morning Star*'s first chapter is situated in an idyllic peaceful Jewish settlement in the twelfth century when King Boleslaw allowed Jewish immigrants to take refuge there, protecting them from the anti-Semitic reigns of Spain and Portugal and other countries and regions (Northern Africa). This harmonious community of the shtetl bears the fictional name of Podhoretz. This peaceful Eden-like haven is eventually rent asunder by the enemies, the two "Pharaohs"—first Russian, then German.

Ultimately, Poland is not portrayed in this novel as the mythical homeland of the author's grandparents, however, as the narrator quickly destroys the myth of a harmonious and peaceful "nest." Ancestral Poland was, in reality, a conglomerate of different ethnicities, run by different "rulers" and with various movements existing even among Jews (Hassidism, Bundists, secular Jews, etc.). The narrative features the innocent child, Haïm Lebke, who, much like the sensitive Ti Jean in Simone's novels, observes, high in the sky, the birds leaving in big numbers for unknown places, an omen of threatening massacres yet to come:

> Autumn was at the village gates with its cartfuls of hay and its fruit trees surrounded by flies. A group of children out on the prowl drew [Haïm's] attention. Gathered under a low branch of a pear tree, the little blond peasants were plucking a Volhynia blue jay from the glue that held its feet captive. Then one of them made its little round eyes pop out with his fingernails, and he ripped them out, sharply, one after the other tossed up into the air, the blind bird first headed straight to the sky. Then it came to a halt, uncertain, before circling all over the place, the circles intersected by the straight lines of sudden surges that sometimes propelled it upward, sometimes downward, since it no longer knew if it was going up or down, before it plummeted into a pond where it swiftly sank, like a stone.
>
> An inexpressible anguish seized the boy Haïm, who put the useless flute back in his pocket. It wasn't just the sight of the bird lost in midair. For the first time in his life, he felt utterly lost on this earth . . . the entire community of Podhoretz sunk in darkness, without a landmark.[24]

As in Caribbean dystopian writing about slavery, the structuring metaphor here is the flight of birds whose movements suggest those of an exiled community soon to be dispersed, persecuted, and, finally, exterminated. The narrator constantly reminds us that the idea of "home" is a product of both the imagination and memory that Judaism imprints on him.

In the first chapter of book 1 of *The Morning Star,* the themes of forced exile and the creation of the diaspora are symbolized through the five sons of the Lebke family, who migrate to different continents. One of Haïm Lebke's sons crosses the Atlantic and settles in Latin America. In Argentina, Carlos Gardel makes a living by dancing the tango while Arturo Schuster "presided over the first hesitant steps of the tango."[25] Another son lives in Siberia "among a forgotten tribe"; others make their homes in Africa and Antarctica. There is no such a thing as a specific fixed place for Jews, since, from the inception of the diaspora, the Jewish people experienced a transcontinental migration; consequently, a variety of branches and Jewish communities exist, extending from biblical times to the present.

Indebted to would-be ethnographers such as Abrasza Zemsc,[26] the narrator follows in the footsteps of anthropologists in setting up a global map of the Jewish diaspora: transplanted groups of people, deported communities whose identities are anchored in religious and culinary ritual, music (the violin), and folktales.²⁷ These significant identity markers become the universal language and key characteristics of both the people of Podhoretz (which "had become a kind of Jerusalem")²⁸ and their descendants, who flee the atrocities of the Cossacks.²⁹ We reach the author's own generation with Yaacov's son, Haïm Lebke, who grows up in the first half of the twentieth century, in a small industrial town torn apart by "Moscow supporters and Jerusalem supporters," and whose Jewish community is increasingly fragmented by confrontations between modernists and "Jews from the land of Jewry."³⁰

Book 1 of *The Morning Star* travels back for the first (and only) time to the land of André Schwarz-Bart's parents: Poland. A unified "I" is symbolized through their shared first names. This anonymous forefather, in fact, has as much right to claim to be Schwartz-Bart's father as the author's biological father, who was deported on one of the last trains from Angers to Auschwitz. As the novel unfolds, Schwarz-Bart avoids a folkloric Yiddishland, preferring to stress ethnic cleansing, religious intolerance, and the fact that Jews were outcasts in Eastern European countries well before the Second World War.

The Morning Star, which reads like a circumfession, is ultimately a confession about André's own failures as a writer: Haïm has lived in French Guiana and then in the Caribbean; after publishing a few books, he now lives like a "schlemiel, a man who had lost his shadow."³¹ He says he is "in mourning for literature, in mourning for himself," because he has spent his life trying to answer the impossible question of how to talk about Auschwitz.³² "How to express his impressions of a heap of dead bodies? Or simply: a day in Auschwitz?"³³

But, even when losing faith, experiencing religious and existential crisis, Judaism ties him to the community. For "Haïm was now caught in a web of ties stronger than any ropes, stronger than anything in the world, for they were woven out of tears and cries, gazing eyes, and the hands of children."³⁴ Haïm Lebke's birthplace was already a densely concentrated "colony" for Jews from all over the world: "For these people, Poland had become a kind of Jerusalem, and its mountains, its sky and its rivers dimly throbbed with Yiddish words, in spite of the old men crucified and the women with bristling abdomens in which the Cossacks had sewn live roosters."³⁵ Oscillating between utopian space and heterotopic space, Podhoretz faces several invasions by Cossacks during the nineteenth century, much as the remote Caribbean rural village of Fond-Zombi is threatened by the brutal repression of the colonizer in Simone's novels *Pluie et vent* and *Ti Jean L'Horizon*.³⁶ Moreover, the *morne* is the setting for both

Simone's postabolition novels and André's *A Woman Named Solitude*. In *A Woman Named Solitude,* the massacre of the three hundred resistance fighters (among whom is the very pregnant Solitude) takes place on an elevated retreat, called "Matouba," that becomes the hiding place for resistant Maroon (rebel) fighters and Solitude. The epilogue of *A Woman Named Solitude* notably links the text to *The Morning Star*—to the lonely visitor who dwells around the "lieu de mémoire" and is "transported" to the "humiliated ruins of the Warsaw ghetto."

Other places of Jewish remembrance are also freely associated in the Schwarz-Barts' work: Matouba is reminiscent of another remote place in time and space in the history of Judaism, namely Masada.[37] Just as the fugitives in Guadeloupe chose to blow themselves up rather than to surrender to Napoleon's troops, who came to reestablish slavery in 1803, Jews refused to surrender to the Roman emperor and preferred to kill themselves in a mass suicide in 75 AD. In the same way, the opening scene of *The Last of the Just* is of a collective suicide as the only remaining option for Jews who didn't want to convert. From Masada to Matouba, André Schwarz-Bart chronicles mass killings as well as resistance to colonial powers by voluntary, collective suicide; in the process, he illustrates a form of "palimpsestic memory" that Max Silverman has analyzed in French and Francophone fiction and film in which one memory is overlaid by another.[38] Likewise, in the final chapter of *The Morning Star* spatial-temporal connections are even further knotted between ruins separated through time and space. André Schwarz-Bart's oeuvre is so deeply involved with and obsessed by these disparate mass killings that it forges a link between different universes, whereby the plantocracy in the Caribbean comes to resemble the concentration camps in Europe. In both worlds of oppression, the slaughter and large-scale killings are tragedies from which recovery is difficult, if not impossible.

While *The Morning Star* specifically engages with Poland in the centuries, years, and months leading to the destruction of the Warsaw Ghetto, Schwarz-Bart also includes a striking scene in which the narrator links the appalling fate of Jewish children to that of slaves sold in the New World. The "knot of memory" in *The Morning Star* alludes to the human traffic during the terrible years of the German occupation of Poland, when sugar and tobacco were exchanged for children—that is, Jewish children, who were handed over to Nazis.[39] In the same way as Africans were literally bought in exchange for bibelots, alcohol, and weapons, Jewish children were exchanged for food and goods: "What's worth a life, a Jewish life?" the narrator wonders in the prologue.[40] In the poor rural zones of

Poland, the farmer Pan Pawiack and his wife discuss selling Haïm and his siblings together with other Jewish children as though they were talking about cattle to be delivered. Haïm overhears their conversation:

> But something felt very funny about the transaction. It wasn't a question of this or that many zlotys per head, but of sugar and tobacco—currency not in use, to say the least. Paniewka Pawiack only wanted sugar and Pan Pawiack only tobacco. After a hissed exchange of words, they agreed on the following arrangements: two heads at a kilo of sugar a head and two heads at two packets of tobacco a head. . . . Haïm immediately understood who the cattle were here and his chest swelled out like a balloon, and he feared for a moment that he would take off.[41]

In Galicia in the nineteenth century, the Jews suffered conditions that are evocative of the transatlantic slave trade. In this scene, through the exchange of children for tobacco and sugar—two of the main crops of Caribbean plantations—the "Black Atlantic" is invoked in the context of a rural Polish prewar setting. Jewish children whose parents hoped to save them from the Nazis through such negotiations with Catholics were often fooled, their offspring becoming "enslaved" by their adoptive families.

Other reversals and recurrent patterns in the Schwarz Barts' oeuvre link the two traumas: for instance, the phrase "like a balloon" and the motif of "taking off" form a riff that finds echoes in Simone's novels and in *A Woman Named Solitude*. In the opening lines of chapter 7, Solitude feels more and more deluded and unreal, much as Haïm and his siblings do as they beg in the Warsaw Ghetto: "The madness had even reached the sky, which was low, fleeting, cloudy . . . preventing you from really being able to distinguish between sleep and the waking state. Haïm had tried his hand on playing the flute in the streets. But his head was empty, his fingers frozen stiff, and the puny and bitter sounds of the musical instrument had nothing that could hold the attention of passerby."[42] Similarly, in *A Woman Named Solitude*, the narrator explains that "every day Solitude felt emptier and lighter, like a bubble shot through with shimmering light . . . she moved soundlessly among the runaway blacks, like a soap bubble revolving in the mansions of the sky, silently mirroring everything about her. She never opened her mouth or moved her tongue of darkness, except in direct response to the living."[43] Once again, in Simone's *Bridge of Beyond*, the same vanishing experience of an unbearable lightness of being that is experienced by Haïm in the face of the pogrom is described by Télumée, thereby implicitly paralleling Black and Jewish experiences of dehumanization: "Languid and non-existent . . . I fell asleep and dreamed there was a bubble inside my body that filled me up and floated me to heaven. Passers-by looked at me as a kind of apparition. They took the precautions one takes with a spirit enclosed in flesh."[44] According to Michael Dash, this is a typical illustration of "Caribbean marvelous realism."[45] Yet it can also be traced back to East-European Jewish masters such as Franz Kafka and Gustav Meyrink, the author of *Die Golem*, both important sources for the apprentice writer of *The Last of the Just* and *The Morning Star*.[46]

The Question of Palestine

Because André Schwarz-Bart disagreed with many of his Israeli and non-Israeli friends on the question of Palestine, *The Morning Star* could not be published while he was alive.[47] Schwarz-Bart held the view that Israel should have handed back occupied Palestinian territory after the 1967 Seven-Day War. When belatedly awarded the *Prix de Jérusalem* that same year, he found it even more difficult to agree with Israel's policies. To the surprise of his audience, he quoted the Senegalese writer and statesman Léopold Senghor in his acceptance speech, focusing on the mutual respect of traditions, observances, and religious identities:

> Lorsque la nouvelle me fut annoncée, voici plusieurs semaines, j'avoue que je ne compris pas tout d'abord la raison de votre choix. Et puis, en y réfléchissant, il me parut que pour une fois vous vouliez saluer une promesse plutôt qu'un accomplissement. Et puis encore, y réfléchissant davantage, je ne pus m'empêcher d'associer votre décision au livre que nous venons de faire paraître, ma femme et moi [*Un plat de porc aux bananes vertes*]. Dès lors, il me parut évident que vous vouliez marquer votre sympathie à l'égard de la jeune littérature de la Diaspora, comme vous auriez pu le faire, par exemple, en désignant mon cher ami Elie Wiesel. Et il me parut, d'autre part, que vous souhaitiez en même temps rendre hommage à une littérature non moins fraternelle, à vos yeux d'Israéliens, non moins chère à tous les cœurs juifs, et qui nous parle à travers les voix lumineuses du Sénégalais Léopold Sédar Senghor et de Césaire l'Antillais. Certains de nos ancêtres disaient : "Juifs sous la tante, homme dehors." Par votre geste, vous témoignez qu'*en Israël, ces deux termes ne font qu'un.* (italics mine)[48]

> (When I received the news a few weeks ago, I swear that I had difficulty at first in understanding the reasons for your decision. And then, thinking about

it, I realised that, for once, you wished to reward promise rather than accomplishment. On further reflection, I could not help making a link between your decision and the book my wife and I have just published [*Un plat de porc aux bananes vertes*]. After that, it seemed obvious to me that you wanted to show support for emerging literature from the Diaspora, which you could have done, for example, if you had given the award to my dear friend, Elie Wiesel. It also appeared to me that you wanted, at the same time, to pay homage to literature that was no less fraternal to your Israeli eyes, and no less dear to all Jewish hearts, and which speaks to us through the enlightened voice of the Senegalese author, Léopold Sédar Senghor and the Antillean, Césaire. Certain of our ancestors said "Jew in the tent, man outside." Through your gesture you affirm that in Israel, these two terms mean the same thing.)

Addressing an almost entirely Israeli audience, Schwarz-Bart spoke on behalf of Ashkenazi Jews, as well as Africans and Black Jews from Ethiopia, Harlem, and Jerusalem. He called for the dissolution of religious borders and reconciliation among monotheistic religions: all believers are "kindred spirits, Christians, Muslims, Buddhists." Most significantly, he took sides in the Middle East conflict when the settler colony of Israel began to colonize neighboring territories. His aforementioned views, as well as his call for secular education to teach Jews and non-Jews to respect each other, launched him as a new counterprophet, but one whose controversial message was difficult to convey publicly.

Schwarz-Bart's novel *The Morning Star* tackles the question of Palestine directly. Israel, it claims, should welcome Jews and non-Jews, and the war between Israelis and Palestinians that began with the creation of Israel ("Nakbah") should come to an end.[49] In *The Morning Star*, Schwarz-Bart ties together two emblematic places. First, Haïm Schuster visits Israel, "that country a thousand times blessed, a hundred thousand times cursed."[50] The crowds of visitors gathered at the Lamentation Wall in the Old City clearly acknowledge the diverse and hybrid character of Jewishness: "They had come from all the continents, witnesses from all the races and all the traditions, Jews of the East and of the West, white Jews, black Jews, yellow, red, right down to those mysterious Jews from Cochin China, whose eyes seemed to gaze upon a different sky. Falashas from Ethiopia, who still remember the Queen of Sheba; right down to the Jews of Harlem."[51] However, Haïm finds the risk of mass tourism to these holy places disturbing, concluding that this spiritual place of prayer is desacralized by the continual flow of tourists: believers and unbelievers as well as Jews and non-Jews.

Following the Israel section, the text moves on to Auschwitz. Here Schwarz-Bart invents a train journey to its refurbished barracks, with a strange encounter on the train between Haïm Schuster and a mixed-race man, a figure representing Schwarz-Bart's son, Jacques.[52] They discuss racial prejudice and discrimination, and whether they are better off as Blacks and/or Jews, and what happens if they are both? Father and son compare the image of Blacks in Jewish culture and Black Jews in New York and Israel. Through the figure of the mixed-race son, the "unique and the universal" come together as a promise of "reconciliation between living people and peoples who had disappeared."[53] The narrator explains, "The young man told him he was from Guadeloupe, of mixed race, with a Jewish mother and a West Indian father: a two-hundred per center: one hundred percent Jew and one hundred percent black." Whereupon the son asks: "You mean all people have two skins?" And the father answers: "Yes."[54] *The Morning Star* ultimately proves to be André Schwarz-Bart's *adieu* to his own kin, as well as an example of autofiction (Doubrovsky), that posits his vision of the future. Placing Jacques Schwarz-Bart at the heart of the narrative is an appeal for a sustainable transcultural and transatlantic peace and a model of mutual understanding. Through the relationship between himself and his youngest son, André Schwarz-Bart portrays the bonding and intimate relationship between Jews and individuals of color.

Like the African American activist Stokely Carmichael before him, Schwarz-Bart distrusts nationalist claims based on religion and ethnic affiliation.[55] He similarly avoids an exaggerated cult of memorial places (such as Auschwitz). Along with other thinkers of his and the younger generation and the Tune (Tunisian Jew), Albert Memmi, in *Testament insolent*,[56] he is profoundly disappointed by the "sacrosanct atmosphere that surrounds the Shoah."[57] He has serious misgivings about the ways in which a sinister kind of tourism (thanatourism) promotes concentration camps as tourist destinations. What if a site of memory does not offer the possibility of mourning the disappeared? What if the very place has washed out most of the traces of what happened on the spot?

In Schwarz-Bart's eyes, Israel is a mega-shtetl, embracing refugees from Eastern European countries and Russia as well as survivors of the Holocaust and new migrants. By sealing the border, however, they have closed themselves in, forming a ghetto or an overcrowded shtetl-cum-ghetto. With no faith in the future and no end in sight to Israel's hostility toward Palestinians, Schwarz-Bart finally decides to retreat to the settler colony of

Guadeloupe. Somewhat paradoxically, this French overseas *département* provides refuge for an author disillusioned with Israeli settler colonialism.

Fifty Years of Solitude

Simone Schwarz-Bart published *The Morning Star* exactly fifty years after *The Last of the Just* as a promotional gesture to revive interest in her late husband's work. Her decision was conceivably motivated by their common Parisian publisher, Seuil, which hoped that the publication would facilitate a comeback after a long span of frustrating silence (the last publication being a semifictional encyclopedia in six volumes, *Hommage à la femme noire*, 1987, cosigned with Simone). Yet one can hardly say that the author was brought back to life. Some critics held the view that *The Morning Star* should possibly never have been published.[58] Rather than giving in to unhelpful criticism, however, it is surely more constructive to consider the effects this disconcerting narrative may have had on André Schwarz-Bart's reputation. How do readers perceive the connection between Schwarz-Bart's Caribbean (plantation) novels and his Jewish (concentration camp and Auschwitz) novels? And how do we understand the lack of critical attention that *The Morning Star* has received? Does it result from the subject matter, or from the quality of the writing, or perhaps the manuscript's editing?

Like other work from this period by Boualem Sansal and Nancy Huston (Tzvetan Todorov's wife), André "relates" (in a Glissantian sense) post-colonial massacres with the Holocaust, without giving in to the competition of victims and the memory wars. In so doing, he fulfills a promise he made to the victims of both tragedies. His modesty and discretion with respect to his knowledge of these subjects is suggested by his quotation from Exodus in *The Morning Star*: "Blot me from the book you have written."[59] This sentence hints at his wish to disclaim authorship and to favor instead his wife's career. When news of André's death was announced in September 2006, many people in France believed that the author was already dead.[60] This was due to two factors: his retreat following his huge success, and his rather enigmatic coauthorship with his wife—a kind of double reception and deception. While André's work has recently gained renewed attention from a Jewish readership, Simone's work is studied primarily by scholars of Caribbean literature, postcolonial studies, and diaspora studies.[61] This separation of the critical reception and audiences for the Schwarz-Barts' writing runs opposite to the intersections and inclusiveness that André sought to promote with his novels. In André and Simone Schwarz-Bart's writing, Black and Jewish diasporas mirror each other, and "intersections" or "knots of memory," as Rothberg puts it make a vibrant claims for cross-cultural dialogue and mutual understanding.[62] Yet the two-track critical reception of their works detracts from these cross-cultural resonances. Moreover, this kind of double-track critical reception seems to have intensified following André's death. As a result, his sustained interest in feelings of homelessness and a lack of belonging has been overlooked by critics, particularly in Caribbean criticism, whose methodologies have tended to excise the interweaving of Black and Jewish diasporas. Similarly, Jewish-studies scholars have failed to examine the significance of these authors' use of "knot of memory," and the entanglements between histories of oppression in a time of decolonization.

Beginning with *The Morning Star,* and ending with Simone's *Adieu Bogota* (2017), the couple's works continuously intermingled Jewish and Black diasporas.[63] Yet, as Cheyette rightly affirms in *Diasporas of the Mind,* the narrow construction of Jewish studies and postcolonial studies has long divided readers and scholars.[64] As a result, the Schwarz-Barts—a French male Jewish writer and Caribbean woman writer—have been discussed in different scholarly contexts (notable exceptions are Bella Brodzki, Ronnie Sharfman, and myself).[65] By conceiving a "cycle romanesque"—a series of novels mapping the intertwined diasporas—the Schwarz-Barts called on readers to cross boundaries and unfix identities, to displace oneself into the Other, and thereby plead for a world without the dangerous borders that have generated so many conflicts and wars, even ethnic cleansing and genocides. Yet, contrary to this aim, André's readers have fallen into a fragmented approach to his oeuvre and his collaborations with Simone. We are left wondering, What do we lose by this bifurcation of subjects? And what do we stand to gain by reading depictions of African and Jewish displacement as intermingled in the Schwarz-Barts' writing, as individual subjects, born from different histories, but capable of shedding productive light upon one another?

In the first lines of her introduction to *The Morning Star,* Simone Schwarz-Bart testifies to her own restlessness and search for belonging in a reversion of her and her husband's respective identities: "The difficulty, in the meeting of two cultures, via two souls, lies in the temptation for each to topple over to the other side, to vanish into a gaze—a temptation all the stronger if the other's gaze is that of the one you love."[66] This statement is surprising, as André Schwarz-Bart insists on sameness as a guiding philosophy in his relation to the Other. The preface to *L'Ancêtre en Solitude,* the second posthumous novel published under both their names in February 2015, clearly emphasizes her husband's fundamental belief: "Tous les hommes sont mes semblables" (All human beings are like me).[67] It seems as if the search for identity, the quest for plenitude and wholeness, implies a trespassing of boundaries in order not to give in to the victimizing postures that are adopted by one's community.

Themes of the invisible, the unusual and the unnameable were persistently employed by this literary couple in the Caribbean, where the Jewish presence has always been overshadowed, if not blotted out, by a focus on other issues of race and skin color. André Schwarz-Bart—in my view the more imaginative and inventive of the two writers—set himself the task of demonstrating the shared Otherness between Jews and Blacks in dominant white societies. In French Caribbean literature a blatant paradox can be observed. Frantz Fanon's *Black Skin, White Masks* calls attention to the common condition of outcasts—that is, to the Blacks and the Jews, who both suffer discrimination (albeit with the major difference that Jews can pass for non-Jews whereas colored individuals can only, on very rare occasions, pass for whites). There is nevertheless a noticeable reluctance by French Caribbean authors, critics, and readers to acknowledge such connections.

Theorists like Glissant and his followers Patrick Chamoiseau and Raphaël Confiant (discussed in the present collection by Alessandra Benedicty-Kokken) cling to a utopian *créolité,* or Creole identity, but leave little room for a consideration of Jewishness. This tendency contrasts with writers like Emile Ajar (alias Romain Gary, another close friend of A. Zemsz),[68] Louis-Philippe Dalembert[69] and Gaston-Paul Effa,[70] who embrace (Caribbean) Jews within a context of creolization, cross-cultural empathy, and "knots of memory."[71] Nonetheless, in spite of having published *A Woman Named Solitude,*[72] arguably the finest historical novel on slavery, André Schwarz-Bart remained an outsider in the French Caribbean landscape.[73] In *Rétrovolutions*[74] and *Anthropologique,* anthropologist Jean-Loup Anselme warns against praising creolization while its main defenders hold rigid views on how a particular author from a particular background should express himself.[75] He argues that some of the recent utopias and pamphlets promoting a borderless society fail to embrace the Other within our midst. Schwarz-Bart's circumfession *The Morning Star* shows what it meant to feel out of place in the chosen place of exile and among his new adoptive community.

Notes

1. André Schwarz-Bart, *L'Etoile du matin* (Paris: Seuil, 2009), introduction by Simone Schwarz-Bart. See Kathleen Gyssels's reviews in *Europe*, *Africultures*, *Oso*, *Francophonia*, and *Mic Romania*. The absence of reviews in more academic journals, as well as in French Caribbean journals and websites, is noteworthy, and indicative of the narrative's first draft. *The Morning Star*, trans. Julie Rose (London: Overlook Duckworth, 2011). This publication is henceforth referred to as *MS*.

2. Jacques Derrida, "Circomfession," in *Jacques Derrida,* by Jacques Derrida and Geoffrey Bennington (Chicago: University of Chicago Press, 1993).

3. Joyce Block Lazarus, *Strangers and Sojourners: Jewish Identity in Contemporary Francophone Fiction* (New York: Peter Lang, 1991), chapter 3.

4. Bluma Finkelstein, *L'Ecrivain juif et les Evangiles* (Paris: Ed Beauchesne, 1991), 53–60.

5. Elisheva Charlotte Fonrobert, *The New Spatial Turn in Jewish Studies* (Stanford, CA: Stanford University Press, 2009).

6. Elisheva Charlotte Fonrobert, "The New Spatial Turn in Jewish Studies," *AJS Review* 33, no. 1 (2009): 155–64.

7. Serge Doubrovsky invented the term "autofiction" to designate a kind of confession and double-binded narrative which deals with the impossibility of finding a place, be it in fiction or (af) filiation. I quote from *Fils* (Paris: Galilée, 1997), 257: "MA PLACE N'EST JAMAIS LA MIENNE. J'existe." Originally Grasset considered *Fils* "commercialement impubliable" (unpublishable in a commercial sense). Doubrovsky rearranged the scattered versions and published excerpts online.

8. Henri Lefebvre, *The Production of Space* (Oxford: Blackwell, 1994), 131, 142–43.

9. I borrow this term from Lefebvre, *The Production of Space,* 131, 142–43.

10. André Schwarz-Bart, *L'Etoile du matin* (Paris: Seuil, 2009); *MS*, 156.

11. André Schwarz-Bart, *La Mulâtresse Solitude* (Paris: Seuil, 1972), 11.

12. Michael Rothberg, "From 'Lieux de mémoire' to Noeuds de mémoire,'" *Yale French Studies* 118–119 (2010): 3–12.

13. André Schwarz-Bart, *The Last of the Just,* trans. Stephen Becker (New York : Atheneum), 204.

14. A. Schwarz-Bart, 271–72.

15. S. Schwarz-Bart, *MS*, 108.

16. In his private library, I found drafts of plays and operas and read his correspondence with Maurice Delaistier and Elias Tanenbaum (New York), who both wrote operas based on *The Last of the Just*. Letter dated Paris, July 22, no year indicated.

17. For a more extended discussion of Schwarz-Bart's novels, see Kathleen Gyssels, *Filles de Solitude: Essai sur l'identité antillaise dans les auto-biographies fictives de Simone and André Schwarz-Bart* (Paris: L'Harmattan 1996).

18. Eric Sundquist, *Strangers in the Land: Blacks, Jews, Post-Holocaust America* (Harvard: Harvard University Press, 2005).
19. Boris Cyrulnik, *Sauve-toi, la vie t'appelle* (Paris: Odile Jacob, 2002), 166.
20. A. Schwarz-Bart, *L'Etoile du matin*, 155.
21. Jacques Derrida, *The Work of Mourning*, ed. Pascale-Anne Brault and Michael Naas (Chicago: University of Chicago Press, 2001).
22. S. Schwarz-Bart, *MS*, 25.
23. S. Schwarz-Bart, 23.
24. S. Schwarz-Bart, 64–65.
25. S. Schwarz-Bart, 45.
26. Kathleen Gyssels, "Abrasza Zemsz, Portrait of an Existential Jew by Richard Marienstras," *Journal of Jewish Identities* (2019). Schwarz-Bart hints at a "gang (which) had moved to a hotel in the rue Llhomond" and formed a "secret society" losing "themselves in more and more dubious conjectures about the possible future of the globe" (152). David, Marco (who commits suicide) and Alexis might refer to Abrasza Zemsz, Piotr Rawicz, and Richard Marienstras, respectively. Elise Marienstras confirmed the friendship and help that André Schwarz-Bart received in the making of what would become the first bestselling postwar novel on the Holocaust (Elise Marienstras, nonpublished interviews in Paris, 2017). I express my gratitude to Elise Marienstras for her precious information.
27. See Kathleen Gyssels, "Man, this food is a real Afro-Dizziac!—le manger créole dans *Pig Tails'n Breadfruit* (Austin Clarke) et *Un plat de porc aux bananes vertes* (Simone et André de Schwarz-Bart)," in *Food in Postcolonial and Migrant Literatures*, ed. Michela Canepari and Alba Pessini (Berlin: Peter Lang, 2012), 195–220. The intersection of both novels is assured through a hallucination of Mariotte: she *thought* to have seen Moritz Lévy (at the end of *Un plat de porc aux bananes vertes*). While Mariotte reappears as protagonist and first-person narrator in *Adieu Bogota*, there is no trace of Moritz. However, André Schwarz-Bart possessed a manuscript entitled *Les enfants du XX ième siècle* in which Mariotte's granddaughter marries Moritz Levy's grandson, both eventually committing suicide, and bringing both cycles back to completion.
28. S. Schwarz-Bart, *MS*, 48.
29. S. Schwarz-Bart, 48.
30. S. Schwarz-Bart, 54.
31. A. Schwarz-Bart, *L'Etoile du matin*, 155. This declaration opens chapter 2, book 2: Haïm Schuster used to be a modest Caribbean novelists who identified strongly with his character, Mariotte, and had lived across the Caribbean and France.
32. A. Schwarz-Bart, *L'Etoile du matin*, 155.
33. S. Schwarz-Bart, *MS*, 177.
34. S. Schwarz-Bart, 73.
35. S. Schwarz-Bart, 48.

36. Foucault defined the ship as a "heterotopic space" that is compatible with the Black Atlantic's site for imagination and resistance in both Black and Jewish Diasporas. New, alternative worlds are simultaneously imaginable and utopias. Michel Foucault, "Des espaces autres," in *Architecture, Mouvement, Continuité 5* (October [1967] 1984): 46–49, reprinted in *Dits et écrits* (Paris: Gallimard, 1994).

37. To the multilingual author, Matouba is reminiscent of the biblical "Masada," the mountainous area where, in 75 AD, nine hundred Jews preferred suicide to giving in to the Roman emperor.

38. See Max Silverman, *Palimpsestic Memory: The Holocaust and Colonialism in French and Francophone Fiction and Film* (New York: Berghahn, 2013).

39. Rothberg, "From 'Lieux de mémoire' to 'Noeuds de mémoire.'"

40. S. Schwarz-Bart, *MS*, 17.

41. S. Schwarz-Bart, 97–98.

42. S. Schwarz-Bart, 114.

43. Simone Schwartz-Bart, *A Woman Named Solitude*, English translation of André Schwarz-Bart, *La Mulâtresse Solitude* (Paris: Seuil, 1972), trans. Ralph Manheim (Syracuse, NY: Syracuse University Press, 2001).

44. Simone Schwarz-Bart, *Pluie et vent sur Télumée Miracle* (Paris: Seuil, 1972), trans. Barbara Bray as *Bridge of Beyond* (New York: New York Review Books Classics, 2013), 102–3.

45. Michael Dash, "Marvelous Realism: A Way Out of Négritude," *Caribbean Studies* 13, no. 4 (1974): 57–70, http://www.jstor.org/stable/25612571.

46. As I demonstrate in *Marrane et marronne*, Kafka's works and words are hinted at through metamorphosis, place names (*Schlosse*) and most of all his marvellous realist style.

47. Edward Said, *The Question of Palestine* (New York: Vintage, 1979). Regular opinion pieces based on this essay were translated for *Le Monde diplomatique*. Said was widely read in France by Edgar Morin and Memmi, who echoes Schwarz-Bart's remark on the Lamentation Wall and the occupation of Palestinian territory in *Le Testament insolent* (Paris: Odile Jacob, 2008).

48. André Schwart-Bart, "Acceptance Speech Prix de Jérusalem," 1967. In Francine Kaufmann, "A Schwarz-Bart," Francine Kaufmann, *Edition française du Jérusalem Post* 817, 21–27 (November, 2006): 17.

49. Both Said and Schwarz-Bart stopped using the term "Diaspora" from the time that "Nakba" generated the Palestinian Diaspora. See Patrick Williams, "'Naturally, I reject the term "diaspora"': Said and the Palestinian Dispossession," in *Comparing Postcolonial Diasporas*, ed. Michelle Keown, David Murphy, and James Procter (New York: Palgrave, 2009), 83–103.

50. S. Schwarz-Bart, *MS*, 170

51. S. Schwarz-Bart, 170.

52. S. Schwarz-Bart, 178–80.

53. S. Schwarz-Bart, 178.

54. S. Schwarz-Bart, 179.

55. https://libraries.ucsd.edu/farmworkermovement/ufwarchives/sncc/26-September%201967.pdf (accessed June 11, 2017).

56. Albert Memmi, *Testament insolent* (Paris: Odile Jacob, 2010).

57. S. Schwarz-Bart, *MS*, 187.

58. Steve Donoghue writes in *Open Letters Monthly* (May 7, 2011) as follows: "This gets to the heart of the matter, the question of whether or not an author's reticences (and failures) are also an inviolable part of his legacy. Readers will eagerly consume these new passages from Schwarz-Bart, naturally—I wish we had ten writers of his greatness working today, or fifty. But for reasons known only to himself, he didn't, or couldn't—produce this book while he was alive. As grateful as we are for the words, we can wonder if his widow should have respected that." https://www.openlettersmonthly.com/book-review-the-morning-star/ (accessed July 4, 2016).

59. S. Schwarz-Bart, *MS*, 133.

60. http://www.lemonde.fr/disparitions/article/2006/10/02/andre-schwarz-bart-ecrivain-de-la-shoah-est-mort_818907_3382.html (accessed October 2, 2006).

61. On the tenth anniversary of his death, the Memorial de la Shoah in the Rue du Temple, Paris, organized a special tribute evening reserved for Jewish participants only, the exception being Guadeloupean novelist and poet Daniel Maximin, who literally gate-crashed the event. Belatedly informed about the event, I was not allowed to join either. http://www.akadem.org/sommaire/themes/culture/litterature/shoah-et-litterature/andre-schwarz-bart-le-courage-de-resister-23-09-2016-83864_404.php (accessed May 6, 2019).

62. Rothberg, "From 'Lieux de mémoire' to 'Noeuds de mémoire.'"

63. This latest novel, cosigned André and Simone, again suffers from misrepresentations in the promotional announcements. While it includes a section pertaining to the transportation camp in Saint-Laurent de Maroni (French Guiana), the novel is presented as set in 1930 (before the war) and presents Mariotte as a worker in an elder house. Moreover, Claire Julliard reproduces in her review these factual errors. Claude Julliard, "Mémoires d'une rêvoteuse: *Adieu Bogota*, par S. et A. Schwarz-Bart," *Nouvel Obs* 2753 (2017): 70. In the rare reviews in France, one fails to see the irony of the title: the "adieu" normally associates with nostalgic, yet positive, "souvenirs," yet Mariotte has lived the most horrifying experience, tortured and raped by a dog in the prison cells of Bogota. See Kathleen Gyssels, *Il Tolomeo* 19 (December 2017): https://edizionicafoscari.unive.it/it/edizioni/riviste/il-tolomeo/2017/1/schwarz-bart-andre-schwarz-bart-simone-2017-adieu-/.

64. Bryan Cheyette, *Diasporas of the Mind: Jewish and Postcolonial Writing and the Nightmare of History* (New Haven, CT: Yale University Press, 2014).

65. Bella Brodzki, *Can These Bones Live? Translation, Survival, and Cultural Memory* (Stanford, CA: Stanford University Press, 2007); Ronnie Scharfman,

"Exiled from the Shoah: André and Simone Schwarz-Bart," in *Auschwitz and After. Race, Culture, and the Jewish Question in France*, ed. Lawrence Kritzman (New York: Routledge, 1995), 250–63; Kathleen Gyssels, *Marrane et Marronne : la co-écriture réversible d'André et Simone Schwarz-Bart* (Leiden: Brill, 2014).

66. S. Schwarz-Bart, MS, 11 (introduction).

67. "All human beings are like me," in *L'Ancêtre en Solitude*, trans. Kathleen Gyssels (Paris: Seuil, 2015), 11. This second posthumous novel was awarded the Grand Prix de l'Association des Écrivains de la Caraïbe at the 2015 Festival of Caribbean Authors in Guadeloupe, presided over by Daniel Maximin.

68. Gary Romain, *Le judaïsme n'est pas une question du sang* (Paris: L'Herne, 2005). See Kathleen Gyssels, "Les Gary de Goyave," *Continents Manuscrits* 7 (2016): 1–9.

69. Louis-Philippe Dalembert, *Avant que les ombres s'effacent* (Paris: Sabine Wespieser, 2017).

70. Gaston-Paul Effa, *Rendez-vous avec l'heure qui blesse* (Paris: Gallimard, 2015). See Kathleen Gyssels, "Elégies de Raphaël Elizé," *Etudes Caribéennes* 7 (2016): https://coma.revues.org/714; and Kathleen Gyssels, "Journal d'un déporté martiniquais," *French Studies in Southern Africa* 47 (2017): 72–86. In his latest novel, *Le miraculé de Saint-Pierre*, Effa invents the biography of Cyparis, one of the two or three survivors of the destruction of Saint-Pierre de la Martinique in the volcanic eruption of 1902. The same "natural holocaust" led Marie to flee to Bogota, Columbia.

71. Rothberg, "From 'lieux de mémoire' to 'noeuds de mémoire,'" introduction.

72. The first English translation of André Schwarz-Bart's *La Mulâtresse Solitude*, published by Atheneum, included a preface by Arnold Ramperstad. I contacted Ramperstad about the circumstances in which he was asked to write this preface, and why this important text disappeared from the second translation. He kindly replied by email (June 15, 2017) as follows: "I know nothing about the decision to drop my Intro. I suppose that's the right of the publisher. I've forgotten how I came to be asked to write it in the first place, although it was a welcome challenge and an honor. I'm pretty certain that I never met André, but something tells me that perhaps I met someone close to him. I simply don't recall." As the biographer of Ralph Ellison and Langston Hughes, Ramperstad is surprised to find a white (moreover, Jewish) author speaking in the name of an Afro-Caribbean character and community. Ralph Manheim produced a translation that is, on the whole, faithful, and often graceful, although it translates *nègre* and *négresse* with the more offensive English term "nigger." See Kathleen Gyssels, *Filles de Solitude: Essai sur les (auto-)biographies fictives de Simone et André Schwarz-Bart* (Paris: L'Harmattan, 1996).

73. *Tout-monde* (1993) is a polemic example of how Blacks and Jews are represented as victims of Nazism. Glissants travelogues include the account of a Martinican student who—the reader is led to believe—told Glissant the amazing story of how he miraculously escaped deportation to the concentration camps.

Using the third-person narrative, the narrator, however, comes to provocative, even controversial, conclusions about Black and Jewish diasporas after the war. See Kathleen Gyssels, "Knots of Memory in French Caribbean Literature: Edouard Glissant's 'Nous ne mourions pas tous,'" in *Literary Transnationalism(s)*, ed. Dagmar Vandebosch and Theo D'haen (Leiden: Brill, 2019), 245–63.

74. Jean-Loup Amselle, *Rétrovolutions Essais sur les primitivismes contemporains* (Paris: Stock, 2010). Amselle, himself of Jewish origin, expressed his admiration for Schwarz-Bart in informal talks we had on several occasions at academic conferences.

75. Anthony Mangeon, *Anthropologique: Jean-Loup Amselle, une pensée sans concession* (Paris: Karthala, 2015).

Raphaël Confiant and Jewishness
The Fraught Landscapes of French, Martinican, and Franco-Martinican Intellectualisms

Alessandra Benedicty-Kokken

je t'énonce
    FANON
tu rayes le fer
tu rayes le barreau des prisons
tu rayes le regard des bourreaux
guerrier-silex

(i enunciate you
    FANON
you strike out the iron
you strike out the prison bars
you strike out the gaze of torturers
flint warrior)
—Aimé Césaire, "par tous mots, guérrier silex," 1982

IN AN EARLY twenty-first-century polemic that has remained undertheorized, academician, writer, novelist, and essayist Raphaël Confiant has been taken to task by fellow intellectuals for statements he made about Jews and Jewishness. Confiant's statements about Jewishness, which have shifted over the years, offer a unique opportunity for the study of postcolonial and decolonial discursive spaces and the sometimes fraught and affectively charged intersections between the disciplines of Caribbean studies and Jewish studies.[1] Literary and cultural studies scholar Madelaine Hron has demonstrated that Global Northern public cultures of the late 1990s through the early 2000s interpreted hybridity and multiculturalism through a celebratory lens. In so doing, a "postcolonial cultural industry" read, processed, and "packaged" postcolonial intellectual production in a way that privileged certain writers over others and reduced the complexity of their work through monolithic readings centered on the role of hybridity in shaping a cosmopolitan social model. Accordingly, while some postcolonial writers have enjoyed public success, others who fit less neatly into what in the late twentieth century became a utopic notion of how narratives of hybridity might positively affect cosmopolitanism (which will be further explained below), writers such as Confiant and his Haitian colleague Franketienne remain largely ignored.[2] Moreover, among certain nonpostcolonial writers, there has been from time to time a backlash, leading to accusations that twentieth-century literary culture engages in "a fetishization of all experiences considered genocidal."[3]

The reception of Confiant's writing and the controversy surrounding his alleged anti-Semitism reflect this context in which a postcolonial cultural industry determines *who* gets published and *how* their publications are presented to a reading audience. As I shall delineate in the pages that follow, over the years Confiant actively wrote about questions of hybridity, yet at the same time was accused of making anti-Semitic remarks. Since hybridity was largely celebrated as an aspirational form of realizing more inclusive societies, Confiant's lack of respect for Jewishness countered his narrative of Créolité's openness, a term to which I will return. A close analysis of Confiant's words, and of the contexts in which they have been produced, illuminates Confiant's increased sensitivity to Black-Jewish questions as well as the affective spaces that inform what hemispheric American studies scholar Sarah Phillips Casteel refers to as the "rhetorical oppositionality of 'Black' and 'Jew.'"[4] The present article examines traditional literary texts (i.e., essays and novels) alongside public culture texts (i.e., commentary by politicians or Confiant's public statements on intellectualisms, notably in France). While this essay attempts to understand Confiant's "injurious" remarks about Jews,[5] it inevitably also involves a more general deliberation on the relationships among France, the Caribbean, Martinique, and the broader Mediterranean (which includes Algeria, Israel, and Palestine) and these spaces' connection to French left-wing anti-Semitism.[6]

First let me summarize some of the accusations against Confiant. The most well-known controversy took place in 2006; however, the polemic also reared its ugly head before and after 2006, a year whose events I take up more thoroughly later in this essay. In 2006, Confiant allegedly circulated a document by email entitled "La faute (pardonnable) de Dieudonné" (Dieudonné's [excusable] error), in which he tried to understand why the comedian Dieudonné M'bala M'bala (referred to in the French media by his first name) attended a party hosted by the National Front, a French extreme right-wing party.[7] What most alarmed those who read the email was Confiant's use of the term "les Innommables" (the Unnamables) to refer to Jews. "The Unnamables" is an epithet that, as Confiant's colleague, the late Pierre Pinalie explains, "correspond à ce qui est trop bas ou trop vil pour être prononcé. Il faut donc être vraiment bas et honteusement vil pour jouer sur les mots en utilisant 'innommables' à propos des juifs" (corresponds to all that is so low and vile that it cannot be iterated. One must then be extremely crass and shamelessly despicable to engage in a wordplay that uses "unnamable" to refer to Jews).[8] In an interview on December 9, 2006, Confiant explained that he did not speak ill of Jews, but rather tried to understand why Dieudonné attended the National Front's "Fête 'Bleu-Blanc-Rouge" (Blue-White-Red Party).[9]

The second controversial episode, dating from 2012, involves Confiant's online op-ed "Une certaine lâcheté intellectuelle . . ." (A certain intellectual cowardice . . .), which analyzed the walkout of French rightwing members of parliament in response to comments made on February 7, 2012, by Socialist Party member Serge Letchimy, president of the Regional Council of Martinique.[10] In February 2012, interior minister Claude Guéant "caused a political uproar for saying that, 'contrary to what the left's relativist ideology says, for us, all civilisations are not of the same value.'"[11] In response, Letchimy likened Guéant's statements to Nazi ideology, stating: "Vous nous ramenez à ces idéologies qui ont donné naissance aux camps de concentrations" (You bring us back to those ideologies that gave rise to the concentration camps). In his op-ed, Confiant explains that he finds the Holocaust absolutely horrific; however, he also asserts that Jews in French society have been accorded a certain privileged position that is not conferred upon other groups who historically have suffered. Confiant analyzes Letchimy's reactions to then Interior Minister Guéant. Confiant acknowledges the suffering of the "Juifs d'Europe"; at the same time, he accuses the French intellectual sphere of privileging and even fetishizing the experience of the Holocaust in such a way that the experience of suffering groups who are not Jewish is rendered unimportant, or at least less important.[12] For example, as will be further elaborated on, he looks at how the word *Shoah* creates a distancing effect whose result is to mitigate the severity of the crime against humanity, whereas "the Holocaust" for most Europeans is more clearly representative of the fact that the event was indeed a genocide.

Following these two episodes, critics responded, including Pierre Assouline, a prominent (and also controversial) French intellectual who has served on the selection committee for the Prix Goncourt, the most prestigious French literary prize, and who also managed the prominent literary website *La République des Livres;* Jacky Dahomay, a political philosopher and professor at the Lycée de Baimbridge in Guadeloupe and a member of the Haut Conseil à l'intégration (High Counsel for Integration, an office housed under the French Prime Minister); Rafael Lucas, a Haitian and French literary scholar, Maître de conferences at the University of Bordeaux III, and specialist in Lusophone literatures; and Paris-based psychiatrist and psychoanalyst Jeanne Wiltord.[13] Although none of the aforementioned accuses Confiant outright of anti-Semitism, each situates him in a discursive space that unfairly undermines Jews and Jewishness. For example, Patrice Louis, a journalist who has written for *Le Monde,* questions Confiant's behavior: "S'agit-il d'un soutien mûrement réfléchi? D'un dérapage du romancier à succès?" (Are we dealing with a carefully deliberated claim? Or the sloppy slip of the tongue of a novelist whose success has gone to his head?).[14] Lucas qualifies Confiant's statements as "affirmations hasardeuses, de généralisations absurdes et injurieuses, le tout couronné d'une énorme prétention baignant dans le ridicule" (risky assertions, absurd and injurious generalizations, which are topped off by a pretentious mockery itself saturated in ridicule).[15] Assouline accuses Confiant of a "délirant développement historique" (delirious account of historical events).[16] Moreover, the incidents also led to the schism of a friendship between Confiant and Pinalie, Confiant's colleague in linguistics at the Université des Antilles et de la Guyane, not to mention weakened professional ties between Martinican intellectuals Jean Bernabé and Patrick Chamoiseau.[17]

This essay's intention then is twofold: first, to consider the complex circumstances surrounding the accusations of anti-Semitism against Confiant, and, second, to argue that the scholarly treatment of the scandal surrounding his work points to an extreme paucity in our ability to deal with questions of Otherness, difference, race, and religion. Perhaps Dahomay states the challenge best when he writes, "Mais on ne peut en rester à cette indignation spontanée. Il faut comprendre. Comment expliquer qu'un intellectuel, dans les Antilles d'aujourd'hui, puisse en arriver là?" (But we cannot content ourselves with such spontaneous indignation. We must understand. How do we explain that an intellectual in today's French Antilles can get so carried away?).[18] The present essay offers a response to Dahomay's call. If indeed the eschewing of Confiant from more general discussions about French Antillean humanism has to do with the discomfort surrounding Confiant's commentary about Jewishness, my hope is that this essay offers a more sustained reflection on Confiant's place in a broader landscape of cultural politics, which silently—but violently—pits minority groups against each other.

If Confiant's stance as a Martinican intellectual has been vehemently "indépendantiste" (independentist), and, as such, anti-French, his work as both a novelist and as a public intellectual has nonetheless been constantly informed by a French intellectual sphere. In other words, to understand the polemics around Confiant is also to dig deeply into some of the more fraught topics that haunt contemporary France; to inextricably link France and Martinique to each other; and to involve Martinique in a larger post-French Empire, a "Francophone" landscape in which France remains an important post- and neocolonial presence in many of the former colonies. To disentangle the sources of such controversial confusion, toward the end of this essay I examine two separate but not unrelated "topics": Frantz Fanon's role as a Martinican intellectual, practicing psychologist and psychoanalyst, and freedom fighter for the Algerian anticolonial struggle; and debates and historical contexts concerning Jewishness in Martinique.

Despite the published criticisms of Confiant by Assouline, Dahomay, Lucas, and Wiltord, university-based scholars who directly work on Confiant's literary oeuvre as well as scholars who have written on Confiant in the past have yet to engage in any official capacity with the controversy. Moreover, as Louis writes, a few days after the circulation of the 2006 alleged anti-Semitic remarks, the Martinican public sphere demonstrated extreme discomfort with what had purportedly taken place: "les élites et les élus martiniquais observent un silence total, comme si la violence de la polémique n'était pas arrivée jusqu'à eux" (Martinican elites and elected officials have remained completely silent, as if the violence of the polemic had not yet reached them).[19]

While holding Confiant accountable, this essay inscribes itself as a more general meditation on the quite complex challenges of Michael Rothberg's call for "multidirectional memory."[20] While Confiant might stand rightly accused of a confused historical account, it is also true that until very recently very little scholarship has dealt with a late twentieth-century history of the relationship between African and Jewish diasporas.

While Jean-Paul Sartre's *Anti-Semite and Jew* (1945), Frantz Fanon's *Black Skin, White Masks* (1952), and Aimé Césaire's *Discourse on Colonialism* (1950, 1955) directly engage the question of Jewishness, it has only been recently that a well-informed discussion has emerged that takes account of exchanges between Africana intellectualisms on the one hand, and Jewish intellectualisms on the other.[21] To compare Fanon's and Césaire's canonical aforementioned post–Second World War texts to texts published from the late 1980s to the early 2000s by Martinican-born writers such as Confiant or Glissant is to note a certain absence of sustained discussions of Jewishness in relation to Blackness. William F. S. Miles, a political scholar whose research focuses on postcolonial borderlands as well as the legacy of Jewishness in postcoloniality, observes that, in their well-known manifesto *Éloge De La Creolite* (*In Praise of Creoleness*, 1989), Martinican-based writers Jean Bernabé, Patrick Chamoiseau, and Raphaël Confiant left Jewishness out of their purview, despite the important relationship of Jewishness to Martinique's colonial and more contemporary histories—a point to which I return in the second part of this article.[22] Thanks, however, to recent scholarship by Miles, but also notably by Casteel, whose book *Calypso Jews: Jewishness in the Caribbean Literary Imagination* (2016) traces philo-Semitic strains in Caribbean literary discourse, it becomes clear (as I argue further on) that Martinique's connections to Jewishness are particularly vexed.[23] This essay seeks to understand the debate around Confiant through the lens of such recent scholarship.

In Praise of Creoleness: The Ironies of Proclaiming Hybridity

My deliberations begin by situating Confiant intellectually, offering the reader an overview of his lifework thus far, as well as his reception within the literary public sphere. Despite Confiant's prolific output of novels and essays, his work has received little scholarly attention in comparison to that of Chamoiseau or Glissant. Yet understanding Confiant's often virulent stances regarding Jewishness, combined with his belligerent perspectives on other issues—such as contemporary Martinican culture, including LGBT rights and the scandal around chlordecone (kepone, an insecticide used in banana farming that has proven to cause significant health risks including cancer and birth defects)[24]—is essential to interpreting the present-day relationship between Martinique and France.[25]

Confiant is the author of more than thirty works of fiction, including novels, historical fiction, and short-story collections written in French and in Martinican Creole, for which he has received esteemed literary prizes.[26] In addition, he is the author or coauthor of several extremely influential book-length essays on literature and politics. In 2013, Confiant was appointed the doyen (dean) of the Faculté des Lettres et Sciences Humaines de l'Université des Antilles et de la Guyane, an important fact for two reasons: first, he has continued[27] to play a key role in defining university curriculum; and second, despite his vehement criticism of France and his independent politics, he has continuously worked as a public servant in his university, a public French institution.

Although the scandal hit the mainstream media in 2006, the accusations of anti-Semitism date back to 1991, when the jury of the Prix Goncourt were deliberating on who would win the esteemed literary prize. According to Confiant, it would seem that the jury members were aware of comments on Jewishness that he had made in the newspaper *Antilla*.[28] In 1991 Confiant was a semifinalist for the Prix Goncourt, a result that is perhaps directly related to our present discussion of how Jewishness figures into his reception by the French public sphere. In fact, Confiant's problematic 2006 remarks and his later 2017 tribute to writer Pierre Combescot are couched in his bitterness over having lost the Goncourt to Combescot, who was the other semifinalist. In an interview and in an elegy for Combescot, Confiant maintains he lost the award because of accusations of anti-Semitism. His sincere praise for Combescot comes in the form of a rare moment of vulnerability in which Confiant admits that he is not as good a writer as the late Combescot. Yet, with characteristically Confiantian irony, he argues that even if he did not deserve the Goncourt on the basis of aesthetic merit, politically he did. That is, it can be inferred from Confiant's 2017 tribute to Combescot that, in terms of identity politics, it was due time for a French Antillean writer to win the award.[29] Confiant even comments on the fact that a year later, in 1992, Chamoiseau, one of his two coauthors of *In Praise of Creoleness*, won the award for the novel *Texaco*.

Most striking is what seems to be a disconnect between Confiant's vitriolic remarks on Jewishness in the French and Martinican public spheres and his advocacy for *créolité*. In 1989, Confiant gained worldwide renown as one of the three authors of the oft-cited *In Praise of Creoleness*, a seminal work of Caribbean criticism. The ideas put forward by *In Praise of Creoleness* are considered to align with the various postcolonial theories of hybridity, which gained intellectual currency in the late twentieth century. That said, the term *créolité* is also often conflated or confused with the range of ways in which writers have grappled with the implications of Creole culture.³⁰ Moreover, the fact that, in English, *creolité* is translated as *creoleness* further associates (and not necessarily appropriately) their work with Édouard Glissant's more opaque term *créolisation*.

Drawing on Adlai Murdoch's most recent work on the topic, I use the term *créolité* here to refer to specific arguments advanced in *In Praise of Creoleness*. Reflecting on the critiques of the past twenty-five years since *In Praise*'s first publication, Murdoch at once invokes the openness associated with créolité and the reasons for which the project of créolité sabotages itself.³¹ Murdoch explains that the "broad claims made by the *créolistes*" were pronounced with the right intentions, notably to nurture "this evolving mosaic of difference," which works to "emphasiz[e] pluralism of being as the core of a postcolonial subjective position," and to "demonstrate[e] the anathema of fixity and singularity."³² Yet, as Murdoch points out, their very desire to define a specifically Creole way of being in the world, without clearly deliberating on how such an identity was (or was not) specifically Martinican, and, notably, without explicitly putting the term into conversation with Glissant's *créolisation*, Stuart Hall's writings, or even scholarship in linguistics or folklore, has resulted in their discussion pitting identitarian politics against difference. Murdoch concludes, "It is in fact the cultural turn embodied and embedded in créolité that, paradoxically, subtented many of the broad claims made by the *créolistes* and gave expressive focus to the ethnocultural matrix of the movement."³³ Even if Confiant and his two coauthors assert the uniqueness of Martinique as resting precisely in its openness, in so doing they put forth a national(ist) discourse that, in turn, excludes those who fall outside the parameters of an essentialized vision of what the Martinican should be.³⁴

The Scandals: Jewishness and Confiant's Media Presence

Having outlined Confiant's career and the importance of *In Praise of Creoleness*, let me return to a more detailed account of the anti-Semitism controversy that stemmed from Confiant's defense of the comedian Dieudonné. In order to understand Confiant's 2006 statements about Jewishness, it is worthwhile outlining Dieudonné's political trajectory, a context that also informs this essay's final consideration of the rapport of Martinique with the question of Israel and Palestine. In the late 1990s and early 2000s, under the name of the party he founded, the Parti des utopistes or Liste des Utopistes (translated by Günther Jikeli as "Utopians"),

Dieudonné ran for office several times. He sought to better represent the "jeunes des cités populaires" (inner-city youth).[35] According to historian and sociologist Günther Jikeli, at "the European Parliament elections in 2004, he was a candidate for the extreme left-wing party Euro-Palestine, which he left shortly afterward due to disagreements with party leaders over his alliances with the extreme right."[36] In the years since, the French public sphere and the French government have accused Dieudonné of anti-Semitism. On January 6, 2014, France's interior minister, Manuel Valls, issued a "circulaire" (memorandum) to police prefectures allowing them to ban any of Dieudonné's shows at their discretion if they considered them a threat to public safety, putting a supposed security agenda before the right to freedom of speech.[37]

In France, Dieudonné came to fame performing with Élie Simon, a Jewish comedian whose acts drew from stereotypes of religious, racial, and cultural categories of marginalized groups. Since the privately aforementioned circulated document "La faute (pardonnable) de Dieudonné" (Dieudonné's [excusable] error) is not available, we cannot know how Confiant "excused" Dieudonné for his association with the National Front. While there is no consensus regarding the reason for Dieudonné's attendance at this event or his continued relationship to the National Front, the media and scholars such as Jikeli reflected on the National Front's strategy for garnering votes.[38] The strategy of the National Front, which is known for actively seeking to attract members of communities marginalized from other political parties, was to target votes of Arabs and/or Muslims whose interests were perceived as unaligned with those of Jewish voters. Yet, in recent years, according to journalist Amanda Borschel-Dan, as mainstream French political parties were unable to address the concerns of Jewish communities, certain Jewish voters have also committed their votes to the National Front.[39]

Within this context, Dieudonné's allegiances seem to be part of what Jikeli describes as sentiments "based on associations and obsessions rather than logic."[40] As noted above, Dieudonné is against racism. Politically, he stood against it, and in 1997 he presented himself as a candidate for legislative election on the part of Le parti des Utopistes (Utopians Party) against the National Front candidate. Again, in 2000, he attempted to run as the Utopians' presidential candidate, but did not receive sufficient support to present himself as a candidate.[41] The National Front is the right-wing party whose platform includes anti-immigration policies and anti-Semitism. However, after receiving criticism for offensive use of stereotypes, especially against Jews, but also against Catholics, Dieudonné began to engage more and more with the National Front, the party against which he had once campaigned. In other words, to try to gauge Dieudonné's political leanings through those he makes fun of is futile, for he makes fun of almost everybody. That said, in his political speech he is most virulent against Jews.

An episode that took place in March 2005 involving the eminent Martinican writer and politician Aimé Césaire offers a further context in which to understand Confiant's interest in Dieudonné. In March 2005, after performing in Fort-de-France, the departmental capital of Martinique, Dieudonné was attacked in a parking lot, possibly by Israeli nationals.[42] Césaire, who at the time had retired from politics, received Dieudonné.[43] *Le Monde* correspondent Pierre Louis writes: "Le vieux sage lui avait rappelé son souhait 'que nos spécificités alimentent l'Universel, et non le particularisme ou le communautarisme,' mais c'est l'image des deux hommes dans les bras l'un de l'autre qui était restée" (The aging wise man had reminded him [Dieudonné] of his hope "that our specificities nourish the Universal, and not particularism or communitarianism," but the image of the two men in each other's arms is what remained).[44] The "jeunes Juifs" (young Jews) who had attacked Dieudonné were sentenced to six months in prison, and a few of them had their sentences mitigated.[45] It was against the background of this 2005 incident that, about a year later in the autumn of 2006, Confiant wrote the email in which he addressed "Dieudonné's (excusable) error" and "tried to understand"[46] Dieudonné's attendance at a National Front party.[47]

Bitterness, or Confiant in His Own Words

To better understand the fuller context of Confiant's statements, let us look at the December 9, 2006, interview in which he defends himself against accusations of anti-Semitism. Confiant states:

> Mes ancêtres n'ont pas pratiqué l'Inquisition. Ils n'ont pas fait de pogroms, de rafles du Vel d'Hiv' ni de chambres à gaz, donc je refuse tout net, quand je suis face à eux, d'avoir le moindre sentiment de responsabilité ou de culpabilité. Que les Européens se sentent coupables face à eux, c'est normal ! Toute cette mauvaise conscience a fait qu'il est devenu presque impossible de nommer ces personnes. Vous pouvez dire ou écrire sans aucun problème "de confession bouddhiste", "de confession chrétienne" ou "de confession musulmane", mais il suffit que vous indiquiez la religion de ces personnes pour que vous soyez immédiatement accusés d'antisémitisme ou que vous soyez traînés en

justice. C'est inacceptable ! Le journal "Antilla" a subi 2 ou 3 procès, je crois, pour les avoir nommés. Cela, c'est le premier point. Le deuxième, c'est que ce qui se passe en Palestine,[48] le massacre du people palestinien, est scandaleux venant de gens qui ont subi la Shoah il y a à peine un demi-siècle. Cela aussi, je le dénonce!

(My ancestors did not practice the Inquisition. They did not engage in the pogroms, the Vel d'Hiver roundups, or the gas chambers, so when confronted by such people, I categorically refuse even the slightest sentiment of responsibility or fault. That Europeans feel culpable in their confrontations with them, of course! All this bad faith has made for a situation in which it is virtually impossible to name these individuals. Without a problem, you can say or write "of a Buddhist denomination," "of a Christian confession," "of Muslim belief," but all it takes is to utter the religion of these persons and you are immediately accused of anti-Semitism, or you can even be taken to court. It is unacceptable. *Antilla* magazine has been sued two or three times, I think, for having named them. That is my first point. Second, what is happening in Palestine, the massacre of the Palestinian people is scandalous, notably from those who were subjected to the Shoah just barely half-a-century ago. And I also denounce that!)

It is clear from this interview that Confiant is *not* a Holocaust denier; in fact, he recognizes not only the Holocaust but also that of a more historically far-reaching history of anti-Semitism, notably of the Inquisition and the pogroms. He declares a need to be more clear-cut in how histories of genocide are told, and he suggests that the way the story of the Shoah has been recounted obfuscates the actual tragic facts in such a way as to deflect blame from the guilty party. For example, in the aforementioned 2012 blog post that repeats many of the same offensive terms, he analyzes the use of the word *Shoah:*

Alors pourquoi masquer derrière un mot hébreu mystérieux et incompréhensible, une chose qu'il est si simple de nommer: la destruction des Juifs d'Europe. Là c'est clair ! Là tout le monde comprend ! Là, je sais qui a été la victime et qui a été le bourreau, tandis qu'avec Shoah, tout devient subitement opaque.

(So why use a mysterious and incomprehensible Hebrew word to dissimulate something that can be stated in a quite simple manner: the destruction of the Jews of Europe. Now that is clear! Now everyone understands. Now I know who the victims were as well as their executors, whereas with the Shoah, everything becomes immediately opaque.)[49]

What we can surmise from these two texts are the following facts: Confiant definitively accuses the perpetrator—Europeans of Christian backgrounds; he clearly denies any responsibility for himself or those with whose heritage he identifies (i.e., he sees himself clearly as African diasporic and in no way Jewish, a question to which I shall return in the final parts of this essay); he does not mention non-Jewish victims of the Holocaust; and he points to a reluctance on the part of the French public sphere to admit wrongdoing.[50] Thus, he in fact reinforces claims for recognition and reparation on the part of, in Confiant's words, "Jews of Europe," a nomenclature that he does not use in 2006, but only in 2012, suggesting that, by the early 2010s, he had begun to pay closer attention to how he referred to Jews.

It then becomes apparent that it is *not* the meaning of Confiant's words that so upsets those who criticize him, but, rather, their tone, as well as the imprecision with which he makes references to the history of the Holocaust. For example, Lucas takes Confiant to task for declaring that Claude Lanzmann "invented" the word *Shoah*.[51] I might argue here, however, that what Confiant notes is nothing more than the fact that Lanzmann made an artistic choice to innovate documentary filmmaking around the lived experience of the Holocaust in such a way that a Hebrew word hitherto unfamiliar to a European audience was given meaning outside of its use by the Israeli state, which, according to Lucas, had used the word since 1949.[52]

If both Confiant's tone in 2006 and 2012 and his negligence as regards Jewish culture and history may be understood as an indication of anger, we must then ask: Is Confiant's antagonism explicitly geared toward Jews? Could it be that what Confiant is upset about are the implications of what it means for Lanzmann's film to have met with such success? Or is he even more basically objecting to the fact that financial and institutional conditions have existed in such a way as to enable the production of a certain number of narrative films and documentaries about the Holocaust, but not, say, about slavery? As with his discussion about the conferral of the 1991 Prix Goncourt on Combescot, Confiant is not undermining either Lanzmann's or Combescot's artistic practices.[53] On the contrary, as is clearly evidenced by Confiant's elegy for Combescot, whose writing he states is superior to his own, Confiant gestures instead to two problems: first, that the Jewish experience of tragedy and oppression has received far more attention in the mainstream than that of the Africana experience; and, second, that in order to achieve such attention, certain artistic choices were made to which Confiant objects—notably, the mystification and aestheticization of the Holocaust. The latter of Confiant's criticisms, then, is in alignment with critics who, for example, find fault with Giorgio Agamben's or Alain Badiou's writings on Jewishness and the Holocaust.[54] Could it be that the object of Confiant's dismay is a culture industry that places artists and intellectuals associated with certain ethnic and/or racial identities in a particular role, so that Jews and Blacks are first conscripted into a generalized category of Otherness that can create a sense of solidarity but that increasingly pits them against one another in a relationship of competitive victimhood?

The more general question is: Does Confiant (as his critics suggest) purposefully nurture a belligerent attitude toward Jews so as to gratuitously feed competitive memory? Or is he working through a complex matrix that involves not just Blackness, Jewishness, and whiteness, but also questions especially of Arabness and Muslimness? Certainly, he is the inheritor of a literary history in French (Jean-Paul Sartre, Aimé Césaire, Frantz Fanon, and even Maryse Condé), which has for the most part respectfully engaged the "rhetorical oppositionality of 'Black' and 'Jew.'"[55] That said, unlike his contemporary Condé, he writes and works from Martinique, rather than, say, New York, where Condé, born in Guadeloupe, has spent a good part of her career; he is dedicated to staying in, working from, and writing about Martinique. As such, his comments on Jewishness, and more generally on a culture industry that seems to favor Jewishness—or at least privileges a certain expression of Jewishness—need to be understood in the context of Martinican intellectualism and society.

Conflating Contexts, a Dearth in Scholarship: Fanon, Palestine, and the History of Jewishness in Martinique

On December 6, 2005, almost a year before Assouline, Dahomay, and Wiltord published their online criticisms of Confiant, a group of twenty-four public intellectuals, including the politician and intellectual Christiane Taubira as well as political philosopher Achille Mbembe and political scientist and philosopher Françoise Vergès, signed their name to a document titled "Déclaration des 24" (the Declaration of the 24), which was published by *Le Monde*. In it they warned against sloppy narratives that accuse Jews of complicity in the slave trade, and that seek to explain at once Israel's mistreatment of Palestinians and the inability of France to recognize its violent colonization and withdrawal from Algeria. In other words, the signatories of the "Declaration of the 24" categorically refuse what they designate as the false notion that there is a "complot juif" (Jewish conspiracy) against those who self-identify as Black, Algerian, Arab, and/or Palestinian. Moreover, the signatories explicitly name Dieudonné as a public figure who promotes such confused and hurtful narratives. Most interestingly, the signatories, albeit subtly, call upon scholars to take up the challenge of creating research projects that help to demystify such conspiracy theories. The signatories write: "La France, heureusement, ne manque pas d'historiens, de sociologues, de politologues—dont beaucoup sont 'issus de l'immigration'—à même d'apporter leur contribution à la lutte contre le double poison de la dérive antisémite et de la dénégation colonial" (Luckily France has its share of historians, sociologists, political scientists—many of whom are "of an immigrant background"—and who are quite capable of contributing to the fight against the double poison represented by anti-Semitic tendencies and colonial denial).[56] The signatories suggest that well-researched journalism on the topic of immigration and intercultural relations, as well as university-funded research, freelance scholarship and historical fiction have the potentiality of existing, but as of 2005 were not yet present, at least in sufficiently disseminated forms. Thanks to the scholarship of Vincent Aaron Brown, Karen Brodkin, Sarah Casteel, Bryan Cheyette, Deborah Eisenberg, Jonathan Israel, Ethan B. Katz, William F. S. Miles, and Ronnie Scharfman, a well-informed discussion has since emerged that courageously complicates, in Casteel's words, "the strict victim/perpetrator binary."[57] Yet, in the case of Confiant—or, more generally speaking, of the French, and even more specifically the Martinican context—the confusion of narratives is particularly difficult to untangle for reasons relating to two topics in particular: the historical presence of Jews in Martinique and Frantz Fanon's Algerian (and, more generally, anticolonial) writing.

A discussion of Jewishness in Martinique is necessarily troubled by a burdened historical understanding of how a *béké* identity (descendants of colonial Europeans, understood to be white) relates to the early Jewish presence on the island. Thanks to Miles's comprehensive history of the presence of Jews in Martinique, it is possible to trace a much more precise, even if still incomplete, history. For example, it is probable that Jewish settlers who had fled Brazil through Recife in the seventeenth century introduced the technical knowledge that allowed for the cultivation of sugar on the island.[58] In the section of *Chronique d'un empoisonnement annoncé. Le scandale du chlordécone aux Antilles francaises (1972–2002)* (The diary of a declared poisoning: The French Caribbean Kepone insecticide scandal, 1972–2002) entitled "Les Békés, leur histoire, leur poids économique" (Békés, their history, and their economic power), Louis Boutrin and Confiant himself emphasize that Jews were among the first cultivators of sugar.[59] Finally, and more recently, as Miles explains, a small but significant Jewish community has established itself in Martinique since the 1970s in a "ripple effect of the Algerian War of liberation that ended in 1962."[60]

As we discover from Confiant's fiction, complicated connections between Martinique and Jewishness also emerge with respect to a more recent historical past: World War II. In 2017, Confiant published a fictional autobiography/biography of Fanon under the title *L'insurrection de l'âme: Frantz Fanon, vie et mort du guerrier-silex* (The insurrection of the soul: Frantz Fanon, life and death of the flint-warrior), a title that references Césaire's poem about Fanon, from which I have drawn the epigraph to this essay. The novel interlaces two narrative modes: chapters that are recounted as an imagined autobiography, in which a fictional Fanon recounts himself in the first person; and chapters told by an external narrator. With this double narrative movement, the novel presents itself as a literary biography of Fanon. I suggest that it is particularly notable that Confiant published his narrative on Fanon, the Martinican figure whom he most admires, roughly a decade after the first criticisms that suggested his insensitivity to the Jewish historical experience. While the novel is most certainly not about Jewishness, it does include significant allusions to Jewishness. For example, in the second chapter, which recounts Fanon's first days upon his arrival at the psychiatric hospital of Blida, the external narrative voice tells of Jacques Azoulay's extreme worry that Fanon might endanger himself by attending to clients in the field, rather than staying in the psychiatric hospital.[61] Here, Confiant clearly makes an effort to include an allusion to Fanon's friendship with Azoulay, a Jewish-Algerian doctor.[62]

A further example of Confiant's invocation of Jewishness as related in particular to the Second World War is the third chapter of *L'insurrection de l'âme*. This chapter is almost entirely an addendum to the historical contexts of one of Confiant's earlier novels, 1988's *Le Nègre et l'Amiral* (The Black man and the admiral), which is set in Martinique during the Second World War. As Miles notes, Martinique under Admiral Robert was characterized by British spies as "very anti-Semitic."[63] In the Fanon novel, published almost thirty years after *Le Nègre et l'Amiral,* and, notably, after the various accusations of anti-Semitism, Confiant's narrators explicitly retell the story of Martinique during the Vichy years so as to include Jews, whom he had mostly omitted from the storyline of *Le Nègre et l'Amiral*. In his Fanon novel, the period in question is recounted by Fanon's first-person narrative voice, which explains how Fanon's mother had taken in the mother of an Italian family that had fled the Mussolini regime. (It is unclear if the Italian woman is Jewish and/or Communist).⁶⁴

In fact, the same chapter of *L'insurrection de l'âme* revisits yet another one of Confiant's previous novels, *Rue des Syriens* (Syrian alley, 2012), explaining that the denizens of the actual street were the focus of Admiral Robert's persecution of

> communistes, les franc-maçons et même la poignée de Juifs installés depuis des lustres en Martinique et que la population avait toujours confondus avec les Syro-libanais, eux en revanche en assez grand nombre et bien installés dans une rue de Fort-de-France, François Arago, qui avait fini par être rebaptisée "rue des Syriens."
>
> (Communists, Free Masons, and even the handful of Jews who ages ago had established themselves in Martinique and whom the population had always mistaken for Syrian-Lebanese, who for their part in quite significant numbers had set themselves up on the François Arago street in Fort-de-France, which in the end had been re-baptized "Syrian Alley.")⁶⁵

In his article on Jewishness in Martinique, Miles explains that "islanders tend to lump all residents of Middle Eastern origin together, distinguishing naught between, say, Muslims of Palestinian origin and Jews from North Africa: all are Syrians. Not even wearing a Jewish skullcap, a *yarmulke*, which several members of the community now do in public, projects religious identification."⁶⁶ Thus, in his 2017 novel about Fanon, by including a discussion of Martinique under the infamous rule of Admiral Georges Robert, Confiant deals more directly with the vexed history of Martinique as regards Jewishness and the Vichy regime, a topic that hitherto his novels had mostly neglected.

Confiant's previous inattention to—or misunderstanding of—Jewishness may in fact have to do in part with Martinique's political role during the Second World War. No other event underscores the particularity of this role and its relationship to the Holocaust than the recent 2017 publication by Haitian author Louis-Philippe Dalembert of the novel *Avant que les ombres s'effacent* (Before the shadows disappear), a fictional literary history of how Haitian consulates issued passports to hundreds of Jews fleeing Nazism. If Haiti was the seat of "la France libre" in the Americas, then Martinique was for all intents and purposes quite the opposite: while Admiral Robert was supposed to safeguard neutrality in

Guadeloupe, Martinique, and Guyana, he in fact collaborated with the Vichy government.

Fanon plays a complex role in Martinican history-making, for, as Miles points out, Fanon is "less well-read in Martinique than outside."[67] The reason for this has to do in part with Fanon's role as an anticolonial revolutionary in Algeria in the decades following Martinique's decision to departmentalize, as such becoming part of the French state. Fanon's itinerary and his lifework—his birth and primary and secondary education in Martinique; his practice as a psychiatrist in France; and his later psychiatric work, research, service, and political activism in Algeria—juxtapose the magnanimous theoretical conclusions put forward in *Black Skins, White Masks* (1952), on the one hand, with an uncompromising call to anticolonialism even at the cost of violence in *The Wretched of the Earth* (1961), on the other. Fanon's trajectory, and the varied shapes of the intellectualism that he nurtured, spin a web that includes the distressed relationship between and among French Catholic Algerians, French Jewish Algerians, Algerian Jews, and Algerian Muslims, not to mention secularists of varying national origins and religious affiliations such as Albert Camus or Saïd Sadi. Notably, Fanon is also a figure who complicates the relationship between "Jews" and "Blacks" in *Black Skin, White Masks*.[68] Confiant, it may be argued, imagines himself the *fils spirituel* (spiritual son) of Fanon. A similar analogy has been made comparing Chamoiseau to the late Édouard Glissant. And, in fact, Fanon's early death in 1961 at the age of thirty-six left Confiant to fend for himself in applying Fanonian intellectualism to an ongoing state of affairs. Whereas Chamoiseau was accorded the privilege of thinking alongside Glissant, who passed in 2011 at the age of eighty-three, Confiant has had to imagine how Fanon would have reacted or behaved in a world that has drastically changed since Fanon's death. How would Fanon have responded to a post-1960s Israel? How would he have understood neoliberalism?

I might even venture the conjecture that Lewis R. Gordon's *What Fanon Said*—published two years before Confiant's novel on Fanon, as well as political scholar Miles's previously mentioned article on Jewishness in Martinique, published both in English in 2005 and updated in French for online publication in 2010 by the journal *Pouvoirs dans la Caraïbe*, which is run out of Confiant's university—might have provided Confiant with a more subtle understanding of how Fanon dealt with Jewishness.[69] For example, Confiant's depiction of Azoulay corresponds to that offered by Gordon, as does Confiant's explanation that, for most Martinicans,

"Syrians" refer generally to citizens of Middle Eastern origin, irrespective of their religion.[70]

Recent scholarship by Casteel, Cheyette, Gordon, Miles, and Rothberg provides models for interpreting the complex ways in which the "dimension of imagination involved in acts of remembrance" takes place.[71] Without a doubt, Confiant's novelistic agenda corresponds to Rothberg's characterization of multidirectional memory as "productive—as producing new objects and new lines of sight—and not simply as reproducing already given entities that either are or are not 'like' other already given entities."[72] The difference between Confiant and most intellectuals—both scholars and novelists, for most of Confiant's anger comes out not in his novels, but in his nonfiction—is that he unabashedly allows himself the space of the affective, whereby he integrates the experience of anger in its most aggressive forms: lashing out; making connections that do not necessarily make sense; and making statements that in all probability hurt someone else.

We're left wondering, Why until recently did he seem to consistently speak out against Jews, and why does he preserve Muslim Algerians, secular Algerians, and Palestinians from his bitterness? We can draw on Miles to answer the question directly and succinctly: "Anti-Israeli, pro-Palestinian sentiment is especially keen in far left and pro-independence circles in Martinique. This may be attributed in part to the limited popularity for outright sovereignty for the island: liberation for Palestine becomes a surrogate for the independence struggle in Martinique. Demanding statehood for the Palestinians is a salve for those not prepared to wrest it for Martinique."[73] In other words, if, as Éric Marty has argued, leftist intellectualism in France demonstrates a new wave of anti-Semitism, then given Miles's politically psychoanalytic analysis of Palestine as a sort of "surrogate" for leftist Martinicans to project their own struggle, it is not surprising that Confiant's discomfort with Jewishness manifests itself in a much more conspicuous manner than that of Agamben or Badiou.[74] Moreover, given the reading of Israel as a colonial project and the accordingly ambivalent relationship of postcolonial studies to Jewishness, especially in the context of Martinique, where on "March 24, 2002, Palestine Day was organized" by the Collective of Martinican Solidarity with the Palestinian People (CSMP, created in 1988), it becomes clearer how Confiant's practice as an intellectual is tightly knitted into both his active participation in Martinican political society and his stance as a political independent. After all, the CSMP was created a year before the publication of *In Praise of Creoleness* (and its exclusion of Jews from its vision of hybridity) and the Palestinian Day took place four years before Confiant's most criticized remarks about Jewishness.

Making Room for Anger?

While Confiant's literary autobiography/biography of Fanon is certainly a project that can be read as the ode of the spiritual son to his spiritual father, it can also be understood as Confiant's working through of how Jewishness today (perhaps also Muslim fundamentalism today, or Arab secularism) fits, and would have fit, into the Fanonian project. Clearly, Confiant has at some level reckoned with the accusations against him of anti-Semitism. Whether or not he regrets what he said or how he said it, and how his words are received by varying parties, remains unclear. Confiant's Wikipedia entry (here I draw from both the French- and English-language versions) reads that he "est issu, par sa mère, d'une famille de petits distillateurs mulâtres de la commune du Lorrain" (on his mother's side he is from a small-scale *mulâtre* distillery family) and "his great-grandfather, Louis Augustin, and his grand-father, François Augustin owned a small rum distillery . . . as well as fifty or so hectares of sugar cane plants."[75] Given that Jews in early colonial Martinique were associated with the sugar industry, could it be that Confiant's genealogy at some level includes Jewish ancestry, as is the case with several other Caribbean authors? Or could we read in Confiant's defiant refusal of "responsibility of fault" for the "Inquisition," "the pogroms," or the "Vel d'Hiver" roundups an ambivalence regarding Martinique's position during World War II? For the writer who has written novels about such a vast set of Martinican experiences, whose literary project has been to imagine into memory so many otherwise forgotten or little-known moments of Martinican history, how is it that he has not written about the first Jews in Martinique? That Confiant is troubled by Jewishness is unquestionable. Might we then read his lack of attention to Jewishness in his novels or his depictions of the "Jewish question" as a sign of his feelings of discomfort?

Ultimately, to judge Confiant as having nurtured a form of competitive memory may be less illuminating than to consider the role of the affective—and, more precisely, the affective space that gives rise to emotions of anger—in the processes by which we construct our political stances. In other words, is there a place for anger in intellectual and scholarly deliberations? Is someone like Confiant allowed to be bitter that recent history and public policy have clearly, at least in the US-American case, done their "level best to shut and double-seal the postwar window of opportunity in African Americans' faces'" while US-American Jews have been able to rise economically?[76] How do we understand the choice of magazines such as *Charlie Hebdo* to protect Judaism from overly offensive satire while refusing to protect Islam from similar forms of discourse?[77] For, in the end, as René Lemarchand argues with reference to Rwanda and Burundi, reconciliation cannot take place without "reckoning," whereby parties-in-conflict confront each other. The question thus remains: What is the place of anger in the process of reckoning?[78] If indeed there is a place for anger, then perhaps we can finally begin to open up our vectors of communication and relation so as not to simply dismiss as delusional the claims of someone such as Confiant, but rather to examine how such affective spaces are undergirded by a complex set of historical factors.

Notes

I cannot thank Heidi Kaufman and Sarah Phillips Casteel, the editors of this volume, enough for guiding this article in a direction such that it respectfully—but honestly—engages a Rothbergian "multidirectional" analysis around such a fraught topic. I also thank Kathleen Gyssels for her generosity and her pioneering work bridging disciplines: without her, I would not have been part of this project. Thank you especially to the students at the Center of Worker Education at City College of New York, whose conversations after screening both Steven Spielberg's *Schindler's List* and *Amistad* pushed me in directions in which I never thought I would have gone. I thank my research group—Kelly Baker Josephs, Christian Flaugh, Kaiama L. Glover, and Maja Horn—for constantly supporting my inquiries. I thank Alicia Montoya, Isabelle Thibaudeau-Boon, and Jeanette den Toonder, who invited me to speak about Confiant at the conference "Colloque Territoires et/ou Mémoires francophones contemporains," which they organized at the University of Radboud in March 2015. I thank Sandra Ponzanesi for her research guiding me through theory that deals meaningfully with the postcolonial culture industry. I thank J. Ryan Poynter and Robert Baron for probing me to go beyond the "conspiracy."

1. The conclusion of this article also examines the space of the affective, wherein the affective is understood as an "active discharge of emotion, the counter-attack," the letting go that precedes a person's capacity to recognize it as a "sensation that has been checked against previous experiences and labeled." Libe García Zarranz, "Transdisciplinary Approaches of Affect Theory," YouTube, https://www.youtube.com/watch?v=za8ew2WgcvA (accessed February 23, 2018)

2. For Franketienne, whose circumstances are much different than those of Confiant—that is, there are absolutely no accusations of anti-Semitism against Franketienne, see Kaiama L. Glover's discussion of the postcolonial culture

industry in *Haiti Unbound: A Spiralist Challenge to the Postcolonial Canon* (Liverpool: Liverpool University Press, 2010), 1–30.

    3. Alessandra Benedicty-Kokken, "Ananda Devi and Dany Laferrière: The Culture Industry, Poverty Discourse, and Postcolonial Literatures in French." *Frame: Tijdschrift* 28, no. 2, The Postcolonial Cultural Industry (Fall/Winter 2015): 31–50.

    4. Sarah Phillips Casteel, *Calypso Jews: Jewishness in the Caribbean Literary Imagination* (New York: Columbia University Press, 2016), 15.

    5. "Rafael Lucas: Fiche personne," Africultures., http://africultures.com/personnes/?no=20069&utm_source=newsletter&utm_medium=email&utm_campaign=438 (accessed August 2017).

    6. Éric Marty, *Radical French Thought and the Return of the "Jewish Question,"* trans. Alan Astro. (Bloomington: Indiana University Press, 2015).

    7. Unless otherwise indicated, all translations are my own.

    8. Pinalie as quoted by Labi in his blog "Les Juifs." I have not been able to find the original source of Pinalie's quote.

    9. His words are: "j'essaie d'analyser le pourquoi de la visite de Dieudonné à la Fête 'Bleu-Blanc-Rouge' du Front National" (I try to analyze the why of Diedonné's visit to the National Front's "Blue-White-Red" Party). The fact that Dieudonné indeed attended the party is logged on the "Dieudonné" Wikipedia entry.

    10. Raphaël Confiant, "Une certaine lâcheté intellectuelle. . . ." *Parti des indigènes de la République,* February 12, 2012, http://indigenes-republique.fr/une-certaine-lachete-intellectuelle/ (accessed May 3, 2019).

    11. Devorah Lauter, "French Interior Minister Claims Some Civilisations 'Superior,'" *Telegraph,* February 5, 2012, https://www.telegraph.co.uk/news/worldnews/europe/france/9062473/French-interior-minister-claims-some-civilisations-superior.html (accessed March 26, 2019).

    12. Rafael Lucas, "Droit de réponse de Rafael Lucas à un article de Raphaël Confiant," *Mediapart,* February 15, 2012, https://blogs.mediapart.fr/david-gauzere/blog/150212/droit-de-reponse-de-rafael-lucas-un-article-de-raphael-confiant (accessed December 14, 2018).

    13. See "idées" article by Jacky Dahomay, titled "L'innomable Raphaël Confiant? Par Jacky Dahomay," December 2, 2006, https://www.lemonde.fr/idees/article/2006/12/02/l-innommable-raphael-confiant-par-jacky-dahomay_840723_3232.html (accessed 26 March 2019); Rafael Lucas, "Fiche personnelle"; and interview between *Franceinfo* and Jeanne Wiltord, "L'invention de la langue créole a sauvé les exclaves d'un état de déshumanistaion (Jeanne Wiltord, psychiatre et psychanalyste)," https://la1ere.francetvinfo.fr/invention-langue-creole-sauve-esclaves-etat-deshumanisation-jeanne-wiltord-psychiatre-psychanalyste-526727.html (accessed March 26, 2019).

    14. Patrice Louis, "Raphael Confiant et les 'Innomables,'" *Le Monde,* December 1, 2006, http://www.lemonde.fr/societe/article/2006/12/01/en-martinique

-raphael-confiant-appuie-dieudonne_840819_3224.html (accessed August 11, 2017).

15. Rafael Lucas, "Droit de réponse de Rafael Lucas à un article de Raphaël Confiant, posted by David Gauzère," Mediapart, February 15, 2012, https://blogs.mediapart.fr/david-gauzere/blog/150212/droit-de-reponse-de-rafael-lucas-un-article-de-raphael-confiant (accessed March 26, 2019).

16. Pierre Assouline, "Le problème avec Confiant," Le blog de Pierre Assouline, December 1, 2006, http://passouline.blog.lemonde.fr/2006/12/01/le-probleme-avec-confiant/ (accessed April 28, 2015). Nota bene: The article has been taken offline. However, in his blog, which reacts to the 2012 episode, Rafael Lucas also uses the term "délire" to refer to Confiant's historical analyses. Lucas writes, "Dans ce genre de délire verbal, les faits historiques maltraités côtoient des simplifications d'évènements dramatiques de l'Histoire et des insultes généralisées" (In this sort of verbal delirium, badly deliberated historical facts stand alongside dramatic oversimplifications of historical events as well as general insults.) See Rafael Lucas, "Droit de réponse de Rafael Lucas à un article de Raphaël Confiant."

17. William Labi. "Les Juifs . . . les innomables," WilliamLabi, December 3, 2006, http://williamlabi.blogspot.nl/2006/12/les-juifs-les-innomables.html (accessed September 25, 2007).

18. Jacky Dahomay, "Raphaël Confiant, nouveau cas de 'lepénisation' victimaire: *L'innommable Raphaël Confiant?*" Histoire Coloniale, December 9, 2006, https://histoirecoloniale.net/Raphael-Confiant-nouveau-cas-de.html (accessed December 11, 2018).

19. Louis, "Raphael Confiant et les 'Innomables.'"

20. Michael Rothberg, *Multidirectional Memory: Remembering the Holocaust in the Age of Decolonization* (Stanford, CA: Stanford University Press, 2009), 1.

21. I use the term "Africana" to refer to what the Barnard College Africana Studies Department designates as a "multidisciplinary approach to the study of the history, politics, cultures, and literatures of Africa and of the African Diaspora in the Americas, Caribbean and Europe," whereby the experience of African Americans, Africans in the Americas, and the notion of diaspora, as well as research taking place in Africa, come together. The gesture of the word Africana is not to privilege any one place of intellectual production over another, and to privilege the relationships between and among scholars, regardless of whether or not they are diasporic. "Africana Studies," Barnard College, Africana Studies Department, https://africana.barnard.edu/africana-studies (accessed September 25, 2017).

22. William F. S. Miles, trans. Loïza Nellec–Miles, "La créolité et le juifs de la Martinique," *Pouvoirs dans la Caraïbe* 16 (2010): 129. The article was first published in English, but updated for the French publication: William F. S. Miles, "Caribbean Hybridity and the Jews of Martinique," in *The Jewish Diaspora in*

Latin America and the Caribbean: Fragments of Memory, ed. Kristin Ruggiero (Brighton, RU: Sussex Academic Press, 2005): 139–62.

23. Casteel, *Calypso Jews*.

24. Louis Boutrin and Raphaël Confiant, *Chronique d'un empoisonnement annoncé. Le scandale du chlordécone aux Antilles francaises (1972–2002)* (Paris: L'Harmattan, 2007), 65.

25. See, for example, Vanessa Agard-Jones's work on the use of kepone in big-business agriculture in Martinique or Justin Izzo's work on Confiant's novel *Le Nègre et l'Amiral*. Also, note the essays that are part of the 2015 special section of *Small Axe* titled "Rethinking Aimé Césaire," guest edited by Eric Prieto, as well as the essays that are part of the 2017 special section in *Small Axe* titled "Eulogizing Creoleness? Rereading *Éloge de la Créolité* and Caribbean Identity, Culture, and Politics" (2017) edited by Martin Munro and Celia Britton, in which authors such as Adlai Murdoch and Carrie Noland consider how prominent Guadeloupean and Martinican scholars (who were born after Césaire—writers such as Maryse Condé, Édouard Glissant, and, notably, Patrick Chamoiseau, with whom Confiant coauthored two essays) have engaged with Césaire's legacy, as well as the more general questions of anticolonialism, postcolonialism, memory, commemoration of slavery, and/or sovereignty. Specific scholars who have recently presented academic papers on Confiant are: Savrina Chinien (University of the West Indies, St. Augustine), Shanaaz Mohammed (Florida State University), Laura Cassin (Université des Antilles et de la Guyane), and Suzanne Crosta, (McMaster University).

26. He has received the Prix November (1991), the Premio Literario Casa de las Américas (1993), the Prix Carbet (1994), and the Prix de l'Agence Française de Développement (2010).

27. Confiant was named "doyen" in April 2013, but in March 2018 self-identifies as no longer occupying that role. As this essay goes to press, the Affaire Ceregmia has become an important topic of debate, to which Confiant has contributed. "Raphaël Confiant nouveau Doyen de la Fac de lettres," Overblog, April 19, 2013, http://elsie-news.over-blog.com/article-politiques-publiques-martinique-raphael-confiant-nouveau-doyen-de-la-fac-de-lettres-117202780.html; "Université : Raphael Confiant est consterné par l'attitude de la 'DGS de l'UA," Antilla, March 24, 2018, http://antilla-martinique.com/universite-raphael-confiant-est-consterne-par-lattitude-de-la-dgs-de-lua/; and "Affaire Ceregmia : les trois professeurs tentent de retrouver leurs postes," FranceInfo, February 21, 2018, https://la1ere.francetvinfo.fr/martinique/affaire-ceregmia-trois-professeurs-tentent-retrouver-leurs-postes-561311.html. The access date for all of the above is March 26, 2019.

28. See interview between the online publication Bondamanjak (BMJ: http://www.bondamanjak.com) and Raphaël Confiant (RC) related through the website ProChoixNews, August 11, 2017, http://www.prochoix.org/cgi/blog/index.php/2006/12/09/1062-confiant-sur-l-anti-Semitisme-et-le-racisme (accessed May 3, 2019).

29. See Raphaël Confiant, "*Les filles du Calvaire* et *Eau de café*, finalistes du prix Goncourt 1991," Montraykréyol, June 28, 2017, http://www.montraykreyol.org/article/les-filles-du-calvaire-et-eau-de-cafe-finalistes-du-prix-goncourt-1991 (accessed August 18, 2017), as well as the interview conducted with Confiant in December 2006, "Confiant sur l'antisémitisme et le racisme," Prochoix.org, December 9, 2006, originally published on Bondamanjak.com.

30. Adlai Murdoch's 2017 article offers the most up-to-date summary of the evolution of the terms *creole, créolité,* and *créolisation,* a succinct narrative that not only honors the complexity of this history, but also problematizes it in new ways. Adlai Murdoch, "Créolité, Creolization, and Contemporary Caribbean Culture," *Small Axe* 52 (2017): 180–98.

31. Perhaps, as Maeve McCusker writes, *In Praise*'s "celebratory rhetoric should be seen not only as premature but as profoundly misplaced. And from this perspective, perhaps the most striking index of the *Éloge*'s failure is the fact that its most energetic proponent now would appear to be not any one of its three signatories but the béké Roger de Jaham" (232). McCusker recounts how békés have used the "rhetoric around multiplicity" (227) to build a civil society that appears to open itself up to the majority of citizens of Martinique, especially on the website *Tous Créoles!,* but in fact uses *In Praise*'s language to continue a supremacist order under a lexicon that seems more expansive toward Martinique's nonbéké community. Maeve McCusker "All Creoles Now? Béké Identity and *Éloge de la Créolité,*" *Small Axe* 52 (2017): 220–32.

32. Murdoch, "Créolité," 185. Murdoch cites Stephan Palmié, "Creolization and Its Discontents," *Annual Review of Anthropology* 35 (2006): 440, 443.

33. Murdoch, "Créolité," 185.

34. Perhaps *In Praise of Creoleness*'s problem is one of genre, for, as Michal Obszyński has argued, *In Praise* is a "manifestaire" (manifestatory) text, and as such cannot practice what it preaches. Michal Obszyński, *Manifestes et programmes littéraires aux Caraïbes francophones: En/jeux idéologiques et poétiques* (Leiden: E. J. Brill, 2016), 21.

35. "Dieudonné," Wikipedia, https://fr.wikipedia.org/wiki/Dieudonné (accessed August 20, 2017).

36. Jikeli, "A Framework," 53.

37. Wikipedia. "Dieudonné."

38. The National Front is the right-wing party whose platform includes anti-immigration policies and anti-Semitism. However, after receiving ongoing criticism for excessively offensive use of stereotypes, especially against Jews, but also against Catholics, Dieudonné began to engage more and more in dialogue with the National Front, the party against which he had once campaigned.

39. Amanda Borschel-Dan, "As French Jews vote for Le Pen, A Case of the Enemy of my Enemy?" *Times of Israel,* December 8, 2015, https://www.timesofisrael.com/as-french-jews-vote-for-le-pen-a-case-of-the-enemy-of-my-enemy/ (accessed March 26, 2019).

40. Günther Jikeli, "A Framework for Assessing Antisemitism: Three Case Studies (Dieudonné, Erdoğan, and Hamas)" in *Deciphering the New Antisemitism,* ed. Alvin H. Rosenfeld (Bloomington: Indiana Univeristy Press, 2015), 53–54.

41. There are certain requirements to become a presidential candidate, such as collecting five hundred signatures from French citizens and establishing an account for campaigning. I do not know which of the eligibility factors Dieudonné did not meet.

42. "Agression de Dieudonné à Fort-de-France," *Le Monde,* March 2, 2005, http://www.lemonde.fr/societe/article/2005/03/02/agression-de-dieudonne-a-fort-de-france_400003_3224.html (accessed August 22, 2018).

43. The meeting may be seen on YouTube. Madame Monfort, "DIEUDO 2005-03-06 RFO Martinique—Rencontre Aime Cesaire & Dieudonne," March 6, 2005, https://www.youtube.com/watch?v=15PcLLb6Ol0 (accessed August 22, 2018).

44. Louis, "Raphael Confiant et les 'Innomables.'"

45. Miles, "Créolité et les Juifs," 129. The English version of the article, published in 2005, does not mention Dieudonné. The French version, published in 2010, includes a vague reference to the incident against Dieudonné in Fort-de-France. I have not been able to find much informaton about the specific perpetrators, except that there were four of them and three held Israeli passports. It is not clear if they hold dual citizenship with France or if they live in Martinique. For a series of news reports on the legal cases, see the YouTube link that edits them together: https://www.youtube.com/watch?v=5W0u8f_SoqE.

46. Without doing more research interviewing Confiant and those who read his emailed document about Dieudonné, it is impossible for me to pass judgment on Confiant and, notably, to gauge his motivations in writing about the comedian.

47. I have not been able to get a copy of Confiant's "La faute (pardonnable) de Dieudonné." In the interview on December 9, 2006, Confiant explains that the text that he authored, was "non publié dans la presse écrite, ni posté sur un quelconque site-web ou blog" (not published, nor published online), and only circulated "auprès d'une trentaine de personnes par Internet, texte" (but only circulated among thirty or so persons by internet). He explains that he does not speak ill of Jews, but rather that he tries to understand why the French comedian Diedonné M'Bala M'Bala might have attended the right-wing National Front "Fête 'Bleu-Blanc-Rouge." Confiant interviewed by Bondamanjak.

48. For an explanation and analysis of the notion of "s'indigner" as related to the Palestinian cause, see Christian Doumet, "Que veut dire s'*indigner* ?" *Contemporary French and Francophone Studies* 16, no. 2 (March 2012): 197–204.

49. Confiant, "Une certaine lâcheté."

50. For the most recent and comprehensive account of the polemics around "apologisme" as regards Vichy, see Lia Brozgal and Sara Kippur, *Being Contemporary: French Literature, Culture, and Politics Today* (Liverpool: Liverpool University Press, 2016).

51. Lucas, "Droit de réponse"; Confiant, "Une certaine lâcheté."

52. Lucas.

53. It is interesting to note that one of the major films on the Middle Passage, *Amistad* (1997) is by Steven Spielberg, released just four years after his film about the Holocaust, *Schindler's List* (1993).

54. See, for example, Laurent de la Durantaye on Agamben, Bruno Chaouat, Éric Marty, or Maurice Samuels as regards Badiou's essay "Uses of the Word 'Jew,'" originally published in French in 2005. Laurent de la Durantaye, *Giorgio Agamben: A Critical Introduction* (Stanford, CA: Stanford University Press, 2009); Bruno Chaouat, *Is Theory Good for the Jews?* (Liverpool: Liverpool University Press, 2016); Marty, *Radical French Thought and the Return of the "Jewish Question"*; Maurice Samuels, "Alain Badiou and Antisemitism," in *Being Contemporary: French Literature, Culture and Politics Today*, eds. Lia Brozgal and Sara Kippur (Liverpool: Liverpool University Press, 2016): 107–26.

55. Casteel, *Calypso Jews*, 15. See Casteel's excellent third chapter on Condé's novel *I, Tituba, Black Witch of Salem*, first published in French in 1986.

56. Christiane Taubira, et al., "Déclaration des 24, 'Démons français,'" YouTube, December 5, 2005, https://www.lemonde.fr/idees/article/2005/12/05/demons-francais_717596_3232.html (accessed March 26, 2019).

57. Casteel, *Calypso Jews*, 14.

58. As Casteel's work shows, it is possible that Benjamin d'Acosta d'Andrade, a protagonist in Condé's *I, Tituba, Black Witch of Salem*, is in part based on the first Jewish settler in Martinique, a Sephardic Jew who was born in Portugal but spent time in South America. He might have been related to the Amsterdam-based family of Joseph Da Costa, a shareholder in the Dutch West India Company. Furthermore, the first article of Louis XIV's *Black Code* (1685) demanded the expulsion of all Jews from the French colonies. That said, by 1685, the small population, which did not exceed eighty persons, had either fled to Barbados or converted to Christianity (Miles, "Créolité et les Juifs," 132). See also Roget Petitjean, "Les Juifs à la Martinique sous l'ancien régime," *Revue d'histoire des colonies* 43, no. 151 (1956): 138–58. While there is little research on Jews in Martinique, a more important and accessible amount of writing has been produced by scholars studying the presence of Dutch colonization and merchant activity in the Antilles and the Atlantic coast of South America, notably in present-day Suriname, from the mid-1600s to the mid-1700s. See the scholarship of Aviva Ben-Ur, Jonathan Boyarin, Jane S. Gerber, Josette Capriles Goldish, Laura Arnold Leibman and Sam May, and Jessica Vance Roitman.

59. Boutrin and Confiant, *Chronique*, 65.

60. Miles, "Caribbean Hybridity," 145.

61. Raphaël Confiant, *L'insurrection de l'âme: Frantz Fanon: vie et mort du guerrier-silex* (Paris: Caraïbéditions, 2017), 38.

62. In the nonfictional world, Azoulay, who passed away on June 5, 2011, indeed served as a psychiatrist at Blida as Fanon's intern. He conducted and

completed his thesis work under Fanon in 1954. See Philippe-Jean Catinchi. "Jacques Azoulay, psychiatre," *Le Monde,* June 9, 2011, http://www.lemonde.fr/disparitions/article/2011/06/09/jacques-azoulay-psychiatre_1534033_3382.html (accessed August 20, 2017); and Numa Murard, "Psychiatrie et politique: Frantz Fanon à Blida," Centre de sociologie des pratiques et des représentations politques, Université Paris Diderot, October 2008, http://www.csprp.univ-paris-diderot.fr/IMG/pdf/murard.pdf (accessed August 20, 2017).

63. Miles, "Caribbean Hybridity," 142.

64. Confiant, *L'insurrection,* 66.

65. Confiant, 66.

66. Miles, "Caribbean Hybridity," 149.

67. Miles, 151.

68. Fanon acknowledges that whiteness has acribed Jews with a certain proclivity for all that is associated with the mind (i.e., a capacity for intellectual activities). In contrast to the Jew, however, whiteness has not only assigned Blackness to certain individuals, but also has attributed certain capacities that are of the physical body (i.e., not of the mind). Moreover, Fanon shows how Blackness, unlike Jewishness, is forever doomed by its skin: the fact that the person who is not white can never pass for or into whiteness. In present-day scholarship, Fanon's work on "black skin" serves as the foundation on which theories of the "flesh" are being deliberated on by Kaiama L. Glover, Hortense Spillers, or Alexander Weheliye.

69. Gordon identifies as an "Afro-Jewish philosopher, political thinker, educator, and musician." Lewis Gordon, "Biography," October 1, 2017, http://www.lewisrgordon.com/biography/ (accessed March 26, 2019).

70. Gordon writes, "Many who actually volunteered and who were closely associated with Fanon, such as Jacques Azoulay and Alice Cherki, were Jewish, which led to Fanon's being in constant battle against anti-Jewish sentiments in the ranks." Lewis R. Gordon, *What Fanon Said A Philosophical Introduction to His Life and Thought* (New York: Fordham University Press, 2015), 104.

71. Rothberg, *Multidirectional Memory,* 19.

72. Rothberg, 8–9.

73. Miles, "Caribbean Hybridity," 154.

74. Marty, *Radical French Thought,* 63, 66.

75. I paraphrase Stéphanie Mulot: Mulâtre initially refers to those persons born of a Black mother and a white father, but by the nineteenth century refers to a set of social behaviors associated with the social class of *mulâtre.* Stéphanie Mulot, "Chabines et métisses dans l'univers antillais: Entre assignations et négociations identitaires," *Clio: Histoire, femmes et sociétés* 27 (2008): 115.

76. Karen Brodkin, "How Jews Became White Folks: And What That Says About Race in America," in *Race, Class, and Gender in the United States: An Integrated Study, Ninth Edition,* ed. Paula S. Rothenberg and Kelly S. Mayhew (New York: Worth, 2014), 50.

77. Deborah Eisenberg, "Read the Letters and Comments of PEN Writers Protesting the Charlie Hebdo Award, put online by Glenn Greenwald," The Intercept, April 27, 2015, https://theintercept.com/2015/04/27/read-letters-comments-pen-writers-protesting-charlie-hebdo-award/ (accessed November 4, 2015).

78. René Lemarchand, *The Dynamics of Violence in Central Africa* (Philadelphia: University of Pennsylvania Press, 2009), 101, 104.

Caryl Phillips's Post-Holocaust/ Decolonized Interstices and the Levinasian Subjective in *Higher Ground* and *The Nature of Blood*

Neil R. Davison

IN MUCH OF his work, Caryl Phillips attempts to explore both the possibilities and limits of humane identifications across lines of colonial histories, identity politics, and racial difference. At the midpoint of his career, this ambition was most significantly realized through his juxtapositions of monologues in novels representing Black and Jewish consciousnesses riven distinctively by personal trauma and the inherited injustices of each of their respective racialized pasts. Critical response to those novels encompassed an early condemnation of his efforts as unethically presumptive: for example, a contextualization of his themes within a postmodern aesthetic "Route, Constellation, and Faultline," and an argument that his work fulfilled "the ethical promise of trauma studies by promoting . . . a critical and self-reflexive empathy as conducive to the establishment of a truly inclusive post-traumatic community marked by openness and respect for otherness."[1] A further discussion, by Wendy Zierler, suggested the works overcome a pattern of competition for victimhood by seeing Otherness as a "contiguity," rather than through a violent eclipsing of pasts in acts of "sameness," a failure of ethics that is the near opposite of Phillips's "pointed asymmetry."[2] Finally, in attempts to read Phillips as one of his generation's most important neohumanists, Bénédicte Ledent has produced a body of work exploring his abstractions as the ground of an "aesthetic of Personalism" emphasizing the "ontological complexity" of the individual in a redefined humanity comprised of "irreducibly multiple categories" and thus confronted through his "polyphonic narratives."[3] Given Phillips's endeavor, a predictable common thread in many of these approaches is their dutiful, yet brief—or even unnamed—allusions to the work of Emmanuel Levinas and his influential concepts of Otherness, the Face, and intersubjectivity.

Rather than placing Levinas in the critical margins of Phillips's work, this essay explores what I understand as the author's postracial neohumanism as a direct literary case study of Levinas's ethics-as-first-philosophy. Through very different methodologies, both writers attempt to express or define a program that begins by deconstructing Enlightenment humanism and its attendant racism, colonialism, alienation, and violence. For Levinas, this challenge demands a wholesale revision of Western rationalism as a primary ground of the existentialist phenomenology he encountered in his teachers Edmund Husserl and Martin Heidegger. But as a lens into Phillips's interest in decolonized diaspora identities, Levinas's alterity (*Autrui*) and *before-time* consciousness of being (the *Il y a*) also suggest links to Homi Bhabha's influential concept of colonial hybridity. Both the philosophy and postcolonial theory originate in the *fracture* and *denucleation* of the subject, albeit on very different planes of formulation: Bhabha's arguments are founded on the assertion that hybrid identities of the marginal and interstitial contaminate and subvert the power of colonialist narratives/selfhood; Levinas's concepts of being through the Other and the subjective as relational rather than ontological begin with the fracture, within the experience of time, of the ego-derived self.[4] In Phillips's novels, dialogue between Jewish and colonized Black voices, as a key portal into his neohumanism, parallel Levinas's dynamic of how the Face is the necessary position of ethics. In his choice of Jewish voices, Phillips may also be indebted to Levinas's positioning of selected imperatives of the Hebraic ethic as the Western root of philosophical alterity (both in complement and opposition to Greek rationalist ontology). This sensibility in Phillips is often prominently detectable in his women characters, who, in an indirect manner, embody Levinas's earliest definitions of "the feminine" as presenting "a face that goes beyond the face" as a sacred absence leading to "the height of dwelling," or the experience of intimacy and inhabitation through the Other.[5] This can be understood, especially but not exclusively, in Phillips's constructions of Jewish women characters, in particular, from the first half of his career.[6] Yet while Bhabha and others rely on the Levinasian intersubjective to engage the dynamics of colonial identity struggle, the liberating potentials of mimicries and hybridity often remain, for all intents and purposes, under the auspices of the nightmares of history. In this manner, it may be that, through Phillips's formalist experimentations in narrative, the novelist achieves a more profound understanding of Leviniasian ethics than much postcolonial theory has yet to present.

Since his debut in the late 1980s, Phillips has been recognized by critics as one of the most aesthetically complex writers from an Afro-Caribbean heritage who has taken up race and historical injustice as his subject matter. This is especially true of his focus on Jewish characters and anti-Semitism as a site of Otherness used in turn to investigate the racism of the colonial and decolonized eras. Jewish historical struggles, both pre- and post-Holocaust, have indeed allowed not only Phillips, but other writers in this genre, oblique strategies for deconstructing racialized identities toward the reassembly of more capacious diaspora consciousnesses. This potentially transformative drama is often staged in such works through the perspectives of émigré families from former imperial peripheries who, in seeking liberal enfranchisement and prosperity in the metropole, encounter racial exclusions and prejudice. Over the past decade, such works have now also been repeatedly positioned as essential to understanding pre-Holocaust anti-Semitism and colonialism as a twin lens through which to view race and diaspora in the decolonized present.

While Phillips's work emphasizes this lens, in interviews as late as 2012 he also asserts that he has never seen himself as a *racial* writer per se, at least not politically; rather, he fashions himself a postmodern neohumanist whose work remains intent on rising above imperialist and nationalist paradigms of self in order to confront the postmodern fluidity of identity in his characters—be they men, women, white, Black, Brown, Jewish, or gentile. He takes umbrage with key critical works in the field, such as Paul Gilroy's *The Black Atlantic,* preferring to see the ocean as a blended *human* place of both trauma and endeavor (implying the possibilities of interstice) rather than defined solely by how its historical role in the slave trade has been unjustly eclipsed by a critique of the Enlightenment that focuses on anti-Semitism and the Holocaust.[7] Phillips stated that he "would never teach anything that is called 'the black Atlantic' because I believe in the Atlantic. I believe in the reality of the Atlantic because I've crossed it a couple of times on water, but I'm not sure I believe in looking at anything in the world through the narrow prism of 'black.'"[8] Despite being a writer whose subject is unarguably the decolonized West, in such statements Phillips would seem to be in a kind of postcolonial limbo; his view of the Atlantic places him just outside of arguments such as those of Frantz Fanon's *Black Skin, White Masks* (1952), in which Negrophobia and anti-Semitism become mainstays of the "'Manicheanism delirium' of Western metaphysics" and yet are ranked into unequal and unbridgeable differences. Phillips might, for example, disagree with Fanon's assertion that the threatening Black body of racism, when set against the insatiably acquisitive "white" Jewishness of anti-Semitism, reveals how "facile liberal assimilationism" or rationalist universalism can allow Jews to pass culturally, but remains ineffectual against the pathologic fear of the white gaze at the Black body.[9]

As a critique of Enlightenment humanism through the lens of racialized characters, Phillips's work nonetheless lies in the shadow of postcolonial theorists like Fanon, Aimé Césaire, and Hannah Arendt. As Ben Ratskoff notes in his contribution to this volume, Césaire argued in *Discourse on Colonialism* (1955) that, at the end of the bourgeois facilitation of slavery and colonialism, "there is Hitler . . . at the end of formal humanism and philosophic renunciation, there is Hitler" (37). Césaire borrowed Arendt's "boomerang effect" concept to assert how colonialism dehumanized the colonized and colonist alike toward the return of that brutality to the Continent in the form of fascism—imperialism turned in on itself to enslave and destroy "white" European Jewry.[10] Influenced by Césaire, Fanon extended such arguments in his parsing of the differences between hatred of Jews and Blacks; but it was Arendt who first theorized that late nineteenth-century imperial "race societies" and their semilawful bureaucracies set the ground for domestic totalitarianism. Arendt's work, however, stands accused of the failures of the Enlightenment project to see race beyond the savage/civilized binary, and thus to understand imperialism as a "biopolitical event" that decimated colonial lives that she indeed acknowledges were subjugated by, but not necessarily essential to, the progress of modern European civilization.[11] Along with Fanon's psychoanalytic discussions, such theories form a kind of textual ground zero of the essential yet knottiest points of this cross-racial dialogic.[12]

Early in his career Phillips turned to Fanon as an authority in his work. In *Higher Ground* (1989), *Wretched of Earth* becomes part of a litany of Black consciousness-raising texts cited by the incarcerated Rudy Williams, the voice of 1960s Black Panther radicalism, who also relates his imprisonment through metaphors of the camps.[13] In *A New World Order* (2001), Phillips introduces Fanon as "a sensitive Martiniquan doctor," inaccurately promoted by publishers as Sartre's henchman, who was rather "arguing for *human dignity [with] racial origins [as] a subsidiary issue*" (italics mine).[14] After hearing Enoch Powell's infamously racist "Rivers of Blood" speech in his youth, Phillips learned about the Holocaust and identified its racism with his own diaspora condition. He soon encountered Fanon, who became for him his own "Old Testament and New

Testament"; while visiting his birthplace of St. Kitts, he later learned that his maternal grandfather was Emmanuel de Fraites, a Jewish trader "with Portuguese roots that reached back to the island of Madeira."[15] Through this revelation about his mixed heritage, Phillips further understood himself as representative of the islands' colonial multiplicity: "Wherever one happens to be in the Caribbean, at least two or more continents and cultures have already provided the bedrock upon which one's identity has been forged."[16] This multicultural exceptionalism now included his own Jewish roots, and this may have become a stepping-stone for him into a postracial humanity in which Jewish history is reasserted as essential to that understanding. I contend here that this new vantage point readily equates to the nonreciprocal responsibility toward the Other in Levinas's relational subjective.

In this *binocular* sense of race and diaspora, Phillips thus inherits foundations of postcolonialism but struggles as well to overcome some of their theoretical limitations. Through confronting what he believes to be a postracial present, Phillips's fiction implies the need for a consciousness founded on the overcoming of colonial or reappropriated racialized selfhood toward a present where "we are all unmoored," "our identities are fluid," and "belonging is a contested state"; in such a space, identities based on Old World master narratives of tribe and homeland are indeed continuously "riddled with vexing questions."[17] This ahistorical ambiguity, and the open ground of the interpersonal it presumes, can be seen as a lay approach to Levinas's early argument that *"totalities"* (history, politics, politicized subjectivities, etc.) project violent sameness and control over the other as Other.[18] This time-oriented (both historical and personal) posture short-circuits alterity—in the manner Levinas claims the ontological ipseity of Heidegger's *a prior Dasein* does—by disallowing a posteriori disruption of being, a resultant substitution, and the same-and-other recognition of "the Good," relationally.[19] Many of the encounters Phillips constructs can be read as attempts to represent the Levinasian *Face* as it commands the ethical in reasserting the Other's vulnerability (presence in the eyes, starvation in the mouth, etc.) spontaneously as the sign of a philosophical human subject outside of historical contingencies. This is in part what Levinas meant in his famous dictum that ethics is "first philosophy" before it is sociological, political, or religious. Levinasian alterity challenges ontology through the event of "exposedness," a state that denuclearizes *a prior* being-in-time (as opposed to Heidegger's assumption that essence pre-dates entity); the encounter with the Other is thus a "nakedness" beyond ego's reliance on the past, which Levinas calls the "otherwise than being" of the subjective.[20] Alphonso Lingis explains that in the philosopher's arguments

> subjectivity is opened from the outside, by contact with alterity. Before subjectivity is a locus positioned by being for its own manifestation, it is a support called up or provoked to respond to alterity. Before it is a devotion to Being, it is a subjection to the Good. "No one is good voluntarily"—the good is not the correlate of an axiological option or valorization. Before finding itself a freedom in the free space opened by the play of being and nothingness, where an exercise of options is possible, subjectivity is a subjection to the force of alterity, which calls for and demands goodness of it.[21]

Many of Phillips's characters appear in *approach* to "the Good" through conversational events that push them beyond the racialized traumas of their ontological insularity.

Ledent's work argues that Phillips's early novels invoke "a new brand of humanism, leading in turn to a revised conception of British identity."[22] She suggests this "could easily be called 'Diasporic' humanism," but refines the title by distinguishing that being a member of a diaspora people is not the single, necessary agent of how we receive this philosophy through his fiction. Rather, his humanism promotes "complexity and ambivalence over simplification and order [and that] far from exhibiting an abstract and intellectualized notion of Man, it focuses on concrete individual subjectivities whose multiplicities and imperfections provide a profoundly humane insight into humanity."[23] This understanding is "revisionary since it simultaneously deconstructs and constructs humanism" through the marginal figures whom Phillips invests with such "complex and unpredictable webs of allegiance" that they cannot coalesce into any kind of homogenous body, ideological or racist.[24] She concludes that instead of widening the categories of the human, inverting them as a returned racialist view, or even dismissing them as "meaningless as some postmodernist would do," Philips rather offers us humanity through subjectivities of "irreducibly multiple categories" of identity bounded by history.[25]

In discussing *Nature of Blood,* Michael Rothberg concludes that "the novel emerges as an exploration of ambivalent modes of belonging and exclusion in which accidental contiguity plays a greater role than correspondences of historical essences."[26] Comparing Phillips's work to André Schwarz-Bart's *A Woman Named Solitude,* Rothberg asserts that while the latter attempts a passé sense of "parallel minoritization as a form of coalitional rationality . . . Phillips, by contrast, writes from a situation in which tensions between minority groups have produced an austerely ethical *stratified* map of minoritization" (167). But, as noted above, Phillips reads Fanon as a neohumanist because "as his comments on Semitism make clear . . . his sympathies traverse all boundaries, imaginary and otherwise," and this can hardly be an acknowledgment of stratification alone.[27] Efraim Sicher and Linda Weinhouse see Phillips's concerns as "the exclusion of the outsider, on the one hand, and the migrants' loss of home when they are cut off from their own people, on the other," and argue that *Nature of Blood* suggests "suffering from racial persecution can be a shared human experience that should not be defined by difference of skin color but can be imagined by those that were not there"; they conclude that his work in general "invites us to engage with issues of 'historical distinctiveness,' such as the relation of the Holocaust to other histories of racism, and of 'national distinctiveness,' such as the relation of cultural production to writing identity."[28] Sarah Phillips Casteel argues Phillips's beginnings as a writer find their germ in his reading of Anne Frank's *Diary* and identification with victims of the Holocaust as becoming a "surrogate memory" to serve in place of his own nebulous Caribbean past.[29]

Thus what Ledent calls Phillips's "ontological complexity" (78) moves furthest from the racial/postcolonial critique of Enlightenment and toward the intersubjective. Yet alterity in Levinas cannot be described as any complexity of self-knowledge in isolation; rather, the Other is the very disruption of rationalist freedom that "calls into question *my* joyous possession of the world" (italics mine).[30] The Other's urgent need is sustained by this disturbing incomprehensibility that dislocates the ego's projection of self into a *Totality*.[31] Phillips's pattern of aligning and yet distancing characters from disparate ethnic backgrounds within a unified piece of fiction suggests this direction in and of itself; if the characters don't often achieve this ethic, Phillips himself as a writer nevertheless approaches it in the endeavor to represent, in dialectic, the alienation of individuals damaged by modernity who desire to bracket race in hopes of intimacy. As mentioned in my opening, Phillips's women characters, in particular, yearn to share their trauma in a manner that begins with the disorienting yet consciousness-raising position of the Other. Despite their suffering, these characters refuse to surrender to the inherent cowardliness, and indeed subtle aggression, of the isolating ego that presupposes the subjective as a rational, immanent, or transcendent. Rather, they hope to achieve alterity across racial lines by initially seeing beyond those very lines, in what is not a denial of history or racial injustice, but more a sustained bracketing at the moment of the relational experience.

This desire to reformulate subjectivity through the relational present can be read as an incipient phenomenological overcoming of the ontological, in which the latter, discovering freedom as an awareness of an essence that pre-dates it, reduces the other to the same.[32] Phillips's characters are often in a process toward experiencing the Other beyond this binary of difference/sameness. In this, subjectivity arrives through a commitment to one's fellow human established prior to and continuing after the locus of consciousness that experiences it; alterity in this manner pre-dates rationalism; indeed, in Levinas's view, prior to the rise of twentieth-century phenomenology, alterity finds its roots in the West in the Hebraic ethic—that is, the "difficult freedom" of responsibility for the Other built into the assumptions of sacred humanity in the Law. *Being* in Levinas thus rises to a level of existence outside of internal time-consciousness or the impulse to conceptualize time through the finality of death. Desire for the absolute—unquenchable as compared to physical desires—outweighs measurability and thus tasks the subject to "think more than it thinks."[33] This estranging gravitas, which derives from the Other's *illeity* or unending withdrawal from any equivalency to the I, becomes an experiential metaphysics Levinas names *Infinity*. In this, *Face* demands a relation that ends in a spontaneous awareness of a sacredness undefinable through *totalities* and beyond conceptualizing; Levinas in fact calls religion, which he imagines as a verb, simply "the bond that is established between the same and the Other without constituting a *totality*."[34]

Phillips's fiction often employs a novelistic parataxis in which individual mimetic sections form a collage of voices, as opposed to conventional dialogue or connective narrative tissue. In *Higher Ground* and *The Nature of Blood,* this form indirectly aligns the histories of slavery, racism, and the African diaspora with the Jewish diaspora, the Holocaust, and early Zionism. Yet, through this, Phillips retreats from comparative insights that might provoke historical or sociological parity or, worse, competition for victimhood. Rather, his inflected use of juxtaposition and interstice suggests a speculative, open encounter that assumes racial identity struggle as constitutionally different form group to group, and yet simultaneously often demoted to a secondary position in active relation. These interstices offer parallels to the sustained strangeness of alterity, through which the subject is "uprooted from history" and ethics "do not arise within a totality nor . . . establish a totality" but remain both semiopaque and urgently destitute ("*La nudité du visage est dénûment*").[35] In employing interstice rather than intersection or projection, Phillips initially attempts in form to reimagine, through idiosyncratic yet racialized voices, each group's past as *contiguous* rather than overlapping, exchangeable, or antagonistic. In these works, however, the promise of such characters' physical intimacy most frequently dissolves under the resurgence of their separate racial traumas. Interstices between these voices thus open the approach to the Other, but also signal how difficult the ethical can be to achieve between members of historically persecuted racialized groups. Phillips's construction of the necessary grounds of this possibility, however, still points to Levinas's *dwelling* as an Eros that draws from yet moves beyond voluptuousness toward the quotidian *infinity* of loving relations. Phillips's use of interstices here becomes a humane negative space replacing the more common racialized projections or rationalist ego-utility of politics that often substitute for the subjective.

Higher Ground: See Me, Feel Me

Higher Ground was Phillips's third novel and first attempt at paratactic form. Prior to this he published *Final Passage* and *A State of Independence,* both third-person narratives examining poverty, hybrid identities in the postcolonial Caribbean, and emigration to London. *Higher Ground* was thus his first departure in both form and historical content. "Heartland," the first section, is a first-person narrative relating the struggles of a coastal tribesman conscripted by slave traders as an interpreter in an unnamed eighteenth-century African locale. Forced to be complicit in that violence, he rescues a young native girl from rape at the hands of his sadistic overseer, Price. The narrator hides and plans to marry her, only later to witness her forced sexual submission to a young soldier he had befriended at the slave fort. Price soon discovers the hidden girl, knocks the narrator unconscious, and takes her to be boarded on the outgoing ship. The narrator concludes his story with the hope of all slaves that someday they might return to their homes; heartbroken and eventually standing himself on the trading block, he realizes he exists only in the limbo of a fractured present and a past that "has fled over the horizon and out of sight."[36] These passages reiterate the brutality of the slave trade as *nearly* superseded by the vacuum of identity that is the diasporic condition. The second section, the epistolary "Cargo Rap," chronicles the autodidactic politics of a Black convict in 1967–68, before and after the Martin Luther King Jr. assassination. His letters engage generational changes within the struggle and allow his Black Panther radicalism an unanswered victory over the mollifying attitudes he denounces in his parents and siblings. He not only frames imprisonment through allusion to the Gestapo and "the camps," but alludes to Jews as well, as in his explanations of the Gospels ("[he] messed with Jews and got what was coming to him").[37] Yet such references remain metaphoric or metonymic within his imposed isolation.

The eponymous third section thus suggests a narrative that overcomes the first two. Here the lives of immigrants in postwar England—Irina, a Kindertransport young woman, and Louis, a recent Caribbean émigré—intertwine in a failed attempt to understand the other's alienation. Irina is working at a library after spending the last decade of her adult life in a psychiatric institution. Her narrative moves among the present, her past in Europe, and her first years in England working in a munitions factory. We learn she was sent ahead of her family, who all perished at the hands of the Nazis. During her factory years she is seduced by her foreman, Reg, who later marries her when they discover she is pregnant. Doomed from the start by Reg's struggle with his threatened masculine self-image as someone who sat out the war, the relationship sours just before she loses their unborn child through miscarriage. After this, Irina attempts suicide and is soon after institutionalized. During the period after her release, she notices Louis in the library suffering racist stares. Prior to this, Louis is introduced in a scene paralleling Irina's dispassionate, numbed physical life in her marriage. During his first week in London, Louis combats his loneliness by going to a local nightclub; there, he meets Patty, who invites him to her flat for a tryst. She asks insensitive questions about what it's like being "a colored" and which racial epithets he must endure. During sex, Louis performs robotically, while Patty continues to fetishize him in comments like "what a great color. I look so pallid beside it."[38] The entire scene is one of an Eros bound entirely by the power politics of race. Back in his hostel, the encounter becomes symbolic of the futility of Louis's hopes to assimilate, and he decides abruptly to go home, "where his short, but presently experienced, nightmare would eventually distil down to rum stories about the past."[39]

In the library where she works, Irina notices Louis's "crumpled face," and, anticipating that the librarian and other patrons might cause an "unpleasant scene" because of his presence, suggests Louis might take refuge in a corner pub, where, during her lunch break, she goes to seek him out.[40] After Irina is later notified that she may be forced to reenter the sanitarium, the two meet for a movie night and return to her flat in the book's final, anticlimatic scene. Here, for the first time in his canon,

Phillips places Black and Jewish characters in conversation as twin racial others, each mired in their trauma as such. Yet Irina desires that her face might become a "lesson, a book that she hoped he would want to read, but he looked away from her."[41] This is not an escape into the ego's violence of projection, but an odd inversion of alterity in which the approach to the ethical relies on a passive reciprocity; it is equivalent to suggesting that *Infinity is* the horizon of the relational, but here can only be bracketed by the proviso that "you must go first." Louis's response is perhaps even more a product of the ontological orientation to suffering, in that his gaze only compels him to reenter "his tired mind [and] . . . grappled with the problem of how to go forth and retrieve his own life."[42] Louis remains unsure as to why he has even come, "steels himself" at her touch, and thinks primarily of his impending departure. As one who has perhaps suffered deeper wounds as a survivor, however, Irina continues to attempt to reveal herself as the Other, a starved being who might become the imperative of hospitality, but again only in the invitation: "'You say your name is Louis. I try not to go back in my memory for I have spent a small life writing unanswered letters, do you understand?' Irene laughed out loud 'If you could lick my heart, Louis, it would coat your tongue with salt, a strong and bitter taste. I keep seeing a girl (not I) making up her face, preparing herself for her first date.' Irene paused. The single, cautious flame rose and then flickered and then died."[43] In return, Louis, having taken himself out of the moment, offers only a platitude: "I'm sure everything will be alright. Just don't worry so much, that's all." As she watches him walk away, Irina recovers her childhood German, wishing him under her breath "*a gite nacht . . . Uf Widerzain.*" The dialect conjures and reinserts into the relation the primary ground of her political trauma, through which she reimagines her family's weeks in a transport, in which "they waited and wept and asked for water. To be burned not buried . . . then total silence. Nothing moved. And the new people began to wonder *Harginnen.* 'They're going to kill us.'"[44] To vocalize her survivor's guilt, she recites the Shema as if she herself were inside the boxcar with them. Although Irina longs for a space through which mutual suffering might discover ethical commitment, both characters remain in a sealed sense of internal time consciousness in which diaspora, be it Jewish or Black, means only existential limbo. One exists between the trauma of a refugee present and the diasporic fantasy of a redemptive native space, and the other between the reimagined terror of a past that remains perpetually present. They are locked into a consciousness that frontloads self as an object of unique racial hatreds—a dehumanizing fulcrum of history that disallows, finally, even an *approach* to alterity.

The Nature of Blood: Hath Not a Moor Eyes?

Nature of Blood remains Phillips's most innovative work; its play with traditional narrative form includes a twin-frame vignette focusing on two different members of the same Holocaust survivor family. These sections bookend palimpsestic retellings of *The Merchant of Venice* and *Othello* that isolate racial difference, alienation, and hatred as the center of the drama at the expense of the original plots of each play. The fifteenth-century trial of a group of Venetian Jews for ritual murder in Portobuffole is narrated in the style of medieval chronicle through witness testimony, documents, and dated entries; the form distances Jewish suffering as personal and rather sterilizes it as historical legal record. Yet before the sentence of auto-da-fé is pronounced, the defense argues the incongruity of the charges when set against *Halachic* prohibitions of the consumption of blood—as if Phillips wants to remind his reader that Christian Judeophobia foreshadowed the role bloodlines played in the future yet equally absurd pseudoscientific racial hygiene of Nazi anti-Semitism.[45] The *Othello* section is a first-person character adaptation of Shakespeare's original Moor, here set by Phillips to wander Venice as a kind of premodern flaneur whose perambulations become occasions to reflect on his struggle as an outsider racial parvenu.

Encountering the Ghetto gates, Othello becomes sympathetic to the Jewish situation and perceives it a product of unjust laws that limit freedom and have "herded [them] *en masse* and enclosed in one defenseless pen."[46] The bestial imagery draws on medieval anti-Jewishness while also provoking images of the camps anachronistically. But he is also confounded by the irony of how Jews, "fortunate in their wealth" should "choose to live in this manner," because "surely there was some other land or some other people among whom they might dwell in more tolerable conditions?"[47] Thus, even while sympathetic, he inculpates Jews in their own captivity; shifting from responsibility to blame disallows a confrontation with the other's precise history, let alone an approach to their humanity as other qua Other. Later, however, Phillips leads Othello into business relations with a Venetian Jew, when Othello returns to the Ghetto seeking a scholar to decipher the handwriting of a love letter. Here too the encounter between two racial minorities who might form an ethical bond remains only superficial at best. Although Othello sees only a "weather-beaten, warp-faced Jew ... sitting in the room in which I imagined they celebrated their unchristian service," he nevertheless notes the scholar's silent, dutiful attention to the request and refusal to accept payment for drafting a return letter; from this, and the smile "that played around his thin lips," Othello judges "by the way he looked upon me that he felt a certain sympathy for my predicament."[48] A reader might understand the scene as a shared erotic displacement in which the scholar puts the needs of his visitor before his own; but this is far from the relation of Eros beyond the voluptuous that Levinas imagines as the proximity of the Other.[49]

Prior to this, the opening frame section begins with the first-person narrative of Eva Stern, a survivor of the camps waiting on British emigration quotas. The section interweaves her thoughts about marrying one of her British guards with a precarious yet hopeful future for herself in Palestine. Here Phillips first engages the question of the Jewish diaspora through the lens of Zionism, which resurfaces in the novel's closing section, set in late-twentieth century Israel.[50] Eva recalls how her uncle Stephan had abandoned his family during the war to serve in Palestine, her father's condemnation of his brother, and Stephan's defense that Jews "remained the only people on the face of the earth without their own home."[51] The scene works to introduce the long history of Jewish diaspora, which, after European emancipation, commonly presented Jews with three directions: liberal assimilation, Socialism, or Zionism.

The final sections of the novel continue the Stern narrative by returning to Eva's voice interspersed with Othello's last recognitions. In one of the latter the novel makes its boldest ahistorical move by inserting what seems to be a twentieth-century voice adding a gloss of ridicule and admonition to the general's vain belief that he could somehow fully assimilate into white Europe. Here the voice berates Othello as a "sad black man" chasing after a white woman "like the Black Uncle Tom that you are. Fighting the white man's war for him / Wide-receiver in the Venetian army / The republic's grinning Satchmo hoisting his sword like a trumpet."[52] The anachronisms end with his recalling a Yoruba maxim about a river never knowing that its source will dry, suggesting again a diasporic arc stretching from Africa to the Shakespearean tragedy to Black modernity. But it is again a call toward an ontological self-awakening rather than a breach of an ethic of the interpersonal. Eva's final passages similarly reemphasize memories of her sister, her experience in the camps, and her arrival in London to seek her former British soldier love, who promised to marry her. Discovering he was married all along, Eva becomes hysterical and is committed for psychiatric observation, where her monologue ends in a word salad of memories of her family and the camps.

But it is the long descriptive passages of the camps themselves and Eva's struggle to survive there that become most crucial to my concerns here. For his portrait of life in the Lager, Phillips draws heavily on the details of the *univers concentrationaire* of Primo Levi's *Survival in Auschwitz*. The borrowing is brashly undisguised; no reader familiar with that work would mistake Eva's observations—the camps' confusion of languages, the luck in the size of a bunk partner, the nighttime ritual of the bucket and the warmth of its urine splashing on the legs of the prisoner who empties it, or the central importance of shoes and spoons—as anything other than this.[53] Phillips himself strikes a distant ethical relation here to the Jewish Other in drawing on Levi (instead of his own imaginative powers of projected sameness) as a self-conscious defense against cultural appropriation. Levi's details indeed frame Eva's singular sense of hope in drawing close to another prisoner named Bella, whom she approaches in a position of alterity as the Other who needs to be fed, here literally as well as figuratively. This scenario too echoes and rebuts Levi's assertion that the primary experience of slow starvation in the Lager reduced humans to the "grey zone" of an inhumanly mercenary yet amoral survival: "The Lager *is* hunger. We ourselves are hunger, living hunger."[54] Any act of fellowship there, as Levi reiterates many times, was an ethical act that revived the humanity of the giver more than the receiver.[55] Phillips redoubles that recognition by way of Eva's proximity to Bella as one whose dark skin disturbs/disrupts what might be called the former's Jewish ontology: "I have made a friend. Bella. Bella with the dark complexion. Her eyes fenced by crow's feet that mark her as one that has toiled in the summer sun. (My skin as white as paper.)."[56] Parallel to issues of complexion and class that haunt many ethnic societies, Eva's noting Bella's possibly Sephardic identity as estranging signals here an intraracialized Jewish division overcome, highlighting again the other as Other beyond *totalities*. Bella is also the hunger of the ethical-call to responsibility; "I share my bowl of soup with her. . . . I need a piece of bread. We need a piece of bread."[57] The altered pronoun signals the subjective, not in numbers or the plurality of I's into we, but in the self *surrendered* to Other.[58] More than physical need, the relation provokes Eva's single awareness of being in the camp as now otherwise than being: "I look at my Bella. Her brown eyes clouded by cataracts. I am twenty. Bella, I want to live to love. To believe in something. To believe in somebody. Because of Bella,

I hope with reckless vigour."[59] This is the "spiritual optics" of seeing the Other, in which "the dimension of the divine opens forth from the human face."[60] But Levinas's metaphysics (*Infinity*) is the opposite of myth; it is a quotidian experience void of any magical overcoming of physical reality or nature; rather it is "the dawn of humanity without myth."[61] In this, Eva's subjectivity in Bella is the perfect foil to Nazi racial myths of metaphysically superior beings and bodies. Levi in fact notes on several occasions how the Nazis preened their ideology through observing the physical "demolition" of prisoners as proof of Jewish racial inferiority and a lack of dignity in suffering.[62] Phillips rather suggests a common *human frailty* by employing powerfully visceral imagery to describe Bella's dysentery as she deteriorates and is soon selected for gassing: "Too weak, now, to steal warmth from my body. I press close to her, as though my life might pass into her body like a fever. But she continues to leak. Seepage. The most undignified disease. Flooding the cracks in the wood. Dripping on the faces of the women below. Speckling them."[63] The grotesquery here, however, is *not* borrowed from Levi, but is Phillips's own; the details work to undermine any sentimentality a reader might find in Eva's former expressiveness, which in turn reveals the subjective experience of *Infinity* as occurring through, and not despite, the body's natural state of vulnerability and degradation.

Phillips's final move in the novel opens ethics out into the postcolonial interstices of diaspora. To examine how a post-Holocaust Jewish diaspora might confront the decolonized-refugee limbo between disrupted native-spaces and incommodious immigrant ones, the narrative reintroduces an elderly Stephan, now a retired Israeli physician long separated from his wife. On this occasion, he spends the evening with Malka, a young Ethiopian refugee working as a "dance hostess" in a Tel Aviv club. The section becomes a multilayered scene of ethnic/racial liminality in which Israel's mitigation of the Jewish diaspora fails to resolve the past or its alienating effect on Stephan, while Malka's experience of mirrored diasporas (within the African and yet returned to a native Jewish space) remains also only a disorienting disenchantment with the promise of a recuperated life in a long-lost homeland. Sicher and Weinhouse, along with other critics, read this section as the text's recapitulation of Western paranoia over blood purity based on the assumption that Phillips's knowledge of Operation Solomon was limited to an *International Herald Tribune* article accusing Israeli medical services of discarding refugee transfusions as a racist act rather than, as was accurate, because of the AIDS epidemic in Ethiopia at the time.[64] But the section can also be read as moving beyond what may have been Phillips's incomplete knowledge of the airlift or subsequent attempts to paint him with the brush of anti-Zionist rhetoric that assumes an endemic Israeli racism. A different reading begs seeing the characters' *relation itself* as simultaneously racialized and yet beyond this barrier by way of Phillips's version of the dynamics of the Face. From this perspective, the *totality* that encloses both characters is momentarily defeated just at the apex of their political separations and thus overcomes the historical imbalance of power between them.

The reader first discovers that Stephan's life as a soldier and physician could not erase his guilt: "His only companion was memory . . . [and yet] he now understood that to remember too much is, indeed, a form of madness," and that this most recent liaison with a younger woman was another of his many "inelegant attempts to heal the lesion in his soul."[65] Malka feels she was "taken" to Israel as a passive villager, herded onto buses and brought to "the embassy compound, where [they] were stored like thinning cattle . . . We just let it happen."[66] Although in transit she absorbed the Zionist narrative of the return, her experience of hostel life, poverty, absorption centers, and culture clash have left her bitter and listless; while the government made good on its promise to educate her generation, she remains an unemployed nurse who must lower herself as a kind of semiprostitute in the club. The work itself is of course racially overdetermined through the frame of the hypersexualization of Black women. She now sees her forced emigration as predicated on nationalist lies: "The Holy Land did not betray us. The People did. The man at the hostel said to us, 'Welcome my black brothers and sisters. You are helping us to understand what we are doing here.'" Subsequently, she blames her alienation on this: "You say you rescued me. Gently plucked me from one century, helped me to cross two more, and then placed me in this time. Here. Now. But why? What are you trying to prove."[67] Through those questions, Malka appears to suggest a nationalist ulterior motive behind the humanitarian effort. The obvious implication is that Ethiopian Jews have been used as pawns to reify a Zionist narrative and thus in turn have been dehumanized, albeit indirectly. In addition, just as in *Higher Ground*, here too an erotic energy between two racially different characters at first appears to devolve into an ego-driven projection to control and fix the Other as a knowable sameness, thus seemingly nullifying the approach to alterity.

But while Malka's thoughts are all italicized to indicate a parenthetical inner voice, over dinner she gains the courage to confront Stephan *conversationally*. This can be seen as representation of Levinas's concept of the *saying*: language as an opening to the Other that activates interlocutor relations and reforms sensibility into an atemporalizing expressiveness (as opposed to the *said*—i.e., language that articulates knowledge, which is always predicated on what is past).[68] Malka's opening places Stephan before herself: "You can be honest with me. You don't want us here, do you?" And he replies, "Not *everybody* feels that way"—a minimalist negative that nevertheless suggests her Otherness as beyond race.[69] Later, in their hotel room, now naked and in bed together, Stephan confesses he does not want sex, and he hears "the words fall from his lips. '*I would like to be your friend.*'"[70] This is the *Welcome* of alterity beyond the rationalist ego, and here too an Eros beyond the voluptuous. Malka then admits her willingness to accompany him was based primarily on her perception that he was one "who did not look as though you would hurt me."[71] Although her second motivation (to stay in a hotel for the first time) reiterates divisions of race *and class* between them, the *Welcome* surmounts these as the nonreciprocal duty to feed the Other. These admissions as the *saying* bring them close enough for a single kiss, after which Malka apologizes for preferring only that and nothing more. The lone gesture indicates Stephan's submission to Malka as the unfathomable Other who represents responsibility rather than possession through projection. Since their coupling was in its origins *predicated* on the politics of race and class (her impoverished state driving her to prostitution), and not initially on a Levinasian *Welcome* and *Dwelling*, their mutual retreat from sex, counterintuitively, represents an *approach* to the other qua Other.

After her departure the following morning, Stephan's reflections on Malka's well-being, and not his former loneliness, continue to represent this *approach*. The passage begins with racial difference qua difference, making Malka appear stranger still and thus less capable of being consumed by self's reason:

> During the night, the sheet had slipped down to her waist, which allowed him . . . to examine her skin. If he had been younger, then maybe. But she belonged to another land. She might be happier there. Dragging these people from their primitive world into this one, and in such a fashion, was not a policy with which he agreed. They belonged to another place. He thought of her now, taking the first of the buses that would carry her back to her cramped apartment. And then, upon her arrival, he imagined she would have to endure her parents. And her sister. Their questions. Their unhappiness. But there had been a private adventure. (For both of them). The club, the hotel, the dinner, the bar, the room, the bed. She had lived. She was living.[72]

Her skin marks her difference, and in his gaze he projects onto her the lost authenticity of the native space, perhaps even here racialized through the savage/civilized binary. But his distancing also remains a platform for him to imagine her trauma as someone displaced by a nationalist project blinded to its alienating effects or potential racism against refugees throughout the West—that is, an attempt to imagine her unique suffering. He thus begins to perceive her only relationally, allowing a recognition of her as the Other in how the *Face* provokes her defenseless state and his responsibility to place her needs, nonreciprocally, before his own. He attempts in this manner to imaginatively project himself (sameness) into her struggle, *but fails,* and in this sustains her unsettling difference as the Other. Finally, he recalls what they had together, through relation, in an approach to the ethical; in a synecdoche of the novel's architectonics, Phillips's final sentences employ grammatical parataxis ("She had lived. She is living"): the unalloyed, declarative switch in tense here signals that Stephan has experienced an ethical moment in the living present. Malka thus gains an unforeseen agency in which her presence compels an isolated Stephan toward a reflective moment of speculative responsibility. Will he offstage *act* to relieve her suffering? As a physician, will he help secure her a nursing job? Phillips again leaves such possibilities open but unresolved. But Stephan's partial overcoming the *totalities* that enclose them both so tightly in their own ethnic egoism seems like a beginning, or, at least, a direction.

To echo Stephan's newly sensitized vulnerability, Phillips offers an envoi of the former's memory of a last contact with his beloved nieces in a park in Germany during the war. They had begged him to stay and then skipped away, leaving him "alone on the bench, his arms outstretched, reaching across the years."[73] The image suggests an open wound (recalling Irina and Eva) that sustains history within ontology as a product of the isolated ego. His trauma thus resurges as a memory of the loss and debilitating inauthenticity that underwrites the struggle of all diaspora peoples. While his empathy with Malka's diasporic consciousness and suffering at once appears to collapse racial distance, the encounter also remains constrained by the cruelty and injustices of history (*totality*) rather than surmounting these through the ethical moment in which an-other, racialized or not, becomes *the* Other.[74]

Over the last decade, critical interest in the Caribbean as an epicenter of diasporic struggles has revealed major sinews between the Jewish and Black experience of modernity. But tensions between laying claim to that inheritance, or even the act of renaming the contemporary period the "decolonized/post-Holocaust era," has led to some self-defeating corners. Such rabbit holes go beyond prevalent accusations that scholars of anti-Semitism often demote or elide the African diaspora as equally essential to a critique of the West. A more devastating by-product—drawing on such orientations as identity politics, multiculturalism, hyper–self-reflexivity, strategic authenticities, or reappropriated racialized nationalisms—is that racial ontology, expressed in stratified minoritarian positions, disallows any legitimate understanding or empathy with members of groups different from one's own. As noted in my opening, even Bhabha's work on the colonial intersubjective in the end imagines hybridity as a weapon of resistance against the dominant group's alienating force without a map of interpersonal ethics outside of history. *Histories* thus become the fulcrum of identities based on the deconstruction of the Western master narrative of a rationally progressive modernity in denial of its biopolitical/racist foundations. Caryl Phillips's work, however, is an entrance into a space in which an older notion of an absolute yet nontranscendent humanity is rediscovered through a disturbing yet inviolable individuality that aligns with the Levinasian concept of alterity. To approach subjectivity as ethical only through *active relation* is to renew the sacredness of *the individual* beyond the violent controls of history. One might say that Phillips attempts a postcolonial hat trick: to be critically aware of the histories of racial injustice and their postmodern political antagonisms, and yet, despite this, to approach ethics through an *otherwise than being* that brackets racial essence in the moment of the encounter. Phillips's reliance on interstice in this way suspends a reader's projections of sameness onto the Other and, in that disorientation, opens the possibility of a spontaneous, lived ethic outside of ego, one that remains attainable—beyond all chauvinisms—only through the *absolute Other*.

Notes

1. These three arguments appeared over a ten-year period from 1997 to 2008 in: Hilary Mantel, "Black Is Not Jewish," review of *The Nature of Blood* by Caryl Phillips, *Literary Review*, February 1, 1997, 39–40; Stephen Clingman, "Route, Constellation, Faultline," in *The Grammar of Identity: Transnational Fiction and the Nature of Boundary* (Oxford: Oxford University Press, 2009), 68–102; and Stef Craps, "Linking Legacies of Loss: Traumatic Histories and Cross-Cultural Empathy in Caryl Phillips's *Higher Ground and Nature of Blood*," *Studies in the Novel* 40, nos. 1–2 (Spring/Summer) 2008: 191–202, 192.

2. See Wendy Zierler, "My Holocaust Is Not Your Holocaust: 'Facing' Black and Jewish Experience in *The Pawnbroker, Higher Ground*, and *The Nature of Blood*," *Holocaust and Genocide Studies* 18, no. 1 (2004): 46–67, quotes on 58, 62.

3. Some examples of Ledent's work would include "The 'Aesthetics of Personalism' in Caryl Phillips's Writing: Complexity as a New Brand of Humanism," *World Literature Written in English* 39, no. 1 (2001): 75–84, 77; Ledent, *Caryl Phillips: Contemporary World Writers* (Manchester: Manchester University Press, 2002); and Ledent, "Caryl Phillips and the Caribbean as Multicultural Paradigm," *Moving Worlds* 7, no. 1 (2007): 74–84.

4. I am indebted here to John Drabinski's arguments in *Levinas and the Postcolonial: Race, Nation, Other* (Edinburgh: Edinburgh University Press, 2011), 89–128. For Levinas's concept of being as "essentially alien and striking against us" in the struggle of being (the existent) within existence, see Levinas, *Existence and Existents*, trans. Alphonso Lingis (The Hague: Martinus Nijhoff, 1978), 23.

5. Emmanuel Levinas, *Totality and Infinity: An Essay on Exteriority*, trans. Alphonso Lingis (Pittsburgh: Duquesne University Press), 1969, 152–74, 256–66, quote on 260.

6. For Levinas's discussion of how Hebraism embodies this ethic, see Sean Hand's *Difficult Freedom: Essays on Judaism*, trans. Sean Hand (Baltimore: Johns Hopkins University Press, 1990). For how biblical feminine figures are conceptualized here, see "Judaism and the Feminine," in *Difficult Freedom*, 30–38. Phillips's non-Jewish women protagonists in works such as *Cambridge* (New York: Vintage International, 1991) or *A Distant Shore* (New York: Alfred A. Knopf, 2003) also attempt to position themselves beyond racial divides to draw closer to black male characters.

7. Gilroy accuses Levinas of the oversight he finds in the work of Zymunt Bauman, who he notes "discusses the relationship between racism and anti-Semitism without even mentioning the Americas let alone exploring the significant connections between what he calls the gardening state and the plantation state and the colonial state"; he cites Levinas's "remarks about the qualitative uniqueness of the Holocaust suggest he suffers from the same blind spot." See *The Black Atlantic: Modernity and Double Consciousness* (Cambridge, MA: Harvard University Press, 1993), 213. It stretches credulity to imagine Levinas did not see racism and slavery as social injustices on the scale of anti-Semitism. As a philosopher, however, he opposes the idea that the redress of history, political unities, or programmatic solutions can be ethical prior to or beyond the event of the individual encounter with the Other.

8. Caryl Phillips, "'Who Are You Calling a Foreigner?': Caryl Phillips in Conversation with John McLeod," in *New Perspectives on the Black Atlantic: Definitions, Readings, Practices, Dialogues*, ed. Bénédicte Ledent and Pilar Cuder-Dominguez (Bern: Peter Lang, 2012), 277.

9. See Bryan Cheyette, "Frantz Fanon and the Black-Jewish Imaginary," in *Frantz Fanon's* Black Skins, White Masks: *Interdisciplinary Essays* (Manchester:

Manchester University Press, 2005), 74–99. Quoted material from *Black Skin, White Masks* (New York: Grove, 1967), 183; and Cheyette, "Fanon and Black-Jewish," 83, 95.

10. As Ratskoff also notes, Césaire's translator, Joan Pinkham, chose Arendt's term for the original *choc en retour*. Since the phrase is more accurately translated "backlash," Ratskoff sees the choice as problematic, as it locks Césaire within Arendt's shadow. Although "backlash" has a special connotation in a colonial context, the sentence in which the term first appears does seem to explain Arendt's precise concept. See *Discourse*, 36. Later in the text, Césaire uses the phrase (again translated "boomerang effect") to explain how the colonizer is as dehumanized by his violence as his colonial victim—an observation not exactly included in Arendt's original concept; see 41.

11. For an extended version of this reading of Arendt, see Michael Rothberg, *Multidirectional Memory* (Stanford, CA: Stanford University Press, 2009), 62–63.

12. From *Mask's* opening assertion that "colonial racism is no different from any other racism. . . . Anti-Semitism hits me head on," to conclusions such as "the Jew is feared because of his potential for acquisitiveness," [but] in white fear of the black man, "everything takes place on the genital level," Fanon empathizes with Jews but also fixes the Jewish body as a nonquestion to anti-Semites. See *Black Skin, White Masks*, 88, 156–57.

13. Caryl Phillips, *Higher Ground: A Novel in Three Parts* (New York: Viking, 1989), 70.

14. Caryl Phillips, *A New World Order* (New York: Vintage International, 2002) 133.

15. Phillips, *New World*, 129–30.

16. Phillips, 131.

17. Phillips, 7.

18. Levinas, *Totality and Infinity*, 22, 38, 47, 51–52, 55–56.

19. See *Otherwise than Being or Beyond Essence*, trans. Alphonso Lingis (The Hague: Martinus Nijhoff, 1981), 17, which states, "Heidegger tries to conceive subjectivity in function of Being, of which it expresses an 'epogue'; subjectivity, consciousness, the ego presupposes Dasein, which belongs to essence as the mode in which essence manifests itself."

20. Levinas, *Otherwise*, 81–121.

21. Lingis, introduction to *Otherwise than Being*, xxi.

22. Ledent, "Aesthetics of Personalism," 76.

23. Ledent, 76.

24. Ledent, 77.

25. Ledent, 77.

26. Rothberg, *Multi-Directional*, 164.

27. Phillips, *New World*, 133.

28. Sicher and Weinhouse, *Under Postcolonial Eyes: Figuring the "Jew" in Contemporary British Writing* (Lincoln: University of Nebraska Press, 2012), 137, 138.

29. Sarah Phillips Casteel, *Calypso Jews: Jewishness in the Caribbean Literary Imagination* (New York: Columbia University Press, 2015), 245–50.

30. Levinas, *Totality*, 76.

31. See John Wild, introduction, *Totality and Infinity*, 15: "Totalitarian thinking accepts vision rather than language as its model. It aims to gain an all-inclusive, panoramic view of things, including the other, in a neutral impersonal light like the Hegelian *Geist* (Spirit), or the Heideggerian Being. It sees the danger of an uncontrolled, individual freedom, and puts itself forth as the only rationalist answer to anarchy. To be free is the same as to be rational, and to be rational is to give oneself over to the total system that is developing in world history. Since the essential self is also rational, the development of this system will coincide with the interests of the self. All otherness will be absorbed in this total system of harmony and order."

32. Levinas, *Totality*, 42–48.

33. Levinas, 62–63.

34. Levinas, 40.

35. Levinas, 97, 251.

36. Phillips, *Higher Ground*, 60.

37. Phillips, 76.

38. Phillips, 195.

39. Phillips, 194.

40. Phillips, 197.

41. Phillips, 216.

42. Phillips, 216.

43. Phillips, 217.

44. Phillips, 218.

45. The Hebrew term *Halacha* refers to aspects of the Torah that pertain to law, as differentiated from narrative, censuses, family lines, etc.

46. Phillips, *The Nature of Blood* (New York: Vintage International, 1998), 129.

47. Phillips, *Nature*, 131.

48. Phillips, 141–42.

49. See Lingis, introduction, *Otherwise*, xix–xx. It is interesting to note Clingman's interpretation of this moment as a different kind of failed attempt at empathy across racial perceptions. He argues that "here the Jew and the African both recognize and do not recognize on another, struggling to see one another beyond the eyes of the European third. . . . Othella and Desdemona attempt to find a different and more reciprocal version of their humanity through a mirroring view that circulates among them . . . like a set of varying recognitions and displacements . . . [through which] there can be no fully achieved reciprocity." See Clingman, "Forms of History and Identity in *The Nature of Blood*," *Salmagundi* 143 (Summer 2004): 141–66, quote on 156–57.

50. See Caryl Phillips, *The European Tribe* (New York: Vintage, 2000), 54. Phillips sympathizes with how African Americans might find Jewish empathy

offensive because Jews weren't slaves and have benefited from economic exploitation of the inner city. But he also states "the Jew is still Europe's nigger," and that while he "channeled part of his hurt and frustration through the Jewish experience," he now "finds himself in agreement with the . . . feeling that some of the policies of modern-day Israel, particularly in relation to South Africa, bring 'shame on the Jewish people.'"

 51. Phillips, *Nature*, 75–76.

 52. Phillips, 180.

 53. Phillips, 167–72. For corresponding passages in Levi, see *Survival in Auschwitz* (New York: Collier, 1986), 38, 57, 61–62, 34, 85, respectively.

 54. Levi, *Survival*, 74.

 55. See, for example, Levi, *Survival*, 119–22; or "The Canto of *Ulysses*," 109–15.

 56. Phillips, *Nature*, 179.

 57. Phillips, 179.

 58. See Levinas, *Totality*, 39: "[The Other] and I do not form a number. The collectivity in which I say 'you' or 'we' is not the plural of the 'I.' I, you—these are not individuals of a common concept. Neither possession nor unity of numbers nor unity of concepts link me to the Stranger. . . . [Metaphysics] is primordially enacted as conversation where the same, gathered up in its ipseity as an 'I,' as a particular existent unique and autochthonous, leaves itself."

 59. Phillips, *Nature*, 179.

 60. Levinas, *Totality*, 78.

 61. Levinas, 77.

 62. See, for example, Levi, "Useless Violence," in *The Downed and Saved* (New York: Vintage, 1989), 105–26.

 63. Phillips, *Nature*, 179.

 64. Sicher and Winehouse, *Under Postcolonial*, 126–27. Operation Solomon was a 1991 Israeli military operation to airlift Ethiopian Jews from tribal areas and repatriate them as Israeli citizens.

 65. Phillips, *Nature*, 211.

 66. Phillips, 199.

 67. Phillips, 207–8.

 68. See Levinas, *Totality*, 40–22, 48–49; see also Lingis, introduction, *Otherwise*, xxv–xxvii.

 69. Phillips, *Nature*, 208.

 70. Phillips, 209, italics mine.

 71. Phillips, 209.

 72. Phillips, 210.

 73. Phillips, 212.

 74. Levinas, 52.

Part IV

Contemporary Voices
Narrative and Poetry

Ema

Anna Ruth Henriques

THE CENTENARIAN LAY in the hospital bed, an oxygen mask covering her small, wrinkled face, tubes in one arm, a plaster cast on the other. A slew of people surrounded her, sharing laudatory if exaggerated stories of the old lady who was named Evelyn, but who was now known as Ema.

"Did you know she taught half of the parish to read and write?"

"Not to mention her guiding. Her cookie sales were legendary."

"Never a kinder woman. She gave everyone her time and attention, from the gardener to the Queen."

"How lovely," the old lady said in a muffled chuckle. "This is like attending one's own funeral! Only that the accolades are not falling on dead ears!"

The people's faces tightened. The tightest belonged to four of her five children and their spouses, who stood vigil over her.

"Don't say that, Mummy, please don't . . ."

The youngest, Judy, burst into tears, pressing her palms to her face. The other daughter, Rosalie, pulled in her lips like a snail backing into its shell, fixing a glassy gaze to the wall ahead. Joan, Ema's youngest son's wife, glanced at her sisters-in-law, then right then left and right again, taking the temperature of the room, which, effectively, was all she was permitted to do with her sisters-in-law around. Joan's husband, David, gave a deep sigh as if gearing himself for the heavy lifting of which he was the most capable and willing, and thus always assigned. While Ema's first-born, Ainsley, lifted his gaze to the ceiling and, in spite of his wife Marjorie's substantial arm draped over his shoulder, floated right out of the room.

Richard, her second son and the only one who might have found the humor in his mother's words, was not with them. He lay quietly at the foot of the Spanish guava tree at Stanton, in dust. A marble plaque marked his resting place at his childhood home, engraved with the dates of both his birth and his precocious death at the advent of his fifth decade. It was where and how Ema wanted to be buried herself, in ashes at the foot of a tree in the verdant garden of her own beloved Stanton where she and her husband, Zackie, had raised their five children. But Zackie was an observant Jew (except when it came to roasted pork, which Evelyn had introduced to him unthinkingly at a Sunday-in-the-country lunch during their courtship and now he couldn't resist).

"Jews just aren't cremated," he'd once said when a granddaughter expressed it as a wish of her own.

Evelyn was more a dutiful wife than an adherent Jew. She stood by her husband's beliefs on big decisions, like what to do with a dead body. But then, years later, given Richard's situation, she spoke up to make an exception. Extenuating circumstances, she declared, as he'd died in Mexico. The bureaucratic logistics of air-shipping a body from a non–English speaking developing country to an undeveloped nation known for importation incompetencies were too much to take on in light of the illness and loss. All manner of problems could arise in Jamaica and there was just no accounting for Mexico. Suppose he was held up in customs for weeks when, as a Jew, his body should be buried within two days of death, not to mention if it sat out in a warehouse in the tropical heat for any length of time. Or worse, imagine if they simply lost the body. It would not be the first time. So she and Zackie decided to cremate him. David, at their request, flew to Mexico and brought his elder brother back in hand luggage, safely stored in a tightly knotted plastic bag. At Stanton, under the guava tree, the family said the Mourner's Kaddish while David emptied the bag in a hole in the ground.

"No one should have to bury a child," Evelyn had stated stoically, without a waver to her voice. Her sorrow sat like mortar within the cut-stone bindings of her long-engrained English colonial upbringing, making her adept at suppressing emotions. Jamaica, now independent, had been a colony for most of her life. Over eight generations of her ancestors had been under colonial rule and had adopted English ways. The English arrived in 1652. It was around this time that Evelyn's ancestors were first recorded on the island and that Jews were recorded at all in Jamaica's history, not due to their sudden presence but that they no longer needed to hide their true identities from the nefarious reaches of the Spanish Inquisitors. Those same Jews had negotiated their freedom with the English not for egalitarian reasons but rather because they had aided the English in capturing the island from the Spanish. Now, over eight generations later of peace and integration (a few glitches in between such as clubs with "No blacks, no Jews" signs in place), they had adopted English ways. So, in spite of Evelyn's and Zackie's full-fledged commitment to their identities as Jews, no shiva was sat, no garment torn, though Kaddish was said for Richard.

It was Evelyn's mother, Pearl, alone, who, in mourning, had covered Stanton's mirrors, albeit seventy-five years earlier. Pearl, an anomaly on the island, had been raised in an orthodox household in the small, mostly Jewish town of Shepetovka, Russia. She'd migrated to the States as a young woman in the 1890s, settling in Philadelphia. Mutual friends at the local synagogue introduced petite, pretty Pearl to charming, handsome Ainsley, who was visiting from an exotic tropical island. Pearl was as intrigued with the Jamaican Jew as she was intrepid about the strange, unknown English colony from whence he came. It wasn't long before the two married and set sail to his island home. Along with a brass samovar and a whalebone corset, she brought the old Eastern European Jewish ways with her, preserving each carefully. She kept her corset wrapped in tissue paper—unworn in the tropical heat—on a shelf in a mahogany armoire, and polished her beloved samovar with half a fresh lime each Sunday morning until well into her ninetieth decade. No one touched either of them. Just like no one touched the mirrors once she covered them. Which was shortly after the telegraph arrived less than four years into her marriage announcing the death of her husband.

The time was shortly after World War I, 1919 to be exact. Young Evelyn had recently turned two. Her family lived in the bucolic town of Morant Bay on the southeastern end of Jamaica. Yet Morant Bay was a place that had seen the bloodiest rebellion on the island half a century earlier. In retaliation for continued exploitation, ex-slaves slaughtered farming estate owners. Evelyn's great-grandparents survived thanks to a note penned by the rebel leader, now-national hero Paul Bogle, and now in the archives at the Institute of Jamaica, naming them alone to be spared from the massacre due to their decent treatment of their employees. Ainsley, Evelyn's father, who ran that same farm, had recently sailed to Philadelphia to purchase equipment for the property and secure orders for the following year's crops of bananas and sugarcane. Upon arrival in late March, the healthy, hearty young man of twenty-seven years of age caught a virus. Less than forty-eight hours later, Ainsley became yet another of the fifteen million victims of the Spanish Flu epidemic sweeping the world. The family in Philadelphia shot off a telegram with the sudden, tragic news. By the time the telegram reached Morant Bay, the Philadelphia family had already buried him. Thus, it was that Pearl covered the mirrors.

In Evelyn's childhood home, her mother continued to cover the mirrors. As a result, Evelyn was never one to fuss about her appearance, as long as her short hair was combed, her clothes neatly pressed, her nose powdered, her light-pink lipstick fresh. For one death followed another. Barely a year later, due to the loss of her only son, Evelyn's grandmother Hanna slipped away, her grief-stricken heart giving out. Then, as Pearl unveiled the mirrors, she shrouded them again. After Evelyn's grandfather Ivanhoe buried his beloved wife, his own heart gave out. Neither their bright, engaging granddaughter, Evelyn, nor their devoted daughter, Ivy, least of all their agreeable daughter-in-law, Pearl, could alleviate the heartbreak. Ivy drove her dead father in the back of the farm truck to Kingston for a Jewish burial. She then got to work running the 850-acre estate while widowed Pearl raised young Evelyn.

Pearl drew on the resilience she'd gained from her upbringing. Pearl spent her childhood in a Ukrainian town during the anti-Jewish pogroms. Her father, sensing the situation would worsen, spent his savings on a steamer ticket to the States. He sold coal door-to-door in Philadelphia to earn enough to bring his wife and three children over a year later. After weeks of traveling by freight trains, by foot across country borders, then by cargo ship across the ocean, tiny Pearl, who stood four feet ten inches on her tiptoes, arrived at Ellis Island with an impetigo infection bad enough for the medical inspectors to quarantine her. Determined to get through with her family, she wore her thickly knitted stockings that hid the unsightly mess of her shins during the obligatory health exam. Feigning prudishness to the medical inspectors when told to remove them, she shook her head and burst into tears. Excusing the adolescent for the emotional outburst—thirteen years of age according to her identity card but who in fact was eighteen—the inspector breached protocol and allowed her entry.

Ivy, on the other hand, was a sheltered, pampered child who had boarded at an all-girls college in the countryside and was schooled in piano, poetry, art history, etiquette, and needlepoint. Well-traveled, she visited London and the European continent annually with her family who groomed and expected her to marry a Jewish man of means. Yet her parents held potential suitors to impossible standards. At the time they died, no one had been good enough in their eyes for their daughter. Now in her early twenties and with no prospects in sight, Ivy, who had never worked a day in her life, was suddenly left either to sell or single-handedly run the banana and sugar cane plantation. Ivy seized the reins. She learned to ride—side-saddle, as she only wore dresses—so she could survey the vast fields on horseback, shadowing farm managers and field laborers. Soon, she was balancing the books and negotiating crop prices with overseas buyers.

Young Evelyn, however, needed a formal education. The two women, in their late twenties, also had hopes of marriage for themselves. The sleepy, provincial town of Morant Bay had little to offer in either area. Pearl and Ivy decided to migrate to Philadelphia, where they each had family. Ivy put the properties up for sale, both the Stanton estate and the family home in town where they presently lived, including all its belongings. The house quickly sold along with most of its contents. But the Great Depression in the United States had begun. Investors, especially in agricultural land, held off as the demand for produce dried up. Meanwhile, Ivy closed on the house sale, forcing the family to move. Ivy packed up the remaining furniture—her baby grand piano and her grandparents' enormous, ornately-carved American Oak bed, dresser, and dining set—and trucked them off to the caretaker's old wooden bungalow at Stanton. As the months dragged on and no buyers appeared for the land, she decided the capital city, Kingston, was better than remaining in the countryside. She purchased a few acres, built a house she named Stanton Terrace, and enrolled young Evelyn in an all-girls day school, running the estate from afar.

It was a move they all came to regret and cherish. For, in Kingston, Evelyn met a young man with whom she fell madly in love. A handsome, charming, and cheeky fellow, he was also spoiled by the status of his long-settled, successful, also-Jewish family. Girls and grown women adored him, yet he was loyal to no one but himself. Both his own mother, who was friends with Pearl, and Ivy begged them to keep lovely Evelyn away from him. So, upon Evelyn's graduation from high school that summer, they took her to Philadelphia, where they convinced her to enroll at the University of Pennsylvania, and returned without her to Jamaica.

Evelyn was miserable. She lived with a childless aunt and uncle and subsequently made few friends. The weather was cold and gray, the city dirty and dense with imposing buildings filled with unfriendly people. The trees were dark and leafless for most of the year. She missed the tropical greenery of the countryside, Jamaica's warmth and sunshine, and, most of all, her mother and aunt, from whom she'd never been apart. She wrote letters weekly to them expressing her unhappiness. When they came to see her the following summer, she begged to go back with them. Needless to say, she also missed the young man.

It was a short courtship. The matriarchs on both sides did all they could do to prevent it, but Evelyn was determined to marry him. Not even proof of his infidelities would stop her. A year following her return to Jamaica, she married him at the Kingston synagogue and moved, as was typical of the time, into her widowed mother-in-law's home, a voluminous, verandah-wrapped, shingle-roofed box of a house with a large lawn shadowed by trees. Within little time, she was pregnant, giving birth at that home to baby Ainsley. Her new husband, however, was seldom present, spending his nights at the drinking holes in Kingston or in the arms of other women. Due to one of his intermittent visits, she became pregnant again, this time with Richard. Yet the arrival of more children would not change her philandering husband's ways, so, six weeks after giving birth, Evelyn sent a telegram to her Aunt Ivy asking her to send her car. Evelyn packed her belongings and babies, piled them into Ivy's chauffeur-driven car, and returned to the safe haven of her beloved mother and aunt, who had reinstalled at Stanton.

Evelyn's tumultuous return to Stanton was in fact idyllic. It was the start of World War II. Rationing had begun but the farm provided all Evelyn needed to raise her two young sons. She also had the help of the two matriarchs. Ivy doted on Ainsley, named for her beloved and sorely missed brother. Richard received the attention of his gentle grandmother Pearl, who was well suited to his sensitive disposition. The bucolic farm also afforded the boys a menagerie of animals, two pet dogs, a talking parrot that called out to everyone in perfect mimicry of Ivy's voice, causing everyone from the gardener to the cook to Evelyn to answer and come running; a monkey that lived in the guango tree and chewed on the sticky pods, throwing them down at passersby; a patient cow that the boys helped milk each morning; a coop of skittish hens that laid eggs which they collected each day; and ducks and goats. And Evelyn learned to drive.

The family of five took all their meals together around Ivy's grandparents' table. Each day, they paused for tea on the porch, where they absorbed the sweeping views of sugarcane and banana fields down a verdant valley of the Blue Mountains to the Caribbean Sea. Between breakfast and lunch, Evelyn taught her boys to read and write. As the school situation in Morant Bay had not improved, Evelyn ordered a teaching kit from the Calvert home-schooling company in the States and from that porch gave her boys formal lessons. In the afternoons, she drove them in Ivy's motorcar (before gas rationing required they take a donkey cart) to the beach, where they learnt to swim. In the evenings, the five played cards together—canasta, hearts, and solitaire—encompassed by the sound of a European symphony needling forth from Ivy's parents' gramophone. As they retired to bed, Ivy switched on the shortwave radio, their lifeline to the outside world, that crackled, hissed, but barked out world news via the BBC as well as stations as far as Turkey, even India. Nightfall was when the radio signals came through with the least interference. Through the wooden walls of the house, they were the last sounds Evelyn and her boys heard before slipping into sleep.

When her two boys were seven and five years old respectively, Evelyn's newly married cousin paid a visit from Kingston with her husband as well as his uniformed brother, who was home on leave from the war. The brother, Isaac, had been pursuing pediatric medicine at the American University in Beirut when war broke out. Unable to receive funds from his family in Jamaica to continue his studies or to purchase a passage home, he enlisted with the British Eighth Army, first as a medic, then in intelligence. He was a tall, trim man of six feet four inches in height with smiling blue eyes. The diminutive Evelyn, who was five feet on her tiptoes, said it was the uniform that won her over. He too was smitten. The son of a practicing Syrian Jewish father and a Jamaican Jewish mother, Zackie was religious and wanted a Jewish wife. He wanted children and a peaceful family life. Evelyn fit the bill. Moreover, she came packaged with two young children, who impressed him that afternoon with their knowledge of art history as they sat quietly sharing their books with him on the porch. There were few places more peaceful than Stanton. He asked if he could write to her from the frontline. After two thick stacks of correspondence of his letters to her, and hers to him (that she tied in twine then burnt when he died), they married, showered with Pearl's and Ivy's blessings.

As a wedding present to Evelyn and Zackie, Ivy and Pearl gave them a car and built them a house at Stanton beside their wooden bungalow, separated by a sprawling guango tree. Evelyn chose the design from an American magazine. The three-bedroom home with an inner garden and a porch running the length of the bedrooms would be constructed from cut limestone to withstand hurricanes. However, the builders misread the measurements and halved its proportions. The stonework meant it would be too cumbersome and costly to redo. Neither Evelyn nor Zackie were exacting or demanding of comforts. So broad-shouldered Zackie walked the hallways at an angle when the family of four moved in. Just as his knees reached his chin when he folded himself into the Standard 8 he'd been gifted.

Evelyn continued to tutor the boys, preparing them to enroll at Jamaica College, a boarding school in Kingston. She also gave birth to David, followed by Rosalie, then Judy. As Ainsley and Richard excelled at their high school entrance exams, Richard obtaining the highest grades in the

Caribbean, word spread of Evelyn's teaching skills. Neighboring farm families asked if she could teach their young offspring too. With three more children of her own to educate, Evelyn built a small cinderblock room at the back of the house and opened an unofficial school. Within a short time, the class numbered twelve. Each child then went off to board at various high schools, the girls to a Catholic institution run by nuns, as was the norm even for Jewish families at the time, and where Evelyn and Zackie arranged a driver to take them to synagogue services every Saturday morning. Their youngest son, David, was homesick, so they brought him back from Kingston and enrolled him at the newly formed Morant Bay High School. Upon graduation, in a moment of 1960s Zionist fervor, Evelyn and Zackie sent him off to Israel to join a kibbutz, where his practical mind would be put to good use. Meanwhile, their two elder sons went off to universities in England, the girls heading north to the United States.

Evelyn expected Ainsley, her eldest, to take over Stanton and had insisted he study agricultural sciences. Upon his return from England, the young man lived on the farm but spent much time in Kingston for the sake of a social life. One afternoon at the tennis club in Morant Bay, Evelyn's opponent called over the net, "Evelyn, I understand I must congratulate you."

"Whatever for?" said Evelyn.

"Ainsley, of course. I hear he's been married."

Of course, Evelyn lost the match. She hurried home, placed a few calls, and learned that her eldest son had eloped. That weekend, Ainsley returned to Morant Bay with his non-Jewish new wife (hence, the elopement) who converted shortly after. Three granddaughters followed one after the other to Evelyn's and Zackie's delight.

"I am too young to be called 'Grandma,'" Evelyn stated, and, with residual Zionist zeal, decided to be called Ema. The title meant mother in Hebrew. It presaged an unexpected role. Within just over a year of giving birth to her last child, Ainsley's wife took ill with terminal cancer. Evelyn became a surrogate mother to the young girls, even when the new family moved to Kingston for Ainsley's wife's treatment. She came into to the city to stay with them or brought them back to Stanton during their holidays, she and Zackie parenting the children.

Erratic child-rearing was not enough to occupy Ema, however. She decided to raise chickens and create an egg business. She bought twelve dozen hatchlings and soon she was supplying the town's supermarket with eggs. She realized it was not simply the fostering and care of living creatures that satisfied her. She missed teaching. So, when she discovered her cook was illiterate, she scheduled her for lessons between mealtimes. The gardener followed and, soon after, the man who milked the cows, as well as his wife. But it was children with whom she loved working. She had no qualifications to teach in a traditional classroom, so Zackie had an idea. He observed the practical and social skills their daughters were enthusiastically acquiring as Girl Guides at their boarding school in Kingston. "Start a chapter at the Morant Bay High School," he told her.

Soon, Guiding occupied Evelyn's every waking moment. She attended trainings and jubilees, proudly wearing her uniform. She visited schools and encouraging students to join. She raised funds for the organization, filling her car to the brim with boxes of cookies and coercing everyone she encountered into buying them during the month-long annual cookie sale. If they declined because they had high blood sugar or were dieting, she told them sweetly, "Then buy them for your neighbors. Imagine how you'd give them a lovely surprise and be helping a good cause at the same time."

It was Ivy who'd instilled Ema's philanthropic drive. Over the course of Ema's childhood, Ivy had given away parcels of Stanton's land to farmworkers to enable them to own a home and grow their own food. She'd enlisted the government to assist in building houses for those who were but a few generations removed from slavery. Now, Evelyn fed lunch to a destitute old woman from this housing development located within walking distance from Stanton. The woman had no money, no food, and no living relatives, only the small one-bedroom cinderblock house in her name. The woman came by each day for a hot meal. One afternoon, she did not appear. Evelyn made an inquiry via her gardener to her cook's husband, who pastured his cow behind the house where the grass was thick and high, then on to their son who picked coconuts for her and, between all of them, discovered the old woman had slipped, fallen, and died in the night.

"May God rest her poor, poor soul," said Evelyn sadly.

Until she found out that the woman's next-door neighbor had taken possession of the old woman's house. According to her grapevine news sources, the neighbor had gotten hold of the property deed and this was not the first time that the next-door neighbor had done such a thing, gotten hold of the deeds of dead neighbors.

"A bunch of thieves!" she proclaimed. "If anyone should get the house, it should be the church." With a little more probing, Evelyn discovered that the same neighbor's son had been over at the old woman's house the night before she died.

"Foul play, for sure," she stated.

"Evvie, what are you getting involved for? It's none of our business," said Zackie with more than an ounce of exasperation.

"If it's not our business, whose is it, Zackie? She had not one living relative. We should call the Commissioner of Police," she countered.

"We?" he said.

"Well, you know I need your help."

Zackie had been appointed the Custos, a Commonwealth title making him the Queen's representative for the parish of St. Thomas on the island. He called the commissioner.

"Yes, I need your team to look into something. Yes, my wife is at it again."

Evelyn then picked up the phone and called the town's only mortician.

"Mr. Brown," she said, "would you please hold the body? There is something amiss and I am going to request an investigation."

A week passed before the commissioner concluded, "Not enough evidence for a murder charge, my dear Custos and Mrs. M., but we've repatriated the deed and the church will get the property, and also bury her."

"All's well that ends well," sighed Zackie, while Evelyn shook her head.

Evelyn visited Mr. Brown, the undertaker, weekly. He was not just the mortician, but also the town's butcher. One day, while shopping for a fresh roast, an idea struck her. While rummaging around for her purse, she noticed a half-skein of white wool in her crochet bag left over from a baby blanket she'd made as a gift. Her main crocheting project, though, was a pair of house slippers that she sold as yet another way to raise money for the Girl Guides. Everyone she knew already owned a pair, including Mr. Brown.

"Mr. Brown," she said, earnestly, "what do you or people put on the feet of the dead?"

"Well, shoes, of course. Can't go to heaven barefooted! Got to make a good impression with shiny new soles to get through those pearly white gates," he answered humorously.

"Brand-new, unworn shoes? They're putting perfectly good shoes into the ground? When many people can't even afford school shoes for their children?" she asked incredulously.

"No one wants to bury a loved one in old, mashed-up shoes," he said, sighing sadly, well practiced in sympathetic gestures.

Evelyn's eyes lit up. She reached into her bag and brought forth the pair of her slippers.

"Mr. Brown, remember my slippers, well, here's what we do . . ." she said. "Show them these but tell them I'll make them in pure white, the color of heaven if you will. They're brand new, not very expensive at all, and moreover, the money goes to a good cause. No point in burying good leather shoes. These are far more appropriate. Tell them that." Suddenly, Evelyn had become the shoemaker to the dead.

It was around this time, in his eighty-second year of life, their children grown, grandchildren thriving, that Zackie began to speak of death.

"Evvie," he said one day at the dining table, "Ev, I've been thinking. I'd better go before you as I can't live without you. If you go first, I will have to go out and buy myself a gun and shoot myself." Zackie was a pacifist. Following his war experience, he abhorred violence of any kind.

"Zacks, stop speaking nonsense!" Evelyn shook her head as if to prevent his words from taking hold. But he continued, "Well, I feel it, that I'm in the departure lounge, so I don't think I'll have any need for guns."

"Then I'm canceling your flight," stated Evelyn. "I've had fifty good years with you and I'll be around for at least another twenty years more and I'm not ready to give you up yet."

But he was leaving. He often fell asleep at the lunch table, his coffee cup in hand, spilling the hot liquid all over himself. He still salted his food before tasting it but his appetite was gone. He was losing weight for the first time in his postwar life, his triple chin shrinking to a single flap of skin. His trousers started to fall off and needed belting, his shirts soon could fit two of him, even the sleeves floated around his arms. Ema remarked proudly on his weight loss, attributing it to his reduced appetite. It was late August when he was diagnosed with pancreatic cancer. By mid-October, he was no longer. He slipped away peacefully at home at Stanton, opting for no treatment, given the disease's prognosis and progression. Ema framed a large jolly photo of her beloved Zackie and hung it at eye level across from her chair at the dining table, hip height for anyone standing. This way, three times a day, he would be with her, smiling upon her from the printed paper.

Now, nineteen years later, Evelyn wished to be buried beside her beloved Zackie in the Orange Street Cemetery where both her parents, her aunt Ivy, and her Jamaican grandparents and great-grandparents lay. The cemetery stretched across a city block in a dry and dusty, rough, and run-down section of Kingston, its gravestones parching unsheltered from the Caribbean sun.

"They need trees there," she'd declared a month after her hundredth birthday, contemplating her interment.

"People want to plant flowers but . . . a flower takes a lot of care. A tree just grows."

She thought back to her last morning at Stanton a few days before the fall in the shower in Kingston that had broken her shoulder, stilled her, setting in the pneumonia that had strained her heart. She'd done as was her habit, waking, reaching for the fishing rod positioned behind the bedside table, and poking the rod about at lizards (of which she was petrified) to chase them away. She'd then pulled on her crocheted slippers and stepped out of her ornate oak bed onto the tile floor, crossing it to peer through the open grilled windows to admire her dozens of potted orchids flowering out on the porch.

Orchid plants swayed before her. White, purple, spotted, frilled, pink, yellow ones too. They were what people always gave her for her birthdays, the last twenty-odd ones. Now those same people over the last eleven days had brought her new ones as she lay in the hospital in Kingston. This morning, she was doing much better and could enjoy the orchids. Instead of a mask, she had simple tubes in her nose, her oxygen levels increasing. The flush of pink coming back to her cheeks gave hope to her family that the doctors would discharge her soon. Her children and some of her grandchildren had been standing vigil each day, all day. In the last few days the urgency had lessened. Now, only Ainsley's second wife was present, having brought her a hearty breakfast from home.

"Ema, now that you've had an egg and toast, would you like a mango, a Bombay mango?"

Ema lit up at the offer.

"Oh, yes!" she said, her sweet tooth piqued with glee.

Her daughter-in-law turned to peel and slice the mango. Ema drew in a breath of the mango's fragrant nectar. The thought of the succulent, perfumed fruit was enough to transport Ema back to the countryside. She was back at her beloved Stanton, where her fruit trees flourished. Her joyous heart flooded, a quiet peace overcame her. Ema, as all knew her, was no more.

Meeting with Judith

Cynthia McLeod

IN MY EARLY childhood, my best friend was a Jewish girl. We were together in kindergarten and from grades one through four. It was the turbulent time of World War II, although we didn't really suffer from the war in Suriname, a remote Dutch colony on the north coast of South America.

Jews played an important role in the history of Suriname; the Jewish community was still in existence during my childhood and one of the synagogues stood just opposite our house. My friend Judith was not originally from Suriname but she happened to live in our country because her father, Professor Oppenheim, an agricultural specialist, was sent to the country in 1938. Then the war broke out and the family couldn't leave, which saved them from the war. Judith, who was exactly the same age as I (I'm six days older), had two older brothers who were ten and twelve years older than she. Later she told me that everyone in Holland had advised her parents to leave their sons in Holland because there would be no education for them in such a remote country as Suriname, but the mother insisted that the family should stay together. The sons came along and, according to the mother, they had an excellent education at their Surinamese school.

The family was orthodox Jewish and the father was also the rabbi of the Jewish community during his stay in Suriname. Judith and I were not only together in school, for I was often invited to play at her house; as a result, I experienced quite a lot of Jewish life. I never played there on Friday evenings or on Saturdays, however, because the Sabbath was a holy day, as she explained to me. We were in the third grade when the war ended and, from then on, she often told me that their family would be leaving for Palestine, which as far as I knew was a name from the Bible that I had only heard in Sunday school.

We were in the fourth grade when she did not come to school anymore and I remember how strange I felt in class without my best friend. Later on, when I heard or read about the creation of Israel, life in the kibbutz, and the development of the new state, I often wondered if Judith was part of all that and how she would cope in that faraway country. When I wrote the novel *The Cost of Sugar* in 1984 in Washington, DC, Judith was often on my mind, because so much of what I knew about Jewish life was from what I had experienced in her home long ago and from what she had told me. The novel was published in Suriname in 1987 and in Holland in 1995 and became a great hit. During the many interviews with Dutch journalists, for whom it was surprising that a Black Surinamese woman could write about Jews, one of the questions was always: How was it possible that I knew so much about Jewish life? I kept telling them the history of Jews in Suriname, that three of my four grandparents were children from a Jewish father and a mixed mother, and I always told them that, in my early childhood, my best friend was a Jewish girl. "Where is she now?" was the much-asked question, to which I always answered: "Somewhere in Israel, I guess. I don't know."

During a book signing in a city in Holland, a lady approached me with the words: "Someone in Israel is looking for you." Because I knew nobody in Israel, I answered: "Could that someone be Judith Oppenheim?" "Yes, she is the one. She wants to contact you." I wrote down my phone number and added: "Dear friend from my childhood, I still remember you. Do you remember me too?" Two weeks later I received a phone call. Someone said: "This is Judith Oppenheim!" I shouted: "Judith, this is Cynthia, your friend. Happy Birthday, because two days ago was your birthday." We talked for more than an hour and, to both of our surprise, we remembered everything about each other; it was as if fifty-one years had vanished. "My whole family sits around me, because everyone knows how important this is to me," she said. After this first phone call, we called each other regularly and we mailed each other letters; we both felt the urge to meet, to see, and to touch each other, but I lived in Antwerp and she lived in Tel Aviv.

A month before our sixtieth birthdays, she wrote that she and her husband were going to the United States via Paris, where they would visit an old aunt. Could I come to Paris to meet her? Antwerp is only four hours by train or bus from Paris, so I decided to go. On my way in the bus, somehow the doubts started to come. Wasn't I doing something foolish? How much could we have in common? I knew her more than fifty years ago and we had since experienced totally different lives. But at the bus stop Judith and her husband were waiting for me and it was as if two sisters were meeting after fifty years! The whole afternoon we sat in a bistro close to the Louvre but we saw nothing of the hectic French life because we talked and talked and talked.

Judith remembered everything from her childhood in Suriname; the streets of Paramaribo, the houses, the names of the children in our class, the way we used to walk from home to school, she remembered it all. "My mother kept everything for me," she said, "the schoolbooks, the pictures, my clothes, everything. It was as if she knew that this would make me unique. In our house, my mother spoke a lot about Suriname. I always heard her telling people that my brothers had the best education they could ever have in their school in Suriname and she was sorry that I didn't have the chance to attend the same school. In the beginning in Israel nobody ever spoke about what happened before, as if nobody had any memories. But everyone had memories, the most awful memories of the Holocaust, their time in the concentration camps, the deaths of their relatives. But in the new Israel everyone was utterly busy building their new lives and maintained silence about their past."

"I was maybe forty when people began to talk about their memories, shocking and horrible. I could never speak up, because I had no dreadful memories, I had beautiful memories which didn't fit into the conversation. When I was in my fifties, I slowly started to talk about my memories, wonderful memories because I spent my early childhood in a peaceful country without war, with all kinds of people who lived happily together. And you know what? Nobody believed me! A country like that couldn't exist. They thought that in my mind I had made it far nicer than it was. And sometimes I felt a strong urge to go back to Suriname, to see if it was really so or if I had made it up." She took my hand and asked urgently: "But it was like that, wasn't it? We were together in school with all these children from different ethnicities, we lived and played together with no problems, we always walked alone in the streets without any fear." I smiled and said, "You didn't make it up, it was like that and it still is." Now I understood why she had said, "Everyone knows how important this is for me," in our first telephone call. I was the confirmation that it was true and that she hadn't made it more beautiful in her mind. Judith continued: "You know, all my life, whenever I heard the word 'Peace,' in my mind I saw the streets of Paramaribo and I was sure that 'Paradise' was like our garden in the Heerenstraat. Should I go and see it all again?"

I sat there and looked at my childhood friend while I softly said: "No, you don't need to go. Just cherish your memories." I felt so moved while I watched her and thought: cherish your memories, which make you a unique person in your society. Cherish your wonderful memories about my country. My insignificant small country that was a safe haven for so many Jews during the war, my impoverished but warm Surinamese society that made the difference between life and death for so many human beings, that ensured that this one person could become a unique person in her society, just because of her beautiful memories. Yes, Judith, cherish your memories and keep them in your heart. That's why I shall not tell you that the streets of Paramaribo were not peaceful in the 1980s, when we had a military dictatorship, and from my mouth you'll never hear that they built an ugly concrete stockroom in your former garden, your paradise.

(Translated by the author from the original Dutch)

Jewish-Cuban Poems

Ruth Behar

Dream of Sefarad

Depart and never return
They told us

Forget about Spain
They told us

Do not dare to live in any of our cities, towns, and villages
They told us

Under penalty of death
They told us

Banished, you are banished from all our kingdoms
They told us

We have made quince jam from the fruit of the trees
We have drunk the wine from the sweet grapes
We have bathed in these rivers
We have welcomed with our faith the new moon
We have loved, brought up our children, buried our dead in this red earth
We have written poems in Hebrew, Arabic, Castilian
We have built modest synagogues, nothing comparable to your cathedrals
We have recited prayers for peace with our souls as open as the sea
We have wished for a *mazal bueno* to those who surrendered to your Cross

We have been here for more than a thousand years, generation upon generation
We have put down roots so deep, how can we leave this soil?
Cities with such beautiful names—
Toledo, Barcelona, Segovia, Zamora, Córdoba

Pretend you won't remember us
Pretend you won't miss us
Pretend you won't see us lurking in the shadows

Sefarad is our home, Spain is our Sefarad
Who are you to take Sefarad and Spain from us?

Weep for my people, who are shutting the doors and clasping the keys
Weep for my people, who are filling the boats at the port of Cádiz
Weep for my people, who are sweating in the damp heat of summer
Weep for my people, who are carrying the Torah on their shoulders
Weep for my people, who are glancing back, seeing only a Moor wave goodbye
Weep for my people, who are bemoaning their lives, wishing only to die
Weep for my people, who are going forth into another exile
Weep for my people, who are furious for having loved Sefarad so much
Weep for my people, who are wondering if Sefarad was only a dream

Many autumns have passed
Look—
Already my people are drying their tears
Already my people are bowing to another shore
Already a cry rises from my people:
I won't weep anymore
I won't weep anymore

Hijica, hear the song inside our hearts
It's sweet and sad and beautiful and broken
It's all that we kept:
the nostalgia for the sad breeze of Spain

The Last Perera

In memory of Victor Haim Perera

I still remember our phone conversations late at night
the desk lamp casting a halo in the darkness of my Victorian house
my husband and my little boy sleeping peacefully down the hall
you in California and I in Michigan talking about our shared heritage.
"Ruth, you must claim your Sephardic identity," you'd say. "Ours is a history like no other, promise me you will take it more seriously."
And I, not to offend, always replied, "Of course I will, Victor, I will, I will."
But then we'd hang up and I wouldn't do much of anything you could call

Sephardic, except listen to all the sad lullabies and love songs that no one had
ever sung to me, *A la una yo nací, a los dos me engrandecí, a las tres tomí
amante,*
a las cuatro me casí: alma, vida, y corasón . . . At one I was born, at two I grew up,
at three I took a lover, at four I married: soul, life, and heart . . .

Did I disappoint you, dear Victor?
For you, being Sephardic was chiseled into your bones, when you went to Toledo
the streets felt familiar, you knew without a shadow of a doubt that your ancestors
had been there, and in Salonika, you ran into your ghost, sent to Auschwitz, and
you were absolutely certain you saw with your own eyes how our largest Sephardic
community was devoured and then forgotten in the history books of the Holocaust.
And that time you came to Michigan, invited to speak at a Sephardic synagogue,
you asked me to drive you there, I who fear all the highways of the world. I was in
a panic, hardly breathing, until finally we arrived. We awaited great fanfare in your
honor and discovered that only three old men had come to hear you, but this didn't
sadden you, dear Victor, for they spoke our beautiful dying language, our Ladino.
When we said goodbye, many hours later, we felt we were among the blessed.

Being Sephardic, for you, dear Victor, was your most sacred badge of honor.
But being Sephardic was also a curse that drove your sister to madness.
You imbibed the evil eye in your mother's milk, you said, and you believed it.
And so you would have no children, you would be the last of the Pereras.

Just when I was starting to take the whole Sephardic thing seriously,
you were embarking on a different journey, swimming with the whales.
In the ocean depths you found a world that wasn't cursed, that wasn't spooked.
History no longer weighed you down and evil eyes couldn't find you . . .
Or maybe they could? While swimming you had a stroke. You recovered, but it
wasn't you anymore. Your soul remained intact, sweet, kind, loving. But your mind
had departed. A proud Sefaradí of all times and places, you took your leave early.
The day the Angel of Death arrived you smiled: *Now take me home to Sefarad.*

A Father's Tattoo

He spends his days parking cars
He's a valet at the Betsy Hotel on Ocean Drive
I never learned his name
Yesterday he came with an umbrella to help me out of the car

It was raining the way it rains in the tropics
The rain gets inside you, even your heart is soaking wet
I was grateful for his kindness, kept thanking him
He didn't seem to understand why
He gave me a slip of paper and took the car away
I trusted him, the way you trust a lifeguard

After I was done with my lecture
I returned and gave him the slip of paper
Someone else went to get my car
As we stood waiting I saw a name on his arm
"May I see the name?"
He turned over his right arm
I saw the inside of his arm, soft silky skin
In flowing script it was written:
Carlota

And who is Carlota? I asked
Mi hija, he told me, it was his daughter.
He pulled out his phone and showed me pictures
She is two, she is dressed in a frilly dress, there's a bow in her hair
She is dreamy-eyed, she smiles, she isn't afraid

What kind of father has a tattoo of his daughter's name on his flesh?
I thought of Jews, numbers branded into their flesh by the Nazis
This was different
This was beautiful
This was a kind of love I couldn't fathom
I know the love of the sea, the love of the sun, the love of the moon
I know the love of an open rose, the love of a wide trunk tree
I know the love of the road that takes me places and brings me home
But the love of a father who treats his daughter's name
Like a blessing

That I do not know

Saying Goodbye to La Habana in May

There's always that last day in La Habana.
When I want to fix the city in my memory.

I want to take another walk on the Malecón.
I want to feel the sea wetting my eyelids.
I want to run after the little girl who walks on the seawall
clasping her father's hand, that little girl who was me, long ago.
I want to hear the street musician with his guitar
singing Stevie Wonder's "I Just Called to Say I Love You."
And I want to hear myself sing along with him, I who never sing.

There's always that last day in La Habana.
When I want to sit in a rocking chair and listen to the rain
pouring despondently from the sky, as if the world were about to end.
I want to watch my neighbor Delia caress the potatoes she's thankful for,
the red earth of the island coating her fingers with love.
I want to go searching for eggs with my taxi driver, who also needed some,
both of us standing in line for almost an hour at El Ten Cent on 23 and 10,
each emerging with thirty eggs, happy, the best of friends.

There's always that last day in La Habana.
When I want to lose myself in the hustle and the bustle on Calle Obispo.
A woman sweeps its cobblestones with a broom, and she wears
a flower in her hair, showing off, posing for pictures with the tourists.
I want to feel the palpitations of my heart after too much sweet coffee.
I want to eat an entire plate of ripe plantains, fried in lots of oil.
And not worry about a thing.

There's always that last day in La Habana.
When I want to fill my suitcase with the orange blossoms of the
    flamboyant trees.
I want to believe Caro won't ever die, that she'll braid her beautiful hair
in the morning and unbraid it at night before she goes to sleep, forever
    and ever.
All she wants now is for her son, Paco, to return for a visit from Miami.
It's been eight years, much too long, tell him to come soon, she tells me, soon.

There's always that last day in La Habana.
On Calle 15, where I once lived, the men are finishing their domino game.
Around the corner, at the Patronato synagogue, our sacred Torah is safe.
We Jews have nothing to fear in Cuba.
Estévez has called from Matanzas to wish me a good trip and make me laugh.

Cristy, who's never flown anywhere, has promised to recite a rosary, yet again, so my plane won't crash, and says, "Don't worry, Ruti, you'll get there just fine."

There's always that last day in La Habana.
When I want to still be there, but I know I am already far away.
Tomorrow, I will be struggling to find the words to explain how I feel.
This is my last day in La Habana.

On *The Nature of Blood* and the Ghost of Anne Frank

Caryl Phillips

WHY WOULD A writer from the Caribbean want to write about the Holocaust? Of course, the answer is I don't know, but why not? Is it perhaps because my maternal grandfather was a Portuguese Jew called Emmanuel de Fraites who came to St. Kitts, the island I was born on, by way of the small Portuguese island of Madeira? Perhaps this fact was complicated and made disturbing to me by the realization that he never knew me and, if he did, he certainly never acknowledged me. Did this personal slight in my early life nudge me toward this material? I don't know, but I don't think so. I do, however, know that I ended up in a Caribbean bar the day I finished *The Nature of Blood*. Albeit, a Caribbean bar in Amsterdam. This was an accident of geography, or so I thought. But now I am beginning to wonder. But maybe I should start at the beginning, or near the beginning.

In January 1996 I found myself sitting in a hotel room in Bangkok working on a novel. Bangkok is not Europe, America, or the Caribbean. I like writing in Bangkok because it is highly unlikely that anything will happen on the street or in the hotel that will interfere with my line of thought. If I were to try this same exercise in New York, London, or St. Kitts, something would happen every day that would impinge upon my concentration, and perhaps eventually spill over and affect the book. I can write in these places, but my writing is always in danger from my environment. This is not the case in Bangkok. Both culturally and physically, I have no connection to the country or the people. I am a foreigner in the most radical sense, and I have always imagined that this sense of alienation frees me to concentrate on my work.

However, in Bangkok I was temporarily undone. The novel I was working on was about Europe in the most intimate manner. It was a novel about the Holocaust. But not just this. My primary obsession was the Holocaust, which was—at least in my mind—related to my secondary obsession: race and faith as seen through the prism of sixteenth-century Venice. Othello's Venice, Shylock's Venice. A Venice whose global influence was predominant, but whose domestic policies were rigidly regulated so that the city-state might preserve its racial, religious, and class "purity." In order to write, I needed to be in Bangkok. I needed to be far away from the familiar world.

At first the writing appeared to be flowing, if not freely, then at least purposefully toward some long-hoped-for conclusion. But there was a final piece to the puzzle that was clearly missing, and I could not identify where or, more importantly, when I might find it. And then one Bangkok morning I opened the *International Herald Tribune* and read the story of what had been occurring in Israel with the Ethiopian Jews. It was then that I realized that these days, short of taking oneself off to a desert island, one's writing is always likely to be in danger from one's environment.

According to the paper, it appeared that in recent years black Jews in Israel had been donating blood in the hope that it might be used to save lives. However, the Israeli government, fearful of "diseases" that might be contained in this blood, had instructed the medical teams to dump the "black" blood. The secret practice had now been exposed, and the black Jews were rioting and demanding that this racist practice be stopped. I could barely believe what I was reading. This, it turned out, was the story that would enable me to put the final piece of the narrative puzzle into place and finish my novel.

The novel is, both directly and indirectly, about blood. At its heart is the story of the supposed murder of a Christian child by Jews in sixteenth-century Italy who wanted the child's blood to use in Jewish rituals; and some few centuries later, the story of Nazi Germany's creation of a system that alienated and then murdered those whose blood was "Jewish" and therefore not "pure." The novel is about Europe's obsession with homogeneity, and her inability to deal with the heterogeneity that is—in fact—her natural condition. The practice of using blood as a barometer of acceptability is deeply ingrained in the European consciousness. Long before the present generation of nonwhite immigrants began to suffer from this failure of European imagination, there were others—"white," if you will—who had been identified as "impure" and "less" who suffered too. In other words, wherever one looks in European history, blood has been used as a pretext for the persecution of those whose faces do not fit on the canvas upon which the national portrait has been painted.

When I was fourteen, and growing up in the north of England, I was very concerned with history. And, of course, the kind of history we studied at school was European history. Colonial history was not taught. I like to think that the teachers saw that in an increasingly multiracial Britain it might have been a little difficult, to say nothing of hypocritical, to continue to preach the glories of the Empire to a classroom peppered with brown and black faces. Whether this occurred to the teachers, I do not know. I do know that European history afforded, and still affords, Britain great opportunities for gloating and sneering at the "losers" across the English Channel because, as everybody knows, Britain won both world wars.

One day I came home from school and, having finished my homework, settled down to watch a television series called "The World at War." This particular week the episode dealt with the Holocaust. I have a vague recollection of some footage of Dutch Jews in Amsterdam, and it is certainly possible that some reference was made to Anne Frank. But the overwhelming impression that the program made upon me was shock. Utter numbing shock. This did not make any sense. These were white people who were systematically rounding up and killing other white people. I could not understand it. However, within the next few days I had written my first short story.

The story concerned a young Dutch boy. His parents informed him that he had to wear a Star of David on his coat. This was now the law. But, of course, the boy was intensely upset to learn of this new decree and saw no reason why he should obey. He was, after all, just the same as all the other boys. His parents tried to explain that it was not a mark to be ashamed of and that he should wear the star with pride. Reluctantly, the young Dutch boy agreed. Soon after the boy and his parents were being transported to a camp in a cattle truck, and somehow the boy managed to pry open a small gap in the wall of the boxcar and leap from the speeding train. Unfortunately, he struck his head on a rock as he fell, and he knocked himself unconscious. He was bleeding heavily, and clearly he was in danger of hemorrhaging to death. Luckily, a farmer who was out working in his fields happened to see the sun glinting where it caught his yellow Star of David. He found the boy, bandaged his head, and nursed him back to health. The boy survived.

The Dutch boy was, of course, me. A fourteen-year-old black boy, born in St. Kitts in the Eastern Caribbean, now growing up in working-class Yorkshire in the north of England. I knew that I was different from the other English kids. I was reminded of it every day by the stares in the street, by the way in which shopkeepers dropped my change onto the counter rather than putting it into my hand, by the way in which I could suddenly find myself ostracized by people I had hitherto considered to be my friends. On good days I might be described as a "West Indian" or "Coloured." On bad days I was a "wog" or a "nigger." On really bad days I was invited to simply "fuck off back to where I came from." Clearly, they meant somewhere other than the country whose name was on the cover of my passport.

Watching this program about the Holocaust had a profound effect on me. The last thing I wanted to be reminded of was the fact that I was different. I knew it, and I already worried too much about it, for I was aware that Britain did not celebrate, let alone encourage, difference. This was not the British way. As I watched the program that evening, I realized that around these issues of difference and visibility, things could go horribly, horribly wrong.

Almost twenty-five years later I found myself sitting in a hotel room in Bangkok reading about the racism of Jews toward their own black people, a racism based solely upon visibility and difference. I was reminded again of how appallingly circular history can be, how replete with ironies, how chilling. I had in the course of my research for this novel, visited Israel during the summer of 1995, and had seen some of the problems that faced people who were visibly the "other." A single afternoon on the West Bank was more than enough to convince me that a solution to the so-called Palestinian problem lies someplace in the distant future. Blood. Always blood. Who are you? You are not us. Therefore, we define ourselves, in part, by defining you. Questions about blood can transcend national boundaries with laughable ease. Hitler was not simply concerned with German Jews. And the black Jews, whose blood was officially dashed to the earth, were, of course, Israelis.

I left Bangkok with a reasonably coherent draft of the novel and returned to London. I knew what the next step would be. A few weeks in which I would polish the prose, clean up the narrative line, and revise the choice of adjectives. Pedantic, painful work, but there was only one place I had in mind for this task. I now needed to go to a place where my sense of security about what I had written would be vigorously challenged in the most radical and unnerving manner. In Bangkok I sought peace from the world. Now I actively needed my writing to be in danger from my environment. On March 13, as it happened my thirty-eighth birthday, I flew from London to Amsterdam with my manuscript, my laptop computer and a portable printer.

Amsterdam was the location of my first story. I imagine that a tangible legacy of that episode of "The World at War" and the story that it gave rise to is that for the past ten years or so I have worked with a large poster of Anne Frank above my desk. In some strange way she was partly responsible for my beginning to write, and as long as I continue to write her presence is a comforting one. In Amsterdam I spent most days working in my hotel room, venturing out only to walk around the park in the misty rain, and then scampering back to my room to continue working. The room-service guys, primarily Surinamese and Arubans, were puzzled by what the "brother" was doing alone in this room with all this computer stuff, books everywhere, and paper scattered over the floor. I overtipped in a panic-stricken attempt to staunch the flow of their questions. And then, after almost two weeks, I wandered out of the hotel and in the direction of the place that I knew I would have to revisit.

I first visited the Anne Frank House nearly twenty years ago, and I remember being puzzled by the geographical relationship of the secret annex to the house. Perhaps I wasn't really puzzled and this was just my elaborate way of avoiding the emotional train that I was sure was about to run me down. This time, as I walked around the house, the emotional train ran me down, and I felt deeply moved and able to submit to the anger and helplessness that coursed through my body as I thought about the lost life of Anne Frank and millions like her. I left Anne Frank's house feeling calmer, in fact strangely serene, and I went next door to the Rum Runners Caribbean Bar and Restaurant. I ordered a beer and sat on a stool and looked around. Next to Anne Frank's house there is now an establishment that is a monument to difference and otherness. And both serving and being served there are a veritable rainbow coalition of faces of all colors, races, and ethnicities. Did this constitute progress? Was Europe finally beginning to deal with "difference?" And why the serene feeling as I left Anne Frank's house?

Sitting in the Rum Runners Bar, I thought about blood. And I decided no. Europe is not finally beginning to deal with "difference." The Netherlands tolerated "difference" back in the thirties, which is why Otto Frank removed his family from Germany and settled in Amsterdam. But it did not help them. And today? Surely it would take only one madman somewhere in Europe to trigger a chain of events that would leave Rum Runners a charred heap of rubble. Then why the serenity? To understand this I had to turn my mind back twenty-five years.

My response to seeing the "A World at War" documentary was to write. A private, annealing act. Writing helps to build a bridge across the space between one's own private (and often fearful) inner world and the external world in which we all have to continue to live. Writing helps the writer to deal with problems—and, if he or she is lucky, to perhaps even understand the nature of the problems.

In the Anne Frank House there was a moment of clarity, for I knew that I finally understood something. I understood that man has an infinite capacity to inflict cruelty on his fellow man and willfully learn nothing from the malign nature of his actions. In short, man learns little from history. Not a pleasant conclusion, but one that helped me to deal with the emotional trauma of being once more in Anne Frank's house. And sitting next door in a warm Caribbean bar on a damp Amsterdam afternoon, I simply felt grateful that I had undertaken the fragmented, obsessional task of writing about "the nature of blood." Doing so had enabled me to achieve a moment of temporary reconciliation with the young Dutch boy of my story of twenty-five years ago, and I also felt that I had repaid a small part of the personal debt that I owed to the remarkable young girl who used to live next door to what is now the Caribbean Rum Runners Bar and Restaurant.

Afterword

Bryan Cheyette

> Granted, the Jews are harassed—what am I thinking of? They are hunted down, exterminated, cremated. But these are little family quarrels. The Jew is disliked from the moment he is tracked down. But in my case everything takes on a *new* guise. I am given no chance. I am overdetermined from without. I am the slave not of the "idea" that others have of me but of my own appearance.
> —Frantz Fanon, *Black Skin, White Masks*, 1952

THERE WAS A time when Frantz Fanon's dismissal of the Nazi onslaught against European Jewry as a "little family quarrel" would have caused outrage. Fanon himself realized this—"What am I thinking of?"—before he rightly characterized the Nazi genocide as that of a people "hunted down, exterminated, cremated." However, even after a second thought, Fanon still described the genocide as a "little family quarrel." What does he mean by this? One clue is his rejection of Freudian (or "white") psychoanalysis built on the foundations of the archetypal "little family quarrel" known as the Oedipus complex.[1] But the wider context for Fanon's statement is his understanding of anti-Semitism and fascism as a matter primarily for the European continent; racism and colonialism are more global. The contrast between the local (Europe) and the global is reinforced by a series of oppositions—Jews and Blacks, inside and out, mind and body—to show the fundamental differences between anti-Semitism and racism ("I am given no chance. I am overdetermined from without").[2]

Despite these reductive binaries, I believe that Fanon's "little family quarrels" can be read less dismissively than first assumed. After all, what Fanon is doing with such provocative statements is decentering the history of Nazism—and, by extension, the Shoah (pace Raphaël Confiant)—so that it can intersect with other forms of oppression such as colonial racism, genocide, and slavery. From the perspective of the twenty-first century, the decentering of the Shoah, as part of a wider colonial project, is something that has been at the heart of, for instance, Paul Gilroy's *Between Camps: Race, Identity and Nationalism at the End of the Colour Line* (2000), Mark Mazower's *Hitler's Empire: Nazi Rule in Occupied Europe* (2008), and Michael Rothberg's *Multidirectional Memory: Remembering the Holocaust in the Age of Decolonization* (2009). My own *Diasporas of the Mind: Jewish and Postcolonial Writing and the Nightmare of History* (2013) recovers the intertwined histories underscoring this twenty-first-century project and shows that such histories were, ironically, part of imaginative literature long before they were recognized by postcolonial and Holocaust scholars. These knotted histories go back to the 1940s and 1950s and include such Caribbean figures as Fanon and his teacher Aimé Césaire, along with Jean Améry, Hannah Arendt, Albert Memmi, Primo Levi, and Jean-Paul Sartre.

Canonical novelists of Caribbean background such as Andrea Levy, V. S. Naipaul, Caryl Phillips, and Zadie Smith all show that Jewish and Caribbean history remains part of the literary imagination into the twenty-first century. As this volume demonstrates, there is a long cultural and social history within the Caribbean that refuses to separate out (or "discipline") Jewish and Caribbean histories. Sarah Phillips Casteel's *Calypso Jews: Jewishness in the Caribbean Literary Imagination* (2016) has rightly shown the ingrained character of Caribbean Creole culture, which mixes Jewish and Caribbean identities, and decenters, above all else, the dominance of Ashkenazic and European literature and history. Along with this collection, *Calypso Jews* engages with the lengthy historical memory of Caribbean culture, which includes 1492 as well as 1939, slavery and colonialism as well as Jewish refugees and the Shoah. Is this because the hybridity of the Caribbean particularly speaks to Jewish hybridity, as Caryl Phillips has argued?[3] Is there a specific Caribbean form of "metaphorical thinking"—seeing "similarities in dissimilars" as Arendt delineated—which in the literary imagination counters boundary-driven disciplinary thinking?[4] It is tempting to privilege the Caribbean as a uniquely creolized space that has incorporated an ambivalent Jewish history (refugees and victims as well as slave owners and colonialists) into its culture. But Fanon, once again, problematizes a too-easy set of "crossings" from Caribbean to Jewish and back again.

At the age of eighteen Fanon volunteered to join de Gaulle's Free French and sailed from Martinique singing, "Hitler, we are going to knock you off your hilltop."[5] By the end of his life, many of his comrades in the Free French were on the other side of the trenches as Fanon joined the Front de Libération Nationale (FLN) to liberate Algeria from colonial rule. Such is Fanon's "impossible life" in the well-known phrase of his North African comrade, the Tunisian-Jewish Albert Memmi.[6] Memmi's portrayal of Fanon's various incarnations has been taken up by Henry Louis Gates Jr. and many recent accounts that wish to see a more Caribbean, "provisional, reactive and local" approach to Fanon rather than his appropriation by "global culture."[7] It was from this "local" perspective that Memmi was to engage with Fanon as a cosmopolitan exile. In his long essay, as well as several shorter pieces, Memmi traces Fanon's various guises as an assimilated "white" French Antillean, a Black West Indian, a revolutionary Algerian nationalist, a pan-Africanist, and a universalizing "new humanist," concluding that it is the very "impossibility" of Fanon's serial transformations that has become "the source of his far-reaching influence."[8]

For Memmi, it was the disavowal of his origins and the people of Martinique in particular that typifies a diasporic Fanon who "broke with France, the French people and Europe."[9] In this reading, Fanon's life becomes something of a family romance, with the surrogate fatherland of Algeria taking the "place of Martinique."[10] Memmi depicts Fanon as a deracinated "Jewish intellectual," which accounts for a succession of invented guises (or conversion narratives) culminating in Fanon's rejection of Algerian nationalism and his turn to pan-Africanism:

> I suspect that Fanon's sudden and intransigent Africanism roused new hostility against him. He might have shared the fate of those Jewish intellectuals who declare themselves universalists and are suspected of cosmopolitanism and even treason; they are not considered sufficiently legitimate members of the community to be permitted such aloofness. For an Algerian so late in the making it was imprudent, to say the least, to put so recent a bond to the test.[11]

There is a strong sense in which the Tunisian Jewish Memmi transforms Fanon into a "family likeness" or an imagined double.[12] But while Memmi's version of Fanon may be considered to be an act of cultural narcissism, it is worth remembering that Memmi was well aware that his reading of Fanon through the prism of a diasporic Jewishness was based on lived experience. Fanon was denounced by Memmi's acquaintance, Dr. Ben Soltan, as a "Zionist" (as well as a "Black Doctor") after a conflict of interest at the Clinique Manouba in Tunis, where Fanon worked for three years following his exile from Algeria in 1956. Soon after working at Manouba, Ben Soltan, the director of the clinic, argued that Fanon was maltreating Algerian and Tunisian patients "on Israeli orders" or as a "spy and ally of the Jews."[13] Two of Fanon's closest colleagues at the clinic were Tunisian Jewish. While these accusations were not taken seriously, Fanon's position was made so uncomfortable that he moved his family off of the hospital grounds. After this episode, Memmi rightly stressed Fanon's discomfort as a Black non-Muslim in Algeria and the fact that he needed an interpreter, although he was learning Arabic, to function as a psychiatrist at the Manouba clinic. The accusation of being an Israeli spy—three years after France's involvement with Israel and Britain in the Suez adventure to neutralize Egyptian influence in North Africa and maintain French colonial control—both reinforced and arose from Fanon's status as an outsider or "European interloper."[14]

Such concerns, which Memmi relates to prevailing and long-standing anxieties about supposedly untrustworthy cosmopolitan Jews (pace Dreyfus) in French colonial culture, were particularly troubling for Fanon. In *The Wretched of the Earth* (1961), for example, Fanon was haunted by the image of the deracinated cosmopolitan (as opposed to the revolutionary "organic intellectual") who was always at risk of becoming a *luftmensch*: "This tearing away [from 'the white man's culture'], painful and difficult though it may be, is, however, necessary. If it is not accomplished there will be serious psycho-affective injuries and the result will be individuals without anchor, without horizon, colourless, stateless, rootless—a race of angels."[15] The deracinated intellectual—"colourless, stateless, rootless"—is contrasted with the organic intellectual, who was "a living part of Africa and her thought."[16] In this reading the figure of the cosmopolitan Jewish intellectual (somewhere between the colonial and decolonial) needed, as Fanon believed, to become an organic part of a decolonized global culture.

The decentering of a foundational European Jewish history—concerning, for instance, migration (as the first "model minority"); the ghetto (from Venice onward); or the "classic" diasporic people—can be productive as well as provocative. After all, decentering can be thought of as another means of decolonizing this largely Westernized narrative.[17] But decolonizing history is not the same as superseding it. As I have shown elsewhere, supersessionist thinking, in relation to Jewish history, has made it much harder than is necessary to find connections in the past and in our most urgent present between different forms of dehumanization (colonialism, slavery, antisemitism and genocide) and between shared forms of suffering.[18] Fanon's "impossibility," containing both the Jewish cosmopolitan and the Afro-Caribbean organic intellectual, dramatizes how Caribbean culture not only creolizes Jewish history but also holds different differences in place. As this collection demonstrates, there is a creolization of Jewish history and culture in the Caribbean but also a Jewish and Caribbean history and culture that resists blending too easily.

To some, however, the very intersection of Jewish and Caribbean histories is morally (and also aesthetically) wrong. If particular national and ethnic histories are conceived as unique, unitary, and uniform, then they are necessarily confined to separate spheres and stand alone. An example of this argument, based on the unbending uniqueness of ethnoracial difference, can be found in Hilary Mantel's notorious response to Caryl Phillips's *The Nature of Blood* (1997). Here she lambasts Phillips for mixing "Black" and "Jewish" history in the guise of Shakespeare's Othello and Shylock: "It is demented cosiness that denies the differences between people, denies how easily the interests of human beings become divided. It is indecent to lay claim to other people's suffering: it is a colonial impulse, dressed up as altruism. The heart may be pure, but more than the heart is needed; good motives sometimes paralyse thought. We are not all Jews. That is a simple fact. It is why the Holocaust happened."[19] Mantel's fear is that by universalizing the Jewish experience other histories will be colonized. In her reasoning, unique racial identities need to be maintained to understand why the "Holocaust happened." Her argument highlights the fear of "the Jew" as an all-encompassing metaphor for victimhood, as "we are not all Jews."[20] Mantel's misguided sense that the longevity and hegemony of Jewish history can deny the "differences between people" leads to what I call the "anxiety of appropriation."[21] In disciplinary terms, such anxiety, however wrong-headed, may well explain why self-designated "new" disciplines—such as diaspora studies, postcolonial studies, and ethnic and racial studies—have needed to supersede a foundational Jewish studies. The richness of this collection, and other work on the Caribbean Jewish nexus, is testimony to a thriving Caribbean culture that has maintained a nonsupersessionist dialogue with Jews, Judaism, and Jewishness.

Despite Mantel's fears, the anxiety of appropriation is hardly a feature of imaginative Caribbean writers. On the first page of V. S. Naipaul's *The Mimic Men* (1967), for instance, there is the figure of Mr. Shylock, whom the young Caribbean exile Ralph Singh (born Ranjit Kripalsingh) mimics in order to give his fluid identity some kind of shape. Zadie Smith's *White Teeth* (2000) similarly uses an all-encompassing, if caricatured, "Jewish" name to counter the idea that Jews and Hindus are model minorities (contra Naipaul) who are worth imitating. That is why *White Teeth* insists on a dismissive account of "Mr. Schmutters and Mr. Banajii . . . merrily . . . weaving their way through Happy Multicultural Land."[22] In both *The Mimic Men* and *White Teeth*, Jewishness enables an exilic or minority Caribbean identity to cohere provisionally in a form of self-appropriation. This perhaps explains why Caryl Phillips not only had a "fascination" with "the Jews" but regarded Shakespeare's Shylock as his "hero."[23] In response to an alienated sense of identity in predominately white, racist Yorkshire in the 1970s, Phillips was to eventually claim a Jewish grandfather as part of an imagined genealogy.[24] It was BBC television documentaries on the concentration camps in the 1970s that enabled Phillips to engage with a publically recognized form of suffering that spoke to his family's private suffering in the Caribbean.

Andrea Levy, who also perhaps had a Jewish genealogy, takes the opposite view to Naipaul, Phillips, and Smith and, instead of appropriating Jewishness, goes back to the ambivalence of Fanon.[25] As with Fanon's perverse sense of littleness, the idea of smallness in *Small Island* (2004) is deliberately confused and confusing. From the Empire Exhibition that opens the novel, there is a sense of the "whole empire in little" or in "miniature" which puts everything else in perspective.[26] Is the Caribbean made up of "small islands" other than Jamaica? Or is Great Britain a "small island" outside of its colonies? Perspective rather than identitarian coherence is central to the novel, with smallness and greatness redefined continually by its four main characters. Some characters, such as Gilbert, grow, and some, like Bernard, shrink, depending on the perspective of Hortense and Queenie, respectively. This narrative play enables Levy to turn Fanon's "little family quarrels" into a novel that decenters and decolonizes "white" European anti-Semitism so as to foreground racism and segregation.

Levy's decentered narrative is best illustrated by the introduction of Gilbert, who enrolls in the Royal Air Force at the beginning of the Second World War. Gilbert, born in Jamaica, volunteers to fight for his "Mother Country."[27] While based in Virginia he encounters the American army, organized along Jim Crow lines, and increasingly severe forms of anti-Black racism. He is told by the Americans that "you would never catch no self-respecting white man going into battle with a nigger" and, by the British, that "no white women will consort with you."[28] Gilbert's sense of self is quickly reduced to the words "coloured, black, nigger."[29] Needless to say, Americans do not distinguish between Caribbeans and African Americans as, following Jim Crow, "the American army is very strict about keeping black folks apart."[30] Worse still, American soldiers in Britain also "segregate" the "Mother Country" along racial lines—"Lincoln is a white town"; "Nottingham is a black town"—and "blacks" can only sit at the back of the cinema.[31]

Gilbert ignores such segregation and sits in the middle of the cinema, next to Queenie Bligh, a white woman. As a consequence, a riot ensues against "uppity niggers" and Arthur Bligh, Queenie's brother, is murdered.[32] After Arthur's death, Gilbert begins to contemplate the nature of the war he is fighting:

> Everyone fighting a war hates. All must conjure a list of demons. The enemy. Top of most British Tommies' list would be the army that hated them most—the Nazis. . . . But from that first uneasy hospitality at the American base in Virginia to this cocky hatred that was charging across the room to yell in the face of a coloured man whose audacity was to sit next to a white woman, I was learning to despise the white American GI above all other. They were the army that hated me the most! . . . If the defeat of hatred was the purpose of war, then come, let us face it: I and all other coloured servicemen were fighting the war on another front.[33]

Rather than combatting the hatred of Jews, Gilbert refigures the war so that it is centered on the hatred of Blacks. The decentering of the Shoah is, however, problematized by Gilbert's Caribbean Jewish father, who tells Gilbert, "You could have been Jewish," which was "the worst curse that could befall anyone."[34] After a few rums, his father would "berate [Gilbert's] estranged Jewish mother, father, the Torah, the synagogue and the silly hats."[35] As a result, Gilbert's father became a "fervent convert" who took "Christianity very seriously."[36] Unlike the predominant narrative in *Mimic Men, White Teeth,* and *The Nature of Blood,* it is not identification with Jewishness that resolves a fractured Black identity but conversion to Christianity. By transcending religious Judaism, Jewishness in *Small Island* becomes a racial matter on a par with Blackness: "Anthropoid—[Gilbert] looked to the dictionary to find the meaning of this word used by Hitler and his friends to describe Jews and coloured men. I got a punch in the head when the implication jumped from the page and struck me: 'resembling a human but primitive, like an ape.' Two whacks I got. For I am a black man whose father was born a Jew."[37] This double consciousness becomes a feature of *Small Island* as Gilbert wrestles with the nature of the racial war he is engaged in: "We [are] fighting the persecution of the Jew, yet even in my RAF blue my coloured skin can [not] permit anyone to treat me as less than a man."[38] Not unlike Fanon's

Black Skin, White Masks, the novel has two competing narratives of identification and differentiation. On the one hand, there is Gilbert's strong identification with Jewish persecution: "The picture in the newspaper was of a German Jew. He wore a cloth star on a dirty coat. He walked along a street, hunched and humbled, while non-Jews eyed him with an expression of disgust ... I knew only too well."[39] But, at the same time as this affiliation with his fellow victims, Gilbert cannot decide "which war" or which "front" he is fighting on. Is it the war against anti-Semitism, or the war against racism?[40]

What *Small Island* illustrates, above all, is the audacity at the heart of the Caribbean Jewish nexus. The uneasy familiarity of this intersection, across many centuries, has led to literary risk-taking—or is that risk-making? The in-between nature of Caribbean Jews (other and self, white and Black, colonizer and colonized) may well place them at the heart of a hybrid Caribbean culture. The essays in this important collection illustrate both the dangers as well as the abundant rewards of "metaphorical thinking" in relation to such long-standing "crossings." Seeing "similarities in dissimilars" has given us many transgressive provocations from Fanon to Levy and beyond. But the alternative to such dissimilarities (however flawed) is a diminished capacity to enlarge our global understanding of what it is to be human.

Notes

1. Bryan Cheyette, *Diasporas of the Mind: Jewish and Postcolonial Writing and the Nightmare of History* (New Haven, CT: Yale University Press, 2013), 68–71 and chapter 2.

2. See Cheyette, *Diasporas of the Mind,* 54–68, for a reading of these binaries.

3. After discovering that he was related to a "Jewish trader with Portuguese roots," Caryl Phillips concludes that "the cultural hybridity that is the quintessentially Caribbean condition had certainly marked my person." Phillips, *A New World Order: Selected Essays* (New York: Vintage, 2001), 130.

4. For Arendtian "metaphorical thinking," see Cheyette, *Diasporas of the Mind,* chapter 1.

5. Cited in David Macey, *Frantz Fanon: A Life* (London: Granta, 2000), 92.

6. Albert Memmi, "The Impossible Life of Frantz Fanon," *Massachusetts Review* (Winter 1973): 9–39.

7. Henry Louis Gates Jr., "Critical Fanonism," *Critical Inquiry* (Spring 1991): 457–58 and 457–70; and also Macey, *Frantz Fanon.*

8. Memmi, "The Impossible Life of Frantz Fanon," 30.

9. Memmi, 19.
10. Memmi, 24.
11. Memmi, 32.
12. Albert Memmi, *Dominated Man: Notes Towards a Portrait* (Boston: Beacon, 1968), 16. See also Gates, "Critical Fanonism," 465–470.
13. Macey, *Frantz Fanon,* 313–17; and Memmi, "The Impossible Life of Frantz Fanon," 26.
14. Gates, "Critical Fanonism," 468. See also Peter Geismar, *Frantz Fanon* (New York: Dial, 1971), 133–34.
15. Frantz Fanon, *The Wretched of the Earth* (1961), trans. Constance Farrington (New York, 1963), 175.
16. Fanon, *The Wretched of the Earth,* 167.
17. Santiago Slabodsky, *Decolonial Judaism: Triumphal Failures of Barbaric Thinking* (New York: Palgrave Macmillan, 2014).
18. Bryan Cheyette, "Against Supersessionist Thinking: Old and New, Jews and Postcolonialism, the Ghetto and Diaspora," *Cambridge Journal of Postcolonial Literary Inquiry* 4, no. 3 (2017): 424–39.
19. Hilary Mantel, "Black Is Not Jewish," *Literary Review* (February 1997): 40.
20. "We are not all Jews" echoes Hanif Kureishi's short story "We're Not Jews" in *Love in a Blue Time* (London: Faber & Faber, 1997), 41–51. See also Wendy Zierler, "'My Holocaust Is Not Your Holocaust': 'Facing' Black and Jewish Experience in *The Pawnbroker, Higher Ground,* and *The Nature of Blood,*" *Holocaust and Genocide Studies* 18, no. 1 (Spring 2004): 46–67.
21. Cheyette, *Diasporas of the Mind,* 32–40.
22. Zadie Smith, *White Teeth* (New York: Penguin, 2000), 398.
23. Caryl Phillips, *The European Tribe* (London: Faber & Faber, 1987), 55, 66.
24. Phillips, *A New World Order,* 130, and n4 above. See also Stephen Clingman, *The Grammar of Identity: Transnational Fiction and the Nature of the Boundary* (Oxford: Oxford University Press, 2009); and Clingman, "Other Voices: An Interview with Caryl Phillips," *Salmagundi* 143 (Summer 2004): 112–40.
25. Sarah Phillips Casteel, *Calypso Jews: Jewishness in the Caribbean Literary Imagination* (New York: Columbia University Press, 2016), 4.
26. Andrea Levy, *Small Island* (London: Headline Review, 2004), 2.
27. Levy, *Small Island,* 158.
28. Levy, 132–33.
29. Levy, 151. There is a parallel here with Frantz Fanon, who was also racially abused in Paris after fighting for the Free French.
30. Levy, 158.
31. Levy, 159–60.
32. Levy, 187.
33. Levy, 177.
34. Levy, 129.

35. Levy, 129.
36. Levy, 130.
37. Levy, 129.
38. Levy, 186.
39. Levy, 130.
40. Levy, 193.

Contributors

RUTH BEHAR is the Victor Haim Perera Collegiate Professor of Anthropology at the University of Michigan. She is the recipient of a MacArthur "Genius" Grant, a John Simon Guggenheim fellowship, a Distinguished Alumna Award from Wesleyan University, and an honorary doctorate in Humane Letters from the Hebrew Union College. Her books include *The Presence of the Past in a Spanish Village; Translated Woman: Crossing the Border with Esperanza's Story;* and *The Vulnerable Observer: Anthropology That Breaks Your Heart.* She coedited *Women Writing Culture,* one of the first books to call attention to women's creative ethnographic writing in anthropology. Ruth frequently visits and writes about her native Cuba and is the author of *An Island Called Home: Returning to Jewish Cuba* and *Traveling Heavy: A Memoir in between Journeys,* which explores her Cuban Jewish heritage. She is the editor of the pioneering anthology *Bridges to Cuba* and coeditor of *The Portable Island: Cubans at Home in the World.* Also a creative writer, she is the author of a coming-of-age novel, *Lucky Broken Girl,* and a bilingual collection of poetry, *Everything I Kept/Todo lo que guardé.*

ALESSANDRA BENEDICTY-KOKKEN is Lecturer at the University of Amsterdam and the Archimedes Institute at the Hogeschool Utrecht, as well as at Utrecht University and University College Utrecht. Previously she was an Associate Professor at the City College of New York and the Graduate Center (City University of New York). She is the author of *Spirit Possession in French, Haitian, and Vodou Thought: An Intellectual History* (Lexington Books, 2015). She is second editor of *Revisiting Marie Vieux Chauvet: Paradoxes of the Postcolonial Feminine* (2016), a special issue of *Yale French Studies;* and coeditor of *The Haiti Exception: Anthropology and the Predicament of Narrative* (Liverpool University

Press, 2016). She is currently Series Editor for Brill's Caribbean Series. She served for four academic years as Director of the MA in the Study of the Americas at the City College of New York (CUNY), a 30-credit MA and BA/MA program. She also helped to launch the Human Rights Forum at the City College of New York. Previously, she worked at the Cultural Services of the French Embassy in New York as Director of Development (2007–9) and at the Québec Government Office in New York as Attachée for Inter-Governmental and Academic Affairs (2004–7).

SARAH PHILLIPS CASTEEL is Professor of English at Carleton University, where she is cross-appointed to the Institute of African Studies and the Institute for Comparative Studies in Literature, Art and Culture, and where she co-founded the Centre for Transnational Cultural Analysis. The recipient of a Polanyi Prize and a Horst Frenz Prize, she is the author of *Second Arrivals: Landscape and Belonging in Contemporary Writing of the Americas* (University of Virginia Press, 2007) and the coeditor of *Canada and Its Americas: Transnational Navigations* (McGill-Queen's University Press, 2010). Her most recent monograph, *Calypso Jews: Jewishness in the Caribbean Literary Imagination* (Columbia University Press, 2016), won a Canadian Jewish Literary Award.

BRYAN CHEYETTE is Chair in Modern Literature and Culture at the University of Reading, and a Fellow of the English Association. He is the editor or author of ten books, including *Diasporas of the Mind: Jewish and Postcolonial Writing and the Nightmare of History* (Yale University Press, 2013), which was a 2013 *Times Higher Education* Book of the Year and includes a chapter on Frantz Fanon, Aimé Césaire, and Albert Memmi. He is also a Series Editor for Bloomsbury (*New Horizons for Contemporary Writing*) and has published over seventy chapters in journals and books. He has lectured widely throughout the United States and Europe and has held visiting positions at Dartmouth College, the University of Michigan, and the University of Pennsylvania. He writes regularly for the *Times Literary Supplement* and is working on a short book on the Ghetto for Oxford University Press and a longer book on Israel Zangwill.

NATALIE ZEMON DAVIS is a social and cultural historian of early modern times, especially attentive to working people, women, Jews, and encounters between European and non-European peoples. She has taught at the University of California, Berkeley, and is currently the Henry Charles

Lea Professor of History Emerita at Princeton University and Professor of History at the University of Toronto. Her books include *The Return of Martin Guerre* (1983), *Women on the Margins: Three Seventeenth-Century Lives* (1995), *The Gift in Sixteenth-Century France* (2000), *Slaves on Screen: Film and Historical Vision* (2000), and *Trickster Travels: A Sixteenth-Century Muslim Between Worlds* (2005). She is currently making a study of slavery in the Dutch colony of Suriname, examining both Jewish and Christian plantations. Among her publications is "Regaining Jerusalem: Eschatology and Slavery in Jewish Colonization in Seventeenth-Century Suriname," *Cambridge Journal of Postcolonial Literary Inquiry*, 3, no. 1 (2016): 11–38.

NEIL R. DAVISON is Professor of Modernism, Irish Studies, and Jewish Cultural Studies in the School of Writing, Literature, and Film at Oregon State University in Corvallis. He is the author of *James Joyce, Ulysses, and the Construction of Jewish Identity* (Cambridge University Press, 1996; paper edition with foreword by Anthony Julius, 1998), *Jewishness and Masculinity from the Modern to the Postmodern* (Routledge, 2010), and scholarly articles on Joyce, modern Irish literature, the Holocaust novel, Emmanuel Levinas and literature, and other topics related to culture, race, and gender in the twentieth century. His work has also recently turned to Afro-Caribbean/Jewish connections in the novels of Andre Schwarz-Bart and Caryl Phillips.

DAVID GANTT GURLEY is Associate Professor of Scandinavian and Director of the Harold Schnitzer Family Program in Judaic Studies at the University of Oregon. He received his PhD from the University of California, Berkeley, in 2007. His first book, *Meïr Aaron Goldschmidt and the Poetics of Jewish Fiction*, examines one of Denmark's greatest nationalistic writers as first and foremost a Jewish artist and explores his relationship to the Hebrew Bible and later Rabbinical traditions, such as the Talmud and the Midrash, as a form of poetics. He is currently working on a study of the Wandering Jew legend in Long Romanticism, from Goethe to Hawthorne. A central aim of both projects and his research at large is to illuminate the mechanisms whereby Jewish thought is reawakened in the European consciousness.

KATHLEEN GYSSELS teaches at Antwerp University, where her main fields are African and Jewish Diaspora literatures. She wrote her PhD—*Filles de Solitude, Essai sur l'identité antillaise dans les (auto-)biographies fictives de Simone et André Schwarz-Bart* (L'Harmattan, 1996)—on André and Simone Schwarz-Bart's oeuvre. She has published widely on comparative issues in the postcolonial Francophone and Caribbean field and interrogates processes of canonization in African American and Caribbean literatures: *Sages sorcières? Révision de la mauvaise mère dans Beloved (Toni Morrison), Praisesong for the Widow (Paule Marshall) et Moi, Tituba (Maryse Condé)* (Lanham University Press, 2001); *Passes et impasses dans le comparatisme postcolonial caribéen: Cinq traverses* (Honoré Champion, 2010); *Marrane et Marronne: la co-écriture réversible d'André et Simone Schwarz-Bart* (Brill, 2014); and *"Black-Label" ou les déboires de L. G. Damas* (Ed. Passages, 2016). Two other monographs are about to be released: *"Mine de riens" ou L. G. Damas, le passant intégral* (Ed. Passages, 2019) and *L'antillectuel L.G. Damas: "a ti pas" vers une France décoloniale* (Brill, 2019). She has published in *Prooftexts, European Judaism, Yod,* and *Journal of Jewish Identities*. Her last articles on the Schwarz-Bart's posthumous novels appeared in *Dalhousie French Studies, Il Tolomeo,* and *Shofar*.

ANNA RUTH HENRIQUES is a multi-talented creator. An award-winning artist, her artworks are in the permanent collections of New York's Jewish Museum and El Museo del Barrio, as well as the National Gallery of Jamaica. She launched her first jewelry collection at Barneys New York and went on to create a top-selling jewelry line, Aayenda, for a postwar, Afghanistan-based nonprofit, Future Brilliance. She is the author and illustrator of *The Book of Mechtilde* (Knopf, 1997) and is currently working on a novel in prose. Born and raised in Jamaica, she graduated from Williams College with a BA, and the University of California, San Diego, with an MFA, where she also starred in Eleanor Antin's film *Man Without A World* (1991).

HEIDI KAUFMAN is Associate Professor of English at the University of Oregon, where she teaches courses in nineteenth-century British literature and digital humanities. She currently holds a University Libraries Digital Humanities Fellowship and serves as the Director of Digital Humanities in the College of Arts and Sciences. She is the author of *English Origins, Jewish Discourse, and the Nineteenth-Century British Novel* (Penn State University Press, 2009) and the coeditor of *Fear, Loathing, and Victorian Xenophobia* (Ohio State University Press, 2013) and *An Uncomfortable Authority: Maria Edgeworth and Her Contexts* (University of Delaware Press, 2004). Currently she is completing a linked monograph and digital project, *The Archive's East End,* focused on the intersection of archival theory and East London cultural formation from 1800–70.

CYNTHIA MCLEOD was born in 1936 in Paramaribo, Suriname, where she spent her youth. She debuted in 1987 with *Hoe duur was de suiker? (The Cost of Sugar)*—a novel dealing with Jewish colonist families in Suriname in the second half of the eighteenth century that became an unexpected and unprecedented best seller in Suriname. *The Cost of Sugar* has been adapted for both stage and screen and has been translated into English, Italian, and German. In 1996 she published her second novel, *Ma Rochelle passée: welkom in el Dorado (Ma Rochelle passée: Welcome to El Dorado)*, as well as a study on Elisabeth Samson, which she later adapted as *De vrije negerin Elisabeth: gevangene van kleur (The Free Negress Elizabeth: Prisoner of Colour,* 2000). McLeod also published *Tweemaal Mariënburg (Twice Mariënburg;* 1997) and *Toen het vakantie was (During the Holidays;* 1999), a children's book, as well as *Tutuba, het meisje van het slavenschip Leusden* (Tutuba, 2013) and *Zenobia. Slavin op het paleis* (2015). In 1998 Cynthia McLeod was decorated as Knight in the Honorary Order of the Golden Palm by the president of Suriname for her writings, and in 2005 she was decorated Officer in the Honorary Order of the Golden Palm. In 2012 she was decorated knight in the Order of Oranje Nassau by the queen of the Netherlands.

INEKE PHAF-RHEINBERGER is Research Associate of the Institute for Romance Languages and Literature at the Justus-Liebig University, Giessen/Germany. Her major areas of study include Caribbean, Latin American, and African literatures. She coedited *A History of Caribbean Literature, Vol. 2: Dutch-Speaking Regions* (with A. James Arnold, 2001) and published *The Air of Liberty. Narratives of the South Atlantic Past* (2008), the first book that discusses the impact of Dutch expansion in early modern history on contemporary authors from Angola, Brazil, Suriname, and Curaçao. A closer look at the intertwined cultural histories of Spanish-and Portuguese-speaking Africa and Latin America was subject of further volumes, *AfriAmericas: Itineries, Dialogues, and Rhythms* (ed. with Tiago de Oliveira Pinto, 2008); *Historias enredadas: Asimetrías con vistas al Atlántico* (ed., 2011), and *Beyond the Line: Cultural Narratives of the Southern Oceans* (ed. with Michael Mann, 2014). She wove those connections together in *Modern Slavery and Water Spirituality:*

A Critical Debate in Africa and Latin America (2017) and coedited the volumes *Literatura e Outras Artes: Construção da Memória em Angola e Moçambique* (with Ana Sobral, 2017) and *Asia en América Latina* (in *Revista de crítica literaria latinoamericana,* with Koichi Hagimoto and Kim Beauchesne, 2018). She also contributed essays to *A Sephardic Pepper-Pot in the Caribbean* (ed. Michael Studemund-Halévy, 2016) and *The Sephardic Atlantic* (ed. Jonathan Schorsch and Sina Rauschenbach, 2018).

CARYL PHILLIPS was born in St. Kitts and came to Britain at the age of four months. He grew up in Leeds and studied English Literature at Oxford University. He began writing for the theater, and his plays include *Strange Fruit* (1980), *Where There is Darkness* (1982), and *The Shelter* (1983). He has written many dramas and documentaries for radio and television, including, in 1996, the three-hour film of his own novel *The Final Passage.* He wrote the screenplay for the film *Playing Away* (1986) and the Merchant Ivory adaptation of V. S. Naipaul's *The Mystic Masseur* (2001). His novels are: *The Final Passage* (1985), *A State of Independence* (1986), *Higher Ground* (1989), *Cambridge* (1991), *Crossing the River* (1993), *The Nature of Blood* (1997), *A Distant Shore* (2003), *Dancing in the Dark* (2005), *In the Falling Snow* (2009), *The Lost Child* (2015), and *A View of the Empire at Sunset* (2018). His non-fiction books are: *The European Tribe* (1987), *The Atlantic Sound* (2000), *A New World Order* (2001), *Foreigners* (2007), and *Colour Me English* (2011). He is the editor of two anthologies: *Extravagant Strangers: A Literature of Belonging* (1997) and *The Right Set: An Anthology of Writing on Tennis* (1999). His work has been translated into over a dozen languages. Formerly Henry R. Luce Professor of Migration and Social Order at Columbia University, he is presently Professor of English at Yale University.

BEN RATSKOFF is a doctoral candidate in Comparative Literature at the University of California-Los Angeles, where he was the 2018–19 Berger Fellow in Holocaust Studies. His academic articles have appeared (or are forthcoming) in *Jewish Studies Quarterly* and *Studies in American Jewish Literature* and his cultural criticism in the *Los Angeles Review of Books, Truthout,* and the *Advocate.* He is also the founder and editor-in-chief of *PROTOCOLS,* a cultural journal for provocative Jewish art and politics.

RACHEL RUBINSTEIN is Professor of American literature and Jewish studies at Hampshire College. Her teaching and research interests range across American literature and culture, with a particular focus on ethnicity, migration, and multilingualism, as well as Jewish and Yiddish literatures. She coedited *Arguing the Modern Jewish Canon: Essays on Literature and Culture in Honor of Ruth R. Wisse* (Harvard University Press, 2008) as well as the forthcoming *Teaching Jewish American Literature* (MLA Publications Committee) with Roberta Rosenberg. She is the author of *Members of the Tribe: Native America in the Jewish Imagination* (Wayne State University Press, 2010). Her current research addresses translation, race, and Yiddish in the Americas.

EFRAIM SICHER is Professor of English and Comparative Literature at Ben-Gurion University of the Negev. He has published widely in the fields of comparative literature and modern Jewish culture. His main research interests include the image of the Jew, contemporary Jewish writing, and the city in literature. His most recent books include (with Linda Weinhouse) *Under Postcolonial Eyes: Figuring the "Jew" in Contemporary British Writing* (2013); (as editor) *Race Color Identity: Discourses about the "Jews" in the Early Twenty-First Century* (2013); and *The Jew's Daughter: The Cultural History of a Conversion Narrative* (2017).

LEONARD STEIN is a PhD candidate in the Centre for Comparative Literature, in a collaborative program with the Anne Tanenbaum Centre for Jewish Studies, at the University of Toronto. His research compares modern literature from the Sephardic diaspora, specifically in representations of al-Andalus and the Spanish Inquisition. He previously served as president and program chair for the Society for Crypto-Judaic Studies, editor for the *University of Toronto Journal of Jewish Thought*, and Broome and Allen Fellow for the American Sephardi Federation.

LINDA WEINHOUSE is Professor of English at the Community College of Baltimore County. Her research focuses on modern Jewish and postcolonial women writers. She has published articles on Doris Lessing, Alice Munro, Nadine Gordimer, Cynthia Ozick, and Anita Desai. Her coauthored book (with Efraim Sicher), *Under Postcolonial Eyes: Figuring the "Jew" in Contemporary British Writing*, appeared in 2013. She is currently working on a book on Doris Lessing and postcolonialism.

Index

abolition, 5, 49, 52, 54, 70, 80, 168; advocates of, 117, 121–22, 128, 135. See also slavery
Adieu Bogota (Schwarz-Bart), 212
Af Inzlsher Erd (Korman), 95
Af Kubaner Erd (Dubelman), 95
Africa, 46, 52, 188; and Africana, 241n21
African religion, 85n26, 138, 165–66. See also religion
Afro-Cubanismo, 98, 108n58. See also Cuba
Agamben, Giorgio, 232, 237
Agard-Jones, Vanessa, 242n25
Algeria: anticolonial revolutionaries in, 236, 302–3; Blacks in, 304; French involvement in, 232; Jews of, 194n11; writing about, 233. See also Algerians
Algerians: French Catholic, 236; French Jewish, 236; Jewish, 236; Muslim, 236–37; secular, 237. See also Algeria
allegory, 53
alleotheta, 53, 58–60; in Danish writers, 64n47
Allgemeine Zeitung des Judentums, 81n2
alloeosis. See alleotheta
Alonso, Eugene A., 139
alterity, 248–66. See also identity
ambivalence, 6, 20, 80, 125
Amerindians, 34. See also Suriname
Améry, Jean, 302
Amselle, Jean-Loup, 219n75
Amsterdam, 32–35, 37–40, 295, 298–300; Blacks in, 40, 299; Jewish Historical Museum in, 115; Jews in, 37, 40, 42, 115, 297; mulattos in, 40
Andersen, Hans Christian, 60, 65n73

Anselme, Jean-Loup, 213
anthropology, 12–13, 136, 143, 149–50, 204
Antilla, 226, 230
Anti-Semite and Jew (Sartre), 225
anti-Semitism: accusations of, 226–32, 234, 237–38; in Caribbean life, xi–xiii, 142, 250, 274; and colonialism, 178, 183–91, 250; controversy of, 227–29; in Danish life, 50; and fascism, 301; in French life, 221, 228, 232–33, 237, 243n38; history of, 230; in literature, 1, 122, 221; medieval, 259; racism and, 250–51, 267n7, 268n12, 306; reactionary, 181; in Suriname, 31–32; in Ukrainian life, 276; and Yiddish-speaking immigrants, 102, 203. See also racism
Antwerp, 32, 286
anusim. See crypto-Jews/crypto-Judaism
Aravamudan, Srinivas, 71, 86n34, 87n46
Arbell, Mordechai, 82n3
Arendt, Hannah, 184–86, 193n8, 251, 268n10, 302
Armitage, David, 79
Arnold, A. James, 194n16
Aronowsky, Eliezer, 18, 91, 95–97, 100–102, 108n63
art: Black figures in European, 116, 125; British, 125; European, 125, 130n7; Jewish figures in European, 116, 125; realist, 119. See also literature
Ashkenazim, 2, 37–38, 40, 127, 135, 159, 209; and *Bildung*, 62n18; in Jamaica, 83n15. See also Jews/Judaism
Assouline, Pierre, 223, 232

Astro, Alan, 95, 102, 107nn33–34
Asia, 188
Assouline, Pierre, 223
Atuei, 98. *See also* Afro-Cubanismo
Auschwitz, 199, 205, 210–11, 291. *See also* concentration camps
Avant que les ombres s'effacent (Dalembert), 1, 235
Azoulay, Jacques, 234, 236, 245n62

Backer, Larry, 97
Badiou, Alain, 232, 237
Baptist War/Christmas Rebellion, 80
Barbados, 114
Barringer, Tim, 84n23
Behar, Ruth, 21, 136–37, 142, 149–50, 289–94
Bejarano, Margalit, 93, 138–39, 144
"Békés, leur histoire, leur poids économique, Les" (Boutrin and Confiant), 233–34
Belisario, Isaac Mendes, xi, 82n6
Beloved (Morrison), xiii
Benedict, Ruth, 182
Benedicty-Kokken, Alessandra, 20, 213
Ben-Ur, Aviva, xii, 15–17, 22, 25n31, 129
Berlin, 33
Bernabé, Jean, 68, 223, 225
Berniker, Pinkhas, 95, 135
Beschrijving van Guiana (Hartsinck), 34
Bettinger-López, Caroline, 137, 142, 149
Between Camps: Race, Identity and Nationalism at the End of the Colour Line (Gilroy), 302
Bhabha, Homi, 91, 96, 249, 266
Bigelow, John, 69
Bijlsma, Roelof, 30, 42
Bindman, David, 131n18
Black Atlantic, 250
Black Atlantic, The (Gilroy), 3, 250
Black Jacobins, The (James), 36
Black-Jewish relations, xii–xiii; concept of diaspora in, 3; in Jamaica, 69–70; literary, 3, 221, 258; sexuality in, 69–70; in United States, 9, 114. *See also* Black Jews
Black Jews: in Israel, 21, 210; in Jamaica, 69; in New York, 210. *See also* Black-Jewish relations
Black Skin, White Masks (Fanon), 213, 225, 236, 250, 301, 308

Blake, William, 117
Block-Lazarus, Joyce, 199
Blyden, Edward Wilmot, 14–15, 46–47, 49, 62n25
Boas, Franz, 182
Bokher, Elye, 90
Borschel-Dan, Amanda, 228
Boutrin, Louis, 234
Bovo D'Antona (Bokher), 90
Boyarin, Jonathan, 7, 129
Brathwaite, Edward Kamau, 13, 68
Braudel, Fernand, 35
Brazil: *conversos* in, 167; Dutch conquest of, 32; Jewish settlers to Martinique from, 233
Bridge of Beyond (Schwarz-Bart), 207
British Caribbean, 5, 81, 114, 156
Brodkin, Karen, 233
Brontë, Charlotte, 113
Brown, Vincent Aaron, 233
Buber, Martin, 199
bürgerliche Verbesserung der Juden, Die (Dohm), 33
Byrne, Bonifacio, 98

Caillois, Roger, 189–90
Calypso Jews: Jewishness in the Caribbean Literary Imagination (Casteel), 156, 225, 302
Camus, Albert, 236
Candide (Voltaire), 39, 44n19
Canvassing for Votes (Hogarth), 124
capitalism, 100, 183–86, 194n11
Cardoze, Grace, 163
Caribbean literary culture, 1–10, 17, 22, 66, 79–81; creolized, 12–17, 69–71, 79–81; Danish Jewish fiction and, 49; francophone, 20; and Jewishness, 114. *See also* literature; writing
Caribbeanness, 21
Caribbean studies, 4, 6–9, 12, 21, 220
Carmichael, Stokely, 210
Carpentier, Alejo, 36
Casteel, Sarah Phillips, 6, 19, 79–80, 156, 221, 225, 233, 237, 245n58, 254, 302
Castro, Fidel, 141, 144–45, 158–59. *See also* Cuba
Catechism of Jamaica: History and Geography of Jamaica (Labatt), 66, 82n3

Catholicism, 34, 92, 138, 148; institution of, 280; mixed, 165; stereotypes of, 228. *See also* Christianity; religion
Césaire, Aimé, 7, 19–20, 59, 65n70, 177–91, 194n16, 220, 225, 229, 232, 234, 251, 302; Jewish themes in work of, 183–86
Césaire, Suzanne, 177
Cesarani, David, 81n2
Chamoiseau, Patrick, 68, 213, 223, 225–26, 236, 242n25
Charlie Hebdo, 239
Cheyette, Bryan, 7, 21, 129, 178, 191, 193n4, 212, 233, 237
choc en retour (boomerang effect), 179, 183–90, 196n36, 251, 268n10. *See also* Arendt, Hannah; Césaire, Aimé
Christianity: and colonialism, 189; conversion to, 22, 50, 63n31, 307. *See also* Catholicism; *Conversos*; religion
Cibber, Theophilus, 121
Civilisation matérielle, économie et capitalisme XVe–XVIIe siècles, tome 3: Le Temps du monde (Braudel), 35
Cliff, Michelle, 6
Cohen, Judah M., 47
Cohen, Robert, 33, 37–38, 40
Coleridge, Samuel Taylor, 88n61
Collective of Martinican Solidarity with the Palestinian People (CMSP), 237. *See also* Martinique
colonialism: anti-Semitism and, 250; British, 66, 68; critique of, 49, 177–91, 248–66; discourse of, 17; economy of, 114; European, 22, 179, 183–90; and modernity, 194n11; and Nazism, 177, 179, 183–90, 193n8, 194n11; power structures of, 116; question of, 19; racism and, 301; rise of, 16; and slavery, 80, 251; society of, 79, 184–85; Spanish, 10, 55, 66, 68; violence of, 67, 80, 183–91; war and, 178; writing about, 36, 79, 114. *See also* coloniality; postcolonialism
coloniality, 179, 183–91, 194n11. *See also* colonialism; racism
Columbus, Christopher, 5, 138, 141
Combescot, Pierre, 226, 231
competitive victimhood, 232, 248, 255
concentration camps, 206, 211, 218n74, 287. *See also* Holocaust
Condé, Maryse, 3, 115, 232, 242n25, 245n58

Confiant, Raphaël, 3, 7, 20, 68, 213, 220–39, 239n2, 242n25, 242n27, 244nn46–47, 301
Contradictory Omens: Cultural Diversity and Integration in the Caribbean (Brathwaite), 68
Conversos, 106n18, 155–58, 167; descendants of, 163–64, 170; history of, 138–43, 152n20, 155–59; Sephardic, 146–47. *See also* Christianity; Jews/Judaism
cosmopolitanism, 221; in French colonial culture, 304
Cost of Sugar, The (McLeod), 21, 29, 286
Cox, Oliver, 182, 193n8
creative writing, 12, 17, 137. *See also* writing
Creole Jews, 6, 14, 16–17, 165–66, 170n4. *See also* Creoles; Jewish creolization
creole languages, 13, 92, 106n16; fiction in, 226; formation of, 66, 68, 70–71; Jamaican, 84n22; Martinican, 226. *See also* creolization
Creoles: culture of, 68–69, 84n23, 225–27; folk tradition of, 203; white, 36; women, 36. *See also* Creole Jews; creole languages
créolité, 20, 68, 213, 221, 226–27, 243n30; advocacy of, 226. *See also* creolization
creolization, 2, 9, 12, 68–69, 154, 213, 227; Caribbean Jewish, 7–8, 12–17, 69–71, 165, 170n4; of Christianity, 165; cultural, 8, 12; ideas of, 68; linguistic, 8, 12; literary, 18, 78–81; studies of, 14. *See also* créolité; Jewish creolization
crypto-Jews/crypto-Judaism, 19, 22, 96, 154, 159; Cuban, 135–51; in fiction, 98, 108n47; history of, 135–51; marking of, 143–45; writing about, 139–40. *See also* Jews/Judaism
Cuba, 18, 21, 89–105; Afro-Cubans of, 18, 89, 91, 95–96, 98, 100, 108n58; colonial, 135, 137, 141, 150; communist, 140–41, 157; freedom fighters of, 103; history of, 97–102, 135–42; immigrant populations of, 96; Jews of, 92–97, 135–51, 157, 200; literature of, 135; modern, 141; nineteenth-century struggles for independence of, 91, 97–100; translations of Yiddish, 102–5. *See also* Cuban Revolution

Cuban Inquisition, 106n18, 137–39, 142. *See also* Spanish Inquisition
Cuban Revolution, 141, 157, 159. *See also* Cuba
Cuban War of Independence, 135, 141. *See also* Cuba
"Cultural Identity and Diaspora" (Hall), 10
cultural theory, 9
Curaçao, 13; Jews in, 37, 114
"Curgy's Funeral, or the Old Time Busha" (Labatt), 67–78
Cyrulnik, Boris, 201

Dabydeen, David, 3, 19, 113–30, 132n29; slave narrative in, 119
Dahomay, Jacky, 223–24, 232
Daily Gleaner. See *Gleaner*
Dalembert, Louis-Philippe, 1–2, 235
Damas, Léon, 179
Danish Caribbean, 14, 18, 46–60, 156, 162; abolition of slave trade in, 47–48, 52
Danish Golden Age, 46–48, 50, 61n1
Danish West Indies. See Danish Caribbean
Dash, Michael, 208
Davis, Natalie Zemon, 13, 24n16, 129
Davison, Neil R., 20–21
Days of Awe (Obejas), 19, 137, 140–44, 147, 149–50, 154, 157, 162–63, 166, 169
D'Costa, Jean, 70, 84n22
de Barrios, Miguel, 42–43
de Certeau, Michel, 141
de Céspedes, Carlos Manuel, 98
"Declaration of the 24," 232–33
decolonization, 212, 250; in France, 197n53; and racism, 250. *See also* Rothberg, Michael
DeCordova, Jacob, 66, 82n5
DeCordova, Joshua, 66, 82n5
DeCordova, Judith, 82n5
de Kom, Anton, xii
de la Durantaye, Laurent, 245n54
de la Luna, Beatrice, 155
de las Casas, Bartolomé, 97, 138
de Lisser, H. G., 4
de Marivaux, Pierre, xi
Demerara (British Guyana), 118, 125–27
den Boer, Harm, 42–43
Denmark, 46–60
de Piedra-Bueno, Andrés, 91, 96–102, 107n38

de Roux, Marie, 182, 195n25
Derrida, Jacques, 194n11, 199, 203
Description topographique, physique, civile, politique et historique de la partie française de l'isle Saint-Domingue (Moreau de Saint-Méry), 35–36
de Vaisseau Bayle, Lieutenant, 177–78, 191
Development of Creole Society in Jamaica, 1770–1820, The (Brathwaite), 13, 68
Diary of a Young Girl, The (Frank), 254
diaspora: African, 2–3, 10, 22, 224, 231, 255, 260, 262, 266; Asian, 10; Black, 212, 216n36, 258, 265; Caribbean poetics of, 12; and hybridity, 154–70; Jewish, 2–3, 10, 22, 81, 156, 158, 166, 169, 200–201, 204, 212, 216n36, 224, 255, 258, 260, 262, 265; of mind, 169; Palestinian, 216n49; postcolonial, 262; race and, 252. *See also* diasporic consciousness
Diasporas of the Mind: Jewish and Postcolonial Writing and the Nightmare of History (Cheyette), 212, 302
diasporic consciousness, 11–12, 169, 250, 265. *See also* diaspora
Dieudonné, 222, 227–29, 233, 240n9, 243n38, 244nn45–47
Discourse on Colonialism (Césaire), 178–80, 183, 191, 194n16, 225, 251
Dohm, Christian Wilhelm, 33
Dominican Republic, 97. *See also* Hispañola
Donnell, Alison, 4, 13
Doubrovsky, Serge, 199, 210, 214n7
Drake, St. Clair, 193n7
Drescher, Seymour, xii
Drumont, Édouard, 178, 183
Drums and Colours (Walcott), 2
Dubelman, Avrom Yosef, 95, 107n33
Du Bois, W. E. B., 193n8
Dürer, Albrecht, 117
Dutch Caribbean, 156
Dutch Republic, The: Its Rise, Greatness, and Fall (1477–1806) (Israel), 29

Echo, The, 66
Eckstein, Lars, 123, 129
Edgeworth, Maria, 86n34
education: enlightened, 41; and German *Bildung*, 62n18, 81n2; in languages, 162; modern, 41

Edwards, Bryan, 86n34
Efigies (Byrne), 98
Eisenberg, Deborah, 233
ekphrasis: discussion of, 131n9; fiction of, 130; postcolonial, 113–30; and representation, 123
Ellison, Ralph, 218n73
El reino de este mundo (Carpentier), 36
emancipation: and abolition, 54; ideology of, 81n2; of Jews, 5, 18, 49, 51–52, 59, 64n36, 260; legal, 191; multiple struggles for, 130; slavery and, 22, 32, 48, 64n44, 70, 76. *See also* slavery
Emery, Mary Lou, 115, 131n22
Enlightenment, 29, 39, 41; colonial, 43; critique of, 250, 254; deconstruction of humanism of, 248–66; principles of, 197n53; and social problems, 44n19
Equiano, Olaudah, xiii
Essai historique sur la colonie de Surinam (Nassy), 5, 17–18, 30–34, 39, 41–43
Esther, Book of, 15. *See also* Purim
Ethiopian Jews, 209, 270n64, 296. *See also* Jews/Judaism
Exodus, xiii, 10, 12, 22, 52, 58–59, 147. *See also* Jews/Judaism
Exodus II (Henriques), 9–10, 11

Faber, Eli, xii
Fanon, Frantz, 7, 179, 193n4, 213, 224–25, 232–38, 246n68, 250–51, 254, 268n12, 301–4, 308, 309n29; autobiography/biography by Confiant of, 234, 238
farce, 77–80, 84n20, 84n24, 87n55. *See also* humor
fascism, 7, 181–82, 193n8, 251; anti-Semitism and, 301. *See also* Nazis/Nazism
Felsenstein, Frank, 123–24, 132n30
feminism, 154
fiction: Caribbean, 108n47, 118, 252; Cuban, 108n47; early modern Danish, 58; modern Jewish, 51–52, 80; postmodern slavery, 119, 122, 129; short, 82n6. *See also* literature
Fielding, Henry, 121
Final Passage, The (Phillips), 256
Finkelstein, Bluma, 199
First Fruits of the West, 10, 66, 81n2
First-Time (Price), 29, 36

Fishkin, Shelly Fisher, 7–8
Fonrobert, Elisheva Charlotte, 199
Forde, Maarit, 85n26
Forrester, Gillian, 84n23
Fort, Bernadette, 120
Foucault, Michel, 216n36
fragmentation: of Judaism, 148; of memory, 140; in writing, 300. *See also* memory
France, 155, 167–68, 191, 221, 224; accusations of anti-Semitism in, 227–32, 237; Algerian involvement of, 232; criticism of, 226; decolonial movements in, 197n53; Nazi occupation of, 177; racism in, 181, 197n53; Vichy government in, 192n1, 235–36
Frank, Anne, 114, 254, 295–300
Frankétienne, 221, 239n2
Frankl, L. A., 65n74
Frederickson, George M., 195n25
French Antilles, 200, 224. *See also* French Caribbean
French Caribbean, 5, 35–36, 42
French Revolution, 5, 37, 52, 163. *See also* France
Freud, Sigmund, 59–60, 301
Frifarvede, De (Hertz), 18, 49, 52–55, 58, 60, 65n66
Frontier Society: A Social Analysis of the History of Surinam (van Lier), xii, 31

Galchinsky, Michael, 120
Garvey, Marcus, 59
Gates, Henry Louis, 73, 84n25, 86n36, 87n53, 303
gender: and rebellion, 161; roles of, 169; and sexuality, 169; substitution of, 53, 162. *See also* sexuality
genealogy: charts of, 145; crypto-Jewish, 138–40; Jewish, 306; questions of, 140. *See also* identity/identities
Gerber, Jane, 5, 70
Germany, 37, 51, 141, 177; fascism in, 181–82
ghetto: Paramaribo, 39; Venice, 114, 259; Warsaw, 206–7. *See also* Jews/Judaism
Gilroy, Paul, 3, 12, 250
Girard, Philippe, 5
Gitlitz, David, 143
Glantz, Yankev, 91
Gleaner, 10, 66, 81n2, 82n5

Glissant, Édouard, 68–69, 213, 218n74, 225, 227, 236, 242n25
Goldberg, David Theo, 182
goldener fontan, Der (Pinis), 95
Goldman, Dara, 147, 160
Goldschmidt, Meïr Aaron, 48–50, 52–55, 58–60, 62n23, 65n66
Goldschmidt, Ragnhild, 64n40, 64n47
Golem, Die (Meyrink), 208
Gordon, Lewis R., 236–37, 246nn69–70
Guadeloupe, 20, 199–202, 210, 232, 236; fugitives in, 206
Gurley, David Gantt, 18, 80
Gutshteyn, M., 93
Guyana, 236
Gyssels, Kathleen, 20

Haiti: immigrants from, 97; and "la France libre," 235. *See also* Hispañola; Saint-Domingue
Haitian Revolution, 52, 56. *See also* Haiti
Halevi, Judah, 148, 160–61
Hall, Stuart, 10–11, 156, 162, 165, 196n42, 227
Hallett, Mark, 132n23
Hansen, Philip, xi
Harlot's Progress, The (Cibber), 121
Harlot's Progress, A (Dabydeen), 19, 113, 116, 118–19, 121–29
Harlot's Progress, A (Hogarth), 113–14, 116–17, 117, 121, 131n13
Harshav, Benjamin, 90
Hartsinck, Jan, 34, 36–37
Hatuey, 91, 97–102. *See also* Cuba
Hatuey (Pinis), 91–92, 95–103
Hatuey (Sellén), 98
Hatuey: Memory of Fire (London and Thoron), 102–5
Havana, 95, 100–101, 104, 106n18, 138, 148, 161, 292–94. *See also* Cuba
Havaner Lebn, 94–95, 98
Hayes, Isaac, 59, 65n70
Hearne, John, 6
Hebrew Intelligencer, 81n2
Hebrew language, 13, 22, 90, 144, 269n45. *See also* Jews/Judaism
Heffernan, James, 123, 133n40
Heiberg, Johanne Luise, 64n47
Heidegger, Martin, 249, 252
Heilman, Robert B., 77–78
Heine, Heinrich, 52, 60, 64n40

hemispheric American studies, 7–8. *See also* Jewish American studies
Hemshekh oyf Kubaner Erd (Ran), 96
Henriques, Anna Ruth, 9–10, 21, 273–84
Hep-Hep riots (1819), 48. *See also* anti-Semitism
Herejes (Padura), 136
Hernández, Marie Theresa, 141–42, 149, 152n20
Hertz, Henrik, 18, 46–60, 62n23, 65n66; and Jewish community, 63n31, 63n36; travels of, 62n24
Hesse, Barnor, 182, 195n24
Hetsch, G. F., 61n2
Heuman, Gad, 5
Higher Ground (Phillips), 248–66
Hilgartner, Judith Lang, 104
Hintzen, Percy H., 68
Hirschfeld, Magnus, 182, 195n25
Hispañola, 97. *See also* Dominican Republic; Haiti
history: African, 199, 201; of Atlantic, 79, 129; buried, 140–43; Caribbean, 23n5, 305; colonial, 21, 47, 182, 297; of Cuba, 89, 92, 97–102; Danish colonial, 47; European, 296–97; family, 140, 144; Jewish, 23n5, 25n31, 129, 135–51, 156, 178–79, 182, 199, 201, 206, 231, 302–5; literary, 4, 7, 12, 16–17, 29, 42; oral, 138–39, 141, 143–44; records of, 12, 140–41; traumas of, 1. *See also* memory
History of Jamaica (Long), 70, 74–75
History of the People of Trinidad and Tobago (Williams), xii
Hitler's Empire: Nazi Rule in Occupied Europe (Mazower), 302
Hoffman, Alice, 19, 154–55, 162–65, 169
Hogarth's Blacks: Images of Blacks in Eighteenth Century English Art (Dabydeen), 113, 118, 122
Hogarth, Walpole, and Commercial Britain (Dabydeen), 113, 120, 127
Hogarth, William, 19, 113–30; Blacks in, 113, 116, 118, 126; Jews in, 113–14, 118, 121, 126, 131n13, 132n24
Holland, 285–88, 299
Holocaust: artistic portrayal of, 231–32; colonial massacres and, 211; colonial turn in studies of, 179; ghosts of, 198;

history of, 231, 255, 291; impact of, 1, 21–22, 114, 141, 201–8, 222–23, 230, 295–300; and Jewish problem, 183; memorial of, 202; memory of, 19, 115, 129, 203, 287; and Middle Passage, xiii; non-Jewish victims of, 231; racism and, 251, 254; survivors of, 210, 259–60; writing about, 295. *See also* anti-Semitism; refugees
Hommage à la femme noire (Schwarz-Bart), 211
Howe, Irving, 87n55
Hron, Madelaine, 220
Hughes, Langston, 178, 218n73
humor: dramatic, 77; failure of, 76; light, 78; physical, 78. *See also* farce
Hurwitz, Edith, 81n2
Hurwitz, Samuel J., 81n2
Husserl, Edmund, 249
Huston, Nancy, 211
hybridity: cultural, 8, 157, 225–27, 302, 308n3; diaspora and, 154–70; Jewish, 302; and multiculturalism, 220–21; narratives of, 221; postcolonial theories of, 226, 266; and syncretism, 18, 91; vision of, 238. *See also* identity/identities

iconotexts, 118, 120–21
identity/identities: *béké*, 233; Black, 307; diasporic, 154, 156, 201, 249; ethnic, 48, 155–56, 162; of European Jews, 50; hidden, 22, 135–51, 158; hybrid, 165, 169, 256; inheriting of, 145–48; *Juban*, 136, 150–51; markers of, 205; multiple, 155, 252; postcolonial, 154, 156; postmodern, 156, 250; postracial Cuban, 100; racial, 154–55, 255; racialized, 250; religious, 154, 162; Sephardic, 261; sexual, 154–55, 157, 162; as social construct, 164; transmission of, 135–51; vacuum of, 256. *See also* hybridity
Ilan (Olinsky), David, 138
illness: from disease, 123, 262, 283; and medicine, 42, 72–78; and poison, 74–76, 86n39. *See also* medicine
"Imaginary Homelands" (Rushdie), 154
Impressionism, 169
"In a finsterer tsayt (tsum shvartsn andeynkung fun petlyoren)" (Pinis), 103

India, 154
indigeneity, 2–3, 103, 158–59, 169. *See also* Indigenous peoples
indigenization, 13, 169. *See also* creolization
Indigenous peoples, 9; in Cuba, 89, 97–103, 142, 166; rebellion of, 97; spirits of ancestors of, 169. *See also* indigeneity
Indo-Caribbean, 17, 201
In Praise of Creoleness (Bernabé, Confiant, and Chamoiseau), 68, 226–27, 237, 243n31, 243n34
Inquisition. *See* Spanish Inquisition
insurrection de l'âme, L': Frantz Fanon, vie et mort du guerrier-silex (Confiant), 234–35
Interesting Narrative of the Life of Olaudah Equiano, The, or Gustavus Vassa, the African (Equiano), xiii
intermediality, 115, 118, 121, 129
International Herald Tribune, 262, 296
Introduction à une poétique du divers (Glissant), 68
Irish Caribbean, 4
irony, 226
Islam, 239. *See also* religion
Island Called Home, An: Returning to Jewish Cuba (Behar), 21, 136, 149–50
Israel: Black Jews in, 21, 296; homeland in, 199, 202, 209; kibbutz in, 280, 285; Palestinians in, 21, 208–11, 232; politics of, 7, 208–9, 227–29; spiritual homeland of, 137, 154, 156. *See also* Jews/Judaism; Palestinians/Palestine
Israel, Jonathan, 4, 29, 37, 233
I, Tituba, Black Witch of Salem (Condé), 245n58
Izzo, Justin, 242n25

Jamaica, xi, 5; Black culture of, 67; colonial, 10, 274; geography of, 66; history of, 66, 80; immigrants from, 97; Jewish culture of, 70, 79–80; Jews in, 114, 273–84; race relations in, 67–70, 80; Spanish conquest of, 10
James, C. L. R., 36, 193n8
James, Marlon, 1–2
Jew, A (Goldschmidt), 48, 60, 65n66
Jewish American literature, 7–9, 92. *See also* literature

Jewish American studies, 3, 7–9. *See also* hemispheric American studies
Jewish Atlantic: historiography of, 115; history of, 3, 6, 79, 81, 129; synagogues of, 46–47
Jewish-Black relations. *See* Black-Jewish relations
Jewish creolization, 7–8, 12–17, 69–71, 165–66, 170n4. *See also* Creole Jews; creolization
Jewish mulattos, 37–40. *See also* mulattos
Jewish Naturalization Bill of 1753, 116
Jewishness, 3–4, 6–9, 13, 131n8, 143–46, 213, 221, 225–29; and Atlantic slavery, 130n5; Caribbean invocations of, 129, 220–39; concealment of, 60, 158; de-essentialized sense of, 160; diaspora, 2–3, 10, 22, 81, 156, 170n4, 303; engagement with, 124, 199; history of Martinican, 232–38; hybridity of, 209; literary discourse about, 20, 58, 114, 120, 127, 129; performed, 51; and revolution, 159; as survivalist creed, 164; veneer of, 62n22. *See also* identity/identities; Jews/Judaism
Jewish planters, 13, 16, 114; in Suriname, 30, 32, 34. *See also* plantation
Jewish Question, The (Blyden), 14–15, 46
Jewish slaveholders, xii, 2, 13–14; cruelty of, 32. *See also* slavery
Jewish slave traders, 4, 47, 61n12. *See also* slave trade
Jewish studies, xi, 4, 7, 12, 21, 114–15, 220, 305. *See also* Jews/Judaism
Jews and Blacks in the Early Modern World (Schorsch), xii
Jews in Another Environment: Surinam in the Second Half of the Eighteenth Century (Cohen), 37
Jews/Judaism: Caribbean, 2, 5, 29–43, 252; Cuban, 135–51; diasporic, 161; Dutch Caribbean, 115; European, xii, 135, 138, 205; hostility to, 187, 205; Masada in history of, 206, 216n37; observance of, 274; religion of, 135–51, 205; remembrance in, 206; rituals of, 13, 22, 144–48, 158, 204, 274–75; and satire, 239; stereotypes of, 228; suffering and, 2, 164; traditions of, 160. *See also* Jewishness; port Jews; religion
Jikeli, Günther, 228
Jodensavanne, 4

Johnson's Dictionary (Dabydeen), 19, 113, 116–19, 124–30
Johnson's Dictionary (Johnson), 77, 80, 87n48
Joseph, E. L., 3
Joubert, Joseph, 136
Jubanidad, 135–51. *See also* Cuba
Jude, Der (Hertz), 51–52
Judíos nuevos en Amsterdam: Estudio sobre la historia social e intelectual del judaísmo sefardí en el siglo XVII (Kaplan), 40

Kadish, Rachel, 155
Kafka, Franz, 59, 208
Kandiyoti, Dalia, 8
Kaplan, Yosef, 40, 42–43
Katz, Ethan B., 233
Kaufman, Heidi, 18, 131n15
Kelley, Robin, 180–81, 192n3, 193n8
Kevane, Bridget, 148
King René's Daughter (Hertz), 51
Kiron, Arthur, 79, 83n15
"knots of memory" (Rothberg), 206, 212–13. *See also* memory
Korman, David, 95
Korn, Bertram W., 66
Kozer, José, 136
Kristobal Kolon (Glantz), 91
Kriz, Kay Dian, 70, 84n20
Kubaner Lider (Dubelman, Berniker, and Aronowsky), 95
Kunin, Seth, 143, 150
Kyrre, Hans, 50–51, 63n32

Labatt, Philip Cohen, 3, 18, 66–81, 81n2, 85n26; marriage of, 82n5; in synagogue records, 83n15
Labatt, Robert, 69
Lalla, Barbara, 70, 82n8, 84n22
language: and alterity, 263–64; colonialist, 181; racist, 181; universal, 205
Lanzmann, Claude, 231
Last of the Just, The (Schwarz-Bart), 198, 200–201, 206, 208, 211, 214n16
Lawton, I., 66, 83n15
Ledent, Bénédicte, 248, 253–54
Légitime Défense, 177
Lemarchand, René, 239
Letchimy, Serge, 222
Levi, Primo, 261–62, 302
Levien, Sidney, 5–6

Levinas, Emmanuel, 20, 199, 248–66, 267n4, 267nn6–7
Levine, Robert, 92–93
Levy, Andrea, 10, 302, 305–6, 308
Levy, Lital, 8
liberalism, 182, 185
Lingis, Alphonso, 253
literary criticism, 12. *See also* literature
literatura sefardí de Amsterdam, La (den Boer), 42
literature: Afro-Caribbean, 67, 71, 79; Black figures in European, 1–2; British, 79; Caribbean, 1–9, 66–67, 71, 198, 201, 211, 213; colonial, 1–2; creolization in, 18, 78–81; Cuban, 89–105, 136; English, 66; French, 232; imaginative, 12; Jewish figures in European, 50–52, 60, 114; multiethnic, 155; postcolonial, 2, 6, 198; Sephardic, 43, 115; Spanish, 42; transnational, 155, 198. *See also* Caribbean literary culture; fiction; poetry; satire; short story; writing; Yiddish literature
London: emigration to, 256–57, 260; prostitution in, 116, 118; Sephardic Jewish community in, 83n15
London, Frank, 92, 103–4
Long, Edward, 70, 74–75
Long Song, The (Levy), 10
Louis, Patrice, 223
L'Ouverture, Toussaint, 5
love: destiny of, 169–70
Love à la Mode (Macklin), 121
Love, Anger, Madness: A Haitian Trilogy (Vieux-Chauvet), 154
Lucas, Rafael, 223, 231, 241n16
Lyon Johnson, Kelli, 142

Maceo, Antonio, 91, 97–102
Maceo (Aronowsky), 91, 96–97, 101, 108n63
Macey, David, 192n1
Machado, Gerardo, 100–103. *See also* Cuba
Mackandal, 36. *See also* Maroons
Macklin, Charles, 121
Madagascar, 200
Mantel, Hilary, 305
Maria, Lady Nugent's Diary (Nugent), 70
Marianne (de Marivaux), xi
Maroons: attacks of, 34–35; ethnography of, 13; peace with, 38; revolts of, 5–6, 36, 206; Saramacca, 29

Marranos, 6. *See also* Sephardic Caribbean
Marriage of Opposites, The (Hoffman), 19, 155, 162–64, 167, 169–70
Martí, José, 92, 97–98, 135–36, 161–62
Martinique, 35, 178–79, 182, 220–39, 303; cultivation of sugar in, 233–34; history of Jewishness in, 232–38; independence struggle in, 237; Jewish community in, 234, 238, 245n58; poisonings in, 75, 86n39; uniqueness of, 227; Vichy regime in, 177, 234–35
Marty, Éric, 237
Marxism, 177, 192n3
Maximin, Daniel, 201, 217n61
Mayol, Humberto, 136
Mazower, Mark, 302
Mbembe, Achille, 232
McClellan, James E., 35, 42
McCusker, Maeve, 243n31
McGarrity, Maria, 4
McKay, Claude, 178
McLeod, Cynthia, 3, 21, 29, 38, 115, 285–88
medicine: forms of, 72, 78; and poison, 74–76, 86n39; in Suriname, 42. *See also* illness
meguila, 16. *See also* Jews/Judaism
Memmi, Albert, 210, 302–4
memory: of Holocaust, 19, 115, 129, 203; multidirectional, 178, 183, 224, 237; recovery of, 137, 148–51; role of, 137; transmission of, 137–39, 143. *See also* history; "knots of memory"; multidirectional memory
Mendelsohn, Adam, 79
Mendieta, Ana, 162
Ménil, René, 177
Merchant of Venice, The (Shakespeare), 259
mestizaje, 14. *See also* creolization
métissage, 199. *See also* creolization
Mexico, 167, 274
Meyrink, Gustav, *Die Golem*, 208
Miami, 95, 137, 139; Cuban Jewish community in, 149, 157. *See also* United States
Middle Passage, xiii, 245n53. *See also* slave trade
midrash, 60. *See also* Jews/Judaism
Mignolo, Walter D., 183, 194n11

Miles, William F. S., 225, 233–37
Milgrom, Genie, 19, 137, 139–40, 143, 146
Mimic Men, The (Naipaul), 305, 307
Minoristas, 98. *See also* Afro-Cubanismo
Miron, Dan, 62n22
Mirvis, Stanley, 69, 83n16
Miss Lucy in Town (Fielding), 121
modernity, 266
Monde, Le, 229, 232
Morant Bay Rebellion, 5, 80, 275
Moreau de Saint-Méry, Médéric, 35–36, 42
Morning Star, The (Schwarz-Bart), 198–213
Morrison, Toni, xiii
Mr. Burchardt and His Family (Hertz), 50
mulâtre, 238, 246n75. *See also* mulattos
mulattos, 35–40; free, 39, 55. *See also* Jewish mulattos; *mulâtre*
Mulatto, The (Andersen), 60, 65n73
multidirectional memory (Rothberg), 178, 180, 224, 237, 239, 302. *See also* memory
multilingualism, 105
Muñoz, Juan, 152n24
Murdoch, Adlai, 227, 242n25, 243n30
"Muse of History, The" (Walcott), 2
My 15 Grandmothers (Milgrom), 19, 137, 139

Naipaul, V. S., 302, 305–6
Nassy, David de Isaac Cohen, xi–xiii, 6, 17–18, 29–43, 44n19
Nassy, Samuel, 34
Nathanson, M. L., 48, 50, 63n35
National Front, 191, 222, 228–29, 240n9, 243n38. *See also* fascism
nationalism, 60, 265; Algerian, 303; Cuban, 97–102; German, 181; Martinican, 227; Ukrainian, 109n72; white, 190–91. *See also* fascism
"Nationalisme français, Le" (de Roux), 182
Nature of Blood, The (Phillips), 21, 114, 248–66, 295–300, 305, 307
Nazis/Nazism: anti-Semitism of, 259; colonialism and, 179–90, 193n8; history of, 301; ideology of, 222; racial myths of, 179, 262, 296; rise of, 181, 185–90; violence of, 182, 185, 301. *See also* anti-Semitism; fascism; nationalism
Nègre et l'Amiral, Le (Confiant), 234–35, 242n25

Nègres et Juifs au XVIIIe: le racisme au siècle des Lumières (Pluchon), 200
Negrophobia, 250–51. *See also* racism
Nesbitt, Nick, 65n70
New Christians, 138. *See also* Christianity
New World Order, A (Phillips), 251
Ninon (Hertz), 51, 62n23
Nochlin, Linda, 134n69
Noland, Carrie, 242n25
Norich, Anita, 90
North Africa: Egyptian influence in, 304; Jews of, 93, 235, 303

Obama, Barack, 104
obeah, 71–78, 84n22, 85n26, 87n46. *See also* religion; tricksters/tricksterism
Obejas, Achy, 3, 19, 22, 137–38, 140–43, 147–50, 154–58, 161, 164, 169, 171n26
Obras Completas (Piedra-Bueno), 96
O'Callahan, Evelyn, 4, 67
Occident and American Jewish Advocate, 81n2
O'Connor, Flannery, 1
One Hundred Years (Hertz), 51
"On the Sea" (Halevi), 161
Opinión Nacional, La, 136
Origins of Totalitarianism, The (Arendt), 184, 193n8
Ortiz, Fernando, 89
Othello (Shakespeare), 259
Other Hogarth, The: Aesthetics of Difference (Fort and Rosenthal), 120
Oyfgang, 93–94, 98, 100–101, 103
"Oyfn Inzele" (On the island) (Gutshteyn), 93–94

Padmore, George, 193n8
Padura, Leonardo, 136
Palestinians/Palestine, 21, 208–11, 227–30, 232–38, 285; liberation for, 237; problem of, 298. *See also* Israel
pan-Africanism, 14, 303; politics of, 3
Paris, 163, 167–70, 170n4, 179, 191
Passover, 10, 146–47. *See also* Jews/Judaism
patois languages. *See* creole languages
Paton, Diana, 85n26
Paulson, Ronald, 132n29
Penn, Asher, 95, 97, 99–100, 105. *See also* Pinis, Oskar
Pépin, Ernest, 201

Perera, Victor Haim, 290
Perez Firmat, Gustavo, 89–90
Petliura, Symon, 109n72. *See also* anti-Semitism
Phaf-Rheinberger, Ineke, 5, 17–18
phenomenology, 249, 255
Philadelphia, 42, 83n15, 275–77
Phillips, Caryl, 3, 7–9, 20–21, 114, 248–66, 269n50, 295–300, 302, 306, 308n3
Phillipson, Ludwig, 81n2
Pinalie, Pierre, 222
Pinis, Oskar, 18, 91, 95, 97, 100–104, 135. *See also* Penn, Asher
Pinkham, Joan, 184–85, 187, 268n10
Pissarro, Camille, 155, 163, 168, 170n4
plantation: planters of the, 13, 16, 30, 32, 34, 114; and plantocracy, 71, 80, 206. *See also* Jewish planters
Pluchon, Pierre, 200
Pluie et vent sur Télumée Miracle (Schwarz-Bart), 202, 205
Poe, Edgar Allen, 53
"Poésie et connaissance" (Césaire), 179–80
poetics: Black surrealist, 177; Caribbean, 19
poetry, 12; Cuban-Yiddish, 89–105; French, 179–82; Jewish-Cuban, 289–94; and knowledge, 179–80. *See also* literature; poetics
Poland, 199, 202–3, 205–7
politics: of anticolonialism, 180; of anti-Semitism, 227–29; autodidactic, 256; of class, 264; identity, 226, 266; independent, 226; of race, 264
port Jews, 10, 79, 114, 124; Sephardic, 129. *See also* Jews/Judaism
Portugal: anti-Semitism in, 203; Surinamese colony of, 29–43
Portuguese Jewish Nation, 29–43; archives of, 34; military activities of, 34. *See also* Suriname
Portuguese New Christians, 32
postcolonialism: foundations of, 252; ideology of, 169, 221; theory of, 178–79, 194n11, 250; writing about, 114, 129. *See also* postcolonial studies
postcolonial studies, 7, 114–15, 211, 305. *See also* postcolonialism
postmodernism, 250
Pouvoirs dans la Caraïbe, 236
poverty, 256, 288

Powell, Enoch, 251
Practice of Everyday Life, The (de Certeau), 141
Price, Richard, 13, 29, 36
Prince, Mary, 117
Pringle, Thomas, 117, 121–22
print culture, 10, 79
Purim, 15–16. *See also* Jews/Judaism

Rabbi of Bacharach, The (Heine), 52
race: and diaspora, 252; and ethnicity, 48; and imagination, 46–60; power politics of, 257; science of, 182; and slavery, 48, 52; as social construction, 195n25; stereotypes of, 68, 71, 118–19. *See also* racism
racism: and anti-Semitism, 250–51, 267n7, 268n12, 306; asymmetries of, xi–xiii, 298; in canonical authors, 1; colonial, 7, 195n25, 250; and colonialism, 301; contradictions of concept of, 179–82; critique of, 248–66; as dogma, 182; European, 22, 178–82; French, 179–82, 197n53, 228; history of, 255; ideology of, 193n8; Israeli, 263; Nazi, 177–91; and society, 187–88, 195n25; Western liberal definition of, 182. *See also* anti-Semitism; Negrophobia; race
Racism: A Short History (Frederickson), 195n25
"Racism's Alterity: The Afterlife of Black Sociology" (Hesse), 182
Ragen, Naomi, 155
Ramchand, Kenneth, 66–68
Ramperstad, Arnold, 218n73
Ran, Leyzer, 95–96
Rassismus (Hirschfeld), 182
Ratskoff, Ben, 7, 19–20, 251, 268n10
refugees, 147; Eastern European Jewish, 96, 210; racism against, 265; Russian Jewish, 210; Yiddish-speaking, 92, 96
religion: Afro-Caribbean, 85n26, 138, 146, 166; ancestral, 140; Jewish, 135–51, 205; in Levinas, 255; mystical, 155; reconciliation in, 209; rules of, 169. *See also* African religion; Christianity; Islam; Jews/Judaism; spiritualism
Renan, Ernest, 181, 190
representation: nature of, 119; racial, 119; reliability of, 128. *See also* literature
République des Livres, La, 223

resistance: and obeah, 71–78; and rebellion, 5, 36, 68, 71–73, 76, 78, 163; and revolt, 5, 36, 163; and signifying, 71, 73, 77–78, 80, 85
"Rhyme of the Ancient Planter, The. Altered from Coleridge" (Labatt), 88n61
Robert, Admiral Georges, 235–36
Roberts, Neil, 14
Rodrigues, Janelle, 85n26
Romanticism, 50
Rosenthal, Angela, 120
Rosenzweig, Franz, 169
Rosh Hashanah, 147. *See also* Jews/Judaism
Rothberg, Michael, 7, 178–79, 181, 193n8, 200, 212, 224, 237, 239, 253, 302. *See also* "knots of memory"; memory; multidirectional memory
Rubinstein, Rachel, 18, 21, 135
Rue des Syriens (Confiant), 235
Ruins (Obejas), 157
Rupert, Linda M., 13
Rushdie, Salman, 136, 154
Ruskin, John, 115

Sadi, Saïd, 236
Said, Edward, 216n47
Saint-Domingue (Haiti), 35–36, 42, 167, 200; historiography of, 35. *See also* French Caribbean; Haiti; Hispañola
Samson, Elisabeth, 38
Sanchez Porro, Reinaldo, 95
Sansal, Boualem, 211
Santería, 138, 165–66. *See also* religion
Sartre, Jean-Paul, 225, 232, 251, 302
Sasportas, Isaac, 5–6
satire, 116, 118, 239. *See also* literature
Savage, John, 75, 85n26
Schachter, Allison, 8
Scharfman, Ronnie, 180, 233
Schorsch, Jonathan, xii, 25n31, 129
Schouten, Gerrit, xi
Schouten, Hendrik, 38–39
Schreier, Benjamin, 9
Schwarz-Bart, André, 7, 20, 198–213, 215n26, 253
Schwarz-Bart, Simone, 20, 198–99, 201–7, 211–12
Sefarad, 289–90, 291. *See also* Sephardim; Sephardism

Seidman, Naomi, 91
Selections from the Miscellaneous Posthumous Works of Philip Cohen Labatt (Lawton), 66, 82n6
Sellén, Francisco, 98
Senghor, Léopold, 179, 196n42, 208–9
Sephardic Caribbean, 6, 18–19, 125, 154–70, 170n10; cousin marriage in, 172n40; in Danish Caribbean, 47; and European art history, 130n7; history of, 8, 10, 18, 115; trade networks of, 115; writing about, 115. *See also* Marranos; Sephardim
Sephardic Expulsion, 10, 22, 32, 42, 83n15, 115, 138, 140, 167. *See also* Sephardim
Sephardim, 2, 10, 37–40, 127, 138; and colonial economy, 114; French-speaking, 93; in London, 83n15; and marriage, 40–41; in Martinique, 245n58; romanticization of, 158; and sexual relations, 69–70, 83n16, 163–64. *See also* Sephardic Caribbean
Sephardism, 155–56; in Amsterdam, 40, 42; Caribbean literary, 42, 115; idealization of, 171n17. *See also* Sephardic Caribbean; Sephardic Expulsion; Sephardim
settler colony, 198–213. *See also* colonialism
sexuality: in Black-Jewish relations, 69–70, 83n16; and exploration of Cuba, 159–60; gender and, 169; and identity, 154. *See also* gender
Shakespeare, 91, 113, 259, 305–6
Shoah. *See* Holocaust
short story, xv, 66–67, 70–71, 297; collections of, 225. *See also* literature
Shponka, Yaakov, 98, 100–102
shtetl, 198–213; return to, 201–8
Shylock, 296, 305–6. *See also* Shakespeare
Sibylla Merian, Maria, xii
Sicher, Efraim, 19, 254, 262
signifying: Henry Louis Gates, Jr. on, 73, 84n25; resistance and, 71, 73, 77–78, 80, 84n25, 85
Signifying Monkey, The (Gates), 73, 84n25
Silverman, Max, 206
Silverstein, Stephen, 135
Simon, Élie, 228
Simpson, Hyacinth M., 82n6

Sketches of Character in Illustration of the Habits, Occupation and Costume of the Negro Population in the Island of Jamaica (Belisario), xi
slave narrative, 22, 49, 52, 231; Afro-Caribbean, 71, 156, 221; in Hogarth novels of Dabydeen, 117, 121–24, 127–29; traditions of, 68, 81, 130n5, 255–56. *See also* slavery fiction
slave rebellion, 5, 36, 68, 163. *See also* slavery
slavery: African, 14, 48–49, 124; Caribbean dystopian writing about, 204; colonialism and, 80, 251; critique of, 78, 80; Cuban, 100, 103; emancipation from, 76–77; female, 39; history of, 255; Jewishness and, 130n5; psychology of, 80; public discourse about, 114; and race, 48, 52; and resistance, 36, 71–73, 76, 78; signifying in, 84n25; transatlantic, 1–2, 207; transnational, 7–8, 155, 198; and violence, 71–74, 76–78, 80; writing about, 22, 36, 64n44, 66–67, 71. *See also* abolition; emancipation; slave rebellion; slave trade
slavery fiction, 22, 36, 64n44, 66–67, 71, 204; postmodern, 119, 122, 129. *See also* slave narrative
slave trade: Atlantic, 124, 207, 250; banning of, 47–48, 52, 61n11; Danes in, 61n11; Jews in, 61n12, 232; violence of, 256. *See also* Jewish slave traders; Middle Passage; slavery
Small Island (Levy), 306–8
Smith, Zadie, 302, 305–6
Snyder, Holly, 70
Solkin, David, 131n13, 132n24, 132n26, 132n29
Spain: anti-Semitism in, 203; Hapsburgs of, 42; immigrants from, 92, 161, 203; literary tradition of, 97. *See also* Spanish Inquisition
Spanish conquest, 103. *See also* Spain
Spanish Flu epidemic, 275
Spanish Inquisition, 2, 5, 19, 22, 42, 140–41, 155–58, 163, 200, 274; in Cuba, 106n18, 137–39; victims of, 102; violence of, 10, 103. *See also* anti-Semitism
spiritualism: African, 165; Caribbean, 165; Christian, 169; native, 169. *See also* religion

State of Independence, A (Phillips), 256
Stavans, Ilan, 49
St. Croix, 49, 54–55, 62n25
Stein, Leonard, 19, 154
stereotypes: of Blacks, 68, 71, 118–19; of Catholics, 228; of Jews, 228, 239
Stern der Erlösung, Der (Rosenzweig), 169
Stewart, Dianne M., 71
St. Kitts, 114, 252, 295, 297
Stowe, Harriet Beecher, 91
St. Thomas, 46–47, 49, 55–56, 60, 62n25, 162–63, 166–68; history of Jews of, 61n4, 61n6
St. Thomas Synagogue, 46–47, 60, 61n5
sugar, 35; cultivation in Martinique of, 233–34
Suriname: Christians in, 34, 39–40; colonial, 13–14, 29–43, 285–88; history of, 31, 33; Jews in, xi, 14–16, 21, 30–34, 37–40, 114, 285–88; slaves in, 16, 31–32, 39; social mobility in, 41; urbanization of, 37–38
Suriname Friends of Letters, xi. *See also* Suriname
surrealism, 177, 179, 190
Survival in Auschwitz (Levi), 261
synagogues: Caribbean, 115; Cuban, 141; sand-floor, 61n5, 166, 172n51; Sephardic, 291. *See also* Jews/Judaism

Taubira, Christiane, 232
tefillin, 146, 158, 161. *See also* Jews/Judaism
"Telescope" (Henriques), 11
Testament insolent (Memmi), 210
Texaco (Chamoiseau), 226
Thackeray, William Makepeace, 1–2
Thoron, Elise, 92, 103–4
Ti Jean L'Horizon (Schwarz-Bart), 205
transculturation, 18, 89, 95. *See also* Cuba
tricksters/tricksterism: forms of, 77, 87n50; Jamaican, 66–81; and trickery, 67, 72–77, 84n24, 87n50, 128
Tropiques, 177–78, 183, 191, 192n3
Tropishe Likht: Lider un Poemen fun Kuba (Dubelman, Berniker, and Aronowsky), 95
Tshutshinsky, Asher, 95
Turner (Dabydeen), 115
Turner, J. M. W., 115

Uncle Tom's Cabin (Stowe), 91, 106n14
United States: Cuban immigrants in, 89, 95–98, 138, 157; exceptionalism of, 92; immigration in, 93, 275, 277; relations of Cuba and, 104–5; territory of, 46; Yiddish writers in, 91
US Virgin Islands, 162

Vanity Fair (Thackeray), 1–2
van Lier, R. A. J., xii, 31–32
Velasquez, Diego, 97, 103
Venice, 114, 259, 296
Vergès, Françoise, 232
Vienna, 33
Vieux-Chauvet, Marie, 154
Vink, Wieke, 14
Viswanathan, Gauri, 16
Voice of Jacob, 81n2
Voltaire, 39–40

Wagner, Peter, 116, 118–19
Walcott, Derek, 2, 6, 115, 118, 130n7
Weinhouse, Linda, 19, 254, 262
Welsh, Sarah Lawson, 13
West Indies: colonial, 124; migration to, 200; politics in, 56
What Fanon Said (Gordon), 236
White Teeth (Smith), 305–7
Whitman, Walt, 91, 106n14
Wiesel, Elie, 196n31, 208–9
Wij Slaven van Suriname (de Kom), xii
Williams, Eric, xii
Williams, Rudy, 251
Wiltord, Jeanne, 223, 232
Wolff, A. A., 48
Woman Named Solitude, A (Schwarz-Bart), 200, 203, 206–7, 213, 253

women: freedom of slaves who are, 39; historical novels by, 155; Jewish American, 154–70; writing of contemporary Caribbean, 170n1. *See also* feminism
world literature, 8, 178. *See also* literature
World War II, 234–35, 238, 278, 285, 306
Wretched of the Earth, The (Fanon), 236, 304
writing: academic, 113, 245n58; anti-colonial, 178, 233; Black, 193n7; about colonialism, 36, 79, 114; crypto-Jewish, 139–40, 149, 157; and ethnicity, 53, 200, 212, 231; and identity, 254; polemical, 179; postcolonial, 17, 129, 221; and power, 6; as recovery, 148–51; of Sephardic Jews, 42; about slavery, 22, 36, 64n44, 66–67, 71, 204; writing back and, 258, 279. *See also* Caribbean literary culture; creative writing

Yiddish language, 22, 90–91, 102–5; translations into, 106n14. *See also* Yiddish literature
Yiddish literature, 18, 89–105; tradition of, 22, 90, 203. *See also* literature
Yiddish press, 100; in Cuba, 135
Yidishe Velt, Dos, 100
Yom Kippur (Day of Atonement), 6, 46, 147–48, 161, 166. *See also* Jews/Judaism

Zeitlin, Aaron, 95–96
Zierler, Wendy, 248
Zionism, 7, 14, 156, 169, 255, 260, 263, 280
Zong massacre, 124

RECENT BOOKS IN THE SERIES

New World Studies

Caribbean Jewish Crossings: Literary History and Creative Practice
Sarah Phillips Casteel and Heidi Kaufman, editors

Mapping Hispaniola: Third Space in Dominican and Haitian Literature
Megan Jeanette Myers

Mourning El Dorado: Literature and Extractivism in the Contemporary American Tropics
Charlotte Rogers

Edwidge Danticat: The Haitian Diasporic Imaginary
Nadège T. Clitandre

Idle Talk, Deadly Talk: The Uses of Gossip in Caribbean Literature
Ana Rodríguez Navas

Crossing the Line: Early Creole Novels and Anglophone Caribbean Culture in the Age of Emancipation
Candace Ward

Staging Creolization: Women's Theater and Performance from the French Caribbean
Emily Sahakian

American Imperialism's Undead: The Occupation of Haiti and the Rise of Caribbean Anticolonialism
Raphael Dalleo

A Cultural History of Underdevelopment: Latin America in the U.S. Imagination
John Patrick Leary

The Spectre of Races: Latin American Anthropology and Literature between the Wars
Anke Birkenmaier

Performance and Personhood in Caribbean Literature: From Alexis to the Digital Age
Jeannine Murray-Román

Tropical Apocalypse: Haiti and the Caribbean End Times
Martin Munro

Market Aesthetics: The Purchase of the Past in Caribbean Diasporic Fiction
Elena Machado Sáez

www.ingramcontent.com/pod-product-compliance
Lightning Source LLC
Chambersburg PA
CBHW021341300426
44114CB00012B/1032